1985

• The Burger Court •

THE BURGER COURT
The Counter-Revolution That Wasn't

EDITED BY VINCENT BLASI
Foreword by Anthony Lewis

Yale University Press
New Haven and London

Published with assistance from the Kingsley Trust Association Publication Fund established by the Scroll and Key Society of Yale College.

Designed by Nancy Ovedovitz and set in Times Roman type by Eastern Graphics. Printed in the United States of America by Murray Printing Co., Westford, Mass.

Library of Congress Cataloging in Publication Data
Main entry under title:

The Burger Court.
  Includes index.
  1. United States. Supreme Court. 2. Burger,
Warren E., 1907–   . 3. Civil rights—United States.
4. Antitrust law—United States. I. Blasi, Vincent,
1943–
KF8748.B86 1983   347.73'26   83-5858
ISBN 0-300-02941-1   347.30735

        10   9   8   7   6   5   4   3   2

• Contents •

v

• Foreword •

Anthony Lewis

When Warren E. Burger succeeded Earl Warren as chief justice of the United States in 1969, many expected to see the more striking constitutional doctrines of the Warren years rolled back or even abandoned. The reapportionment cases, *Brown v. Board of Education* and the other decisions against racial discrimination, the criminal-law decisions imposing what amounted to a code of fair procedure on the states, the cases enlarging the freedom of speech and of the press: In these, it was often said, the Warren Court had made a constitutional revolution. Now a counter-revolution was seemingly at hand.

It is fourteen years later as I write. Six members of the Warren Court are gone, replaced by nominees of Republican presidents: Nixon, four; Ford, one; Reagan, one. And what has happened to those controversial Warren Court doctrines? They are more securely rooted now than they were in 1969, accepted by the Burger Court as the premises of constitutional decision-making in those areas. Of course particular results have swung away from the trend apparent before 1969; of course this decision or that has disappointed those who welcomed the changes of the Warren years. But there has been nothing like a counter-revolution. It is fair to say, in fact, that the reach of earlier decisions on racial equality and the First Amendment has been enlarged. Even the most hotly debated criminal-law decision, *Miranda,* stands essentially unmodified.

The Burger Court approved busing as a judicial remedy for school segregation. The Burger Court made the press virtually immune to "gag orders" forbidding publication of stories about pending criminal cases and said that newspapers could not be made to balance critical stories by publishing replies; it held unconstitutional a state tax imposed on newspapers alone and held for the first time that the press and the public have a right to observe certain public proceedings, in particular trials.

There was a decision day toward the end of the 1982 term that symbolized the commitment of the Burger Court to the spirit of the Warren doctrines. On May 24, 1983, the Court decided by a vote of 8 to 1 that racist private schools are ineligible for tax exemptions because they are not "charitable" in the common-law sense of advancing agreed public policy. The opinion of the Court, rejecting arguments to the contrary by the Reagan administration, was written by Chief Justice Burger. "Racial discrimination in education," he said, "violates a most fundamental national policy." That same day Justice Sandra Day O'Connor, President Reagan's appointee, wrote the opinion for a 5 to 4 majority holding that a state violated the due process clause of the Fourteenth Amendment when it revoked a convicted burglar's probation for failure to pay a $550 fine, without giving him alternatives to prison or showing that he had not made a bona fide effort to raise the money. It was an innovative decision right in the tradition of Earl Warren's egalitarian approach to criminal justice.

How has it happened, this extraordinary continuity of doctrine? Why have judges appointed by conservative presidents clung to the libertarian principles of the previous judicial generation or even enlarged upon them? These questions are evoked again and again in the mind of the reader who explores the work of the Burger Court in this book's fascinating analyses.

An irony must be part of the answer. Conservative judges—meaning by that term those who are more cautious in lawmaking—are naturally committed to the doctrine of *stare decisis*. It follows logically that they should respect a precedent once established, even though they opposed that result during the process of decision. For such a true conservative as Justice John Marshall Harlan, that consideration was certainly a factor; he might warn in dissent against what he foresaw as the baleful effects of a decision, but he would hesitate thereafter to subject it to constant relitigation. He valued stability over perfection.

A psychological truism supports *stare decisis*. Yesterday's surprise becomes today's commonplace. That is true of life generally in a changing world and of judicial life in particular, for it is the nature of the judicial process in our legal system to use yesterday's innovation as the accepted premise, the platform for further decision. Not only most judges but virtually all lawyers reason that way: incrementally consolidating the past into the future. It is the lawyer's way of thinking, taught in law schools.

Moreover, the public believes it is entitled to a certain reliance on constitutional decisions of the Supreme Court—and judges sense that. Reconsideration of doctrine in light of changed circumstances is one thing; our view of race was different after Hitler from what it had been in 1896, when *Plessy v. Ferguson* was decided. Reconsideration after a few years, in light of changed judges, is another.

It is also true that doctrines seen as radical when they first appear in Supreme Court opinions have a way of turning out to feel familiar and right. The decision that state legislators and members of the federal House of Representatives must be elected from districts of roughly equal population did force a lot of change—but it was change quite acceptable to the public. The United States still has much racial injustice, and much hypocrisy on the subject, but few Americans would want to go back to the rule of *Plessy v. Ferguson* and have the Supreme Court say that segregation in public facilities meets the Constitution's demand for "the equal protection of the laws." Probably the most bitterly disputed decision of the Burger Court is *Roe v. Wade,* the abortion case. But if it were overruled, by the Court itself or by constitutional amendment, would the American public easily accept now the criminal prosecution of women or doctors involved in abortions?

However conservative their political outlook, very few judges today are prepared to break boldly—radically—from prevailing constitutional doctrines. On the Supreme Court, only Justice William Rehnquist really goes back to first premises in his opinions and is willing to rethink doctrines in terms of a personal constitutional ideology. He is today's equivalent of Hugo Black—at the other end of the judicial spectrum.

Perhaps this is only a transitional period. Perhaps Justice Rehnquist will be joined by others as ready as he is to uproot established doctrine. Then the Burger years might be seen in history as no more than what Justice Holmes called "that period of dry precedent which is so often to be found midway between a creative epoch and a period of solvent philosophical reaction."

But as it stands, the Burger Court is doing what comes naturally to judges in the post-Warren era: trimming here and there, notably where egalitarianism looks to have costly consequences, but also building on the cases of the 1950s and 1960s when the spirit moves it—and doing so without any great concern for "self-restraint." That was the approach so often advocated in dissent by Justice Felix Frankfurter, who remembered that willful conservative judges had brought the Court to the edge of disaster in 1937 in their resistance to the New Deal.

One thing to be learned from these essays is that the great conflict between judicial "restraint" and "activism" is history now. Today's commentators on the Supreme Court are not survivors of the New Deal struggle, and neither are the justices. They comment and they decide without much self-conscious concern for whether this is a proper role for the Court.

We are all activists now. So this fascinating book tells us. Activists for what is a different question. Vincent Blasi, in his powerful summing-up, finds the Burger Court to be without the energizing moral vision of its predecessor; it is a rootless activism, he says. Martin Shapiro, telling us cheerily that the critics are never satisfied with the Supreme Court, nevertheless thinks we are better off arguing about the wisdom of what the Court does than wishing it had been done by someone else.

The great puzzle of American democracy has always been why so much should be done by judges, and ultimately by nine of them, appointed for life. After fourteen years of the Burger Court, the puzzle is more mesmerizing than ever.

The Society of American Law Teachers

The Society of American Law Teachers, the sponsor of this book, was founded in 1975 to represent the interests and concerns of teachers of law. The organization facilitates the efforts of law teachers to improve the capacity of the legal profession to serve societal needs, particularly as that capacity is affected by the quality and direction of legal education and legal scholarship. Over the years, the Society has testified in public forums in favor of affirmative action in law school admissions, in opposition to efforts to restrict the jurisdiction of the federal courts on such controversial issues as abortion and school prayer, and in favor of continued funding of the Legal Services Corporation. The Society has sponsored conferences and panel discussions on the future of legal education, access to the federal courts, the concept of equality, goals in law teaching, tenure standards for law professors, and clinical legal education. The book Looking at Law School, *designed to introduce law study to prospective and beginning law students, was published under the auspices of the Society. Each year the Society honors one member of the law teaching community for enduring contributions to the profession.*

• Preface •

This book presents a series of commentaries on the performance of the United States Supreme Court since Warren Burger became chief justice in 1969. Typically, the advent of a new chief justice signals more of a change in the public image of the Court than in the content or character of its work product. No modern chief justice, and least of all this one, has dominated the court over which he has presided. It is nonetheless a common expedient to use changes in the identity of the chief justice as dividing lines for demarcating segments of Supreme Court history.

Moreover, from the standpoint of the attitudes of the presidents who tried to shape the Court in recent years, Warren Burger serves as an appropriate symbol. Burger was viewed at the time of his appointment as a worthy champion of the conservative legal philosophy of the president who nominated him, Richard Nixon. In addition, Nixon and his personally selected successor, Gerald Ford, named four associate justices to the Court. Another was added by President Ronald Reagan, who like Nixon and Ford professed disenchantment with much of the work of the Warren Court. For the last half of the period under discussion, the Court has been composed of seven jurists nominated by Republican presidents and only two named by Democrats.

Surprisingly, in light of this political background, the last fourteen years have witnessed a series of decisions by the Supreme Court that seem on first view to be antithetical to what might be termed the modern conservative vision of the Constitution, a vision characterized primarily by the insistence on a limited, tradition-bound role for the Supreme Court. The departure from conservative principles, moreover, has not been confined to questions of judicial role. A remarkable number of the substantive results decreed by the Court during this period run counter to basic conservative political tenets favoring crime control over civil liberties, "family values" over the claims of liberty and equality associated with the feminist movement, neighborhood autonomy and states' rights over racial integration, and privacy and patriotism over aggressive, disturbing reporting by the press. At a more personal level, it is of course noteworthy that all three of the Nixon nominees who sat on the case voted against their nominator in the crucial Watergate tapes decision, thereby making his resignation from the presidency all but inevitable. The story of the Burger Court to date, whatever else it might be, is not a tale of a conservative counter-revolution, at least not one of epic proportions or obvious import. If there have been historically significant shifts of premises or institutional dynamics, the movement has been subtle, complicated, not easily perceptible.

In bringing together essays by twelve close students of the Court's work, this book seeks to contribute to an assessment of this somewhat perplexing era. The book is designed to be accessible to nonlawyers and lawyers who claim no special expertise in the areas of law that are covered. The general observations of the distinguished contributors to this volume should also be of interest to specialists.

With two exceptions, each of the chapters in the book offers an overview of one significant area of the Burger Court's work. This format has enabled authors both to provide a narrative survey of a number of important decisions and to identify and comment upon noteworthy themes, trends, and problems. Even with this division, the essays converge in interesting ways. For example, the Burger Court's immensely significant and controversial decision in *Roe v. Wade*, the abortion case, is discussed in five different chapters. Several of the chapters address the basic question of the Supreme Court's proper role in a democratic system of government. In addition to the nine chapters on specific areas of the Court's work, the last two chapters, one by a lawyer and one by a political scientist, present general critiques of the Burger Court that cut across a broad range of doctrinal categories.

No attempt has been made to provide comprehensive coverage of the Burger Court's work. Too much has transpired, on too broad a front. Important areas such as administrative law, securities regulation, environmental law, taxation, voting rights, federal-state relations, the separation of powers, and freedom of religion could well support chapters of their own. Certain of these subjects are discussed in some detail in chapters devoted to more encompassing observations. Others receive no coverage whatever. In addition, the inevitable lead time in the production process has prevented the authors from taking into account the Court's decisions during its 1982–83 term.

The selection of topics and authors has been influenced to some degree by a desire that the book reflect, within a broad range, the concerns and ideals to which the Society of American Law Teachers is dedicated. Even so, the diversity of perspectives is striking. So too is the variety of assessments that emerge. The Burger Court receives high praise from Richard Markovits for its work in antitrust law and measured praise from Ruth Bader Ginsburg for its decisions regarding sex discrimination. Paul Brest (race discrimination) and Theodore St. Antoine (labor law) find the Court's work in their areas difficult to encapsulate but more respectful of traditional liberal values than might have been predicted. Robert Bennett (poverty law) and

Yale Kamisar (criminal procedure) see the Burger Court as stridently conservative in its early years but more balanced recently. Thomas Emerson is alarmed by the Court's consistent lack of realism and penchant for balancing tests in the area of freedom of the press. Several of the authors decry the Court's lack of direction, at times even schizophrenia, in their respective areas. Yet Robert Burt detects a coherent theme—promotion of the traditional authoritarian socializing conception of child rearing—in the Court's family jurisprudence. Norman Dorsen and Joel Gora also find an explanatory principle—respect for private property—that ties together the Burger Court's variegated free speech decisions. Martin Shapiro and I agree that the Burger Court has been activist in nature but has not had the kind of clear-cut agenda that propelled the Warren Court. He attributes this absence of a theme to the breakdown of the New Deal consensus; I attribute it more to the distinctive personnel profile of the Burger Court.

Taken together, these essays indicate that the Burger Court's work does not lend itself to any concise, comprehensive characterization. In certain areas, the recent Court has consolidated the landmark advances of the Warren years. In other areas, a mild retrenchment has taken place. Much of the time, the Court seems to have been drifting. It adds up to a curious but nonetheless intriguing period in the history of a remarkable institution.

• Acknowledgments •

Judith Cox, Paula Franzese, Tracy Goldblum, Alexandra Rebay, and Patricia Root provided invaluable assistance in the preparation of this book. The essay by Norman Dorsen and Joel Gora, "The Burger Court and the Freedom of Speech," appeared in expanded form in the 1982 volume of the *Supreme Court Review*. The essay by Robert Burt, "The Burger Court and the Family," appeared in expanded form in the 1979 volume of the *Supreme Court Review*. Both essays are reprinted here by permission of the publisher of the *Supreme Court Review*, The University of Chicago Press. The profiles of the justices of the Burger Court are based on information provided in Friedman and Israel, eds., *The Justices of the United States Supreme Court*, vols. 4 and 5 (1969, 1978). The photographs of the justices are from the collection of the United States Supreme Court and are reproduced here by permission.

• The Burger Court •

• One •

Freedom of the Press
Under the Burger Court

Thomas I. Emerson

In 1969, when the transition to the Burger Court began, the press as a whole had grounds to feel that its position under the First Amendment was relatively secure. As far back as 1931, the Supreme Court in *Near v. Minnesota* had ruled that, except under certain limited circumstances, the press could not be subjected to restraint in advance of publication, either by a system of censorship or by court injunction. Shortly afterward, in *Grosjean v. American Press Co.*, the Court held that the press could not be subject to any burden, such as a tax, not imposed upon other enterprises. In the *Bridges, Pennekamp,* and *Craig* cases, decided in the 1940s, the Court had made clear that press criticism of the courts was protected, unless presenting a clear and present danger to the administration of justice, in marked contrast to the vulnerability of the press in England. The Warren Court, beginning with *New York Times Co. v. Sullivan* in 1964, had drastically altered the law of libel, assuring the press virtual immunity from damages for false statements, except where the statement was knowingly false or made with reckless disregard as to whether it was false or not. While the electronic media—radio and television—were subject to a licensing system and compelled to adhere to controls such as the fairness doctrine, that result was attributed entirely to the scarcity of facilities and the resulting need for those granted the privilege of owning broadcast stations to operate in the public interest. Even in the sensitive area of national security in time of war, the press had not been put under any formal restrictions.[1]

Despite appearances there were some weaknesses in the position of the press. A number of important issues remained unresolved. And the decisions of the Supreme Court, while generally favorable in results, were based upon doctrines that contained important loopholes. In making exceptions or employing the balancing test, the Court had never firmly closed the door to government intervention in the affairs of the press. Thus it was perhaps the general friendly attitude of the Warren Court, rather than a close analysis of its actual decisions, that gave comfort to the press.

In any event, after more than a dozen years of the Burger Court, much of the press has become seriously concerned. It feels that its First Amendment protections have been eroded and that it is being threatened by various

1

judicial encroachments. Thus in April 1979 the president of the American Newspaper Publishers Association called upon his fellow publishers to "fight to rescue, defend and uphold the First Amendment," saying that the "imperial judiciary . . . is bending the First Amendment at every turn" and has created an "atmosphere of intimidation" for the press.[2]

What, then, has become the status of the press under the Burger Court? An appraisal of the situation requires examination of the Court's rulings in five major areas: (1) libel and privacy; (2) free press–fair trial; (3) restrictions based on national security or other social interests; (4) limitations upon newsgathering; and (5) government regulation designed to improve the functioning of the press.

Before proceeding to this analysis, however, one emerging problem of doctrine should be considered. Does the First Amendment, in specifically referring to "freedom of the press," in addition to "freedom of speech," confer upon the press any special status not available to other institutions, groups, or individuals?

THE SPECIAL STATUS OF THE PRESS

The proposition that the First Amendment should be interpreted to extend special constitutional protection to the press was first clearly advanced by Justice Potter Stewart in an address at Yale Law School in 1974. He suggested that the framers of the Constitution intended to recognize "the organized press," that is, "the daily newspapers and other established news media," as "a fourth institution outside the Government," serving as "an additional check on the three official branches." He concluded that, as such an institution, the press was entitled to enjoy not only "freedom of speech," available to all, but an additional right to "freedom of the press." Justice Stewart's position has received some support from commentators. It has never been accepted by a majority of the Supreme Court, however, and Chief Justice Burger has explicitly rejected it.[3]

The debate over whether the press should receive special protection under the First Amendment has not been a productive one. If the term "press" is narrowly defined, there is no justification for singling it out for special treatment as compared with other institutions or persons who perform similar functions. If the term is broadly defined, the whole concept is stretched beyond any meaning. Nor have any standards been developed for ascertaining just what special rights the press is entitled to receive.

There are other, even more cogent reasons for rejecting Justice Stewart's analysis:

1. If the First Amendment is broken down into its constituent parts—speech, press, assembly, and petition—its scope, force, and power are

greatly diminished. The more effective approach, and one which the Supreme Court has actually taken, is to construe the First Amendment as broadly establishing a comprehensive right to "freedom of expression."

2. A distinction between freedom of speech and freedom of the press makes sense only in the context of a balancing approach to the First Amendment. If one seeks a more precise standard for measuring First Amendment rights, such as a full protection theory, the dichotomy between the "institutionalized press" and other communicators is not helpful.

3. There are dangers in affording the press special privileges, especially if the press is defined as the mass media. Special responsibilities are likely to follow.[4]

All in all, therefore, it is better to consider "the press" as simply one feature of an integrated system of freedom of expression. There are times when the nature of the "institutionalized press" requires that its particular advantages in communication, and the particular function it performs, be taken into account. This occurs primarily where there are physical limitations upon the process of newsgathering, as where access to the scene of a natural disaster must be restricted to a few persons, or where there are limits upon the number of persons who can be accommodated on the president's plane. In such situations it makes sense to give access to a representative of the "institutionalized press," who is in a better position to carry the news to the general public than an ordinary citizen. But this is quite different from visualizing the press as broadly entitled to unique privileges. On this issue the Burger Court's treatment of the press seems entirely correct.

LIBEL AND PRIVACY

In libel law the legacy handed down by the Warren Court was of prime importance to the press. Prior to 1964, Supreme Court dicta had it that false and defamatory statements were completely outside the purview of the First Amendment. The vulnerability of the press under this legal doctrine was evident in the first case in which the Court squarely addressed the problem. In the midst of the civil rights struggle in the South, the *New York Times* published an advertisement sharply criticizing government officials in Alabama for the manner in which they had attempted to suppress persons engaged in protest against racial discrimination. Some of the statements made in the advertisement were not accurate. A high-ranking police official in Montgomery, Alabama, sued the *New York Times* in the Alabama state courts and won a verdict of $500,000. The United States Supreme Court, in the landmark decision of *New York Times Co. v. Sullivan*, held that the Alabama libel law did not meet the requirements of the First Amendment.[5]

Justice Brennan's opinion for the majority of the Court was based essentially upon the proposition that the system of freedom of expression contemplates that "debate on public issues should be uninhibited, robust, and wide-open" and that a rule of law requiring the press or others to guarantee the truth of all their assertions "dampens the vigor and limits the variety of public debate." The Court concluded that public officials could not recover damages for a defamatory falsehood unless they could show that the statement had been made with "actual malice"—in other words, "with knowledge that it was false or with reckless disregard of whether it was false or not." Three justices, including Justices Black and Douglas, would have gone further and held that a public official could not prevail in a libel suit regardless of whether "actual malice" had been proved.[6]

The decision in *New York Times Co. v. Sullivan* was noteworthy because it did not attempt to resolve the issue by a balancing test but rather undertook to focus on the purposes served by the First Amendment, the dynamics of limiting expression, and the realistic need for protection of the system against inhibiting or repressive measures. In this it conformed closely to full protection theories. On the other hand, the decision left open a number of questions, including the application of the rule to persons who were not public officials and the problems involved in proving "actual malice."

In a subsequent series of cases the Supreme Court extended the "actual malice" rule to "public figures" and in 1971 to all matters "of public or general interest." By this time, however, the Court was seriously fragmented. In 1974, with the arrival of two new justices, the Court turned sharply in the other direction. In *Gertz v. Robert Welch, Inc.* a majority of the Court, returning to a balancing test, held that the "actual malice" rule should be limited to public officials and public figures and that, in libel suits brought by "private individuals," the state or federal government could adopt any rule so long as it required at least a showing of negligence on the part of the defendant. This position was reaffirmed two years later by a 6 to 3 vote in *Time, Inc. v. Firestone.* Moreover, the Court adopted a very narrow definition of "public figure": in *Gertz* a well-known Chicago lawyer, who had been active in various controversial public issues, and in *Firestone* a socially prominent woman, who had been involved in a widely publicized divorce case, were held not to be public figures. Later decisions also excluded from the category of public figures a director of research at a state mental institution who had published widely in scientific journals and had received over half a million dollars in federal funds for a research project, and an individual convicted of criminal contempt for failing to appear before a grand jury investigating espionage.[7]

In *Herbert v. Lando*, the Supreme Court filled in some of the gaps left in the administration of the "actual malice" rule. Lieutenant Colonel Anthony Herbert had received extensive publicity during the Vietnam War when he had accused his superior officers of covering up reports of atrocities and other war crimes. Subsequently, in CBS's television program "60 Minutes" and in an article in the *Atlantic Monthly*, Herbert's version of the events was vigorously challenged and it was suggested that he had made the war-crime charges to explain his being relieved from his command. Herbert brought suit for libel and, conceding that he was a "public figure" and thus had to prove "actual malice," sought in discovery proceedings to inquire into the mental states and editorial processes of those responsible for the publications. The Court, 6 to 3, upheld the right to make such inquiries. The majority admitted that probing into the thoughts, opinions, and conclusions of the publisher had some chilling effect but concluded that this was inherent in the "actual malice" rule and was "consistent with the balance struck by our prior decisions." To the argument that such questioning would render impossible full and frank discussion in making editorial judgments, the majority held that the editorial process was entitled to First Amendment protection but not where there was a specific claim of injury from a false statement. As to the burdens placed upon publishers by elaborate discovery proceedings and the costs of litigation, the majority answered that only "complete immunity from liability from defamation" would relieve this impact.[8]

Thus the Burger Court has largely abandoned the approach of the Warren Court, which, giving the First Amendment a preferential status, looked closely at the actual effect of government restrictions imposed by the libel laws. Rather the Burger Court has returned to a balancing posture and has marched down the hill through the gaps left open by its predecessor. As a result the present state of libel law has greatly weakened the position of the press. So far as reporting on public issues is concerned, where neither a public official nor a "public figure" is involved, the press is subject to libel suits, which, as the Court said in *New York Times Co. v. Sullivan*, "dampens the vigor and limits the variety of public debate." Where the "actual malice" rule does apply, there is no protection against the costs of defending libel suits or the inhibiting effects of probing into a writer's or an editor's state of mind, professional standards, or editorial discussions. Furthermore, it is apparent that there has been a dramatic increase in the number of libel suits brought against the press, including some of a purely nuisance character, and that damages awarded and legal costs have soared. The question still remains whether, as Justices Black and Douglas thought, the law of libel is inherently incompatible with the First Amendment.

In privacy law the main constitutional issues remain unresolved. It is clear that protection against intrusions upon personal privacy, either by the government or by nongovernment organizations or individuals, is rapidly becoming a major task for our legal institutions. At most points there is no conflict between the emerging right of privacy and freedom of the press. On the contrary, the two rights are mutually supportive in that both are vital features of the basic system of individual rights. At other points, there is only a minor likelihood of conflict, as in the law of trespass or the regulation of sound trucks. There are, however, two major areas where an accommodation must be worked out. One concerns the privacy tort, in which suit is brought by an individual against the publisher of matter alleged to invade his or her privacy or in which a government law or regulation attempts to prohibit the publication of facts that are considered to intrude upon privacy. The other concerns the right of the press to obtain information from the government, where invocation of right-to-know principles to force disclosure may run squarely into the claim of an individual that data about one's personal affairs should not be disseminated to others.

Neither the Warren Court nor the Burger Court has squarely addressed these issues. In *Time, Inc. v. Hill* the Warren Court, and in *Cantrell v. Forest City Publishing Co.* the Burger Court, discussed the problem, but those cases actually were concerned more with misrepresentations of fact (and were therefore more like defamation) than with a pure invasion of privacy. In *Cox Broadcasting Co. v. Cohn*, a state statute prohibiting the publication of the name or identity of a rape victim was held invalid insofar as it applied to a broadcasting station that had obtained the name from court records which were open to public inspection. The Court emphasized that it was dealing only with a situation where the information was already available in public records. Similarly, the Court has not passed upon the right of the press to obtain information from the government about the private affairs of an individual, except in connection with the interpretation of the statutory exemption for privacy in the Freedom of Information Act.[9]

While the press looks with some alarm to the possibility of adverse rulings on these issues, it would seem doubtful that its fears are well grounded. Neither the Burger Court nor any other court is likely to carry the constitutional right of privacy to a point where it seriously interferes with an institution as powerful as the press. Even if the right of privacy is given preference over the First Amendment, the scope of that right is likely to be very narrowly defined.

FREE PRESS–FAIR TRIAL

The problem of reconciling the First Amendment right to freedom of the press with the Fifth and Sixth Amendment rights to a fair trial before an impartial jury is one of long standing. In general, various devices are available to assure a fair trial without imposing restrictions upon press coverage of events. These include change of venue, postponement of the trial, careful scrutiny of prospective jurors, warning instructions to the jury, sequestration of jurors and witnesses, and, as a last resort, reversal of conviction and a new trial. Such measures were encouraged by the Warren Court and it did not have occasion to rule beyond that point.[10]

Two other methods of preventing prejudicial publicity are available, however, and these do directly affect the press. One is to prohibit the publication of information by the press, and the second is to withhold information from the press. The Burger Court has dealt with both.

In *Nebraska Press Association v. Stuart*, one of the major decisions of the 1975–76 Term, the Burger Court considered the prohibition device. Following a notorious murder of six members of a family, and prior to trial of the alleged culprit, the Nebraska courts issued an order restraining the press from publishing any facts about the case that implicated the defendant. The Supreme Court unanimously reversed. The result was an important victory for the press, but the manner of reaching it left the press less satisfied.[11]

Chief Justice Burger, writing for a majority of five, observed that "prior restraints on speech and publication are the most serious and least tolerable infringement on First Amendment rights." Nevertheless, he went on, the rule against prior restraint is not absolute and hence the question is whether there is a serious and likely danger to the fairness of the trial. This issue, in turn, depends upon what is shown with respect to "(a) the nature and extent of pretrial news coverage; (b) whether other measures would be likely to mitigate the effects of unrestrained pretrial publicity; and (c) how effectively a restraining order would operate to prevent the threatened danger." Examining the record with a highly skeptical eye, Chief Justice Burger concluded that the state had not met "the heavy burden of demonstrating, in advance of trial, that without prior restraints a fair trial will be denied."[12]

Justice Brennan, with Justices Stewart and Marshall concurring, took the position that a prior restraint upon publication was never permissible as a means of securing a fair trial. Justice Stevens was doubtful, but inclined to agree with Justice Brennan.

Government measures to withhold information from the press raise somewhat different questions. Certainly the First Amendment right to publish is more fully protected than the First Amendment right to obtain information that the government does not wish to disclose. Thus there would seem to be little doubt that the government may legitimately instruct its police, prosecutors, court attendants, and other employees not to give out information that might prejudice a potential defendant in obtaining a fair trial. The federal Department of Justice has long imposed such restrictions. On the other hand, some limits on the government's right to withhold information or to conduct proceedings from which the public is excluded are not only implicit in the First Amendment right to know but appear to be mandated by the Sixth Amendment requirement of a public trial. These issues reached the Burger Court in 1979 in *Gannett Co., Inc. v. DePasquale*.[13]

The *Gannett* case involved the disappearance and apparent murder of a resident of a Rochester, New York, suburb. The case received substantial, but not inflammatory, attention in the Rochester press. Prior to trial of the accused, a motion to suppress evidence, including statements made to the police, was set for hearing. On request of the defendants' counsel, concurred in by the prosecution, the trial judge ordered the exclusion of the public and the press from the hearing. A challenge by the newspapers involved was overruled by the New York courts. The United States Supreme Court, in a 5 to 4 vote, affirmed.

Justice Stewart, writing for the majority, ruled that the Sixth Amendment right to a public trial is for the benefit of the defendant alone, that the right can be waived by the defendant with the agreement of the prosecution and the court, and that "members of the public have no constitutional right under the Sixth and Fourteenth Amendments to attend criminal trials." Justice Blackmun, speaking for the dissenters, argued that the Sixth Amendment was intended for the benefit of the public as well as the defendant and could not be waived by the defendant. He acknowledged that there were qualifications on the right of the public to attend criminal trials, and specifically that the public could be excluded from a pretrial suppression hearing where "necessary in order to ensure that a defendant not be denied a fair trial as a result of prejudicial publicity flowing from that hearing." Justice Blackmun contended, however, that any exception should be "narrowly drawn" and exclusion permitted only after a careful balancing of all the factors involved.[14]

On the First Amendment issue, both majority and dissenters declared that they did not find it necessary to decide whether there was a First Amendment right of access to criminal trials. In fact, however, both sides did severely limit any First Amendment protections. Justice Stewart took the position that, even if a First Amendment right existed, there was no violation of that right because (1) the protesting newspapers had been afforded an opportunity to be heard by the trial judge; (2) the trial judge properly "balanced the 'constitutional rights of the press and the public' against the 'defendants' right to a fair trial'"; and (3) the denial of access was "not absolute but only temporary." Justice Blackmun stated that "[t]o the extent the [First Amendment] protects a right of access to the proceeding, the standards enunciated under the Sixth Amendment suffice to protect that right."[15]

Following the *Gannett* decision four of the justices engaged in an unusual public debate over the scope of the Court's ruling. Chief Justice Burger contended, as he had in a concurring opinion, that the case stood only for the proposition that the public and the press could be excluded from pretrial suppression hearings, not necessarily from criminal trials generally. Justices Powell, Stevens, and Blackmun disagreed. Justice Stewart's opinion seems clearly to hold that there is no Sixth Amendment right of access across the board. Although Chief Justice Burger "joined" in the Stewart opinion, his vote was necessary to make a majority and hence final resolution of the issue remained in doubt.[16]

The *Gannett* case aroused intense criticism in the press, a criticism echoed by many legal commentators. While the scope of the ruling was not entirely clear, the decision plainly ranked as one of the most antipress utterances of the decade. At worst it allowed a trial judge to exclude the public and the press from all criminal proceedings virtually at will. At best it afforded a pale and weak constitutional protection. Far from establishing an absolute right of the press to attend judicial proceedings, it made no effort to limit exclusion to the narrowest possible grounds. Nor did the Court take into account the pressures upon trial judges to close the courtroom in many situations or the fact that their decisions would be virtually unreviewable. Not unexpectedly, following the *Gannett* case the press began to report an increasing number of exclusions.

The following year, in *Richmond Newspapers, Inc. v. Virginia*, the Supreme Court substantially changed its tune. In that case the defendant, accused of murdering a hotel manager, had been found guilty at his first trial but the conviction was reversed because a bloodstained shirt alleged to have belonged to him had been improperly admitted into evidence. Two succeeding trials ended in mistrial, the second because a juror had told other jurors about the first trial. At the fourth trial the defendant's counsel asked that the proceeding be closed to the public and the press. The prosecutor stated that he had no objection. The judge thereupon, without making any formal findings, granted the motion. The Supreme Court, by vote of 7 to 1, held the closure of the trial proceedings to be unconstitutional.[17]

Although the seven justices in the majority issued six opinions, they were in general agreement on the basic constitutional doctrine and its application to the facts of the particular case before them. The Sixth Amendment was not invoked; it was apparently assumed that the *Gannett* case had settled the point that, in trial as well as in pretrial proceedings, the right to a public trial extended only to the defendant and not to the public or the press. Rather the decision was placed upon First Amendment grounds. Chief Justice Burger, in one of the two main majority opinions, reasoned that, historically, criminal trials had been "open to all who cared to observe"; that this openness was not a mere "quirk of history" but served important functions "under our system of justice"; and, quoting right-to-know language in previous decisions, that "the First Amendment can be read as protecting the right of everyone to attend trials so as to give meaning to [its] explicit guarantees" intended to assure "freedom of communication on matters relating to the functioning of government." Acknowledging that the Constitution nowhere explicitly "spells out" such a guarantee, Chief Justice Burger observed that the Court had previously found that "certain unarticulated rights were implicit in the enumerated guarantees."[18]

Justice Brennan, writing the other main majority opinion, agreed that the First Amendment assured the public and the press a right of access to trial proceedings. His basic position was that the First Amendment "has a *struc-*

tural role to play in securing and fostering our republican system of self-government"; debate on public issues should not only be "uninhibited, robust, and wide-open" but "must be informed." Justice Brennan recognized that the "correlative freedom of access to information" could not be provided a "categorical assurance" of protection equal to that afforded the right to communicate. In this area, the Court must invoke its powers "with discrimination and temperance." He suggested two principles to guide the Court. First, "the case for a right of access has special force when drawn from an enduring and vital tradition of public entree to particular proceedings or information"; second, in deciding individual cases "what is crucial . . . is whether access to a particular government process is important in terms of that very process." Analyzing "historical and current practice" with respect to the openness of trials and weighing "the importance of public access to the trial process itself," he found that both principles led to First Amendment protection.[19]

Having enunciated the basic doctrine the majority had no difficulty in applying it to the case before them. Both main opinions devoted only a single paragraph to this problem. Chief Justice Burger merely noted that "the trial judge made no findings to support closure; no inquiry was made as to whether alternative solutions would have met the need to ensure fairness; there was no recognition of any right under the Constitution for the public or press to attend the trial." Hence he found it unnecessary to determine what "overriding interest articulated in findings" might justify closure. Similarly, Justice Brennan stated that "[w]hat countervailing interests might be sufficiently compelling to reverse [the] presumption of openness need not concern us now." Thus the Court, while making it clear that the right of access to trials was not absolute, did not undertake to explore the nature of the exceptions.[20]

The *Richmond Newspapers* case is noteworthy on several grounds. For one thing, the Supreme Court was plainly demonstrating a more friendly attitude toward the press than it had exhibited a year before in the *Gannett* case. More important, the *Richmond Newspapers* case was the first in which the Court actually upheld a First Amendment right to obtain information that the government wished to withhold, a matter discussed below. So far as access of the press to criminal trials is concerned, the outcome of the *Richmond Newspapers* case is likely to be that the press will seldom be excluded on the ground that prejudicial publicity might result in an unfair trial. Although the Court did not accord the press an absolute right to be present, in a trial the alternative of sequestering the jury and witnesses is always available. Hence few occasions for banning the public or the press should arise.

With regard to pretrial proceedings the press is not in as favorable a position. Under the *Gannett* rule it may not rely upon the Sixth Amendment right to a public trial, and its rights under the First Amendment are uncertain. The Supreme Court found in *Gannett* that, historically, pretrial hearings have never been characterized by the same degree of openness as actual trials. Hence it is not clear that the Court would hold the First Amendment applicable at all. If a First Amendment right is ruled to exist, it will be subject to exceptions on a case-by-case basis where "overriding" or "countervailing" interests are found to be present. And the alternative of sequestration of the jury, affording automatic protection to the defendant's interests, will not be available. Under such circumstances the press will have no assurance that its First Amendment claim will prevail. Since only a small percentage of criminal cases ever get to trial, and since many are for all practical purposes decided at the preliminary hearing stage, important aspects of the criminal justice process may not be open to the public or the press.

In one fair-trial controversy of long standing the Supreme Court has come down largely on the side of the press. The issue involves the use of television, radio, and photographic equipment in the courtroom. In 1965 the Court overturned the conviction of Billie Sol Estes, charged with having engaged in a notorious swindle, on the ground that he had been denied a fair trial because parts of the proceedings had been broadcast on television and radio. From the six opinions rendered in the case it was not entirely clear whether the broadcasting of trial proceedings constituted a denial of due process per se, or whether a constitutional right would be infringed only in particular cases such as the one before the Court. In 1981 the Burger Court resolved the matter in favor of the press. In *Chandler v. Florida* it unanimously upheld an experimental program in the Florida courts that allowed broadcast and photographic coverage of trials, subject to certain guidelines and under the control of the trial judge. The result has been to open the door to a privilege long sought by the press.[21]

RESTRICTIONS ON PUBLICATION BASED ON NATIONAL SECURITY OR OTHER SOCIAL INTERESTS

The Burger Court has not fully expressed itself on the question of what restrictions, if any, can be imposed upon the press with respect to the publication of information that may affect national security. One major decision in this area, the *Pentagon Papers* case, was rendered in 1971, during the early years of the Burger Court, and did not lead to any definite doctrine. The other major decision, *Snepp v. United States*, involved only one aspect of the question. Nevertheless, certain general conclusions as to the attitude of the Burger Court can be drawn.

The *Pentagon Papers* case, officially known as *New York Times Co. v. United States*, arose when the *New York Times*, the *Washington Post*, and other newspapers began publication of a series of articles based on the Pentagon Papers, a highly classified history of the Vietnam War made available to them by a former government employee who had access to the documents. The government sought an injunction, claiming that publication would cause "grave and irreparable injury" to the United States. The case reached the Supreme Court in less than two weeks. In a 6 to 3 per curiam opinion, the Court denied the government's request on the ground that it had not met "the heavy burden of showing justification for the imposition of such a restraint."[22]

Each of the nine justices wrote a separate opinion setting forth his reasons for supporting or opposing the conclusion reached. Justices Black and Douglas asserted that under no circumstances did the government have power to "make laws enjoining publication of current news and abridging freedom of the press in the name of 'national security.'" Justice Brennan agreed, but with the reservation that an exception might be permissible in the limited area of information concerning tactical military operations. Justices Stewart and White took the position that a prior restraint would be justified only on a showing of "direct, immediate, and irreparable damage to our Nation or its people." Justice Marshall, without reaching the basic First Amendment issues, based his conclusion upon the fact that Congress had never authorized the executive branch to invoke the jurisdiction of the courts to prevent the publication of national security information. The three dissenting justices thought the courts should exercise only a very limited review when the executive branch had determined that disclosure "would irreparably impair the national security."[23]

The result reached in the *Pentagon Papers* case gave significant support to freedom of the press. Certainly a contrary conclusion would have dealt the press a devastating blow. But the theoretical position of the press does not appear strong. Justices Black and Douglas are no longer on the Court. It seems safe to assume that a substantial majority of the present Court would not go beyond the position taken by Justices Stewart and White. Thus the press would be subject to an injunction whenever the government could persuade a court that publication would cause "direct, immediate, and irreparable damage" to national security and would be subject to a temporary restraining order whenever the government made that allegation. This is, indeed, just what happened in the *Progressive* case, where the *Progressive* magazine was "temporarily restrained" from publishing an article on the manufacture of the hydrogen bomb for seven months before the government's suit for an injunction was ultimately withdrawn.[24]

The *Snepp* case developed from the practice of the Central Intelligence Agency, the Department of Defense, the State Department, and a growing number of other agencies requiring that their employees, as a condition of employment, sign a statement agreeing that they would not publish any information or material relating to the agency, either during or after their employment, without specific prior approval of the agency. The validity of such an exaction, and its application to various types of information, raise crucial questions under the First Amendment. Not only are drastic restrictions imposed upon the employee's or former employee's freedom of expression but the device cuts off the public from an enormous volume of information, ideas, and opinions relating to the activities of an ever-expanding government. Moreover, the requirement of silence can readily be utilized by the agency as a protective screen to hide errors, incompetence, illegalities, or corruption. In addition, the mandate is hardly likely to be enforced equally between friends and critics, or between the Kissingers and the Snepps. And it relies for administration upon a system of prior censorship— a highly disfavored procedure under traditional First Amendment doctrine.

Despite the urgency of these issues the Burger Court, in *United States v. Marchetti*, declined to address them. Marchetti, a former employee of the CIA, had coauthored a book entitled *The CIA and the Cult of Intelligence*, which was sharply critical of CIA operations. When the government learned that Marchetti was about to publish the book, it sought an injunction to compel him to submit the manuscript to the CIA for approval. The lower courts granted the injunction and the Supreme Court denied review. When the CIA thereupon ordered 168 deletions (reduced from an initial claim of 339), Marchetti went back to court. The Court of Appeals for the Fourth Circuit, however, upheld the government's contention that any classified material could be suppressed even though the validity of the classification had not been established. Again the Supreme Court denied review.[25]

The *Snepp* case also involved a former CIA employee. In this case, however, Snepp's book *Decent Interval*, a critical account of the last days of the United States forces in Vietnam, had already been published without approval by the CIA. The government brought suit for an injunction requiring Snepp to submit any further writings to the CIA for advance clearance and asking for an order imposing a "constructive trust" for the benefit of the government upon all profits that Snepp might receive from publishing the book. Snepp asserted, and the government conceded for purposes of the case, that the book contained no classified information. The Supreme Court, without waiting for briefs or hearing argument, issued a per curiam opinion affirming issuance of the injunction and ordering Snepp to pay over to the government all his earnings from sales of the book. The Court dealt with the First Amendment issues only in a brief footnote. It simply said that Snepp had "voluntarily signed the agreement that expressly obligated him to submit any proposed publication for prior review" and that the government had "a compelling interest in protecting both the secrecy of information important to our national security and the appearance of confidentiality so essential to the effective operation of our foreign intelligence service." Justices Brennan, Marshall, and Stevens dissented.[26]

Apart from the highly unusual procedure followed, the Burger Court's handling of the *Snepp* case is remarkable in that the majority refused to acknowledge that any substantial First Amendment issue was at stake. It accepted the agreement imposed by a government agency upon its employees as if it were an ordinary contract between two private persons, rather than a serious encroachment upon the constitutional right of the employees to communicate and of the public to obtain vital information. At the same time it upheld, almost casually, a system of prior restraint. It made no effort whatever to limit government control over information affecting "national security" to the minimum necessary for the performance of governmental functions. And its theory of a "constructive trust" over information the government asserted to be confidential could conceivably be applied not only to authors but to editors, publishers, and others, thereby in effect creating an official secrets act.

All in all there is not much in the Burger Court's record to give the press any substantial hope that the Court will give it vigorous support in a conflict with the government over the demands of national security.[27]

In two other cases, not involving national security or former government employees, the Burger Court did strike down restrictions upon the publication of information concerning government activities. *Landmark Communications, Inc. v. Virginia* concerned a Virginia statute that made it a criminal offense to divulge information with respect to proceedings before the Virginia Judicial Inquiry and Review Commission, a state body authorized to hear complaints regarding the disability or misconduct of a state judge. The *Virginia Pilot*, utilizing lawful methods in obtaining the information, published an article that accurately reported on a pending inquiry before the commission. A conviction under the statute was unanimously reversed by the Supreme Court. Chief Justice Burger, writing for the Court, weighed and balanced in considerable detail various social interests advanced by the state in support of its restriction. He ultimately concluded that those interests were not "sufficient to justify the encroachment on First Amendment guarantees" and resolved the issue in favor of publication.[28]

The Court came to a similar conclusion in *Smith v. Daily Mail Publishing Co.* Here a West Virginia statute prohibited the publication in any newspaper of the name of any youth charged as a juvenile offender, except with the permission of the juvenile court. The defendant newspapers, after obtaining the information from interviews of witnesses at the scene, published the name and picture of a high school student who had shot and killed a classmate. The Court unanimously struck down the statute as a violation of the First Amendment. Chief Justice Burger, citing the *Landmark* case and the *Cox Broadcasting* case, stated the law to be that "if a newspaper lawfully obtains truthful information about a matter of public significance, then state officials may not constitutionally punish publication of the information, absent a need to further a state interest of the highest order." The Court then examined the interest of the state in protecting the anonymity of the juvenile offender and found it "not sufficient to justify the application of a criminal penalty" to the newspapers. This time the balancing was brief and indeed cursory. Justice Rehnquist, who balanced more elaborately, came to the opposite conclusion but concurred in the judgment because the statute prohibited only publication by a newspaper, not by radio, television, or other forms of communication.[29]

The results in both cases upheld the press. But again the press cannot take complete comfort from the Burger Court's approach to these problems. Obviously, the balancing process can go either way and, in the *Daily Mail* case, seems hardly to have been taken seriously.

LIMITATIONS ON NEWSGATHERING

An increasing number of issues involving the press relate not to the right of the press to publish but to its right to gather and process the news. Even if direct prohibition upon the dissemination of news were wholly eliminated, governmental regulation that impaired the capacity of the press to obtain information, or to make editorial judgments about what to publish, could have a critical impact upon the functioning of the system of freedom of expression. In recent years problems of this nature have come to the fore in three connections: (1) protection of confidential sources in judicial proceedings—the so-called reporter's privilege; (2) use of investigative methods by the government that expose the press to harassment; and (3) the right of the press to obtain information from the government. Decisions of the Burger Court in these areas have not, on the whole, been favorable to the press.

Reporter's Privilege

Journalists have a long tradition of refusing to reveal information or sources of information when they have obtained material under a pledge of secrecy. They have felt that their function as part of a free press cannot be effectively performed on any other basis and they have been ready to go to jail in order to maintain their position. Without question, the pledge of confidentiality, and the capacity to honor it, are crucial to most investigative reporting. Whether it be an investigation of organized crime, the drug scene, a militant political organization, or corruption or incompetence in government, much information vital to public decision-making would not be made available if reporters could be forced, often by powerful and hostile officials, to reveal the identity of their informants, produce their notes, or otherwise disclose details of their inquiry. On the whole, the courts and government prosecuting officials have recognized the journalists' position and confrontations have been rare. It was inevitable, however, that sooner or later the issues would be presented for constitutional adjudication and this finally occurred in 1972, in the case of *Branzburg v. Hayes*. The decision of the Supreme Court is typical of the Burger Court's approach to the newsgathering rights of the press.[30]

The *Branzburg* case involved three reporters. One had written two stories about the local drug scene. Another had been admitted to a Black Panther headquarters when a police raid was anticipated. And a third had covered the activities of the Black Panthers and other black groups. All were called by grand juries investigating possible violations of criminal laws but refused to testify about information they had obtained in confidence. Before the Supreme Court they did not "claim an absolute privilege against official interrogation in all circumstances," but only that they should not be forced to appear or testify unless substantial grounds were shown for believing that they possessed important information necessary to the proceedings and not available from other sources. The Supreme Court, in a 5 to 4 decision, rejected their claim.[31]

Justice White, writing for the majority, acknowledged that newsgathering did "qualify for First Amendment protection": "[W]ithout some protection for seeking out the news, freedom of the press could be eviscerated." "But," he went on, "these cases involve no intrusions upon speech or assembly, no prior restraint or restriction on what the press may publish, and no express or implied command that the press publish what it prefers to withhold." In that situation, he found, "the sole issue before us is the obligation of reporters to respond to grand jury subpoenas as other citizens do." Utilizing a balancing process he concluded: "[W]e perceive no basis for holding that the public interest in law enforcement and in ensuring effective grand jury proceedings is insufficient to override the consequential, but uncertain, burden on newsgathering that is said to result from insisting that reporters, like other citizens, respond to relevant questions put to them in the course of a valid grand jury investigation or criminal trial."[32]

Justice Powell, whose vote was necessary to make up the majority of five, somewhat qualified the stark position taken by his majority colleagues. In his view, "if the newsman . . . has reason to believe that his testimony implicates confidential source relationships without a legitimate need of law enforcement," the court should strike the "balance of these vital constitutional and societal interests on a case-by-case basis."[33]

Justice Stewart, writing for himself and Justices Brennan and Marshall, charged that "[t]he Court's crabbed view of the First Amendment reflects a disturbing insensitivity to the critical role of an independent press in our society" and that it "thus invites state and federal authorities to undermine the historical independence of the press by attempting to annex the journalistic profession as an investigative arm of the government." Concluding that "First Amendment rights require special safeguards," these three dissenters took the position that "when a reporter is asked to appear before a grand jury and reveal confidences," the government "must (1) show that there is probable cause to believe that the newsman has information that is closely relevant to a specific probable violation of law; (2) demonstrate that the information sought cannot be obtained by alternative means less destructive of First Amendment rights; and (3) demonstrate a compelling and overriding interest in the information."[34]

Justice Douglas, also dissenting, was alone in his view that "a newsman has an absolute right not to appear before a grand jury": "Forcing a reporter before a grand jury will have two retarding effects upon the ear and the pen of the press. Fear of exposure will cause dissidents to communicate less openly to trusted reporters. And, fear of accountability will cause editors and critics to write with more restrained pens."[35]

Following *Branzburg* the number of instances in which reporters were called upon to produce materials obtained in confidence greatly increased, but the Supreme Court did not undertake to review any further cases. The impact of the *Branzburg* decision was made clear when the Court refused to intervene in the Myron Farber case. Farber, a reporter for the *New York Times*, had made an investigation of a series of mysterious deaths in a New Jersey hospital. As a result of his articles in the *Times*, further inquiry was undertaken by the New Jersey authorities and Dr. Mario E. Jascalevich was indicted for murder. The defense attorney for Dr. Jascalevich subpoenaed all the notes, statements, pictures, and other materials in the possession of Farber and the *New York Times* for possible use on cross-examination. The trial court ordered that all these documents be produced, so that it might determine whether any information contained therein was relevant to the defendant's case. Farber and the *New York Times* refused and were cited for contempt of court. Two Supreme Court justices refused a stay, thereby making a review impossible. In the end Farber spent forty days in jail and the *Times* paid $285,000 in fines and $750,000 in legal fees. Dr. Jascalevich was acquitted. [36]

The attitude toward the press exhibited by the Burger Court in the *Branzburg* case is in sharp contrast to that displayed by the Warren Court in *New York Times Co. v. Sullivan*. Instead of concern that the press remain "uninhibited, robust, and wide-open," the Burger Court is satisfied if the press is not subjected to "official harassment." Rather than making a realistic appraisal of the inhibitions imposed on the press arising from the rule of law under consideration, the Burger Court casually concludes that "the evidence fails to demonstrate that there would be a significant constriction of the flow of news to the public" from compelling disclosure of confidential sources. In place of formulating doctrine upon the basis of the impact of the proposed rule upon effective performance by the press of its First Amendment function, the Burger Court is content to balance that function vaguely against the "public interest in law enforcement" and does not even impose a requirement of "compelling reasons" in order to override First Amendment rights. And without attempting at least to limit as much as possible the occasions when First Amendment rights are to be infringed, the Burger Court (except for the Powell qualification) rejects all efforts to confine demands for the production of confidential materials to the most necessary and urgent situations.

It should be noted, moreover, that even if the position of the Stewart minority were accepted, there would remain, as is true of the decision in *New York Times Co. v. Sullivan*, serious unanswered questions. The minority solution, while it leaves open the possibility that in individual cases a lower court could strike the balance in favor of the reporter's privilege, in effect withholds virtually all constitutional protection. Since the newsgatherer can seldom know in advance under what circumstances a court will allow him to keep a pledge of confidence, he cannot rely upon any constitutional right to make such a pledge. In that situation the privilege is of little use, and investigative reporters must rely upon the power and the will of the press to resist government encroachment. Only Justice Douglas squarely faced these problems.

Intrusive Government Investigating Techniques

The second aspect of newsgathering that has come under the scrutiny of the Supreme Court concerns government investigative methods that affect the operation of the press. The approach of the Burger Court to this problem has been similar to its attitude to reporter's privilege. The main case is *Zurcher v. Stanford Daily*, decided in 1978.[37]

The *Stanford Daily* case grew out of a student demonstration on the Stanford University campus that ended in a clash with the police. Two days later the *Stanford Daily*, a student newspaper, published stories and photographs relating to the episode. The following day the local district attorney obtained a search warrant and four police officers conducted an exhaustive search of the *Daily*'s offices, including its photographic laboratories, files, desks, and wastepaper baskets. The *Daily* brought suit in federal court under section 1983 for violation of its constitutional rights. The district court upheld the *Daily*'s contention. It ruled that a search warrant, allowing a physical raid on the *Daily*'s offices without prior notice, was valid under the Fourth Amendment "only in the rare circumstance where there is a *clear showing* that (1) important materials will be destroyed or removed from the jurisdiction; *and* (2) a restraining order would be futile." Otherwise the prosecuting officials would have to obtain evidence by issuing a subpoena, which gives the recipient notice and opportunity to contest and involves no physical search by the police.[38]

The Supreme Court reversed, 5 to 3, with Justice Brennan not participating. Justice White, writing for the majority, held first that the Fourth Amendment permitted searches of third-party premises for evidence even though the owner of the premises was not suspected of any criminal activity. He then went on to consider the application of that rule to a situation where the search was directed against newspaper offices, thus bringing into play the additional safeguards of the First Amendment. Justice White ruled that consideration of First Amendment values demanded only that the courts apply warrant requirements "with particular exactitude" and that no further protection was necessary. He was not persuaded otherwise by the close historical links between the First Amendment and the Fourth Amendment, both of which were designed to protect freedom of the press; by a series of Supreme Court decisions holding that searches impinging upon First Amendment rights, such as a search for allegedly subversive or obscene literature, were subject to special limitations; by Supreme Court decisions requiring that prior restraints upon publication, if allowed at all, must be accompanied by special procedures for notice and hearing; or by basic First Amendment doctrine requiring that the least drastic means be utilized. While he recognized the possibility that "confidential sources will disappear and that the press will suppress news because of fears of warranted searches," he nevertheless concluded: "Whatever incremental effect there may be in this regard if search warrants, as well as subpoenas, are permissible in proper circumstances, it does not make a constitutional difference in our judgment."[39]

Justice Stewart, accompanied by Justice Marshall, dissented. He stressed that the "most immediate and obvious First Amendment injury caused by such a visitation by the police is physical disruption" and elaborated on the burden to the press resulting from the possibility of disclosure of information received from confidential sources. Noting that affidavits in the record attested to this impact, he argued: "Despite the Court's rejection of this uncontroverted evidence, I believe it clearly establishes that unannounced police searches of newspaper offices will significantly burden the constitutionally protected function of the press to gather news and report it to the public." Justice Stevens also dissented, believing that a warrant for search of third-party premises should issue only upon a showing of probable cause that the evidence would otherwise be destroyed.[40]

Justice Stewart's warning with respect to the impact of police searches upon the press understates the case. In the course of everyday operations the news media frequently obtain information that might constitute evidence of violation of law. Under the *Stanford Daily* rule, prosecutors and others are authorized to obtain a warrant that would allow them to break into a news office, without notice, and to search the entire premises looking for evidence. It is hard to think of any conduct by government that would pose a greater threat to freedom of the press. Any news enterprise that appeared to be probing too deeply into government corruption, or that criticized or offended the government in some way, would be subject to harassment by prosecuting authorities. Judicial supervision of the issuance of warrants is likely to be a formality and, in any event, cannot control the actions of the police once they are inside the premises to be searched. Moreover, in all but the most exceptional circumstances a subpoena would accomplish the purpose of obtaining evidence. There is no need for such a crude and dangerous use of governmental power.

Thus far prosecutors and the police do not appear to have taken advantage of the opportunities presented to them by the *Stanford Daily* case. Yet there is no guarantee that this forbearance will continue in future periods of tension.

That the Burger Court's decision in *Stanford Daily* is not an aberration would seem to be confirmed by its actions in two subsequent cases. In *Reporters Committee for Freedom of the Press v. American Telephone and Telegraph Co.*, the Court of Appeals for the District of Columbia upheld the right of government investigators to obtain from the telephone company the records of telephone calls made by reporters, no notice being given to the person whose records were thus inspected. The Supreme Court refused to review the case, over the dissents of Justices Brennan, Stewart, and Marshall. And in *Smith v. Maryland*, the Court in a 5 to 3 decision upheld the right of government investigative authorities, without any need for obtaining a warrant, to arrange with the telephone company for installation of a "pen register," which would record all telephone numbers dialed from a particular phone. The majority, ruling that no search within the meaning of the Fourth Amendment was involved, did not even mention the First Amendment. The vulnerability of journalists to use of the pen register was noted only in dissent.[41]

Right to Obtain Information
from the Government

The third aspect of newsgathering—the right of the press to obtain information from the government—raises frontier issues in First Amendment law. The Supreme Court has long held that the First Amendment protects not only the right to communicate but the right to know, that is, the right to read, to listen, to see, and otherwise to receive communications. Thus in *Lamont v. Postmaster General*, decided in 1965, the Warren Court upheld the right of citizens to receive "foreign communist propaganda" from abroad without having to notify government authorities that they wished such mail to be delivered to them. A powerful constitutional argument can be made that the right to know also embraces a right to obtain information from the government in order to communicate it to others. One of the principal functions of the First Amendment—to facilitate the participation of citizens in self-government—requires full access to government information. In short, the issue presented is whether there is a constitutional basis for limiting secrecy in government.[42]

In addition to the national security issues raised in the *Marchetti* and *Snepp* cases, previously discussed, the question has been presented to the Burger Court in a series of cases involving the right of the press to have access to prisons for the purpose of informing the public about conditions existing in those institutions. The first two cases, *Pell v. Procunier* and *Saxbe v. Washington Post*, were inconclusive; the Court simply held that the regulations there challenged afforded sufficient access to the public and the press. In *Houchins v. KQED, Inc.*, however, the Court dealt squarely with the basic issue.[43]

In the *Houchins* case the regulations governing the Santa Rita jail in Alameda County, California, afforded only occasional and limited rights of visitation to the public and to the press. Television station KQED sought an injunction to allow its reporters reasonable access, including the right to use photographic and sound equipment and to conduct inmate interviews. The lower courts upheld the claim but the Supreme Court, by a 4 to 3 vote, reversed. There was no majority opinion.

Chief Justice Burger, with Justices White and Rehnquist joining, wrote the plurality opinion. He held that (1) "[n]either the First Amendment nor the Fourteenth Amendment mandates a right of access to government information or sources of information within the government's control"; and (2) "the media have no special right of access to the Alameda County Jail different from or greater than that accorded the public generally." The opinion is not wholly clear whether Chief Justice Burger meant that under no circumstances was there any First Amendment right to government information, or whether he intended to confine his opinion to a right of access to prisons and similar institutions.[44]

Justice Stewart concurred in the judgment of reversal but upon different grounds. He agreed that the "First and Fourteenth Amendment do not guarantee the public a right of access to information generated or controlled by government" and that the press has no right of access "superior to that of the public generally." Once some public access is granted, however, the "special needs of the press" must be considered, and that requires allowing the press to utilize its usual methods and equipment. Hence Justice Stewart would have allowed partial relief.[45]

Justice Stevens, along with Justices Brennan and Powell, dissented. In their opinion, "information gathering is entitled to some measure of constitutional protection," "not for the private benefit of those who might qualify as representatives of the 'press' but to insure that the citizens are fully informed regarding matters of public interest and importance." Conceding that "there are unquestionably occasions when governmental activity may properly be carried out in complete secrecy," they asserted that this did not apply to the "policy of concealing prison conditions from the public." Their dissent represented the first clear-cut statement by justices of the Supreme Court that government secrecy must yield at some points to the demands of the First Amendment. Justices Marshall and Blackmun did not participate in the decision.[46]

In addition to the prison cases, the Burger Court dealt with the right of access to government information in *Gannett Co., Inc. v. DePasquale*, already discussed. There, despite the support provided by the Sixth Amendment right to a public trial, the majority, and to a lesser extent the minority, gave short shrift to First Amendment rights of the public and the press to attend criminal pretrial proceedings and perhaps regular trial proceedings.[47]

A year later, in *Richmond Newspapers, Inc. v. Virginia*, also discussed previously, the Supreme Court modified its stonewall position. The *Richmond Newspapers* case, as Justice Stevens observed in his concurring opinion, was "a watershed case" in that "never before has [the Court] squarely held that the acquisition of newsworthy material is entitled to any constitutional protection whatsoever." The decision clearly opens up important new perspectives. Nevertheless, it should be noted that the precise issue before the Court was a relatively narrow one. The question for consideration was whether a trial judge could exclude the public and the press from a criminal trial "upon the unopposed request of a defendant, without any demonstration that closure is required to protect the defendant's superior right to a fair trial, or that some other overriding consideration requires closure."[48]

The position taken by the Supreme Court in *Richmond Newspapers* was reaffirmed the following year in *Globe Newspaper Co. v. Superior Court*. The *Globe* case involved a Massachusetts statute that provided for the exclusion of the press and the public during the testimony of a minor, the victim in a sex-offense trial. Justice Brennan, writing for a majority of five, reiterated that "the press and general public have a constitutional right of access to criminal trials" and expanded upon the rationale of the previous decision: "The First Amendment is thus broad enough to encompass those rights that, while not unambiguously enumerated in the very terms of the Amendment, are nonetheless necessary to the enjoyment of other First Amendment rights." Justice Brennan also made clear, however, that while "the right of access to criminal trials is of constitutional stature, it is not absolute." The Massachusetts statute was struck down because it was general and mandatory, but the right of access could be limited where "necessitated by a compelling governmental interest, and is narrowly tailored to serve that interest."[49]

There are no clear indications from *Richmond Newspapers* and *Globe* how far a majority of the Court is prepared to go in supporting a constitutional right of the press to obtain information from the government. Chief Justice Burger's opinion in *Richmond Newspapers* ties the access right very closely to government proceedings customarily open to the public, and expressly distinguishes the prison cases on the ground that penal institutions are not "open" places. Justice Brennan takes a much broader view, and his analysis in terms of the structure of the governmental process potentially opens the way for extensive application of the First Amendment. Both wings of the Court, however, make it clear that the First Amendment right, whatever its scope, is subject in individual situations to "overriding" or "countervailing" interests.[50]

The ultimate destination of the Burger Court in this area thus remains unknown. On the whole, despite *Richmond Newspapers*, the prognosis is not favorable. So far, implementation of the right to know, in the sense of the right to obtain information from the government, has come almost entirely from the legislative branch. Thus federal and state freedom of information acts require that many government records be open to public inspection, and sunshine laws provide that meetings of public bodies be open to public attendance. The Burger Court has taken the first steps toward judicial progress, but whether it will proceed much beyond its holding in the *Richmond Newspapers* case is by no means clear.[51]

GOVERNMENTAL REGULATION TO IMPROVE THE OPERATION OF THE SYSTEM OF FREEDOM OF EXPRESSION

One of the major weaknesses in our system of freedom of expression has long been the lack of diversity in the mass media resulting from the concentration of control in the hands of a single economic, political, and social group. A remedy for this distortion that would be compatible with a free system has not been easy to find. In general two types of measures have been proposed. One is the breaking up of monopoly control through the use of antitrust laws and similar legislation. The other is government regulation that will assure greater access to the facilities of the mass media for diverse points of view. In recent years the development of cable television has afforded a new opportunity for dealing with the diversity problem. The Burger Court has given cautious approval to antitrust measures but has prohibited or discouraged efforts to assure greater access.

In the antitrust area the principal attempt to limit concentration of control of the mass media has been undertaken by the Federal Communications Commission (FCC). After a lengthy rule-making procedure, the FCC adopted regulations barring future initial licensing or transfer of broadcast facilities where a radio or television station and a daily newspaper located in the same community were under common ownership. Existing newspaper-broadcast combinations were allowed to continue except in sixteen "egregious cases" where the combination consisted of the sole newspaper and the sole broadcasting station in the locality. For all practical purposes, the regulation constituted a very modest effort to achieve more diversity. Upon review, the Court of Appeals held that the FCC had not gone far enough and required dissolution of most existing combinations. In *Federal Communications Commission v. National Citizens Committee for Broadcasting*, the Supreme Court unanimously (Justice Brennan not participating) restored the original FCC order.[52]

The problem of assuring wider access to existing facilities has been more controversial, and the status of the electronic media has diverged substantially from that of the print media. In 1969, in the early days of the Burger Court, the decision in *Red Lion Broadcasting Co., Inc. v. FCC* upheld the FCC equal time provisions, requiring broadcasting stations to give equal time to all political candidates if they gave time to one, and the fairness doctrine, requiring that broadcasting stations give adequate coverage to controversial public issues and that such coverage be fair in representing opposing views. These requirements were held to be justified under the First Amendment solely on the ground that the physical facilities for broadcasting (the wavelengths or channels) were limited and that therefore the government could license facilities on the condition that they be operated in the public interest. A few years later, in *Columbia Broadcasting System v. Democratic National Committee*, the Burger Court refused to carry access requirements further. It ruled that broadcast licensees were not required by the First Amendment to accept political advertisements, even though they customarily accepted commercial advertisements. Justices Brennan and Marshall dissented.[53]

In 1974 the issue of mandatory access to the print media was presented to the Supreme Court in the case of *Miami Herald Publishing Co. v. Tornillo*. Here a Florida statute required newspapers to give candidates for public office who had been attacked in their columns a right to equal space for reply. The court unanimously struck down the statue as an unwarranted invasion of First Amendment rights.[54]

The position of the Burger Court in *Tornillo* would appear to be entirely correct. Implementation of a right of reply throughout the print media would surely lead to substantial governmental interference in the operations of the press. Likewise the distinction between the print press and the electronic press, so far as equal time or fairness is concerned, would appear to be justified. In principle, the scarcity of broadcasting facilities creates a government obligation to maintain some rules for operation in the public interest. And in practice there are advantages to having at least one branch of the mass media free from government supervision of any kind. On the other hand, the refusal of the Court in the *Columbia Broadcasting* case to interpret the First Amendment as imposing more effective rules of access seems highly questionable.

As just noted, the solution to the problem of developing diversity in the electronic media would appear to lie in the expansion of cable television. By using wires instead of channels, the scarcity of physical facilities is virtually eliminated. The FCC has approached these opportunities in cable television very gingerly, fearing to disrupt the established broadcasting industry. Nevertheless, it finally promulgated regulations requiring cable television stations having 3,500 or more subscribers to maintain, at a minimum, twenty channels in operation and to devote four of those channels to public, governmental, educational, and leased uses. In *FCC v. Midwest Video Corp.* the Burger Court, 6 to 3, struck down the regulation. Narrowly construing a provision of the Communications Act of 1934, which prohibits the treatment of a licensee as a "common carrier," the Court held that the FCC lacked jurisdiction to adopt the access requirements.[55]

If one reads the *Columbia Broadcasting* and the *Midwest Video* cases together, it is clear that the promotion of greater diversity in radio and television will have to come from legislative rather than judicial encouragement.

CONCLUSION

Taken as a whole, the record of the Burger Court does not indicate that an "imperial judiciary" has created an "atmosphere of intimidation" for the press. But it does give cause for serious concern. The press no longer receives the vigorous support given it by the Warren Court. In Justice Stewart's words, the Burger Court has taken a "crabbed view" of the First Amendment and has exhibited a "disturbing insensitivity" to the role of the press. In doing so it has significantly reduced the protections afforded the press by the First Amendment. And its methods of dealing with First Amendment problems bode ill for the future.

If one looks at the results of the decided cases, it is apparent that the Burger Court has upheld the press most strongly when the issue involved direct governmental regulation of the right of the press to publish or not to publish. *Nebraska Press Association* and *Tornillo* show the Burger Court at its most supportive. But even in this area the Court has withdrawn protection at important points, as in the libel cases and, to a substantial degree, in national security situations. With respect to the corollary, but equally important, right to gather news, the Burger Court has been unsympathetic and largely negative. It has recognized a First Amendment interest here but has treated it as wholly secondary and subordinate to other social interests. *Branzburg, Stanford Daily, Houchins*, and *Gannett* all testify to this, and it is by no means clear that *Richmond Newspapers* and *Globe* represent a change of heart. Finally, so far as concerns affirmative promotion of a healthy and diversified press, the Burger Court has been unwilling to move. *Columbia Broadcasting* and *Midwest Video* reflect the reluctance of the Burger Court to advance to new positions.

If one examines the basic philosophy, legal doctrines, and operating techniques of the Burger Court, several conclusions stand out. In the first place, the Burger Court has either forgotten or ignored the most fundamental tenet of First Amendment theory, namely, that freedom of expression occupies a special status in our constitutional structure. To a major degree, other rights in our democratic system originate in, flow from, or are dependent on the rights to freedom of speech, press, assembly, petition, and other forms of expression. Not only has the Burger Court failed to come forth with any ringing affirmation of the First Amendment, but it has consistently treated First Amendment values as simply one additional social interest, on a par with numerous other constitutional or social interests. The decisions in *Branzburg, Stanford Daily, Houchins, Herbert,* and *Gannett* all flow from this premise. The decision in *Snepp* goes even further in ignoring and subordinating First Amendment values.

Second, under the Burger Court there has been a consistent deterioration of First Amendment doctrine. Far from attempting to formulate clearer and more precise standards, which would impose firmer controls on police, prosecutors, and lower courts, the Burger Court has tended to allow existing standards to become vague and diluted. Thus the prior restraint doctrine was needlessly watered down in *Nebraska Press Association.* The almost universally applied balancing test is even more amorphous than ever, as the *Landmark* and *Daily Mail* cases illustrate; no attempt has been made to refine it or give it more precise content. And most surprising of all, even if one concedes that there is justification for declining to adopt a rule of absolute protection, the Burger Court frequently refuses to limit exceptions to clear and urgent cases or to impose any requirement that a less drastic alternative be utilized. *Snepp, Branzburg, Stanford Daily,* and *Gannett* all authorize unnecessary infringements upon First Amendment rights.

Third, the Burger Court has lost that feeling for the dynamics of the system of freedom of expression which was the hallmark of the Warren Court. The impact upon the press of journalists' inability to pledge confidentiality, police raids on newsrooms, investigators' procurement of telephone records, and the probing of the mental states or editorial judgments of publishers often receives only cavalier treatment. (*Tornillo* is an exception.) Nor does the Burger Court seem concerned with framing administratively workable rules. The result of this lack of realism on the part of the Burger Court is bound to be an increasing gap between the rights of the press as laid down in the marble halls of the Supreme Court and its rights under workaday conditions.

All of these factors make the legal future of the press look somewhat bleak. Nevertheless, the press remains a strong and vigorous institution in our society. It survived the tirades of Vice President Agnew, the wrath of President Nixon, and the manipulations of Watergate. In fact, it emerged stronger and more dedicated from that experience. Yet for some time to come it may have to rely less upon the courts and constitutional rights and more upon its own power and spirit.

• Two •

The Burger Court and the Freedom of Speech

Norman Dorsen and Joel Gora

THE FREE SPEECH LANDSCAPE

On January 7, 1972, Lewis F. Powell and William H. Rehnquist were sworn in as associate justices of the Supreme Court. That brought to four the number of justices appointed by Richard Nixon; it also brought to full complement the judicial and political institution that we refer to in this book as the "Burger Court." In the years that have passed since then, there have been only two changes in personnel—Justice Stevens has replaced Justice Douglas and Justice O'Connor has replaced Justice Stewart—and these changes, despite Justice Douglas's prominent views on free speech, have not had a major impact on the Court's First Amendment rulings. It is accordingly appropriate to examine these decisions to determine whether they can be explained by any general theory of First Amendment liberties.

What landscape did the Supreme Court survey in early 1972? Even a casual analyst might have been struck by a remarkable series of free speech decisions rendered almost simultaneously less than a year before. It is well known that certain years produce memorable wines; it is less well known that certain volumes of the *United States Reports* produce vintage decisions. In First Amendment terms, number 403, which covers the period from June 7 to June 30, 1971, is a vintage volume. It begins with a characteristically careful analysis by Justice John M. Harlan, in which he held that California could not punish as disorderly conduct the public display, in a Los Angeles courthouse, of the words, "Fuck the Draft." Justice Harlan said:

> For, while the particular four-letter word being litigated here is perhaps more distasteful than most others of its genre, it is nevertheless often true that one man's vulgarity is another's lyric. Indeed, we think it is largely because governmental officials cannot make principled distinctions in this area that the Constitution leaves matters of taste and style so largely to the individual.[1]

Although the authors are closely associated with the ACLU, the views expressed here are personal and not necessarily those of the ACLU.

An earlier version of this essay was delivered by Professor Dorsen as the 1979 Cooley Lecture at the University of Michigan Law School. Some of the ideas in this chapter are explored at greater length in Dorsen and Gora, *Free Speech, Property and the Burger Court: Old Values, New Balances,* 1982 SUP. CT. REV. 195.

Volume 403 ends, appropriately enough, with the *Pentagon Papers* case, in which the Supreme Court defended the First Amendment's basic purpose against a direct assault. In his separate opinion in that case Justice Black said:

> Only a free and unrestrained press can effectively expose deception in government. And paramount among the responsibilities of a free press is the duty to prevent any part of the government from deceiving the people and sending them off to distant lands to die of foreign fevers and foreign shot and shell. In my view, far from deserving condemnation for their courageous reporting, the . . . [newspapers] should be commended for serving the purpose that the Founding Fathers saw so clearly.[2]

These two cases capped a number of other speech-protective rulings that led free speech partisans to experience unaccustomed satisfaction. The Court adopted what appeared to be a rigorous standard for testing restraints on political advocacy and in the process overruled one of the most scorned decisions of an earlier era;[3] it took some positive steps to cope with the "intractable" obscenity problem under normal First Amendment criteria;[4] and it accorded the media broad protection against defamation suits arising out of news stories on "matters of public or general interest."[5] Free speech advocates could be forgiven the measure of optimism they felt as they scanned the scene.

But beneath the surface trouble brewed. The precise condition of the First Amendment, if closely analyzed, was more uneven and less happy than appeared. A legacy of older and restrictive rulings remained on the books. Perhaps more important, First Amendment doctrine was, in the view of the nation's foremost scholar on the subject, in "chaos." In 1970, at the very time of some of the notable free speech victories described above, Thomas Emerson decried the lack of a coherent First Amendment policy:

> At various times the Court has employed the bad tendency test, the clear and present danger test, an incitement test, and different forms of the ad hoc balancing test. Sometimes it has not clearly enunciated the theory upon which it proceeds. Frequently it has avoided decision on First Amendment issues by invoking doctrines of vagueness, overbreadth, or the use of less drastic alternatives. . . . The Supreme Court has also utilized other doctrines, such as the preferred position of the First Amendment and prior restraint. Recently it has begun to address itself to problems of "symbolic speech" and the place in which First Amendment activities can be carried on. But it has totally failed to settle on any coherent approach.[6]

If the Supreme Court is guilty of doctrinal confusion, it is "guilty with an explanation," or rather with a series of explanations. Because free speech issues arise in a wide variety of contexts, the development of an all-inclusive theory is not easy. The Supreme Court—aware of the tendency of litigants to press principles to the limit of their logic—tries to retain flexibility by resisting broad formulations that can return to haunt it. Furthermore, attempts to restrict speech rarely appear as heavy-handed repression; more often they seem to be the product of well-meaning officials trying to cope with difficult problems and offering national security, public order, or private sensibilities as plausible justifications for any infringement of speech. In addition, the historical antecedents of the First Amendment provide no guidelines. The Framers were mainly concerned with problems of censorship and seditious libel,[7] and it is unclear how they intended the new Constitution to resolve even these questions much less the full range of free speech problems that have emerged since their time.[8]

Despite these factors, which account for the doctrinal chaos described by Emerson, attempts have been made by judges, teachers of law and political science, and lawyers to develop a persuasive theoretical framework for the solution to free speech problems. Some of these individuals are not particularly sympathetic to First Amendment claims, or perhaps more accurately, they are responsive to the values offered to justify limitations on speech. On the other hand, there are scholars who seek, through a variety of formulations, to provide as much protection of freedom of speech as possible with as much certainty of application as possible. One of these scholars, Laurence Tribe, has presented a fascinating "two-track" route to this end,[9] and there have been other approaches, such as a "revitalized" clear-and-present danger test applicable to all forms of speech,[10] or a rule absolutely forbidding controls of speech based on content,[11] or the "presumptive unconstitutionality of content discrimination,"[12] or a "heavily negative presumption" against control of public speech.[13]

One or a combination of these theories may ultimately prevail, but at present there is no consensus among scholars on the best formulation or even the best direction to be taken, and there is certainly no sign that the doctrinal confusion that existed at the inception of the Burger Court has abated.

This chapter has two aims: first, to offer for consideration what we believe to be an apparent underlying theme of the Burger Court's freedom-of-speech decisions, and second, to present a tentative approach of our own that we think would lead to more satisfactory results. In line with our second objective, it should be made clear (if it is not already) that we favor the maximum protection of freedom of speech. Indeed, the idea that we shall shortly advance will be called the "maximum protection" theory.

A NEW FREE SPEECH VARIABLE: PROPERTY

In trying to understand what has happened in the Supreme Court since early 1972, one is faced with a bewildering variety of seemingly disharmonious decisions. The Burger Court's free speech cases sometimes contract earlier rulings of the Warren Court, sometimes expand them, and in some instances dramatically chart new ground.

What can one make of all this? Upon first undertaking to catalog the Burger Court's free speech rulings, we despaired of identifying anything like a coherent profile. Eventually, however, our reading began to disclose an unusual pattern of decision. A closer look indicated that the pattern was real, and if not all-encompassing, at least remarkably consistent.

This pattern can be summarized in one word: property. With few exceptions, the key to whether free speech will receive protection depends on an underlying property interest, either private or governmental. In other words, throughout the past decade the values of the First Amendment have been protected, it appears, mainly when they have coincided with property interests; conversely, free expression has received diminished protection when First Amendment claims have appeared to clash with property interests.

In presenting this property hypothesis we do not, of course, deny the relevance of other factors in these free speech cases. The copious scholarly commentary that exists is a testimonial to their variety. Our goal, very simply, is to trace an apparently close fit in Burger Court decisions between property interests and First Amendment results. The significance of this finding, indeed its validity,[14] is for others to judge.

Speech and Property in Tandem

Let us first examine a series of rulings in which the First Amendment interests were sustained. In *Spence v. Washington*,[15] the conviction of a man who had taped a peace symbol on an American flag that he owned was invalidated. The Court explained: "A number of factors are important in the instant case. First, this was a privately owned flag. In a technical property sense it was not the property of any government. . . . Second, appellant displayed his flag on private property."[16]

In a second case, a law that compelled a citizen to place on his car a license plate bearing what he considered an offensive ideological message was invalidated, in part, on property grounds. Said the Court: "We are thus faced with the question of whether the State may constitutionally require an individual to participate in the dissemination of an ideological message by displaying it on his private property in a manner and for the express purpose that it be observed and read by the public. We hold that the State may not do so."[17]

These two cases perhaps represent a yeoman's perspective on the importance of personal property. But *First National Bank of Boston v. Bellotti*,[18] decided in 1978, has broader property implications. There the Court for the first time expressly recognized the free speech rights of an entity that embodies the quintessential modern form of property—the corporation—by holding that the state cannot prohibit a corporation from spending its funds to express corporate views on referendum issues, even when these issues do not "materially affect" the corporation's business or property. The Court rejected the state's asserted interests in preventing corporate domination of the political process and in protecting shareholders who do not concur in their corporation's views.

Perhaps the *Bellotti* case would have been treated differently if the suit had been brought at the instance of dissenting shareholders. It then would have been similar to another Burger Court First Amendment case, *Abood v. Detroit Board of Education*,[19] where the Court refused to permit labor unions to use the fees of nonunion dissenting members of the bargaining unit in taking stands on public issues unrelated to collective bargaining.

Another case in which substantial property interests were involved is *Buckley v. Valeo*,[20] the campaign finance decision. In rejecting portions of a congressional electoral reform bill, the Court held that those whose personal wealth and property permit them an enlarged opportunity to speak on partisan campaign issues cannot be restricted in the interests of electorate equality. The Court said: "[T]he concept that government may restrict the speech of some elements of our society in order to enhance the relative voice of others is wholly foreign to the First Amendment." Although the Court did uphold congressional restrictions on certain forms of campaign financing, largely because of its fear of corruption, it did so with full recognition of the "speech" interests that election contributions were found to embody.

The Court took the *Bellotti* and *Buckley* principles one step further in a 1980 decision invalidating public service commission restrictions on the right of a regulated utility company to insert in monthly bills to consumers material that expressed the utility's viewpoint on "controversial matters of public policy."[21] In holding, 7 to 2, that the utility could include bill inserts describing the benefits of nuclear power, the Court sounded a number of notes on the property theme. First, it reaffirmed the broad First Amendment protection for corporate speech that it had granted in 1978, saying that restriction of corporate speech on controversial public issues "strikes at the heart of the freedom to speak." Second, the Court had to decide whether the commission could exclude certain kinds of subject matter from discussion in the utility's billing statements. In holding that it could not, the Court distinguished earlier cases allowing government to ban certain messages from *its* property from the right of the utility to use *its* own property to communicate its views:

In [these] cases, a private party asserted a right of access to public facilities. Consolidated Edison has not asked to use the offices of the Commission as a forum from which to promulgate its views. Rather, it seeks merely to utilize *its own billing envelopes* to promulgate its views on controversial issues of public policy. . . . [T]he Commission's attempt to restrict the free expression of a private party cannot be upheld by reliance upon precedent that rests on the special interests of a government in overseeing the use of its property.[22]

This rationale also illustrates a distinction, which we shall discuss shortly, between government's broad control over speech activities conducted on its property and its diminished control over speech emanating from or utilizing private property.

The broadest category of Burger Court decisions in which property and speech interests were combined is that of the commercial speech cases. In 1942 the Court established new doctrine by holding that "the Constitution imposes no . . . restraint on government as respects purely commercial advertising."[23] This holding remained relatively undisturbed until 1975 when, in *Bigelow v. Virginia*,[24] the Court ruled, in the context of advertising of abortion services, that commercial speech merited some constitutional protection, the precise extent depending on whether the public interest in the speech outweighed the state's need for regulation. In 1976 the Court buttoned down its new doctrine in a case involving price advertising of prescription drugs. It held that such speech, which does "no more than propose a commercial transaction," is nevertheless entitled to First Amendment protection, although at the same time it said that for "commonsense" reasons commercial speech could be regulated in ways that would be intolerable for other forms of speech.[25]

In 1977 the Court went a step further by providing a then unclear degree of protection to the advertising of legal services.[26] That same year, in *Linmark Associates v. Willingboro*,[27] a unanimous Court relied on the earlier cases to strike down a different sort of commercial communication. Over strong objections by the NAACP Legal Defense Fund, but with the support of the ACLU, the Court invalidated an ordinance prohibiting the posting of real estate "For Sale" or "Sold" signs on private property that had been enacted by a municipality to stem what it perceived as the flight of white homeowners from a racially integrated community.[28]

Finally, in 1980, the Court reaffirmed and reformulated its rules governing commercial speech. In another case involving a public utility,[29] the Court, this time by a vote of 8 to 1, invalidated a public service commission ban on utility advertising that promoted the use of electricity, holding it an impermissible restriction on commercial speech, defined as speech "related solely to the economic interests of the speaker and its audience." Indeed, the Court's formula for protecting commercial speech seemed so potent to Justice Rehnquist, the sole dissenter, that he was moved to complain: "The test adopted by the Court thus elevates the protection accorded commercial speech that falls within the scope of the First Amendment to a level that is virtually indistinguishable from that of noncommercial speech."[30]

The message of the decisions in the utility cases is clear—a strong reaffirmation of the Burger Court's doctrinal willingness to protect corporate speech and commercial speech, and the property-related interests that they represent.

Speech and Property in Tension

In the above cases, free speech and property interests were united and free speech was upheld. Let us see what happens when the speech interest and property interests conflict. In one rather amusing case a closely divided Supreme Court denied First Amendment protection to a news station that ran a fifteen-second clip of the act of a "human cannonball."[31] The majority recognized a property interest in the value of the publicity surrounding the stunt and held that the media were not privileged to "broadcast a performer's entire act without his consent." It rejected any analogy to defamation actions on the ground that the publicity tort protects money-making activities and not merely a plaintiff's reputation or mental well-being.

In a second case, the Court considered an ordinance that required advance notice in writing to the police by "any person desiring to canvass . . . or call from house to house [for] a recognized charitable [or] political . . . cause." This was not a permit requirement but was "for identification only." Although the ordinance was struck down on vagueness grounds, six justices rejected the free speech claim in dicta.[32] Relying on "the householder's right to be let alone" in enjoyment of property, they concluded that "vagueness defects aside, an ordinance of this kind would ordinarily withstand constitutional attack."[33] A similar approach was taken more recently in a case involving a local ordinance that prohibited door-to-door solicitation by charitable organizations that devoted more than 25 percent of their revenue to organizational expenses. The Court reaffirmed its recognition that such solicitation, even though involving political and charitable causes, can be regulated by government in order to protect the privacy of homeowners against fraud, crime, or annoyance. The particular ordinance was invalidated, however, because the 25 percent limitation did not bear a sufficiently substantial relationship to achieving such goals.[34]

Finally, the Court addressed the issue of residential picketing in a case that involved a challenge by a civil rights group prevented by an Illinois statute from demonstrating on the public sidewalk in front of the private home of the mayor of Chicago.[35] Although the case raised broad issues as to whether residential neighborhoods can be placed off limits to free speech, the Court invalidated the statute on equal protection grounds, because the law exempted certain kinds of labor dispute picketing from the general prohibition on residential picketing. Justice Brennan, writing the majority opinion, found the case "constitutionally indistinguishable" from a 1972 decision in which the Court had thrown out a comparable Chicago ordinance[36] that also selectively proscribed picketing on the basis of its message.

Significantly, the Court expressly left unresolved the question "whether a statute barring all residential picketing regardless of its subject matter would violate the First and Fourteenth Amendments."[37] And in dictum the majority strongly indicated the broad protection that it would afford to the privacy of the home, even against free speech claims, where the ban on residential picketing was content-neutral:

> We are not to be understood to imply, however, that residential picketing is beyond the reach of uniform and nondiscriminatory regulation. . . . The State's interest in protecting the well-being, tranquility, and privacy of the home is certainly of the highest order in a free and civilized society.[38]

Thus, while the Court's decision invalidated a ban on residential picketing at the behest of free speech claimants, the precise holding was that the exception to the statutory protection of residential privacy was unjustifiable. Equally revealing is Justice Rehnquist's dissenting opinion, which was joined by Chief Justice Burger and Justice Blackmun, expressing the view that the states may protect residential privacy even at the expense of free speech values:

> [T]he [demonstrators] have no fundamental First Amendment right to picket in front of a residence. . . . An absolute ban on picketing at residences used solely for residential purposes permissibly furthers the state interest in protecting residential privacy. The State could certainly conclude that the presence of even a solitary picket in front of a residence is an intolerable intrusion on residential privacy.[39]

The permissibility of a nondiscriminatory ban on residential picketing was left open by the majority and flatly approved by the dissent.

The "public forum" cases constitute an especially significant line of decisions rejecting First Amendment claims of access to either private property or government property. In a series of holdings, the Burger Court, expressly overruling Warren Court precedent, has permitted large facilities open to the public to exclude speech activity if the owner—corporate or governmental—so wishes.

With respect to private property, the first precedent was decided in 1946. In *Marsh v. Alabama*[40] the Court held that merely because a corporation owned title to a town, it could not impair the public's interest "in the functioning of the community in such a manner that the channels of communication remain free." In 1968 the Court extended *Marsh* by striking down a state court injunction banning peaceful labor picketing of a store in a privately owned shopping center.[41]

Enter the Burger Court. In 1972 it held that a shopping center owner could constitutionally forbid the on-site distribution of handbills, in that case antiwar leaflets.[42] In purporting to distinguish the 1968 case, the Court said that "the invitation extended to the public" here was simply one "to come to the Center to do business with the tenants" and not an "open-ended invitation" to use it "for any and all purposes." The opinion went on: "this Court has never held that a trespasser or an uninvited guest may exercise general rights of free speech on property privately owned and used non-discriminatorily for private purposes only."

In 1976 the Court eschewed any pretense of distinguishing the first shopping center case by overruling it and confining *Marsh v. Alabama* to its facts.[43] In response, the dissenting justices attacked the majority's "overly formalistic view of the relationship between the institution of private ownership of property and the First Amendment's guarantee of freedom of speech."

In 1980, however, the Court decided another shopping center case that involved a seemingly direct clash between property rights and free speech interests.[44] The case concerned an attempt by a pro-Israel group to solicit petition signatures at a typical shopping center, privately owned, though open to the general public. The group was rebuffed by an even-handed shopping center ban on all such activity. Blocked by the overruling of *Logan Valley Plaza* from asserting a First Amendment right of access, the group persuaded the California Supreme Court that the state constitution's guarantee of "liberty of speech," coupled with the state's general police power to regulate the uses of private property in the public interest, permitted the state court to fashion a rule allowing access to shopping centers in order to vindicate state-protected free speech rights. In reaching that result, the California Supreme Court held that the Burger Court's restrictive shopping center public forum decisions had not recognized a federal constitutional property right to exclude free speech activity but had simply refused to recognize a First Amendment right of access. The state court dissenters disagreed, observing that the Burger Court had, as a matter of constitutional law, subordinated free speech interests to the property rights of shopping center owners.

The Supreme Court, speaking through Justice Rehnquist, unanimously affirmed. The Court ruled that the state restriction of property rights in favor of state-recognized free speech rights was permissible and did not deprive the shopping center owner of property rights. In reaching this result, the Court provided a primer on property and free speech. It treated *Lloyd Corp. v. Tanner*, the 1972 shopping center case, as having protected private property rights against a First Amendment right of access for speech purposes. That decision, whose continuing validity was not questioned by the Court, did not limit the state's general police power to regulate property rights:

> In *Lloyd* . . . there was no state constitutional or statutory provision that had been construed to create rights to the use of private property by strangers, comparable to those found to exist by the California Supreme Court here. It is, of course, well established that a State in the exercise of its police power may

adopt reasonable restrictions on private property so long as the restrictions do not amount to a taking without just compensation or contravene any other federal constitutional provision.[45]

Next, having concluded that the 1972 case was not in point, the Court addressed the shopping center owner's claims that the state restriction of the right to exclude speakers from the shopping center premises constituted a "taking" of property without just compensation and deprived the owner of property without due process of law. In a statement that evokes memories of a law school property course, the Court noted that "one of the essential sticks in the bundle of property rights is the right to exclude others" and agreed that there had been a "taking" of that right by the state court's recognition of a state right to engage in free speech on shopping center property. But, the Court reasoned, this was not a taking in the constitutional sense, under the Fifth Amendment's takings clause, because it did not "unreasonably impair the value or use" of the property as a shopping center or interfere with "reasonable investment backed expectations." The Court also found no deprivation of general property rights, given the traditionally broad state power to define and reorder such rights.

At first glance, the 1980 shopping center case, a major victory for free speech values, would appear to confound our thesis that the Burger Court has preferred property rights over free speech interests. And, indeed, the result of the decision is that demonstrators will be able to circulate leaflets and petitions on shopping center grounds against the owner's wishes. But close examination reveals that the decision is not a victory for First Amendment claims over property rights.

There are several grounds for this conclusion. First, the Court left undisturbed the 1972 holding in the *Lloyd* case that First Amendment rights of access to private property will not prevail over state-sanctioned rights to exclude. Except where a state has chosen, as California did, to withdraw the right to exclude from the "bundle of property rights," the 1972 decision will control.[46] Second, had the Court reversed the California court's restriction of the shopping center owner's right to exclude, it would have had to employ the due process clause to place severe limits on the state's ability to define and condition property rights. Such a ruling would have altered settled doctrine governing the state's exercise of the police power over property rights. In short, the Supreme Court in *PruneYard* did not vindicate First Amendment rights over property rights; rather, it upheld the expansive power of states to define and to expand or contract property rights.[47]

The other strand of "public forum" cases involves government property. The constitutional principle was stated most vividly in Justice Roberts's plurality opinion in the 1939 case of *Hague v. CIO*.[48] Rejecting a property-centered conception of the First Amendment, he said: "Wherever the title of streets and parks may rest, they have immemorially been held in trust for the use of the public and, time out of mind, have been used for purposes of assembly, communicating thoughts between citizens, and discussing public questions."

Under the Warren Court, this reasoning was often applied to invalidate governmental restrictions on use of the streets for First Amendment purposes, including demonstrations before a State House,[49] the home of a mayor,[50] and an army recruiting station.[51] The Burger Court, on the other hand, has adopted a narrower view and thus choked off further development of the principle, most notably in cases allowing the army to prohibit political speeches and leaflet distribution in areas of a New Jersey military post that were open to the public[52] and permitting the air force to require prior command approval before allowing servicemen to circulate petitions on the base.[53]

One important public forum case tends to confirm our property analysis in two distinct ways. In *Lehman v. City of Shaker Heights*[54] the Court sustained a municipal ban on political advertising on city-owned buses while nevertheless allowing commercial advertising to be displayed. The Court both sanctioned municipal dominion over its property as a sufficient basis on which to restrict free speech and discriminated in favor of commercial speech over political speech. An analogous ruling sustained a flat ban by broadcast networks on paid public issue announcements at a time when commercial advertising was being accepted.[55]

A related series of cases concerns the rights of prisoners and military personnel. Both groups are virtually powerless in property terms and both are physically confined—one absolutely and the other relatively—on government-owned property. Although property concepts may play only a partial role here, it is not surprising under our theory that the Burger Court has turned back the claims of these groups to First Amendment protection.[56]

A 1981 case confirmed the current Court's willingness to accord government broad power to restrict speech rights that conflict with its property interests. In *United States Postal Service v. Council of Greenburgh Civic Associations*,[57] the Court held that local civic groups did not have a First Amendment right to place unstamped leaflets and literature in residential mailboxes. Justice Rehnquist's rationale was that although the homeowner pays for the mailbox, the government controls it through the plenary power to regulate its use. Rather than merely acknowledging that government regulation overrides the homeowner's property interests in the mailbox, the Court analyzed the case in terms of government ownership of the property in question. Pointing to earlier decisions restricting free speech rights on government property, the Court reaffirmed its view that "[t]he First Amendment does not guarantee access to property simply because it is owned or controlled by the government." Having thus compared the government's interest in a mailbox to its control over property to which it has title, the

Court saw no need even to consider whether the challenged restrictions could pass muster as "time, place and manner" controls. Government ownership of the postal system settled the issue.

Thus, whether the property is owned or controlled by a private party or by government itself, property interests will be paramount to First Amendment rights.

The Burger Court's rulings on obscenity involve more complex relationships between property and speech. Properly understood, however, these decisions, too, lend support to our thesis.

Probably the most important holding is *Young v. American Mini Theaters*,[58] which, strictly speaking, is not an obscenity case at all. The Court upheld a Detroit zoning ordinance which differentiated between motion picture theaters that exhibited sexually explicit "adult" movies and those that did not. The ordinance required that "adult" theaters not be located within 1,000 feet of any two other theaters or within 500 feet of a residential area. An "adult" theater was defined as one that presented "material [that emphasized] matter[s] depicting . . . 'Specific Sexual Activities' or 'Specified Anatomical Areas.'"[59] This definition, which is interestingly elaborated in further definitions, does not of course meet the constitutional definition of "obscenity," as all nine justices recognized.[60] Nevertheless, a 5 to 4 majority upheld the ordinance, relying in part on a finding of the Detroit Common Council "that some uses of property are especially injurious to a neighborhood when they are concentrated in limited areas." Justice Powell's concurring opinion seems even more clearly dominated by property considerations. He viewed the case simply as "an example of innovative land-use regulation, implicating First Amendment concerns only incidentally and to a limited extent."

Obscenity cases usually involve conflicting property interests—the rights of commercial purveyors of books and motion pictures versus the rights of property owners in the surrounding community. The latter prevailed in the *American Mini Theaters* case. By contrast, when the proprietor of a drive-in movie showing suggestive films succeeded in invalidating a restrictive ordinance, the property interests of the community were not as weighty—the screen was on a busy highway and visible only from two adjacent streets and from a little-used church parking lot.[61]

The most important obscenity decisions of the Burger era have rejected a major challenge to the notion that there exists a distinct category of "obscene" speech, which can be regulated in ways constitutionally unacceptable for other forms of expression. In these decisions, the majority slighted the free speech values at stake by relying on the proposition that the Court is not "a super-legislature to determine the wisdom, need, and propriety of laws that touch economic problems, business affairs, or social conditions."[62]

To explain these decisions adequately one must look beyond property interests. *Stare decisis* played a part because of earlier obscenity decisions, as did a moralistic strain that has surfaced in the Burger Court, both in the separate opinions of individual members and in some rulings of the Court as a whole. An example of the latter—also at the expense of First Amendment values—is a decision that upheld FCC regulation of a radio monologue that was found to be "indecent but not obscene" because it included seven "dirty words."[63] This decision can also be explained in terms of a concern for the privacy of the home—also in part a property conception. But the net result in these cases is that speech interests are subordinated to protect residential or commercial property from exposure to speech and its effects.

Many of these themes can be observed in two other recent decisions of the Burger Court. Property and speech interests were arrayed in a complex fashion in the Court's 1981 decision on whether municipalities could restrict billboards in order "to safeguard and enhance property values" and improve "traffic safety and the appearance of the city."[64] At issue was a complicated San Diego ordinance that generally permitted occupants of property to use "on-site" billboards to advertise their own products or services, but not to advertise for others, and that restricted "off-site" billboards depending on the message displayed. A four-justice plurality found it constitutionally permissible for a city allowing on-site billboards to restrict off-site billboards used for commercial messages. To that extent, the city's preference for the property and speech rights of on-site advertisers was allowable, and speech emanating from property was therefore afforded protection. Restricting off-site commercial billboards was found justifiable, however, because of the city's aesthetic and land use interests, and those generalized interests in preserving property values took precedence over speech rights. But insofar as the ordinance allowed some commercial billboards while restricting historically noncommercial messages, the plurality concluded that there was unjustified content discrimination and invalidated the ordinance. The plurality was joined by Justices Brennan and Blackmun, the only two justices who believed that urban aesthetics did not justify the restrictions on an important medium of communication.

Dissenting, the chief justice insisted that the city's interests in "eliminating distracting and ugly structures from its buildings and roadways" and "eradicat[ing] . . . ugly and dangerous eyesores" were ample justification for limiting speech. Justice Rehnquist was of a similar view. Justice Stevens also stressed the property theme in concluding that billboards could be banned in the interest of "enhancing property values."

The billboard decision demonstrates two of the themes we have observed. First, government will be allowed to favor the speech and property interests of occupants of the particular property by permitting most on-site billboards. But beyond that, when speech interests conflict with property values protected by government through aesthetic zoning, speech will take second place to "enhancing property values" and preventing "ugly and dangerous eyesores."

The Court also favored property rights over speech-related interests in *Loretto v. Teleprompter Manhattan CATV Corp.*[65] The case involved a New York statute that required landlords to permit cable television companies to install wires on the landlord's property so that tenants could subscribe to the service. The statute was based on the state's interest in "rapid development of and maximum penetration by a means of communication which has important educational and community aspects." A landlord filed suit, claiming that the statute authorized a physical trespass on her property and therefore was a "taking" without compensation. The New York Court of Appeals, 6 to 1, rejected her claims, but the Supreme Court reversed. The Court held that the trespass sanctioned by the New York statute constituted a traditional taking of property interests not justified by the state's concern with facilitating tenant access to an important new form of communication. Once again, property rights carried the day.

A DIFFERENT APPROACH: MAXIMUM PROTECTION OF SPEECH

Our thesis is that the factor of property appears to have played a surprisingly significant role in the Burger Court's free speech decisions. This conclusion does not denigrate the importance of private property in our society, which many believe to be central to the preservation of civil liberty. The man or woman with assets is a more independent individual, both in regard to personal dealings and in resisting or coping with the state. He or she is more likely to speak out, challenge authority, and, if necessary, hire a good lawyer.

While individual ownership of property has been linked to civil liberty, that is very different from the Burger Court's practice of linking property concepts to protection of free speech. We see no basis in principle for preferring property interests over speech values.

How, then, do we believe the First Amendment should be interpreted in order to achieve its grand purposes?

These purposes are well known and can be easily summarized. The first is individual fulfillment through self-expression. Justice Brandeis put it well: "[T]he final end of the State [is] to make men free to develop their faculties."[66] The second major justification stresses the concept of democratic self-government. This theory of free speech was powerfully formulated by Alexander Meiklejohn and, in a well-known passage, was underlined by Justice Brennan, who affirmed the "profound national commitment to the principle that debate on public issues should be uninhibited, robust, and wide-open."[67] The third major purpose of the First Amendment is to advance knowledge and reveal truth—this is its purifying quality. Justice Holmes's metaphor was that "the best test of truth is the power of the thought to get itself accepted in the competition of the market."[68] And finally, freedom of expression is a method of achieving a more adaptable and hence a more stable community, of maintaining "the precarious balance between healthy cleavage and necessary consensus."[69]

These are the classic purposes of the First Amendment. Individually they are strong; together they mount a compelling case for free expression. Only two considerations need be added to fill out the premises on which we would base interpretation of the speech clause.

The first is an additional or at least a collateral First Amendment purpose. It transcends any preference for political ideas, the search for truth, or even the high goal of encouraging individual self-expression and focuses on the effect of ideas and information on those who receive them. It has loosely been called the "right to know," and it has been described impressively by Vincent Blasi:

> Perhaps the most important beneficial consequence of unregulated expression is simply the stimulation individuals receive from a diverse reading and listening fare; this stimulation may contribute to human happiness directly, and hence be thought to have value quite apart from its relationship to the search for truth.[70]

The second consideration is of a different sort—the *intensity* and *sensitivity* with which one adheres to the above purposes.

In the course of our considerable exposure to both academic discourse and courtroom combat relating to free speech, we have rarely found a person who openly belittles the worth of the constitutional guarantee. To the contrary, everyone professes to support it. Why, then, the sharp differences among judges and scholars? We suggest that these differences turn not merely on whether the disputants agree with purposes of the First Amendment but rather on the degree to which they embrace them. Intensity cannot of course be measured, but it is palpable in judicial opinions, law review articles, and even the briefs of lawyers. As Justice Stewart observed about hard-core pornography, one knows it when one sees it.

Contrast, for example, Justice Holmes's opinion in *Schenck*[71] with his dissent in *Abrams*.[72] Compare the opinion of Justice Harlan in *Barenblatt*[73] with the Harlan opinion in *Cohen v. California*.[74] Stack up the opinions of Justice Frankfurter against those of Justices Black and Douglas, and the articles of Alexander Bickel and Philip Kurland against those of Thomas Emerson and Harry Kalven, Jr. The differences are only partly intellectual.

It should be clear that we are not extolling mere emotionalism, but rather a simple yet compelling confidence in speech values and a full sensitivity to their significance. The words of Justice Brandeis in *Whitney v. California*, which cannot too often be repeated, are a stirring embodiment of these qualities:

Those who won our independence . . . valued liberty both as an end and as a means. They believed liberty to be the secret of happiness and courage to be the secret of liberty. They believed that freedom to think as you will and to speak as you think are means indispensable to the discovery and spread of political truth; that without free speech and assembly discussion would be futile; that with them, discussion affords ordinarily adequate protection against the dissemination of noxious doctrine; that the greatest menace to freedom is an inert people; that public discussion is a political duty; and that this should be a fundamental principle of the American government.[75]

These are our premises for a theory that would protect free speech to the maximum. We use the phrase "maximum protection" because we do not assert that freedom of speech is "absolute." Certain kinds of speech can severely damage individuals or institutions, including the government itself. Those who would formulate a persuasive free speech theory must take account of this reality.

The elements of our "maximum protection" theory are as follows:

1. The content of communication is entitled to the fullest protection possible and can be restricted only where the identified harm resulting from such communication plainly cannot be remedied, mitigated, or prevented by "more speech." Again, the best statement of this prime element is one made by Justice Brandeis: "If there be time to expose through discussion the falsehood and fallacies, to avert the evil by the processes of education, the remedy to be applied to more speech, not enforced silence."[76]

2. Communication that surely will cause the harm sought to be averted can be restricted, but only if it comes within one of a few rigorously defined categories. Examples of speech that might be restricted are: the revelation of "hard-core" national security information, relating, for example, to tactical military operations, blueprints of advanced military equipment, or secret codes; the revelation of a valid trade secret; a material or fraudulent misrepresentation of products, goods, or services—for example, the mislabeling of a poison as aspirin; and intensely assaultive speech that is the verbal equivalent of a slap in the face—for example, a vulgar phone call.

A free speech theory that ignores the impact of such communication will be self-defeating. It is far better to recognize the realities in fashioning constitutional rules.

3. Speech can be placed in such categories only upon the most demanding showing, comparable to that required to overcome the "heavy presumption against [the] constitutional validity" of prior restraints.

4. So-called time, place, and manner restrictions on speech are to be gauged by a rigorous form of compelling interest test. Such restrictions are tolerated in order to provide for content-neutral "rules of the road." But to guard against the pretextual use of such rules to deny speech any effective

forum, the rules must be subjected to strict scrutiny and shown to be carefully tailored and necessary to serve the interests being asserted.

5. First Amendment "procedural" rules—the presumptive invalidity of prior restraints, the doctrines against overbreadth and vagueness, and the requirements of scrupulous procedural safeguards—should remain firmly in place. These rules are protective devices under almost all First Amendment theories to assure adequate "breathing space" for free speech and to avoid the more obvious forms of infringement.

These are the five elements of the "maximum protection" theory, which is designed to confine permissible limitations on expression within the narrowest channels. Under such a theory restrictions are tolerable only upon the most rigorous procedural and evidentiary showings, and only with regard to types of speech where the harm is complete upon publication or utterance and cannot be remedied or mitigated by further communication.

CONCLUSION

It is perhaps not wholly surprising to find an apparently close link between the Burger Court's free speech decisions and its attention to traditional property interests. As has been observed elsewhere,[77] a major theme emerging from a decade of Burger Court jurisprudence is a reemergence of an older concept that the primary office of civil liberties is to safeguard property and contract. That, too, is unsurprising since during most of our two-century-old experiment in "ordered liberty" the protection of property and contract has been viewed as a cornerstone of the protection of liberty.[78]

We do not suggest that free speech and property are inherently antithetical. Although they may frequently conflict, the values inherent in those concepts play a critical role in the maintenance of democracy. But there are potent differences between property interests and free speech values, and they have to do with priorities and attitudes.

In terms of priorities, the Burger Court has been respectful of free speech interests principally when those interests have coincided with or furthered the protection of property, and thus the Court has afforded protection to corporate speech, commercial speech, and even iconoclastic individual speech when personal property has been utilized to convey the message. But the Court has been suspicious of free speech when it has appeared to conflict with traditional proprietary rights asserted by individuals, corporations, or even government. In such instances, free speech has been treated as simply one factor to be weighed in the balance, with no recognition that speech should be first among equals in the pantheon of liberty.

In terms of attitudes and imagery, free speech and property rights are different kinds of liberty. The protection of property is bottomed on the protection of "settled expectations" within the larger context of a model of society that is orderly, stable, and rational. Such a vision of society is apparently congenial to the Burger Court and its partisans. Affording maximum protection for free speech, by contrast, is often risky, for it may result in disorder and instability. But in our view the alternative of viewing free speech as just another "value" among many presents a graver danger. We would cast our lot with the risk-takers: Justice Brandeis of *Whitney*, Justice Douglas of *Brandenburg*, and Justice Harlan of *Cohen*, whose faith in freedom was expressed as follows:

> The constitutional right of free expression is powerful medicine in a society as diverse and populous as ours. It is designed and intended to remove governmental restraints from the arena of public discussion, putting the decision as to what views shall be voiced largely into the hands of each of us, in the hope that use of such freedom will ultimately produce a more capable citizenry and more perfect polity and in the belief that no other approach would comport with the premise of individual dignity and choice upon which our political system rests.[79]

• Three •

The Burger Court and the Poor

Robert W. Bennett

The Supreme Court, like any institution of society, can realistically be appreciated only as a part of a larger environment that helps to shape its work. One important part of the Court's environment that is little studied and seldom discussed is the pattern of cases that are brought to it. This part of the Court's environment changed rather abruptly in the late 1960s in a way that continues to have important implications for the poor.

The Supreme Court has significant control over its own agenda. It can only hear cases that are brought to it by litigants, however, and usually only after substantial litigation effort in the lower courts. One of the institutional imperatives of the Supreme Court, of course, is to provide guidance to lower courts for the cases that are coming to them. With this combination of pressures, when the nature of the cases coming to court changes, so almost inevitably does the nature of cases decided by the Supreme Court.

CONCERN WITH PROBLEMS OF THE POOR

Prior to 1965, cases touching the interests of poor people came to the Supreme Court almost incidentally. The Court had defined important procedural protections, including the rights to appointed trial counsel and to a trial transcript for appeal purposes, for many indigent criminal defendants.[1] These developments helped inspire other cases before 1965 about the rights of criminally accused indigents.[2] The opinions in these cases occasionally indicated that discrimination against the poor generally was a matter for special judicial concern. Outside the criminal defense area, however, lawyers for the poor were largely unavailable. As a result, the interests of poor people were usually represented only if they happened to coincide with the interests of civil liberties or civil rights organizations or other groups or individuals with more access to lawyers. In a 1966 opinion striking down Virginia's poll tax, Justice Douglas wrote that "lines drawn on the basis of wealth or property, like those of race, are traditionally disfavored."[3] With regard to matters of wealth or property, however, there really was little of such a tradition.

In 1964 Congress passed the Economic Opportunity Act,[4] establishing the Office of Economic Opportunity. One of that agency's earliest efforts was to fund programs of civil legal services for the poor around the country. That activity continues today under the aegis of the Legal Services Corporation.[5] Indeed, the federal legal services budget grew from about $20 million in 1965 to $321 million for fiscal year 1981. It was scaled back to $241 million for fiscal year 1982 under pressure from the Reagan administration. Federally funded legal services programs were nemeses of Ronald Reagan in his days as governor of California, and he strenuously sought an end to targeted federal funding for them. Thus, even with the decrease in the 1982 budget, the legal services effort demonstrated substantial political staying power.

The result has been that since the late 1960s there has been a large and continuing flow of litigation affecting the interests of poor people, with an impressive portion of it reaching the Supreme Court. Warren Burger replaced Earl Warren as chief justice when this flow was just beginning, and consequently it is the Burger Court's efforts that have judicially molded at least the federal law for the poor today.

One measure of the change legal services programs of the late 1960s brought in the Court's case load is the increase in the number of decisions dealing with the rights and responsibilities of welfare recipients. Large-scale public assistance programs became a familiar part of the governmental landscape in the United States after passage of the Social Security Act of 1934.[6] The Aid to Families with Dependent Children (AFDC) section of that statute, establishing a program of cash assistance exclusively for poor families with children, was not the subject of a Supreme Court decision until 1968. Between 1968 and 1979, however, the Court handed down at least eighteen major AFDC decisions.[7] Since that time the flow of AFDC cases has abated, but this seems to represent more a shift of attention to other welfare programs[8] than any diminished concern with the legal problems of the poor.

WELFARE DECISIONS

Shapiro v. Thompson[9] and *Dandridge v. Williams*[10] are two Supreme Court AFDC decisions that were handed down in the period of transition from the Warren Court to the Burger Court. Together they suggest a deep-seated ambivalence that the Burger Court inherited and still has not resolved. *Shapiro*, decided during Chief Justice Warren's final term on the Court, held that one-year state residence requirements for receipt of public assistance violated the equal protection clause of the Fourteenth Amendment. It made use of the doctrine the Warren Court had been developing that state action discriminating against the exercise of certain "fundamental" rights was to be subjected to strict judicial scrutiny. Most governmental action passes constitutional muster if shown to be a rational means for the pursuit of any legitimate governmental purpose. If an action impinges upon the exercise of fundamental rights, however, the Court has required that the action be necessary to achieve a compelling governmental interest. In *Shapiro* the Court held that durational residence requirements discriminated against the fundamental right of interstate travel and could not withstand the strict judicial scrutiny that had then become appropriate. That assistance for desperately poor citizens was involved also seemed to have significance in the *Shapiro* rationale. The Court never explicitly said that the fact that welfare benefits were at issue called for special scrutiny, but it pointedly began its substantive discussion by noting that "the ability of the families to obtain the very means to subsist—food, shelter and other necessities of life"[11]—was at stake.

Similar willingness to treat subsistence benefits as special recurred the following year in *Goldberg v. Kelly*,[12] with Justice Burger on the Court. In *Goldberg* the Court held that before terminating AFDC benefits, the state must give a hearing to a recipient claiming that the proposed termination is improper. The decision was grounded in the due process clause of the Fourteenth Amendment and was expressly justified by the importance to the recipients of the benefits put in jeopardy. "For qualified recipients," the Court stressed, "welfare provides the means to obtain essential food, clothing, housing, and medical care."[13]

No similar willingness to attach constitutional significance to the importance of welfare benefits for recipients appears in *Dandridge*, decided only two weeks after *Goldberg*. *Dandridge* posed the question whether states could place a ceiling on the amount of an AFDC grant regardless of family size or actual need. Maryland had set a monthly ceiling of about $250, with the result that families of more than six persons could receive no more welfare assistance than families of six. A receptive Court might have reasoned that this discrimination against large families impinged upon a fundamental interest of the recipients in making decisions about family size. Decisions both before and after *Dandridge* have recognized a fundamental right of privacy encompassing interests in childbearing and child rearing. This privacy interest, in combination with the fact that welfare benefits were in issue, suggested a close analogy to *Shapiro*. Instead of exercising strict judicial scrutiny of the Maryland maximum in the manner of *Shapiro*, however, the Court returned to an extreme form of pre-*Shapiro* judicial deference to governmental decisions.

The Supreme Court of the late New Deal had largely withdrawn from serious constitutional review of regulatory measures for business and industry. In one of the most remarkable passages from *Dandridge*, the Burger Court acknowledged that welfare "involved the most basic economic needs of impoverished human beings" but then likened the case constitutionally to the business regulation cases, despite "the dramatically real factual difference" between the two contexts.[14] With economic regulation cases rather than *Shapiro* as the relevant norm, the Court proceeded to find the Maryland maximum justified partly by the work incentive it provided, despite the fact that the heads of the large families whose grants were limited by the maximum were probably less suitable for job placement than were recipients generally.[15] The Court's specific acceptance of this work incentive rationale highlights the contrast with *Shapiro*, since in *Shapiro* the Court rejected a strikingly similar justification advanced for residence requirements. In *Shapiro* the Court had said it was irrational to use residence requirements to provide a work incentive for new arrivals while providing no similar incentive for long-term residents.[16]

The Court concluded the *Dandridge* opinion with a passage that probably tells more about its reason for the decision than does the improbable identification of welfare programs with state regulation of business:

> Conflicting claims of morality and intelligence are raised by opponents and proponents of almost every measure, certainly including the one before us. But the intractable economic, social and even philosophical problems presented by public welfare assistance programs are not the business of this Court. . . . [T]he Constitution does not empower this Court to second-guess state officials charged with the difficult responsibility of allocating limited public welfare funds among the myriad of potential recipients.[17]

The difficulty the Court foresaw is, of course, quite real. There are many disparate views, both within and without the welfare population, about the proper allocation of public assistance funds. Welfare problems may or may not be more intractable than others the Court has faced, but the same difficulties were presented by *Shapiro*. The two cases thus suggest a Court in conflict with itself about its proper role in addressing welfare problems. That conflict continues to the present day and indeed appears to extend to the Court's role in the legal problems of poor people more generally.

RIGHTS VERSUS PRIVILEGES

Another indication of the Court's ambivalence has been its attitude toward the distinction occasionally made in constitutional cases between "rights" and "privileges." The distinction had been used before in the early part of the Warren Court era to justify a refusal of constitutional protections—both procedural and substantive—when the government denied, withdrew, or conditioned a "privilege." Where "rights" were involved, however, constitutional protections attached. Welfare benefits would likely fall on the privilege side of the line if the distinction retained significance, but as government benefit programs grew in societal importance, the prospect of government dominating recipients by conditioning benefits on a willingness to give up what would be constitutional protection in a rights context increasingly seemed repugnant.

In both *Shapiro* and *Goldberg*, the Court explicitly rejected as irrelevant any distinction between rights and privileges.[18] In each, as we have seen, the fact that welfare benefits were at stake seemed to strengthen the plaintiff's case. The 1971 decision in *Wyman v. James*,[19] however, appeared to resurrect the distinction, even though the Court did not use those precise words. *Wyman* involved a challenge to the common requirement in public assistance programs that a caseworker be allowed periodically into the home of each recipient family. Refusal to allow such a home visit often results in complete termination or denial of assistance to the family. The home visit requirement was challenged in *Wyman* as a violation of the Fourth Amendment "right of the people to be secure in their persons, houses, papers and effects, against unreasonable searches and seizures."[20]

The Fourth Amendment reasonableness limitation had earlier caused the Court difficulty outside the core Fourth Amendment concern with searches for evidence of crime. In 1967, however, the Warren Court seemed to have resolved the problem in holding that housing code inspections could not be conducted without a valid search warrant.[21] The Court in that decision rejected as "anomalous" the notion that the Fourth Amendment protected only suspected criminals, saying that "even the most law-abiding citizen has a very tangible interest in limiting the circumstances under which the sanctity of his home may be broken by official authority."[22] The Burger Court has occasionally indulged in a similarly expansive reading of the Fourth Amendment's warrant requirement.[23] In a sharp departure from the pattern, the Court in *Wyman* rejected the Fourth Amendment challenge, concluding that the home visit is neither a Fourth Amendment "search" nor unreasonable. Much of the *Wyman* rationale appears to rest on a treatment of welfare as a privilege.

In reasoning that the intrusion was not a search, for instance, the Court explained that "the visitation in itself is not forced or compelled. . . . If consent . . . is withheld . . . aid . . . never begins or merely ceases, as the case may be."[24] And in its extended discussion of the intrusion's reasonableness, the Court said:

> The [welfare] agency, with tax funds . . . is fulfilling a public trust. The State . . . has appropriate . . . concern in . . . assuring that the intended and proper objects of that tax-produced assistance are the ones who benefit from the aid it dispenses. Surely it is not unreasonable . . . that the State have at its command a gentle means, of limited extent and of practical and considerate application, of achieving that assurance.[25]

An exhange between the *Wyman* majority and Justice Marshall in dissent illustrates the inferior constitutional status to which the decision relegated welfare recipients. The majority's discussion of the visit's reasonableness ended with an analogy to an Internal Revenue Service audit of a taxpayer. The taxpayer must prove his entitlement to a deduction, and if he does not,

the deduction simply is disallowed. "So here," the *Wyman* majority concluded, the plaintiff "has the 'right' to refuse the home visit, but a consequence in the form of cessation of aid, similar to the taxpayer's resultant
additional tax, flows from that refusal."[26]

The majority opinion ended the discussion there, but the analogy cried
out for completion because it made no mention of the home intrusion that
lay at the heart of the recipient's constitutional claim. Justice Marshall took
up the task in dissent. "A true analogy," he insisted, "would be an Internal
Revenue Service requirement that in order to claim a dependency exemption,
a taxpayer *must* allow a specially trained IRS agent to invade the home for
the purpose of questioning the occupants and looking for evidence that the
exemption is being properly utilized for the benefit of the dependent. If
such a system were even proposed, the cries of constitutional outrage would
be unanimous."[27]

The most startling aspect of *Wyman*, however, is the majority opinion's
use of unproved assumptions about the way that home visits operated in
practice and about the plaintiff's personal life. In a footnote reference to
the plaintiff's welfare record, for instance, presumably submitted by the
defendant department but never acknowledged as accurate or submitted to
cross-examination by plaintiff's attorney, the Court characterized the "picture" revealed by the caseworker's notes as "a sad and unhappy one."[28] In
contrast, the Court said that the "caseworker is not a sleuth but rather, we
trust, is a friend in need."[29]

In *Wyman* the Court appeared to view Fourth Amendment "searches" as
requiring a predominantly investigative purpose. It concluded that the home
visit was not a search (and hence that no constitutional protection attached),
despite the fact that the "caseworker's posture in the home visit is perhaps,
in a sense, both rehabilitative and investigative," because the investigative
"aspect . . . is given far more emphasis than it deserves."[30] In dissent,
Justice Marshall explained that the state had repeatedly pointed to the investigative value of home visits in justifying them. Indeed the state had
stressed the need to enter AFDC homes to guard against welfare fraud and
child abuse, both of which are felonies.

Wyman represents the nadir of treatment of the poor in the years of the
Burger Court. The decision is distressing not only because it was badly
reasoned and is inconsistent with the thrust of Fourth Amendment decisions
both before and since. It is most distressing because the public policy
justification for the Court's holding is difficult to fathom. *Dandridge* involved discrimination between one group of welfare recipients and another.
If the welfare budget is assumed to be constant, the dispute in *Dandridge*
highlights the problem the Court specifically mentioned of allocating limited
resources. If the Court holds for one group, another suffers. *Wyman*, on the
other hand, presented no such wrenching problem. If the Court had held that
home visits could not be made compulsory, most recipients would likely

have permitted them rather than agree to meet a caseworker at a less convenient place outside the home. Those who refused the home visits would
just risk caseworker suspicion, which could be pursued by making inquiries
at school or in recipients' neighborhoods. If mandatory home visits did con-
serve welfare funds, the amounts involved were likely to be a small price to
pay for the recipients' ability to say no.

Justice Blackmun was the author of the opinion in *Wyman v. James*, but,
as if to emphasize the Burger Court's ambivalence, he also wrote the 1979
decision in *Califano v. Westcott*,[31] holding unconstitutional a federal AFDC
provision extending benefits to intact families in need because of the father's
but not because of the mother's unemployment. In that opinion, Justice
Blackmun placed specific emphasis upon the fact that the benefits in dispute
were "subsistence payments made available as a last resort to families that
would otherwise lack basic necessities."[32] And he chided the federal government for presenting an argument in defense of the statutory limitation that
invited "a return to the discredited view that welfare benefits are a 'privilege'
not subject to the guarantee of equal protection."[33]

Westcott remains the Court's most recent explicit word on the right–privilege distinction in welfare cases, but the 1980 decision in *Harris v. McRae*[34]
shows that the constitutional law limiting the state's ability to discriminate in
benefit programs is no simple mirror image of the law applicable when the
government imposes what can more comfortably be termed a "burden" or a
restriction that denies a "right." *Harris* involved government refusal to fund
medically necessary abortions in Medicaid programs that did fund medically
necessary procedures more generally. In *Roe v. Wade*,[35] a decision not particularly focused on problems of the poor, the Court had severely limited
the state's power to restrict a woman's ability to obtain an abortion. In
doing so, it had relied heavily on the "fundamentality" of the woman's privacy interest in making the abortion decision. In *Harris*, however, the Court
found that no unusual court scrutiny of the discrimination was required because refusal to fund did not "interfere" with the fundamental right in a
constitutionally significant way. If this part of *Harris* is taken seriously,
Shapiro will be called into question and the law of discrimination with regard to benefits will be cast into disarray. Most likely, however, Harris is a
sport in the law of the poor, understandable more in terms of the Court's
wariness about the sensitive abortion issue than as a wholesale abandonment
of the law of discrimination in welfare programs.[36]

REMEDIES

In *Westcott* the Court was also responsive to the interests of the poor in
the remedy it found appropriate. When state action is found to violate the
equal protection requirement because it extends a benefit to too small a

group, the legislature can either extend the benefit to a larger group or eliminate it altogether. The Court, however, must decide what to order while the legislature has the matter under consideration, and what the Court decides may—by defining a new status quo—influence the result of the legislative deliberations. In *Westcott* the Court majority, over a four-man dissent joined by the chief justice, found extension of the benefit appropriate, based in part upon the "equitable consideration" that "an injunction suspending the program's operation would impose hardship on beneficiaries whom Congress plainly meant to protect."[37]

USE OF OTHER THEMES

Westcott is illustrative of an important strain in the Burger Court's decisions touching the interests of the poor. The Burger Court has been very active in addressing problems of gender-based discrimination, and the Westcott opinion rests heavily on the fact that it involved sex discrimination. In most of the constitutional decisions affecting the interests of the poor, the plaintiffs have prevailed only where there was present another decisional theme with which the Court has felt comfortable. Thus, the Burger Court has built on doctrine developed in the Warren Court years to redress some forms of discrimination against illegitimate children. This has often redounded to the benefit of the poor, as in 1973, when the Court struck down a New Jersey welfare limitation on the ground that it discriminated against families with children born out of wedlock.[38] In 1974, with four post–Warren Court appointees taking part, the Court picked up on the right-to-travel theme of *Shapiro* to hold that Arizona could not impose a one-year residence requirement for receipt by indigents of hospitalization or medical care at a county's expense.[39] The Court has always been more comfortable with procedural than with substantive issues. In 1981, it took the middle ground and decided to leave to case-by-case adjudication the question of whether an indigent was entitled to appointed state-compensated counsel when the state attempted to deprive her of her parental status.[40] That same year, Justice Burger wrote the opinion for a Court unanimous in its conclusion that an indigent was entitled to state-paid blood tests in a paternity action.[41]

THE ROLE OF MIDDLE-CLASS VALUES

Several commentators have chided the Court for pursuing middle-class values in the name of fundamental rights, while ignoring the pressing problems of those, including the poor, with fewer resources to bring to bear on legislative decision-making.[42] Perhaps the most dramatic evidence for the validity of such a charge is the 1973 decision in *San Antonio Independent School District v. Rodriguez*.[43]

The fundamental rights doctrine brought to fruition in *Shapiro* had stimulated an extensive scholarly literature about financing schemes for public education.[44] Prior to *Rodriguez* the Court's decisions had provided little guidance as to the nature of "fundamental rights." The commonsense case for the fundamentality of an interest in education is more than plausible, however, since education contributes so importantly to one's ability to participate in the governance of the nation as well as to function in modern society more generally. It can be seen as closely related to the exercise of the rights to vote, speak, and assemble, all of which have deep roots in constitutional law.

Publicly funded primary and secondary education is found in all states, and its funding scheme is typically defined in state legislation. These legislative schemes frequently ensure a minimum expenditure per pupil but allow local districts willing and able to raise additional funds to spend more than the minimum. The additional funds are often raised by property taxes, and as a result property-rich districts can and do spend more money on education per pupil than property-poor districts. This result is found in many cases even where the property-poor district taxes at a higher rate. The value of the property in a district and the total individual wealth of its inhabitants are by no means equivalent, but they are related to such a degree that public money spent on education is substantially correlated with demographic variations in the wealth of district inhabitants.[45]

Justice Powell wrote the opinion in *Rodriguez*, rejecting an equal protection challenge to a Texas education financing scheme much like that sketched above. Since the correlation of district property value and per capita district wealth was imperfect, Justice Powell found that the discrimination was not against the poor but against "a large, diverse and amorphous class"[46] including even wealthy families living in property-poor districts. Such a class, he insisted, unlike racial minorities, or aliens, or women, is entitled to no unusual protection under the equal protection clause. Nor, he concluded, was education a fundamental right, since it was not a right "explicitly or implicitly guaranteed by the Constitution."[47]

The Court, perhaps especially under Chief Justice Burger, has not been timid in ascribing fundamentality to particular interests not explicitly protected by the Constitution. In *Memorial Hospital v. Maricopa County*[48] the Court followed *Shapiro* in characterizing the right of interstate travel in this way. The monumental abortion decision in *Roe v. Wade*[49] was reached by holding the interest in abortional privacy to be fundamental. The Court in *Rodriguez* characterized *Shapiro* and *Roe* as recognizing interests "implicitly"[50] guaranteed by the Constitution. "Implicit" constitutional protection, however, is always a matter of judgment, and the arguments for implicit protection of travel or abortional privacy seem no stronger than those for education. Against this background the charge becomes plausible that the

Court in *Rodriguez* used the distinction between implicit constitutional interests and those outside the document's protection as a shield to stave off an assault by the poor on the middle-class prerogative of well-financed public schools.

The school financing problem suggests class rivalry in a way that the welfare cases do not, at least at first blush. Welfare problems, as we have seen in the discussion of *Dandridge*, usually arise when the state treats two groups of poor persons differently. If the Court forbids the unequal treatment, the legislature usually retains the option to divide the original welfare budget more equitably among a larger group of recipients. If this is the legislature's response, no interests outside the welfare population are put in jeopardy.[51] If the Court had required evenhanded school financing, in contrast, the result would have been some combination of higher taxes for education and lower public expenditure for education in wealthier districts.

Still, the strains in constitutional decision-making are too varied to allow the charge of middle-class parochialism to stand, at least in any extreme form. The welfare decisions do not really justify the generalization. The problem of birth out of wedlock, to which the Burger Court has been responsive in welfare as well as in other contexts,[52] is hardly the classic middle-class problem. Conversely, the interest of the poor in the ready availability of abortion coincides with a stereotype of what the middle class wants for the poor. Yet, despite its pathbreaking work in constitutionalizing abortion rights, the Burger Court, as already mentioned, has held that it is permissible for a state to refuse to fund even medically necessary abortions in its medical assistance programs for the poor.[53]

The *Rodriguez* decision is perhaps understandable in terms other than those of class conflict. An important prudential constraint in constitutional decision-making is the extent to which a court can provide an adequate remedy once it has defined a wrong. A court's remedial tools are limited. It cannot raise money directly or closely administer an ongoing program. It must depend largely upon its power to order others to take some action, with a contempt citation as its basic enforcement sanction. And once it has defined a wrong, it may breed disrespect for the legal system generally if its remedial powers are not adequate to eliminate, or at least substantially ameliorate, the wrong. Two of the major contributions of the Warren Court to constitutional jurisprudence—the school desegregation and legislative reapportionment decisions—required a willingness to devote extraordinary judicial resources to a continuing process of overseeing the responsive actions of other branches of government. In *Rodriguez* the Court may well have thought that attacking the school financing problem would have required just such an extraordinary devotion of resources; that prospect could have chilled the enthusiasm even of a Court quite appalled by unequal educational financing.

Constitutional decisions show the Supreme Court at its best and at its

worst. It is in constitutional decision-making that the Court has principal
responsibility for developing a coherent body of doctrine. The Warren Court
did not carry a constitutional law for the poor much beyond oversimplified
catchphrases. More than a decade after Warren Burger became chief justice,
the Court still seems caught between repudiating those catchphrases as irrelevant and groping for some manageable constitutional status for the fact and
the by-products of poverty in our society. But if problems of poverty have
not shown the Burger Court at its constitutional best, it appeared at its
worst in *Wyman v. James*, and that was some time ago.

THE FUNCTION OF CONSTITUTIONAL REVIEW

The question of the proper role for judicial review in the name of the
Constitution is never far below the surface in constitutional cases. Why, in
a legislative democracy, should public officials outside the constituted legislative processes be given a form of veto over legislative enactments?
Facing that question repeatedly may yet lead the Burger Court to special
concern for constitutional problems of the poor.

Some would contend that it is the Constitution, not the judiciary, that
forbids the legislature to do some things and that the Constitution's authority
stems from the fact that it was made the premise of all else in American
government, including legislative authority. But that answer is clearly insufficient and is generally recognized as such today. When the judiciary is
charged with enforcing general constitutional commands over time, it is both
inevitable and desirable that the meaning of those commands will evolve over
time and will be a function, at least in some measure, of the value structures of those who are appointed to judicial office.

The judicial veto must search for its justification in a more dynamic
view of American society. The most persuasive justifications are three. First,
all societies develop mechanisms to protect long-run interests against immediate, sometimes destructive, impulses. Judges speaking in the name of the
Constitution can be seen as a check on shortsighted legislation so that
values important to the long-run health of society can be given some breathing space. This is a commonly accepted justification for judicial enforcement of the Constitution, and it has no special significance for the poor.
The second and third justifications, however, do.

The central tenet of our system of government is majority rule. At the
same time, our political and moral philosophical systems treat the good of
the individual as an end in itself and recognize the danger that majorities
will unjustifiably invade individual prerogatives. A judicially enforced constitutional law can be seen to insulate the individual from majoritarian dominance, and the poor, with fewer resources to protect themselves, might be
thought to be in special need of such protection.

A third justification for the judicial veto, in some tension with this second, is that the imperfections of the political process prevent it from expressing even the immediate majoritarian will of the polity. Neither the number of voters in favor of a particular policy nor the intensity of voter preferences determines policy outcomes in a legislative democracy in the manner often ideally assumed. Among the other factors playing a significant role are organization of voters, personal influence with legislators, and money.[54] In each of these respects the poor are likely to be disadvantaged in the political process.

When the interests of the poor, or a particularly weak segment of the poor, have been severely disadvantaged in a political forum, the judiciary can appropriately intervene, if only with a nudge, to readjust the balance. In this sense, poverty is not constitutionally an irrelevance but rather a cause for special judicial concern. The Warren Court started to draw constitutional law toward this ideal; the Burger Court has drawn it back or perhaps has circled around the ideal. But the vision is an enticing one, and it may yet prevail. No court can sit in a democracy to revise all legislative decisions that "unjustifiably" disfavor those with relatively little political power. Our constitutional democracy does demand some court interventions, however, and the most severe burdens placed on the least powerful of our citizens are among the most appropriate objects of judicial concern.

The decision in *Shapiro v. Thompson* is justifiable in these terms. Recent arrivals in the state who applied for welfare would not only likely be severely impoverished and objects of popular prejudice, but they would also be particularly unfamiliar with the levers of influence in the state's political processes. The burden imposed on them by durational residence requirements—total denial of assistance for a full year—was so severe that judicial intervention became appropriate.

The maximum grant limitation in *Dandridge v. Williams*, however, also likely resulted from the inability of large welfare families to have their interests fully weighed in the political process. These families are few in number and are often the object of heightened popular prejudice and misunderstanding. Maryland offered several policy justifications for maximums, but the real reason behind them was probably that they disproportionately imposed the burden of inadequate welfare budgets on a politically weak segment of the welfare population.

THE IMPORTANCE OF ACCESS TO THE COURTS

Even if the Burger Court makes no further progress in formulating a constitutional law explicitly incorporating the problems of poverty, the access to the courts opened by the legal services movement will have been of surpassing significance. Since 1968, for instance, the Court has rendered at

least fourteen decisions interpreting the AFDC provisions of the Social Security Act and implementing regulations of the Department of Health, Education and Welfare.[55] Of these, eight were decisions favorable to the recipient
plaintiffs.[56] The Burger Court, for instance, has held that states cannot set
arbitrary limits to the amount of allowable work-related expenses for AFDC
recipients,[57] cannot presume that a non-AFDC family living with recipients
is contributing a proportionate share of the rent,[58] and cannot deny AFDC–
foster care benefits to children living in a foster care situation with rela-
tives.[59] Some of the decisions interpreting legislation have been legislatively
altered, but many have not. Thus even if the years of the Burger Court
had not seen a single constitutional decision peculiarly affecting the interests of poor people, statutory decisions would have left the poor population
with more "law" on its side than when Warren Burger took his seat on the
Supreme Court.

Continued access to the courts—particularly the federal courts—is essential to consolidation and extension of these gains. In its own decisions affecting court access, however, the Burger Court has been rather insensitive
to the importance of litigation as a vehicle by which the rule of law is made
available to the poor population.

Edelman v. Jordan[60] is the most striking example. The Eleventh Amendment withdraws federal judicial authority over actions "against one of the
United States by citizens of another State."[61] Literally read, the amendment
has no effect in suits against a state by its own citizens, but it at one time
was read as resurrecting a common law rule of sovereign immunity for states,
even against suits by their own citizens.[62] This immunity in turn was later
qualified in an important way by allowing suits for injunctive relief against
state officials acting unconstitutionally, on the ground that they were not
then acting for the state.[63] *Edelman* posed the further question of whether
welfare recipients could obtain back benefits illegally withheld when a federal court awarded prospective injunctive relief.

The narrow language and checkered history of the Eleventh Amendment
left ample room for the decision to go either way. The Supreme Court,
probably out of concern for beleaguered welfare budgets, decided that back
benefits (or other monetary relief against a state) were unavailable in federal
court because of the amendment, unless the state consented or a statute
specifically provided for such relief. But the decision imposes significant
additional litigation burdens in many instances, since state court or administrative actions may sometimes make the back benefits available in a separate
proceeding after the federal suit. But whether back benefits may sometimes
be recoverable elsewhere or not, the *Edelman* limitation gives welfare departments a very substantial incentive to stall litigation and thus lessen the
period for which the benefits will definitely have to be paid. The result is
justice often delayed and sometimes denied, as recipients' lawyers ignore

some grievances because of the delay they know awaits them in federal litigation against a welfare department.

Edelman is a mischievous opinion, but other questionable Burger Court decisions exclude certain types of poor litigants from court altogether. In the 1971 decision in *Boddie v. Connecticut*[64] the early Burger Court held it a denial of due process to prevent indigents from initiating divorce proceedings for failure to pay the court fees and costs for service of process. Justice Harlan wrote the *Boddie* opinion and rested it heavily on the exclusion of indigents worked by the fee requirements "from the only forum effectively empowered to settle their disputes."[65] Depending upon how this emphasis was later used, *Boddie* could have shown the way to lowering monetary barriers to commencement of court action by indigents generally.

The reach of *Boddie* was tested in 1973 in *United States v. Kras*,[66] where a challenge was brought by an indigent to the fees required to initiate a bankruptcy proceeding. The Court rebuffed the challenge, distinguishing *Boddie* because it involved the fundamental interest in marriage and because an overextended debtor could resolve his problems without official court sanction. "However unrealistic the remedy may be in a particular situation," the Court said, "a debtor, in theory, and often in actuality, may adjust his debts by negotiated agreement with his creditors."[67]

Justice Blackmun wrote the opinion in *Kras*. After distinguishing *Boddie*, he undertook to demonstrate the reasonableness of the filing fee requirement by noting that it could be paid in weekly installments of $1.92 or, under some circumstances, $1.28. This much, Justice Blackmun noted, "less than the price of a movie and little more than the cost of a pack or two of cigarettes . . . should be within [plaintiff's] able-bodied reach."[68]

Justice Marshall fairly seethed in dissent:

> It may be easy for some people to think that weekly savings of less than $2 are no burden. But no one who has had close contact with poor people can fail to understand how close to the margin of survival many of them are. . . . A pack or two of cigarettes may be, for them, not a routine purchase but a luxury indulged in only rarely. The desperately poor almost never go to see a movie, which the majority seems to believe is an almost weekly activity.
>
> • • •
>
> It is perfectly proper for judges to disagree about what the Constitution requires. But it is disgraceful for an interpretation of the Constitution to be premised upon unfounded assumptions about how people live.[69]

Kras was soon followed by *Ortwein v. Schwab*,[70] upholding Oregon's $25 appellate court filing fee for judicial review of welfare administrative hearings.

Perhaps the most strained of the Burger Court decisions limiting access to court was *Warth v. Seldin*,[71] decided in 1975. Different groups of plaintiffs in *Warth* brought suit to challenge the zoning ordinances and practices of a town in upstate New York, claiming that they had the "purpose and effect of excluding persons of low and moderate income from residing in the town."[72] The Supreme Court never reached the merits of plaintiffs' claim, however, because it held that plaintiffs did not have the requisite interest in the lawsuit to give them "standing" to pursue it. Low-income plaintiffs claiming they would like to live in the town had no standing, the Court said, because the practices did not injure them "in any concretely demonstrable way."[73] The desire of these plaintiffs to live in the town, the Court explained, "always has depended on the efforts and willingness of third parties to build low and moderate-cost housing."[74]

Another group of plaintiffs alleged that they were effectively excluded from building housing in the town. The Court held that these parties did not show the requisite interest because, with one exception, they had not actively pursued the possibility of building such housing developments. And the single exception had not done so since he had been rebuffed about two and a half years earlier.

There is a decided Catch-22 aspect to the *Warth* decision. If plaintiffs' substantive complaint is taken as true, there is a considerable disincentive for any persons to proceed far enough in their efforts to satisfy the Court's standing requirement. Poor persons and those providing them with goods and services in particular can hardly be expected to devote significant resources to a project before seeking court assurance that an apparent legal hurdle will not prevent the project's successful completion.

Decisions like *Warth* that limit access of the poor to court hinder the effectiveness of legal services programs established and funded by Congress. Substantive statutory protections are often realized only if the courts stand ready to give them force. And even a constitutional law that withholds specific attention to problems of poverty can be put to service for poor clients who raise claims of a more general nature, if they have access to the court system. Conversely, a constitutional law that explicitly and sympathetically incorporates problems of poverty is useless to the poor if they do not have the ability to invoke it.

The Burger Court's limitations on access have not, of course, undone the changes wrought by the legal services movement. But a Supreme Court sensitive to its distinctive role in the governmental structure of the country would place a special premium on court access for the poor. It would do so even if Congress had never established legal services programs.

Access to legislative decision-making is symbolically open to the poor but is often effectively impeded. The Court cannot compensate comprehensively for this handicap, even with a substantive constitutional law fully developed to incorporate concerns for the impoverished. But the Court can compensate for the handicap more fully if it is mindful that limited legislative access for the poor makes access to court all the more important. Even in areas where the poor have made legislative gains, they can, if the courts remain inaccessible, lose those benefits more easily than others in further forums where competing interests vie. The courts are designedly insulated from the usual levers of political influence and thus are particularly charged with ensuring that the benefits of the rule of law reach the nation's poor.

• Four •

The Warren Court (Was It Really So Defense-Minded?), The Burger Court (Is It Really So Prosecution-Oriented?), and Police Investigatory Practices

Yale Kamisar

In one sense the Warren Court's "revolution" in American criminal procedure may be said to have been launched by the 1956 case of *Griffin v. Illinois* (establishing an indigent criminal defendant's right to a free transcript on appeal, at least under certain circumstances)[1] and to have been significantly advanced by two 1963 cases: *Gideon v. Wainwright* (entitling an indigent defendant to free counsel, at least in serious criminal cases)[2] and *Douglas v. California* (requiring a state to provide an indigent with counsel on his first appeal from a criminal conviction).[3] But these were not the cases that plunged the Warren Court into controversy.

Almost everyone accepted, or came to accept, the *Gideon* and *Griffin-Douglas* principles "in principle"—as long as they were limited to judicial proceedings. It was only when the Warren Court decided to carry these principles to the point where they really bite—police investigatory practices—that it met heavy resistance. It was not the Warren Court's efforts to strengthen the rights of the accused in the courtroom but its "activism" in the search and seizure, police interrogation, and pretrial identification areas that led many to believe that it was "too soft" on crime and made this a major political issue in the 1968 presidential campaign.

Did the Burger Court bring the so-called criminal procedure revolution of the 1960s to an abrupt halt? Did it launch a counterrevolution? Has it pro-

---

Because of the large number of "police practices" decisions handed down by the Supreme Court in the past dozen years, especially on the subject of search and seizure, I have not attempted to cover every significant Burger Court case in the area. For more comprehensive treatments of the same general subject matter, see Israel, *Criminal Procedure, The Burger Court, and the Legacy of the Warren Court*, 75 MICH.L.REV. 1320 (1977) and Saltzburg, *Foreword: The Flow and Ebb of Constitutional Criminal Procedure in the Warren and Burger Courts*, 69 GEO. L.J. 151 (1980), two articles I have found especially helpful in preparing this essay. In addition, all significant search and seizure cases are ably treated in LaFave, SEARCH AND SEIZURE: A TREATISE ON THE FOURTH AMENDMENT (1978), and the annual pocket parts to this three-volume work.

moted "law and order" without regard to the procedural rights of the accused or the suspected? Or has the Burger Court, no less than its predecessor, been the victim of grossly exaggerated criticism? One cannot intelligently answer these questions without first reexamining, if only briefly, the Warren Court's performance in the "police practices" phases of criminal procedure.

A HARD LOOK AT THE WARREN COURT'S PERFORMANCE

"The history of the Warren Court," it has well been said, "may be taken as a case study of a court that for a season determined to employ its judicial resources in an effort to alter significantly the nature of American criminal justice in the interest of a larger realization of the constitutional ideal of liberty under law."[4] But the Warren Court did not, and did not strive to, reform American criminal procedure nearly as much as is commonly supposed. Although it was often accused of being overly solicitous of criminal suspects, the Warren Court legitimated challenged law enforcement tactics on more occasions than is generally realized. Despite its public reputation as a bold, crusading court, more often than not its criminal procedure decisions reflected a pattern of moderation and compromise. Some examples follow.

The Use of Spies, Undercover Agents, and Electronic Surveillance

The Warren Court found no constitutional restrictions on the government's power to employ spies and undercover agents. Some members of the Court sought to draw a constitutional distinction between the government's use of "friends," "associates," and other secret agents equipped with electronic devices and its use of secret agents operating without such equipment, contending that "[e]lectronic aids add a wholly new dimension" to police spying activities.[5] But a majority of the Warren Court took the position (a viewpoint the Burger Court was to share) that one who speaks to another not only takes the risk that his listener will later make public what he has heard but also takes the risk that his listener will electronically record or simultaneously transmit what he is hearing.[6] Neither form of undercover activity, both courts told us, requires reasonable suspicion *or any justification.* For such activities are not perceived as implicating any Fourth Amendment interests.[7]

That in *Katz v. United States*[8] the Warren Court overruled the much-criticized 5 to 4 decision in *Olmstead v. United States*[9] is hardly surprising. For in holding, over the famous dissents of Justices Brandeis and Holmes, that wiretapping (or other forms of electronic surveillance) is neither a "search" nor "seizure," and viewing the protection against unreasonable search and seizure as turning upon the presence or absence of a physical intrusion into enclosures, Chief Justice Taft read the Fourth Amendment "with the literalness of a country parson interpreting the first chapter of Genesis."[10] As the Court pointed out in *Katz*, by the time that case was decided, the underpinnings of *Olmstead* had already been severely eroded.[11]

For many years, however, it had been unclear whether, if and when tapping and bugging were held subject to the requirements of the Fourth Amendment, that amendment would permit *any* electronic surveillance. Indeed, in *Olmstead* the Court may have resolved the constitutional issue the way it did on the premise that a contrary ruling would have precluded even the most closely supervised tapping. There was reason to think that electronic eavesdropping was so intrusive, so indiscriminate, and so incapable of being "particularly described" in advance that if tapping and bugging were held to be "searches" or "seizures," they would necessarily be "unreasonable searches and seizures."[12]

More specifically, once electronic surveillance was deemed Fourth Amendment activity, any proposal for law enforcement tapping and bugging, however carefully circumscribed, would have to reckon with the rule articulated in *Gouled v. United States*[13] that objects of "evidentiary value only" (as opposed to the instrumentalities or the proceeds of crime) are beyond the reach of an otherwise valid warrant. Six months before it overruled *Olmstead*, the Warren Court repudiated the "mere evidence" rule, thus clearing the way for a system of court-ordered electronic surveillance that could meet Fourth Amendment standards.[14] The following year, a Congress bent on "unleashing the police" granted law enforcement authorities broad powers to engage in continuing electronic surveillance for up to thirty days (with extensions possible).[15]

Arrest, Search, and Seizure

In 1961 the Warren Court did, of course, impose the federal exclusionary rule, which bars the use of evidence obtained in violation of the protection against unreasonable search and seizure, on the states as a matter of constitutional law.[16] But the Court was a good deal less exuberant about the exclusionary rule seven years later, when it legitimated the police practice of stopping and frisking persons on less than probable cause to believe they were engaged in criminal activity.[17] In resolving an important and difficult issue in favor of law enforcement—the stop and frisk practice had been widespread but its legality was uncertain—the Court recognized, almost poignantly, that "[t]he exclusionary rule has its limitations . . . as a tool of judicial control."[18]

It took a long time for the Supreme Court to decide whether stopping and frisking on less than traditional "probable cause" could be squared with the Constitution. What if resolution of this issue had been delayed a few years longer? What if the Burger Court, say in 1971, rather than the Warren Court in 1968, had upheld these police practices? In that event, I venture to say, the decisions would have been deemed solid evidence of the changing philosophy of the "emerging Nixon majority," and the opinions of the Court (if they had been the same as those actually written by Chief Justice Warren) would have been denounced by admirers of the Warren Court for "leav[ing] the lower courts without guidance concerning recurrent and related issues" and for "at best, gross negligence concerning the state of the record and the controlling precedents."[19]

The Warren Court's opinions in the stop and frisk cases leave much to be desired. The justices "detoured around" the threshold issue of investigative "stops," one on which the lower courts, lawyers, and police deserved guidance, and discussed only the "frisk" issue; strained a good deal to avoid explaining how the police, after removing an *opaque* envelop from a "frisked" suspect's pocket, could open the envelope to see what was inside; seemed to misunderstand "classical 'stop and frisk' theory"; confused the limited search permitted to uncover weapons that may be used to assault police with the more extensive search permitted when an arrestee is about to be transported to the police station; and seemed to assume that a less restrictive Fourth Amendment test applies when the police act *without* a search warrant (although the Court had repeatedly held to the contrary).[20]

The Warren Court's approach in the 1968 stop and frisk cases contrasts dramatically with the approach it had taken two years earlier in *Miranda*. There, evidently greatly troubled by the lower courts' apparent persistence in utilizing the ambiguity of the "voluntariness–totality of the circumstances" test to sustain confessions of doubtful constitutionality, the Court sought to replace the elusive and largely unworkable old test with a relatively automatic device. But the stop and frisk cases left such a spongy standard, one that allowed the police so much discretion and provided the courts so little basis for meaningful review (at one point the Court said that an officer could frisk when he "observes unusual conduct which leads him reasonably to conclude in light of his experience that criminal activity may be afoot and that the person with whom he is dealing may be armed and presently dangerous"[21]), that these Warren Court decisions must have been cause for celebration in more than a few precinct stations throughout the land.

The same may be said for the Warren Court's holding a year before these decisions in *McCray v. Illinois*,[22] upholding the so-called informer's privilege (the government's privilege to withhold the identity of its informant at a suppression hearing), even when the police act without a warrant (as they did in *McCray*). The Court made plain that the police need not always disclose the informant's identity, but it had virtually nothing to say about when, if ever, they must do so.

Although establishment of a meaningful standard concerning informant disclosure is not a simple task, in *McCray* the Court made no serious effort to strike a fair balance between "the conflicting concerns of informant anonymity and police perjury."[23] In those circumstances where, *apart from* police testimony as to information supplied by an informer, there was insufficient evidence to establish probable cause, for example, the Court would have done well to endorse the in-camera hearing device, thus protecting the government from any significant impairment of necessary secrecy, yet still saving the defendant from what could have been serious police misconduct. If the defendant has fairly put in issue the informant's existence or reliability or the officer's recitation of what he said, "nothing less" than an in-camera inquiry, maintains a leading commentator, "will ensure that the protections of the Fourth Amendment have not been circumvented."[24] But *McCray* offers less, offers virtually nothing, when the police invoke "Old Reliable, the informer."

Police Interrogations and Confessions

At this point, I can hear the cries of protest: What about *Miranda*? Isn't a discussion of the Warren Court's criminal procedure decisions without mentioning *Miranda* like staging *Hamlet* without the ghost?

Miranda, which held that suspects must be informed of their rights, including the right to remain silent and the right to have a lawyer (retained or appointed) present before being subjected to "custodial interrogation," was a most welcome, and the Court's most ambitious, effort to seize the police interrogation–confessions problem by the throat. It did, at long last, apply the privilege against self-incrimination and the right to counsel to "in-custody" questioning. (The prize for ingenuity, it has always seemed to me, should go not to the Warren Court for doing so but to those who had managed for so long to devise rationales for not doing so.) The case did generate "a greater general awareness of rights on the part of suspects" and it did remind the police, quite emphatically, that "their actions are subject to review, that they do not create the rules of interrogation."[25]

Nevertheless, although one would gain little inkling of this from the hue and cry that greeted the case, *Miranda* may fairly be viewed as a compromise between the old voluntariness–totality of the circumstances test (a standard so elusive and unworkable that its safeguards were largely illusory) and extreme proposals that threatened (or promised) to "kill" confessions.

The *Miranda* decision did not, and was not designed to, kill confessions. It allows the police to conduct "general on-the-scene questioning" even though the person questioned is both uninformed and unaware of his rights. It allows the police to question a person in his home or office, provided they do not restrict the person's freedom to terminate the meeting. Moreover, "custody" alone does not call for the *Miranda* warnings. The Court might have held that the inherent pressures and anxieties produced by arrest and detention *and nothing more* are substantial enough to require neutralizing warnings. But it did not. Thus, so long as the police do not *question* one who has been brought, or is being taken, to the station house, *Miranda* leaves them free to hear and act upon "volunteered" statements, even though the "volunteer" neither knows nor is advised of his rights.

On the eve of *Miranda*, there were doubts that law enforcement could survive if the Court were to "project" defense counsel into the police station.[26] But in *Miranda* the court did so only in a quite limited way. It never took what might be called "the final step" (and, as a practical matter, the most significant one)—requiring that a suspect *first* consult with a lawyer, *or actually have a lawyer present*, in order for his waiver of constitutional rights to be deemed valid.

Whether suspects are continuing to confess because they do not fully grasp the meaning of the *Miranda* warnings or whether the police are mumbling, hedging, or undermining the warnings, or whether the promptings of conscience and the desire "to get it over with" are indeed overriding the impact of the warnings, it is plain that in-custody suspects are continuing to confess with great frequency.[27] This would hardly have been the result if *Miranda* had fully projected counsel into the interrogation process—had required *the advice or presence* of counsel *before* a suspect could waive his rights.

Some Final Thoughts about the Warren Court

Many, no doubt, would dispute my view that even *Miranda*, "the high-water mark of the due process revolution,"[28] reflects considerable moderation and compromise. For purposes of this chapter, however, the more important point is that whatever the size of the victory defendants won in *Miranda*, they suffered not a few defeats at the hands of the same Court, especially in its final years. The point may be made another way. In its final years "the Warren Court," I think it may be argued, was *not* the same Court that had produced *Miranda* or *Mapp*. One might say there were *two* Warren Courts: (1) the one most of us think of when we talk about that Court, and (2) the one that so peremptorily sustained the informer's privilege in 1967 and so gropingly upheld stop and frisk practices in 1968. Before it disbanded, the second (and less publicized) Warren Court had begun a process many associate only with its successor—a process of reexamination, correction, consolidation, erosion, or retreat, depending upon your viewpoint.

The change in the Warren Court can hardly be attributed to a change in its personnel. Justice Goldberg (1962), and then Justice Fortas (1965), replaced the less adventurous Frankfurter; Justice Marshall (1967) succeeded the more prosecution–oriented Clark. The change does seem attributable to "the buffeting of rapid historical developments that incessantly place unprecedented strains upon the Court."[29] The last years of the Warren Court's "criminal procedure 'revolution'" constituted a period of social upheaval, marked by urban riots, violence in the ghettos, and disorders on the campuses.[30] The political assassinations and near-assassinations of the late 1960s, both Congress's and presidential candidate Richard Nixon's strong criticism of the Court, the "obviously retaliatory" provisions of the Crime Control Act of 1968, and the ever-soaring crime statistics and ever-spreading fears of the breakdown of public order "combined to create an atmosphere that, to say the least, was unfavorable to the continued vitality of the Warren Court's mission in criminal cases."[31]

There is yet another twist to the story. The performance of the Burger Court, too, has been a good deal more mixed than is generally realized. Indeed, although the patterns are by no means neat, I think it may even be argued that there are *two* Burger Courts.

THE BURGER COURT: SELECTED AREAS OF CRIMINAL PROCEDURE

The "first" Burger Court, the one that most individuals think of as *the* Burger Court, is the one that gutted the Warren Court's "lineup decisions," soon dealt heavy blows to the Fourth Amendment, appeared to be stalking the exclusionary rule, and seemed to be laying the groundwork to overrule *Miranda*. In the past few years, however, a significantly less police-oriented "second" Burger Court seems to have emerged, one that has given interrogation within the meaning of *Miranda* a fairly generous reading, reinvigorated *Miranda* safeguards when a suspect has invoked his right to counsel, re-vivified and even expanded the *Massiah* doctrine[32]—which, although once almost forgotten, has become "the other" major confessions rule—and a court that has underscored the centrality of the search warrant requirement in all investigations with the exception of automobile searches.

Of course, Warren Court developments in the police practices area have by no means escaped unscathed. But in hindsight, with one notable exception (pretrial identification), the fears that the Burger Court would dismantle the work of the Warren Court (or the Bill of Rights itself), and the reports that such dismantling was well under way, seem to have been considerably exaggerated.

Pretrial Identification

Unlike many commentators who have denounced the Burger Court for its "law and order" orientation, Jerold Israel has forcefully argued that "neither the record of the Court nor the tenor of its majority opinions, taken as a whole, really supports a broad movement towards restricting the protections afforded the accused."[33] But even he readily concedes—as I think he must—that the pretrial identification field marks a striking exception to this otherwise reassuring generalization.[34]

Although mistaken identification has probably been the greatest cause of conviction of the innocent, the Supreme Court did not get around to this problem until surprisingly late. When it finally did, in a 1967 trilogy of cases, *Wade, Gilbert*, and *Stovall*,[35] it seemed bent on making up for lost time. Although the Court might have undertaken a case-by-case analysis of various identification situations, as had been done in the confession area in the thirty years prior to *Escobedo* and *Miranda*, only throwing out convictions based on unfair or unreliable identifications, it leapfrogged the fairness stage and applied the right to counsel to pretrial identifications in one swoop. Since "[t]he trial which might determine the accused's fate may well not be that in the courtroom but that at the pretrial [identification, and] [s]ince it appears that there is grave potential for prejudice, intentional or not, in the pretrial lineup, which [absent counsel's presence] may not be capable of reconstruction at trial," the Court deemed counsel's presence at the pretrial identification itself essential to "avert prejudice and assure a meaningful confrontation at trial."[36]

Absent circumstances that presented "substantial countervailing policy considerations . . . against the requirement of the presence of counsel"[37] (perhaps, for example, "alley confrontation," that is, prompt confrontation with the victim or with an eyewitness at the scene of the crime), the 1967 cases seemed to require the presence of counsel at all pretrial identifications. The Court thought it "obvious" that whether "the pretrial confrontation for purposes of identification" takes the form of a lineup or presentation of the suspect alone to the witness, "risks of suggestion attend either form of confrontation and increase the dangers inhering in eyewitness identification."[38]

The pretrial identifications in *Wade* and *Gilbert* did take place after the defendants had been indicted, and the Court did mention this fact. But such references seemed—and most lower courts considered them to be—*merely descriptive* of the facts before the Court in those cases, not meant to limit the operation of the new rule. Although the lower courts gave *Wade* and *Gilbert* a begrudging reception in other respects, only a minority of state courts (and no federal appellate court that addressed the issue) could bring themselves to limit the 1967 cases to postindictment identifications.[39] For nothing in the Court's opinions suggested that the mere fact that a routine station house identification was conducted prior to the filing of formal charges furnished "substantial countervailing policy considerations" against the new rule. Nor did anything in the Court's reasoning suggest that a lineup or showup held before the institution of formal judicial proceedings—which is when most take place—is less riddled with dangers or less difficult for a suspect to reconstruct at trial than one occurring after that point in the criminal process.

But in *Kirby v. Illinois* (1972),[40] the Court did announce a "post-indictment" rule, one that enables law enforcement officials to manipulate the applicability of the right to counsel by conducting identification procedures before the filing of formal charges. Such a rule is not in keeping with a judicial system bent on dealing with the realities of the criminal process rather than its labels. Moreover, it was no secret that not a few state courts and lower federal courts were unhappy with the recent "revolution" in criminal procedure and were watching for signals from the "new Court." A ruling such as that in *Kirby* could only encourage them to commence, or to intensify, efforts to "contain" (or worse) the *Wade* and *Gilbert* decisions in other respects, or for that matter to give other landmark Warren Court decisions similar treatment. The new Court had showed them how.

A year after *Kirby*, the Burger Court struck the *Wade-Gilbert* rule another heavy blow. This time, however, it only confirmed the great weight of lower court authority.

The Warren Court had carved out an exception to the *Wade-Gilbert* rule for pretrial photographic identifications, but apparently a narrow one. In concluding that there was no right to have counsel present at the photo-identifications in *Simmons v. United States* (1968)[41] and, alternatively, that the procedures utilized in that case were not "impermissibly suggestive," the Court stressed, first, that at the time the witnesses viewed the pictures for identification purposes "[t]he perpetrators were still at large" and "[i]t was essential for the FBI agents swiftly to determine whether they were on the right track"; and second, that the witnesses were shown the photographs "only a day [after the bank robbery], while their memories were still fresh."

The majority of lower courts, however, read *Simmons* as permitting counselless photoidentifications even when the suspects were *in custody* and thus available for a corporeal lineup. Most courts took this position even when the defendants had already been indicted and had retained or been assigned counsel—and even when the photographs were displayed not shortly after the crime occurred, as in *Simmons*, but *months* after the suspect had been taken into custody.

The District of Columbia Circuit was the only federal appellate court to apply the right to counsel to postcustody photoidentifications, and it did so in the extraordinary factual setting of the *Ash* case.[42] Although the defendant had been indicted, had been appointed counsel, and *had been in detention for two years prior to trial*, a photoidentification was conducted in the absence of counsel a day before the trial began. It was a photo display that seemed designed more to prompt the witness than to secure an identification. The District of Columbia Circuit deemed the *Wade-Gilbert* rule applicable to these facts, maintaining, quite persuasively I believe, that although retention of the photographs used at the pretrial display for examination at trial may mitigate the dangers of misidentification resulting from the suggestiveness of the photographs themselves, the availability of the photographs at trial provides no protection against the *suggestive manner* in which they may have been displayed or the comments or gestures that may have accompanied the display. Moreover, pointed out the court, since, unlike the lineup situation, the accused himself is not even present at the photo-identification, without the presence of counsel he is even less able to reconstruct what took place at the display than at the lineup.

The Burger Court was unmoved. In *Ash v. United States* (1973),[43] it held that the right to counsel does not apply to photographic identifications whether conducted before or after the filing of formal charges. It added a "personal confrontation" requirement to Sixth Amendment analysis. Throughout the expansion of the right to counsel to certain pretrial stages, maintained the Court in *Ash*, "the function of the lawyer has remained essentially the same as his function at trial"—to furnish the accused "aid in coping with legal problems or assistance in meeting his adversary." Since there is no triallike confrontation involving the presence of the accused at photographic identifications, there is no right to counsel at such proceedings.

In *Ash* the Court seemed to overlook the fact that the right to counsel sometimes exists even when the defendant is not entitled to be personally present.[44] More fundamentally, the Court's analysis seems inconsistent with the original lineup decisions. Although in deciding *Ash*, the Court looked back on *Wade* and *Gilbert* as cases involving triallike confrontations requiring counsel in order "to render 'Assistance' [to a suspect] in counterbalancing any 'overreaching' by the prosecution,"[45] thus implying that counsel is to be an active adversary at this stage, the great weight of authority is to the contrary.[46] Counsel "cannot stop the lineup or see that it be conducted in a certain manner"; "his only recognized function is as a trained observer."[47] Moreover, if a lineup *is* a triallike, adversary confrontation at which the defendant needs aid only his lawyer can provide, is that not true of all lineups, not just postindictment ones? Why, then, did the Court draw the line it did in *Kirby*?

Although *Kirby* and *Ash* crippled the original lineup decisions, abuses in photographic displays and in preindictment corporeal identifications are not, in theory at least, beyond the reach of the Constitution—a defendant may still convince a court that his identification and the circumstances surrounding it present so substantial a "likelihood of misidentification" as to violate due process.[48] But this is no easy task. An "unnecessarily suggestive" identification is not enough; the "totality of the circumstances" may still permit the admission of the identification evidence if, despite the unnecessary "suggestiveness," "the out-of-court identification possesses certain features of reliability."[49] This is an elusive, unpredictable case-by-case standard that was unlikely to be, and has not turned out to be, any more manageable by reviewing courts or any more illuminating to local police than the voluntariness–totality of the circumstances test for admitting confessions that proved so unsuccessful in the thirty years before *Escobedo* and *Miranda*.

A Supreme Court determined to expand or effectuate suspects' rights must do more than hand down landmark decisions. It must also be, as the Warren

Court often was, strong on follow-through, on closing loopholes and block-ing police-prosecution endruns. There is so much resistance to landmark decisions made on behalf of those suspected of crime that a Supreme Court may do considerable damage simply by doing nothing—by not reentering the fray to "rescue" an earlier landmark decision. In the pretrial identifica-tion area, the Burger Court did more damage than that. It not only allowed the lower courts to cut down the 1967 lineup decisions, but it led the way in sharply contracting the *Wade-Gilbert* rule, and, still worse, it contributed significantly to the emaciation of the back-up due process test. It gave aid and comfort to the many lower courts that, in effect, were leapfrogging back over the "fairness" stage to pre-1967 days.

When law enforcement officials violate the prophylactic *Wade-Gilbert* right to counsel rule, the resulting identification evidence may not be unre-liable. But when they *unnecessarily* employ a suggestive identification tech-nique (present a lone suspect to a witness when it would have been feasible to hold a lineup[50] or exhibit a single photograph when they could easily have displayed photos of many different persons[51]), the risk of misidentification is much greater, and this increased risk is gratuitous.[52]

The Burger Court should have excluded all *unnecessarily* suggestive out-of-court identifications[53]—an approach, it recognized, that was favored by almost all scholars of the subject "as essential to avoid serious risk of miscarriage of justice"[54]—*without regard* to such totality of the circumstances factors as the opportunity of the witness to view the criminal at the time of the crime or the level of certainty demonstrated by the witness at the iden-tification. When it rejected this per se approach in favor of the more lenient totality approach, it should have realized, considering the strong pressure on the lower courts "to find means for preserving convictions, particularly in ugly cases,"[55] that many courts would seize, or, more accurately, would con-tinue to seize, on the ambiguity inherent in the phrase "totality of the cir-cumstances" to find all but the most grossly unfair pretrial identifications not in violation of due process, and that the test would give the police little incentive to remove unnecessarily suggestive characteristics from identifica-tion procedures.[56]

The Burger Court's performance in the pretrial identification area may well be the saddest chapter in modern American criminal procedure. This is so not so much because the retreat from the 1967 decisions was so exten-sive, but because these decisions, unlike most Warren Court developments in the area of criminal procedure, were so explicitly designed to protect the innocent from wrongful conviction.[57] The Burger Court, it must be said, has failed badly to deal with a problem that "probably accounts for more miscarriages of justice than any other single factor—perhaps . . . for more such errors than all other factors combined."[58]

Arrest, Search, and Seizure

The Burger Court, it has been pointed out, appears to be far more impressed than its predecessor with "the importance of being guilty" and, in evolving a hierarchy of constitutional rights on the basis of their impact on the reliability of the truth-determining process, seems to have "placed the Fourth Amendment's ban on unreasonable searches and seizures at the bottom."[59] A number of Burger Court search and seizure decisions (but by no means all of them) furnish support for this view. *Stone v. Powell* (1976)[60] certainly does.

In *Stone* the Court commented upon the "long-recognized costs" of the exclusionary rule "even at trial and on direct review"—for example, "deflect[ing] the truthfinding process and often free[ing] the guilty." And it found "no reason to believe [that the rule's] overall educative effect . . . would be appreciably diminished if search-and-seizure claims could not be raised in federal habeas corpus review of state convictions," nor any reason "to assume that any disincentive already created by the risk of exclusion of evidence at trial or the reversal of convictions on direct review would be enhanced if there were the further risk that [convictions] might be overturned in collateral proceedings often occurring years after the incarceration of the defendant."[61] Conclusion: a state prisoner may not be granted federal habeas corpus relief on search and seizure grounds unless he has been denied "an opportunity for full and fair litigation" of the claim in the state courts.[62]

Stone illustrates the tendency of the Burger Court to "narrow the thrust" of the exclusionary rule—for example, to balance the assumed benefits of the rule against its "long-recognized costs" in contexts *other than the criminal trial itself* and to strike the balance in favor of admissibility.[63] In *United States v. Calandra* (1974),[64] the Court held that a grand jury witness could not refuse to answer questions based on illegally seized evidence, deeming the "speculative and undoubtedly minimal advance" in deterrence that might be achieved by upholding such an objection outweighed by "the potential injury to the historic role and functions of the grand jury."[65] And in *United States v. Janis* (1976), the Court refused to apply the exclusionary rule to a federal civil tax proceeding (adjudicating liability under the wagering excise tax provisions) based upon evidence illegally seized by state police, viewing the deterrent force of the exclusionary rule "highly attenuated when the 'punishment' imposed upon the offending criminal enforcement officer is the removal of that evidence from a civil suit by or against a different sovereign."[66]

The Burger Court has also narrowed the thrust of the exclusionary rule by shortening the reach of the "fruit of the poisonous tree" doctrine[67] and by stiffening the "standing" requirements for suppressing the products of

Fourth Amendment violations. There is much to be said for scrapping the
"standing" limitation altogether (although, unfortunately, the Warren Court
declined the opportunity[68]), for "such a limitation virtually invites law enforcement officers to violate the rights of third parties and to trade the escape
of a criminal whose rights are violated for the conviction of others by the
use of the evidence illegally obtained against them."[69] Under the Burger
Court, however, the "standing" barrier seems to have grown more formidable
than ever.[70]

Even more disquieting than the manner in which the present Court has
narrowed the scope of the exclusionary rule is the way in which it has
narrowed the substantive protection provided by the Fourth Amendment. By
taking a crabbed view of what constitutes a "search" or "seizure," the Court
has put no constitutional restraints at all on certain investigative techniques
that may uncover an enormous quantity of personal information.

Although "the totality of bank records provides a virtual current biogra-
phy" of an individual,[71] the decision in *United States v. Miller* (1976)[72] tells
us that a depositor has no "legitimate 'expectation of privacy'" as to the
checks and deposit slips he "voluntarily convey[s] to the banks and expose[s]
to their employees in the ordinary course of business." Thus, when his
records are obtained by means of subpoenas served upon banks at which
he has accounts, "no Fourth Amendment interests of the depositor are
implicated" that can be vindicated by challenging the subpoenas. "The
depositor takes the risk, in revealing his affairs to another, that the information will be conveyed by that person to the Government. . . . [T]he
Fourth Amendment does not prohibit the obtaining of information revealed
to a third party and conveyed by him to Government authorities, even if the
information is revealed on the assumption that it will be used only for a
limited purpose and the confidence placed in the third party will not be
betrayed."[73]

Although the numbers dialed from a private phone "are not without 'content'"—a list of them could "reveal the most intimate details of a person's
life"[74]—in *Smith v. Maryland* (1979)[75] the Court held, relying heavily on the
Miller case, that police use of a "pen register" to record the numbers dialed
from a home phone does not constitute a "search" either. Thus, no warrant
is needed for use of such a device (nor, presumably, "probable cause" or
any cause whatsoever). No less than one who opens a bank account, reasoned
the Court, one who uses the phone "assumes the risk": when Mr. Smith
used his phone, he "voluntarily conveyed numerical information to the telephone company and 'exposed' that information to its equipment in the ordinary course of business. In so doing, [he] assumed the risk that the company
would reveal to police the numbers he dialed."[76]

In deciding *Smith* and *Miller*, the Court seemed to have forgotten that
merely because one gives up *some* privacy for a *limited* purpose, one does

not lose Fourth Amendment protection against government intrusions. "The fact that our ordinary social intercourse, uncontrolled by government, imposes certain risks upon us hardly means that government is constitutionally unrestrained in adding to those risks."[77] One who stays at a hotel, for example, does not enjoy absolute privacy in his room (he gives implied permission to the maids and other hotel personnel to enter his room in the performance of their duties), but he still retains Fourth Amendment protection against unreasonable police entry.[78]

The present Court has also narrowed the protection against unreasonable search and seizure in another important respect—by stretching the concept of "consent." "The easiest, most propitious way for the police to avoid the myriad problems presented by the Fourth Amendment" is to obtain a "consent" to what would otherwise be an unconstitutional invasion of privacy.[79] Thus, the scope of the protection furnished by the Fourth Amendment may vary greatly, depending on how easy or difficult it is for the government to establish "consent." In *Schneckloth v. Bustamonte* (1973),[80] the Court made it easy.

No less than the aforementioned *Stone* case, *Schneckloth* manifests the Court's willingness to downgrade Fourth Amendment rights. The *Schneckloth* court perceived a "vast difference" between those constitutional rights that "protect the fairness of the trial itself" and rights guaranteed under the Fourth Amendment, which "have nothing whatever to do with promoting the fair ascertainment of truth at a criminal trial." Fourth Amendment rights differ from trial rights in that "every reasonable presumption" need not be indulged against relinquishment of Fourth Amendment rights. Indeed, when the police lack sufficient cause to make an arrest or search, "the community has a real interest in encouraging consent."[81]

Thus, when the government seeks to justify a search on "consent" grounds, it need not demonstrate a "knowing and intelligent" waiver of Fourth Amendment rights—this strict standard of waiver is reserved for those rights designed to preserve a fair trial. It need only demonstrate that the consent to an otherwise impermissible search "was in fact voluntarily given, and not the result of duress or coercion, express or implied."[82] According to the *Schneckloth* majority, then, one may effectively consent to a search even though he was never informed—and the government has failed to demonstrate that he was aware—that he had the right to refuse the officer's "request." One need not be protected from loss by *ignorance* or *confusion*, only from loss through *coercion*.[83] After *Schneckloth*, the criminal justice system, in some important respects at least, can (to borrow a phrase from *Escobedo*) "depend for its continued effectiveness on the citizens' abdication through unawareness of their constitutional rights."[84]

Any commentary, however summary, of the Burger Court's performance in the search and seizure area must take into account its treatment of the two major exceptions to the warrant requirement: (1) the search incident to a lawful arrest and (2) the *Carroll* doctrine, often called the "automobile exception."[85]

1. Before the late 1960s, the "search incident to arrest" exception had been applied very broadly—it authorized the warrantless search of an entire house and thus an entire vehicle as well. In one of its final acts, however, the Warren Court significantly contracted the "search incident" perimeter, holding in the 1969 *Chimel*[86] case that it may not extend beyond the "immediate control" or "grabbing distance" of the arrestee at the moment of arrest. But *Chimel* has not fared well in recent years.

In *United States v. Robinson* (1973),[87] the Court upheld a thorough but warrantless body search of a person incident to a valid custodial arrest for a traffic offense, although the search could not be justified by any need to prevent the destruction of evidence, for no evidence of the offense existed, nor by any fear or suspicion that the arrestee was armed or dangerous. Distinguishing *Chimel* as a case that treated the scope of a search *beyond* the arrestee's person and not the right to search the arrestee's person itself, the Court, per Rehnquist, J., held that if a custodial arrest is lawful, a search of the person "requires no additional justification. It is the fact of the lawful arrest which establishes the authority to search."[88]

In *Robinson* the court supported its "bright-line" rule by pointing to the administrative difficulties that would be created if the arresting officer had to make a case-by-case estimate of the likelihood that a search of the person would turn up weapons or evidence. More recently, for similar reasons, the Court adopted another "bright line" rule in *New York v. Belton* (1981),[89] a decision that massively broadens the "search incident" exception, at least in automobile settings. In *Belton* the Court held that, whether or not there is probable cause to believe a car contains evidence of crime, so long as there are adequate grounds to make a lawful custodial arrest of the car's occupants, even though the occupants are handcuffed and standing outside the car, the police may conduct a warrantless search of the entire interior or passenger compartment of the car, including closed containers found within that zone. Thus, warned Justice Stevens, an arresting officer may find reason to take a minor traffic offender into custody "whenever he sees an interesting looking briefcase or package in a vehicle that has been stopped for a traffic violation."[90]

2. In a typical automobile search, the search incident exception and the *Carroll* doctrine overlap. (The same probable cause to believe there is evidence of contraband in the vehicle that triggers the *Carroll* doctrine, which permits a warrantless search of the entire vehicle, including the car trunk, usually points also to the likely guilt of the driver and justifies his arrest and a search incident thereto but not a search of the trunk.) The two exceptions to the warrant clause are conceptually distinct, however. As it was

originally understood and for most of its life, the 58-year-old *Carroll* doctrine permitted police to search a car without a warrant only when there
were *both* (1) probable cause to believe that the car contained evidence of
crime *and* (2) "exigent circumstances," making it impractical to obtain a
warrant. In the 1970s, however, the Burger Court significantly expanded the
doctrine by virtually eliminating the exigent circumstances requirement.
Thus, in essence, the doctrine became simply a "probable cause" exception
to the warrant requirement for automobiles. Even cars that had been removed
to a police station could be subjected to warrantless searches.[91]

The Court implicitly recognized that it had extended the *Carroll* doctrine
—once called the "moving vehicle exception"—far beyond its original scope
by offering new rationales for the doctrine: the "lesser expectation of privacy" in a car and the "severe, even impossible burdens" that would be
imposed upon "police departments of all sizes around the country" if they
were constitutionally required to have available the personnel and equipment
to transport seized vehicles and the facilities to store them, with due regard
for the safety of these vehicles and their contents, until a search warrant
could be obtained.[92] Neither one of these new rationales has much to do with
whether a car is "a fleeting target for a search"—the original grounds for
the doctrine. Moreover, neither rationale is persuasive.[93]

In the 1982 *Ross* case,[94] the Court further extended the *Carroll* doctrine,
utilizing it to sustain the warrantless search of a "movable container" found
in a locked car trunk.[95] One may accept the earlier expansion of the *Carroll*
doctrine and still find fault with *Ross*. What bearing do the inherent bulk
of an automobile and its alleged inherent vulnerability to theft and vandal-
ism (one of the new rationales for the *Carroll* doctrine) have on a suitcase
or package found in a vehicle—an item that can be readily removed and
easily stored safely? What bearing does the alleged "lesser expectation of
privacy" in an automobile (the other new rationale for the *Carroll* doctrine)
have on one's expectation of privacy in a sealed package or a locked suitcase? That containers should receive the protection of the warrant requirement when found outside an automobile (and *Ross* reaffirms that they should)
but lose that protection when placed inside seems bizarre. Surely a person
demonstrates a stronger expectation of privacy when he locks a container in
the trunk of his car. Yet when he does so, it turns out, the container becomes subject to the *Carroll* exception to the warrant requirement.

Nevertheless, I believe the focal point of the criticism of the Court's
handling of the *Carroll* doctrine should not be *Ross*, but the pre-*Ross* cases
expanding the doctrine. The basic issue is not whether (absent "exigent circumstances" making it impractical to seek a warrant) a container found in a
car trunk should be opened without a warrant, but whether (absent "exigent
circumstances") the car trunk itself should be opened without a warrant.
When, in the 1970s, the Court decided the basic issue in favor of law en-

forcement, it took a wrong turn. Although *Ross* dramatizes the potency of
the revised *Carroll* doctrine, when the Court decided *Ross* it only traveled
a bit further down the wrong road.

That the Burger Court delivered some heavy blows to the Fourth Amendment, there can be no denying. It should not be overlooked, however, that
the Burger Court did not "retreat" (as supporters of the Warren Court would
characterize it) on all search and seizure fronts. Indeed, in some instances,
especially in recent years, the present Court has even expanded or invigorated
Fourth Amendment protections.

In *Gerstein v. Pugh* (1975),[96] turning its attention to a long-neglected phase
of the pretrial system and one that was causing growing concern, the Court
necessitated changes in the practice of many states by holding that the Fourth
Amendment requires prompt judicial review of the legality of warrantless
arrests as a prerequisite to "extended restraint on liberty" following such
arrests. In *Payton v. New York* (1980),[97] although a majority of the states
passing on the question had upheld the practice of warrantless arrests in
homes, and despite the protest that the majority was "exaggerating the invasion of personal privacy involved in home arrests" while "fail[ing] to account
for the danger that its rule will 'severely hamper effective law enforcement,'"
the Court struck down a state statute permitting the police to enter a suspect's
home without a warrant in order to make a routine felony arrest.

In *Ybarra v. Illinois* (1980),[98] over the complaint that "such a rule not only
reintroduces the rigidity condemned in [the stop and frisk cases], [but] also
renders the existence of the search warrant irrelevant," the Court held that a
valid warrant to search a tavern (a "one-room bar") and the person of the
bartender for drugs gave the police "no authority whatever to invade the
constitutional protections possessed individually by the tavern's customers."
"[A] person's mere propinquity to others independently suspected of criminal activity does not, without more, give rise to probable cause to search
that person. [The requirement that a search or seizure of a person] be supported by probable cause particularized with respect to that person . . .
cannot be undercut or avoided by simply pointing to the fact that coinci-
dentally there exists probable cause to search or seize another or to search
the premises where the person may happen to be." Nor, held the Court in
Ybarra, over the protest that it was "unjustifiabl[y] narrowing" the rule of
the stop and frisk cases, does the officers' need to protect themselves or
to "freeze" the situation in preparation for the search permit "a generalized
'cursory search for weapons,' or, indeed, any search whatever for anything
but weapons."

It is hard to believe that *Payton* and *Ybarra* would have been decided
the same way, say, in 1973, when the Court decided *Schneckloth* and
Robinson. The tenor of the latter cases is quite apparent—a determination to
grant the police as much leeway as possible, at least as much leeway as

possible within the spacious confines of "bright line" search and seizure law. But the question presented in *Payton* had been expressly left open in several prior Supreme Court cases. Moreover, a majority of the state courts had sided with the police on this issue. And in *Ybarra* no clear precedential hurdle stood in the way of a decision upholding the pat-down search of the tavern's customers.

Ybarra involved the scope of an officer's power to search pursuant to a valid *search* warrant and *Payton* dealt primarily with the need for an *arrest* warrant. More often, especially in recent years, with two notable exceptions (the aforementioned *Carroll* and "search incident to arrest" doctrines), the Burger Court has reaffirmed and fortified the centrality of the *search* warrant requirement. In *United States v. United States District Court* (1972)[99] the Court held, without a dissent, that neither the "domestic security" exception of the 1968 federal electronic surveillance statute nor the inherent powers of the president to defend the government against attempts by domestic organizations to overthrow it "justify departure [from] the customary Fourth Amendment requirement of judicial approval prior to initiation of a search or surveillance." This was one of the first signs that the charges that the new Court was showing only a "law and order" orientation were exaggerated.[100] The Burger Court has also utilized the search warrant requirement to shield commercial buildings,[101] the burned premises of one suspected of deliberately starting the fire himself,[102] and the scene of a murder.[103] Moreover, the Court has emphatically rejected the contention that the warrant clause protects only homes, offices, and private communications.[104]

The present Court's strong commitment to the warrant clause is dramatized by its application of that clause to the "bizarre facts" of *Walter v. United States* (1980).[105] The FBI had lawfully acquired boxes of film that had been mistakenly shipped to a private party. Before the misdelivered cartons containing the boxes of film had been turned over to the authorities, employees of the private party had opened the cartons and had read the descriptive material on each box indicating that the contents were obscene. Nevertheless, the Court deemed the FBI's viewing of the films on a projector an impermissible "search" without a search warrant. "The fact that the cartons were unexpectedly opened by a third party before the shipment was delivered to its intended consignee," observed Justice Stevens, "does not alter the consignor's legitimate expectation of privacy."

Walter does not seem to have caused much of a stir. I venture to say, however, that if the decision had been handed down in 1965 or 1966, not a few critics of the Warren Court would have pointed to it as evidence of a defense-minded Court running wild.

Sometimes a Court's refusal to take advantage of an opportunity to change the law may be as significant as its determination to make the most of that opportunity. Thus, no discussion, however brief, of the present Court's performance in the search and seizure area would be complete without noting those instances where the Court has declined invitations to do serious damage to the Fourth Amendment.

In *Brown v. Illinois* (1975),[106] the Court rejected the contention that the giving of the *Miranda* warnings should purge the taint of any preceding illegal arrest—a view that would have permitted the admissibility at trial of any resulting incriminating statements to be considered without regard to the illegal arrest and thus would have encouraged such arrests.[107] *Brown* was reaffirmed and fortified in *Dunaway v. New York* (1979)[108] and *Taylor v. Alabama* (1982).[109] Moreover, in *Dunaway* the Court fought off other serious challenges to the Fourth Amendment.

The state argued that the "picking up" of Dunaway, driving him down to the police station, and placing him in an interrogation room, where he was in fact questioned, (1) did not constitute a Fourth Amendment "seizure" at all, and (2) if it did, did not amount to an "arrest" and thus could be justified merely on the basis of "reasonable suspicion." The Court emphatically disagreed, pointing out that the state's approach "threaten[ed] to swallow the general rule that Fourth Amendment seizures are 'reasonable' only if based on probable cause."[110]

In *Franks v. Delaware* (1978),[111] the Court blocked still another threat to the Fourth Amendment. The state argued, and the state supreme court had agreed, that under *no circumstances* may a defendant challenge the truthfulness of factual statements made in a police affidavit supporting a search warrant. Fortunately, the Court rejected this no-challenge rule, finding that the arguments for it were essentially "nothing more than a frontal assault upon the exclusionary rule itself."[112] "A flat ban on impeachment of veracity," pointed out a 7 to 2 majority, per Blackmun, J., "could denude the probable-cause requirement of all real meaning." For an officer could deliberately resort to false allegations and, having misled the magistrate, could "remain confident that the ploy was worthwhile." As for alternative sanctions such as perjury prosecutions, contempt citations, or administrative discipline, in *Mapp* the Court had "implicitly rejected" the notion that they are "likely to fill the gap."[113]

It is now plain that "stops" may be justified on less than traditional "probable cause," but in *Delaware v. Prouse* (1979)[114] the state argued that "random stops" of an automobile for license and registration checks need not be subject to any constitutional restraints whatsoever. The Court balked. Understandably, it failed to see how "[t]he marginal contribution to roadway safety" that might result from the challenged practice could "justify subjecting every occupant of every vehicle on the road to a seizure . . . at the unbridled discretion of law enforcement officials." Such discretion "would invite intrusions upon constitutionally guaranteed rights based on nothing more substantial than inarticulate hunches." Only Justice Rehnquist dissented.

Some would dismiss *Franks, Prouse*, and the *Brown-Dunaway-Taylor* line of cases as merely instances where the Burger Court rejected government contentions so extreme that they would not have been advanced without the earlier encouragement of the Burger Court. But a Court bent on dismantling the criminal-justice revolution forged by its predecessor, and prepared to do so by every means short of outright reversals of landmark rulings, would not have considered the government's contentions in the above cases so extreme. Such a Court would have welcomed the opportunities presented by these cases, not spurned them.

Justice Rehnquist did side with the government in *Dunaway, Franks*, and *Prouse*. But he was all alone in *Prouse*, and he was joined only by the chief justice in the other two cases. Justice Rehnquist may be willing and eager to dismantle the work of the Warren Court in the search and seizure area, but it has become increasingly clear that neither he nor he and the chief justice constitute "the Burger Court."

Finally, although at various times there has been serious concern that it was getting into position to do so,[115] the Burger Court has not abolished the exclusionary rule. Although the chief justice launched the most extensive and most powerful attack on the rule,[116] he was hardly alone in expressing disenchantment with the "suppression doctrine."[117] Nevertheless, when, in the summer of 1979, Justice Rehnquist argued at length for the need "to brief the question of whether, and to what extent, the so-called 'exclusionary rule' . . . should be retained,"[118] only the chief justice joined his opinion.

For some time now, there has been considerable support both on and off the Court for a "good faith" exception to the exclusionary rule, that is, for an exception admitting evidence obtained by "inadvertent" violations of the Fourth Amendment or evidence obtained by police who believed in "good faith" that they were acting lawfully and had reasonable grounds for such belief, even though it turned out that they had violated the Fourth Amendment.[119] The Court is much more likely to constrict the exclusionary rule along these lines than to abolish the rule outright. But in *Taylor v. Alabama* (1982),[120] the Court dismissed the argument for such an exception in one sentence: "To date, we have not recognized such an exception, and we decline to do so here."

The exclusionary rule's life may have been furthered by a recent study of some 2,800 federal cases indicating that the "price" exacted by the rule is much smaller than critics of the rule have asserted or assumed: Motions to suppress were filed by only one defendant in ten and denied in the overwhelming majority of cases. Thus, evidence was excluded as a result of Fourth Amendment violations in only 1.3 percent of the cases. Moreover, prosecutions were dropped in less than one half of one percent of the cases because of search and seizure problems.[121] These findings may not only fortify members of the Court already disinclined to abolish the rule, or even to curtail its scope,[122] but may also exert a significant influence on those justices in the "undecided" category.

Police Interrogation and Confessions

Miranda was the centerpiece of the Warren Court's "revolution in American criminal procedure"—and the prime target "of those who attributed the mounting wave of crime to the softness of judges and to their seemingly irrational predilection to shackle the police rather than the criminals."[123] The case "plunge[d] the Court into an ocean of abuse" and was made "one of the leading issues of the 1968 presidential campaign."[124] Almost everyone expected the new Court to treat *Miranda* unkindly. And it did—for (but only for) a decade.

The first blow was struck by *Harris v. New York* (1971).[125] Over the bitter and forceful dissent of Justice Brennan (joined by Douglas and Marshall, JJ.), *Harris* held that statements preceded by defective *Miranda* warnings, and thus inadmissible to establish the prosecution's case in chief, could nevertheless be used to impeach the defendant's credibility if he took the stand. The Court noted, but seemed untroubled by the fact, that some comments in the landmark opinion could be read as barring the use of statements obtained in violation of *Miranda* for any purpose.

Although *Harris* was the more highly publicized decision, a second "impeachment" case, *Oregon v. Hass* (1975),[126] seemed to inflict a deeper wound. Many suspects disclose incriminating information even after the receipt of the *Miranda* warnings. Thus, but for *Hass*, the *Harris* decision could have been explained, and contained, on the grounds that permitting impeachment use of statements acquired without proper warnings would not greatly encourage the police to violate *Miranda*. The somewhat increased probability of obtaining statements by not giving proper warnings, the argument runs, would not furnish the police much incentive to refuse to give the warnings, for such a refusal would prevent the use of any resulting statements in the prosecution's case in chief—and the police are likely to get statements even if they give the required warnings. In *Hass*, however, the police advised the suspect of his rights and he *asserted them*. Nevertheless, the police refused to honor the suspect's request for a lawyer and *continued to question him*. That such a flagrant *Miranda* violation should yield evidence that may be used for impeachment purposes, even if not for the government's case-in-chief, is especially troublesome because under these circumstances, unlike those in *Harris*, it is fair to assume that no hope of obtaining evidence usable for the case-in-chief operates to induce the police to comply with *Miranda*. *Hass*, then, is a more dangerous decision than *Harris*.

Even more disturbing than *Harris* and *Hass* is their recent extension to permit the use of a defendant's *prior silence* to impeach his credibility when he chooses to testify at his trial. Thus, in *Jenkins v. Anderson* (1980),[127] the Court held that a murder defendant's testimony that he had acted in self-defense could be impeached by the fact that he did not go to the authorities and report his involvement in the stabbing. In *Fletcher v. Weir* (1982),[128] it held that even a defendant's *post*arrest silence—so long as he was not given and need not have been given the *Miranda* warnings—may be used to impeach him if he chooses to testify at trial.[129]

As brought out in *Michigan v. Mosley* (1975),[130] police interrogators unwilling to accept defeat have another option if a suspect asserts his right to remain silent (as opposed to his *right to counsel*, discussed below). Under certain circumstances (and what they are *Mosley* leaves painfully unclear), the police, if they cease questioning on the spot, may "try again," and succeed, at a later interrogation session.

Although the language in *Miranda* could be read as establishing a per se rule against any further questioning of one who had asserted his "right to silence,"[131] in *Mosley* the Court held that police questioning may be resumed at least in the following circumstances: (1) the original interrogation is promptly terminated; (2) the questioning is resumed only "after the passage of a significant period of time"; (3) the suspect is given a fresh set of warnings at the second session; (4) a different officer resumes the questioning; (5) the second interrogation is "restricted . . . to a crime that had not been the subject of the earlier interrogation"; and (6) the second interrogation occurs "at another location."[132] The first three circumstances seem to be *minimal requirements* for the resumption of questioning once a person asserts his right to remain silent. They may also be *the only* critical factors, that is, *Mosley* may mean that the first three circumstances suffice without more to eliminate the coercion inherent in the continuing custody and the renewed questioning.[133]

Although in *Mosley* the Court "made clear that the requirement that the police 'scrupulously honor' the suspect's assertion of his right to remain silent is independent of the requirement that any waiver be knowing, intelligent, and voluntary"[134]—thus rejecting the most restricted interpretation of *Miranda* in this respect (an interpretation advanced by Justice White[135])—it would have done better to adopt the position advocated by the dissenters. They argued that either arraignment or counsel must be provided before resumption of questioning of one who has previously invoked the privilege.[136] "Instead, [the Court] in *Mosley* chose to chart a middle course which offers only ambiguous protection to the accused and virtually no guidance to the police or the courts who must live with the rule."[137]

As *Mosley* illustrates, supporters of *Miranda* had to contend not only with the new justices, but with the two *Miranda* dissenters who were still on the

Court: Justice Stewart (until June 1981) and Justice White. Although *Miranda* defined "custodial interrogation" broadly,[138] Justices Stewart and White took the position that *Miranda* applies only to *police station* questioning. *Miranda*, they insisted, "has no relevance to inquiries conducted outside the allegedly hostile and forbidding atmosphere surrounding police station interrogation" but only "guard[s] against what was thought to be the corrosive influence of practices which station house interrogation makes feasible."[139]

Although the above views were advanced in dissenting opinions, the same begrudging view of "custodial interrogation" is reflected in Justice Stewart's opinion for a 6 to 3 majority in *Schneckloth v. Bustamonte*,[140] declining to impose warnings on the "normal consent search": "[Consent searches] normally occur on the highway, or in a person's home or office, and under informal and unstructured conditions . . . immeasurably far removed from 'custodial interrogation.' . . . [T]he spectre of incommunicado police interrogation in some remote station house is simply inapposite."

Justice Stewart's discussion of consent searches in *Schneckloth* raised concern (or, depending upon one's viewpoint, inspired hope) that when the appropriate case came before it, the Court would similarly interpret "custody" or "custodial." In the meantime, *Oregon v. Mathiason* (1977)[141] demonstrated that even *police station* interrogation is not necessarily "custodial." In *Mathiason*, an officer left a note at the suspect's apartment, asking him to call. The suspect did so and, after discussing a convenient meeting place over the phone, agreed to meet the officer in the state patrol office. He came alone. On arrival, he was told that he was not under arrest. Shortly after being taken into an office, the suspect was informed that the police believed that he was involved in a burglary and that his fingerprints had been found at the scene (which was not true). He confessed a few minutes later.

Assuming *arguendo* that Mathiason was not "in custody" at the time the officer first met him and took him into an office, at the point when the police told him that his fingerprints had been found at the scene and that there was other evidence against him he should have been considered "in custody" for *Miranda* purposes. Then, at least, he must have realized (certainly a reasonable person in his position would have) that he was not free to leave. More fundamentally, as dissenting Justice Marshall argued, "faithfulness to *Miranda* requires us to distinguish situations that resemble the 'coercive aspects' of custodial interrogation from those that more nearly resemble [situations such as 'general-on-the-scene questioning'] which *Miranda* states usually can take place without warnings." Yet the Court thought it clear (without the benefit of briefs, oral argument, or a record) that at the time Mathiason confessed, he "was not in custody 'or otherwise deprived of his freedom of action in any significant way.'"

Mathiason is a formalistic, crabbed reading of *Miranda*. Moreover, it is quite confusing. It is unclear, for example, whether the Court was applying a "subjective intent of the officer" approach to custody (if so, it should not have) or *misapplying* a "reasonable person in the suspect's situation" test. It is hoped that *Dunaway* has limited *Mathiason* to situations where a person agrees to meet with the police at a later time and goes to the station house on his own.[142]

Although supporters of *Miranda* were troubled by the Burger Court's confession decisions, they were more alarmed by the tenor of the opinions. The new Court was doing damage to the landmark case, but its general hostility toward *Miranda* thundered louder than its specific holdings. In the early and middle 1970s the only real question seemed to be whether the Burger Court would continue to chip away at *Miranda* or repudiate it outright.

In *Harris*, the Burger Court disposed of the discussion of the impeachment issue in *Miranda* by calling it dicta. But *Miranda* "was deliberately structured to canvass a wide range of problems, many of which were not directly raised by the cases before the Court. This approach was thought necessary in order to 'give concrete constitutional guidelines for law enforcement agencies to follow.' Thus, a technical reading of *Miranda*, such as that employed in *Harris*, would enable the Court to label many critical aspects of the decision mere dictum."[143]

In *Schneckloth*,[144] the Court seemed to look back on the pre-*Miranda* "voluntariness"–"totality of the circumstances" test with something akin to affection: "'[V]oluntariness' has reflected an accommodation of the complex of values implicated in police questioning of a suspect. . . . This Court's [pre-*Miranda* 'voluntary' confession] decisions reflect a frank recognition that the Constitution requires the sacrifice of neither security nor liberty." And it could think of "no reason for us to depart in the area of consent searches, from the traditional definition of 'voluntariness'"—a startling statement for a Court that, seven years earlier, had rejected this very test in the confessions area because it was so elusive, unworkable, and ineffective.

For supporters of *Miranda*, the most ominous note of all was struck by Justice Rehnquist, speaking for the Court in *Michigan v. Tucker* (1974).[145] Although the police had violated *Miranda* by failing to advise Tucker that he would be given free counsel if unable to afford counsel himself, Justice Rehnquist maintained that the interrogation "involved no compulsion sufficient to breach the right against compulsory self-incrimination." He viewed the *Miranda* warnings as "not themselves rights protected by the Constitution," but only "prophylactic standards" designed to "safeguard" or to "provide practical reinforcement" for the privilege against self-incrimination.

In *Tucker* the Court, per Rehnquist, J., seemed to equate "compulsion" within the meaning of the privilege with "coercion" or "involuntariness" under the pre-*Miranda* "totality of the circumstances" test. It seemed to miss the point that much greater pressures were necessary to render a confession "involuntary" under the old test than are needed to make a statement "compelled" under the new. *That was the trouble with the old test.* That was why it was abandoned in favor of *Miranda.*

The whole point of applying the privilege to custodial surroundings as well as to formal proceedings was that the privilege imposed "more exacting restrictions than [did] the Fourteenth Amendment's voluntariness test."[146] Even without applying the severe pressures or utilizing the various strategems that characterized the police conduct in the coerced confession cases, pointed out the Court in *Miranda,*[147] "the very fact of custodial interrogation exacts a heavy toll on individual liberty and trades on the weakness of individuals." Thus, "[u]nless adequate protective devices are employed to dispel the compulsion inherent in custodial surroundings"—and they were not so employed in *Miranda* or *Tucker*—"no statement obtained from the defendant can truly be the product of his free choice."

The Court claimed in *Tucker* that *Miranda* "recognized" that the now familiar warnings "were not themselves rights protected by the Constitution."[148] No, not quite. In *Miranda* the Court recognized only that *protective devices other than the warnings*[149] might suffice to dispel "the compulsion inherent in custodial surroundings." But "unless other fully effective means are adopted"[150] (and there was no contention that they had been in *Tucker*), the warnings *are* rights protected by the Constitution.

A lumping together of self-incrimination "compulsion" and pre-*Miranda* "involuntariness," which seems to be what the Court did in its *Tucker* opinion, amounts to nothing less than "an outright rejection of the core premises of *Miranda.*"[151] Moreover, since the Supreme Court has no supervisory power over *state* criminal justice, if the *Miranda* warnings are not constitutionally based, where do they come from? By stripping *Miranda* of its most apparent constitutional basis without explaining what other bases for it there might be, the Court in the *Tucker* opinion seemed to have prepared the way for the eventual overruling of *Miranda.*

Against the background of such cases as *Harris, Schneckloth,* and *Tucker,* a recent confession case, *Rhode Island v. Innis* (1980),[152] posed grave dangers for *Miranda.* Innis had been convicted, and seemed plainly guilty, of heinous crimes: the kidnapping, robbery, and murder of a cabdriver (by a shotgun blast to the back of the head). He had made incriminating statements while being driven to a nearby police station, only a few minutes after being placed in the police vehicle, and any "interrogation" that might have occurred in the vehicle was very brief and quite mild—much more so than the sustained police station interrogation in *Miranda* and its companion cases, and milder still than "the historical practices at which the right against compulsory self-incrimination was aimed."[153] Moreover, if any "interrogation" had taken place in the police vehicle, it had been conducted by ordinary patrolmen, not detectives skilled in the art of getting people to confess. *Innis,* in short, looked like "a godsend for *Miranda* critics."[154]

To state the facts in more detail: After being warned of his rights three times, the last time by a captain, Innis stated that he wanted to see a lawyer. The captain then ordered him transported to the police station, instructing the three accompanying patrolmen not to question him along the way. Shortly after the trip to the station began, one officer began a conversation with the other officer sitting in front,[155] pointing out that the murder had occurred in the vicinity of a school for handicapped children and expressing the fear that one of the children might find the missing shotgun and injure himself. The second officer voiced similar concern. At this point Innis interrupted the officers and offered to lead them to where the shotgun was hidden. The police brought Innis back to the scene of the arrest, where the captain again advised him of his rights. Innis replied that he understood his rights but that he wanted to retrieve the gun because of the children in the area. He then led the police to the spot where the gun was hidden.

Reviewing Innis's subsequent conviction, the Rhode Island Supreme Court held that the shotgun, as well as the testimony of the officers relating to its discovery, should have been excluded because the police conversation in the vehicle amounted to "custodial interrogation." But Innis was unlikely to prevail in the Burger Court—a Court that up to that point had failed to hold a single item of evidence inadmissible solely on *Miranda* grounds. Indeed, the real question seemed to be not whether Innis would win in the Supreme Court, but how he would lose—and how much damage would be done to *Miranda* in the process. Innis did lose, but, surprisingly, *Miranda* fared quite well.

The Supreme Court might have taken an approach suggested by the White-Stewart dissents in *Mathis* and *Orozco* and limited *Miranda* to custodial *station house* interrogation or its equivalent (for example, a four- or five-hour trip in a police vehicle). Such a ruling might have distressed supporters of *Miranda,* but it could hardly have surprised them. Faithfulness to *Miranda,* the Court might have said, requires application of its doctrine to all custodial station house questioning no matter how brief or mild but not extension of the doctrine to *other* custodial contexts where the potential for abusive and compelling interrogation is significantly less. In non–station house custodial settings, the Court might have ruled, (1) the pre-*Miranda* "voluntariness" test is still adequate to remedy actual instances of coercion, or (2) *Miranda* may sometimes be invoked but only when the police interrogate under conditions that place unusual pressure on the suspect to confess. Justice Stewart, in his opinion for the Court in *Innis,* however, did not pause to consider such an approach to *Miranda*; the only issue deemed worthy of discussion was whether the police conversation in the vehicle constituted "interrogation" within the meaning of *Miranda.*

The Court might have taken a mechanical approach to interrogation and limited it, as some lower courts had,[156] to situations where the police directly address a suspect. It did not do so. It might have limited interrogation to situations where the record establishes that the police *intended* to elicit a response, an obviously difficult test to administer. It did not do this either. The Court might have excluded from its definition of interrogation any police questioning prompted by a legitimate concern for protecting public safety, arguably the officers' motivation in *Innis*. It did not do this either.

Instead, the Court held that "*Miranda* safeguards come into play whenever a person in custody is subjected to either express questioning or its functional equivalent," that is, "the term 'interrogation'" includes "any words or actions on the part of the police (other than those normally attendant to arrest and custody) that the police should know are reasonably likely to elicit an incriminating response from the suspect."[157] Although the *Innis* case involved police "speech," the Court's definition embraces police tactics that do not. Thus, the Court seems to have repudiated the position taken by a number of lower courts that *confronting* a suspect with physical evidence or with an accomplice who has confessed is not interrogation because it does not entail *verbal conduct* on the part of the police.[158]

One may quarrel with the Court's application of the test to the facts before it; it held that Innis had not been subjected to the "functional equivalent" of questioning.[159] One may also criticize the wording of the Court's test. Justice Stewart might have articulated more clearly what I think he meant: "interrogation" includes any police speech or conduct that *foreseeably* might elicit an incriminating statement, or, perhaps better yet, that *would normally be understood as calling for* a response about the merits of the case or that *has the same force as a question* about the merits of the case.[160]

In future cases, of course, the Court may read the *Innis* definition of "interrogation" more narrowly than I do. If I am right, however, in *Innis* the so-called process of qualifying, limiting, and sapping the substance of *Miranda* came to an abrupt halt. I would go further. I would say that in *Miranda's* hour of peril the *Innis* Court rose to its defense.

Concurring in *Innis*, Chief Justice Burger seemed to confirm the view that *Miranda* had weathered the storm. Three years earlier, dissenting in *Brewer v. Williams*,[161] the chief justice had expressed outrage at the *Miranda* doctrine in general and the Court's analysis of interrogation in particular. Although the now famous "Christian burial speech" at issue in *Brewer*[162] seems to fall well within the boundaries of the Court's definition of "interrogation" in *Innis*, in *Innis* the chief justice did not challenge the Court's rather expansive definition of this key term. He raised questions only about the difficulty of its administration. Nor did he renew his attack on *Miranda*. He was content to say that he "would neither overrule *Miranda*, disparage it, nor extend it at this late date."[163]

Miranda continued to fare well in two of the three cases dealing with the subject decided a year after the *Innis* case: *Edwards v. Arizona* and *Estelle v. Smith*.[164]

Estelle v. Smith (1981)[165] arose as follows. Although a judge had ordered the prosecution to arrange a psychiatric examination of Smith, a capital defendant, to determine his capacity to stand trial, the psychiatrist did not merely report to the court on this issue. After Smith was convicted of murder, the doctor testified (indeed he was the government's only witness) at the penalty phase of the capital case. Based in part on the psychiatrist's testimony as to his future dangerousness, Smith was sentenced to death.

The state argued that the privilege against self-incrimination was inapplicable because (1) the challenged testimony was used to determine punishment *after* conviction, not to establish guilt; and (2) Smith's communications to the psychiatrist were "nontestimonial" in nature. Rejecting these contentions, the Court, per Burger, C. J., gave *Miranda* a generous reading.

As far as the privilege against self-incrimination was concerned, the Court could "discern no basis to distinguish between the guilt and penalty phases of Smith's capital trial." The death penalty was a potential consequence of what Smith had told the psychiatrist. "Just as the Fifth Amendment prevents a criminal defendant from being made 'the deluded instrument of his own conviction,' it protects him as well from being made the 'deluded instrument' of his own execution." A criminal defendant who, like Smith, "neither initiates a psychiatric evaluation nor attempts to introduce any psychiatric evidence, may not be compelled to respond to a psychiatrist if his statement can be used against him at a capital sentencing proceeding."[166]

In *Edwards v. Arizona*,[167] the more significant 1981 confession case, the Court reinvigorated *Miranda* in an important respect. Sharply distinguishing the *Mosley* case, the Court held in *Edwards* that when a suspect invokes his right to counsel (as opposed to his right to remain silent), the police cannot "try again." Under these circumstances, a valid waiver of the right to counsel cannot be established by showing "only that [the suspect] responded further to police-initiated custodial interrogation," even though he is again advised of his rights at a second interrogation session. He cannot be questioned anew "*until* counsel has been made available to him, *unless* [he] himself *initiates* further communication, exchanges or conversations with the police" (emphasis added).

There was no dissent in *Edwards*, but concurring Justice Powell, joined by Rehnquist, J., balked at what appeared to be the Court's undue emphasis on "a single element of fact"—"initiation"— among the various facts bearing on the validity of a waiver. But a "standardized procedure" for the resumption of questioning once a suspect has invoked his right to counsel seems quite appropriate in this area.[168] After all, *Miranda* itself is a "standardized procedure" case par excellence.

Although *Miranda* has dominated the confessions scene since it was handed down, it is not the only major Warren Court decision dealing with police interrogation. The decision in *Massiah v. United States* (1964),[169] as clarified by the Burger Court's decision in *Brewer v. Williams* (1977), [170] establishes that once adversary proceedings have commenced against an individual (for example, once he has been indicted or arraigned), government efforts to "deliberately elicit" incriminating statements from him, whether done openly by uniformed police officers or surreptitiously by "secret agents," violate the individual's right to counsel. *Brewer* revivified *Massiah*. One might even say "disinterred" it,[171] for until the decision in *Brewer*, "there was good reason to think that *Massiah* had only been a stepping-stone to *Escobedo* and that both cases had been more or less displaced by *Miranda*."[172]

United States v. Henry (1980)[173] not only reaffirmed the *Massiah-Brewer* doctrine but expanded it by applying it to a situation where the FBI had instructed the secret agent, ostensibly a fellow prisoner, not to question defendant about the crime, and there was no showing that he had. It sufficed that the FBI "intentionally create[d] a situation likely to induce [defendant] to make incriminating statements without the assistance of counsel." The government created such a situation in *Henry*, held the Court (in an opinion by Chief Justice Burger!) when an FBI agent instructed the informant to be alert to any statements made by defendant, who was housed in the same cellblock. "Even if the FBI agent's statement that he did not intend that [defendant's fellow inmate] would take affirmative steps to secure incriminating information is accepted, he must have known that such propinquity likely would lead to that result."

Few, if any, would have predicted it in the mid-1970s, but in the second decade of the Burger Court, *Miranda* is not only alive but in some respects invigorated. Moreover, the *Massiah* doctrine has emerged as a much more potent force than it ever had been in the Warren Court era.

SOME FINAL THOUGHTS

It may well be that the intensity of the civil libertarian criticism of the Burger Court in the police practices area "relates less to what the Court has done . . . than to what the critics fear[ed] it [would] do."[174] When the Burger Court handed down the *Kirby* and *Ash* decisions in the early 1970s, it showed how it could cripple landmark Warren Court rulings without flatly overruling them. But the Court never repeated that performance in the search and seizure or confessions areas. The two most controversial Warren Court criminal procedure rulings, *Miranda* and *Mapp*, did not survive the 1970s unscathed, but in the early 1980s they appear more secure than they have been for a number of years.

A Warren Court admirer probably would say that the new Court did retreat on a number of search and seizure fronts but that it held firm on others and even advanced on some. In the confessions area, again viewed from the perspective of a Warren Court supporter, the Burger Court did inflict substantial damage, especially in the earlier years, but much less than it had been threatening to do. Although at various times in the 1970s a few justices, at least, seemed to be casting a longing eye at the old voluntariness test, the Court's generous reading of *Miranda* in *Innis* and *Edwards* and its even more generous reading of *Massiah* in the *Henry* case "reaffirmed its commitment to controlling police efforts to induce confessions by constitutional rules that look beyond the voluntariness test."[175]

In recent years, especially, the Burger Court has passed up a number of opportunities to cut down Warren Court police practices decisions. Justice Rehnquist, and to a lesser extent the chief justice,[176] would have seized these opportunities, but in recent years these justices have not infrequently seemed as lonely as did Justices Brennan and Marshall in the mid-1970s.

Why the Burger Court's hostility to its predecessor's police practices rulings seems to have subsided is unclear. Perhaps some of the new justices have been "liberalized" by their closeness to these difficult problems. Advocacy of extremely begrudging views of the Fourth Amendment by overconfident or overzealous government lawyers may have led one or more justices to appreciate the need to resist encroachment on the scope of that amendment—and the need for an exclusionary rule. And a recent state supreme court holding that a statement taken from a seriously wounded man lying on his back in an intensive care unit was a "voluntary" confession may have cooled more than one justice's ardor for the pre-*Miranda* totality of the circumstances test.[177]

For reasons that should be apparent to those who have come with me this far, one no longer hears much talk about the "Nixon Court" or the "Nixon bloc." One does hear a good deal of talk nowadays about a "leaderless," "unpredictable," or "fragmented" Court. But the difference between such a Court and one composed mostly of "independent," "uncommitted," and "open-minded" justices is highly elusive. Indeed, it seems to be all in the eye of the beholder.

• Five •

The Burger Court and the Family

Robert A. Burt

In the last decade, family relations have become a substantial part of the Supreme Court's constitutional concerns. In one recent term alone, for example, the Court addressed the constitutional rights of pregnant children to obtain abortions without parental consent,[1] of illegitimate children to intestate inheritance under state law,[2] of fathers to bar adoption of their illegitimate children,[3] of mothers to obtain federal social security support for their illegitimate children,[4] and of husbands to obtain equal claims to alimony from their wives in divorce proceedings.[5] The Court's repeated attention during the 1970s to abortion and gender discrimination,[6] as well as to adoption and foster placement proceedings[7] and disputes between children, parents, and school authorities,[8] has elaborated new constitutional doctrine to adjudicate relations both within the family and between the family unit and outsiders.

One case decided late in the 1970s illuminates central aspects of the Court's contemporary work. In *Parham v. J. R.,*[9] the Court considered whether the Constitution constrains parents who want to confine their children in mental institutions. Although the Court acknowledged the child's "substantial liberty interest" in avoiding unjustified hospitalization, it held that due process protections against parental impositions could adequately be provided through "informal, traditional medical investigative techniques" presided over by "physicians and behavioral specialists." The Court rejected the lower court's requirement of a formal adversarial hearing before a "law-trained or a judicial or administrative officer" designed to protect children, though constitutional norms would require such a process for an adult who protested or who (like most children) lacked the capacity to consent to such confinement.[10]

Chief Justice Burger, writing for the Court majority, rested this holding on "Western Civilization concepts of the family as a unit with broad parental authority over minor children." Justice Brennan, in dissent, was prepared to give special constitutional homage to family status only by postponing adversarial hearings for a "limited period" after a child was admitted to the institution. Beyond this concession, Brennan argued that both children and adults had the same constitutional claims for protection against hospitalization.

An expanded version of this essay appeared in 1979 SUPREME COURT REVIEW at p. 329.

Parham points to the broader context of the Court's family jurisprudence. Although the dispute most directly concerned the prerogatives of parents over children, the case arose only because a professional caretaking bureaucracy agreed with the parents' requests to take custody of their children. The chief justice wrote glowingly of the traditional deference owed to parental authority, but those claims came enmeshed with the authoritative validation of medical professionals and bureaucratic officials. The case thus directly implicates a historically preoccupying dispute regarding the proper judicial role in confronting executive claims for deference on grounds of supposed expertise.

In this regard, *Parham* reveals a central aspect of the Court's contemporary construction of a family jurisprudence: that the Court refracts through the familial prism its fundamental concern with conflicting claims of individual and community, of liberty and authority. Although the Court may speak of a crisis in family structure and authority and may find a sympathetic response in popular attitudes, that shared perception is part of a broader concern in our society. Indeed, current historians who have only recently made the family a subject for rigorous inquiry cast doubt on the accuracy of contemporary claims, which pervade both Court opinions and popular tracts, of the existence of some earlier "golden age" of unquestioned familial authority and stability.[11] This scholarship suggests that current lamentations regarding the decline of parental authority and of familial bonds are an unacknowledged proxy for a different social concern regarding the strength and legitimacy of communal authority generally.

The Court's consitutional jurisprudence of the family, developed during the past decade, can most coherently be understood in this light. Although the justices have been speaking of the proper role of law in regulating family relations, they have implicitly, and occasionally explicitly, addressed in these cases the definition of legitimate social authority generally, asking how legitimacy can be recognized and what is the proper role of the courts and constitutional adjudication in that recognition. The two popularly identifiable ideological blocs on the Courts—the "conservatives" and the "liberals," to use conventionally opaque terminology conventionally[12]—have approached these questions in distinctive ways. Exploring the critical differences and agreements between the blocs in the family relations cases can help to illuminate some important themes in the contemporary Court's constitutional jurisprudence.

THE CONSERVATIVE JUSTICES:
SUPPRESSING CONFLICT BY AUTHORITY'S FORCE

The Court spoke in *Parham* as if it were upholding parental prerogatives against governmental intrusions. Chief Justice Burger acknowledged that some parents harm their children and that state intervention can be justified when children's "physical or mental health is jeopardized." Nonetheless, he said, "The statist notion that governmental power should supersede parental authority in *all* cases because *some* parents abuse and neglect children is repugnant to the American tradition."[13] This is an odd way to describe the issue at stake in *Parham*. Parents there were not seeking to resist governmental power over their children; they were invoking that power by attempting to confine their children in state psychiatric institutions.

This paean to parental prerogatives would have had greater relevance if state officials had sought to impose behavioral controls on children against their parent's wishes. The Court did consider a case two years earlier that directly implicated this principle. School officials had administered corporal punishment to children. In *Ingraham v. Wright*,[14] the Court majority, composed of the same conservative nucleus as in *Parham* (but here joined by Justice Stewart, with Justice White in dissent), ruled that school officials were free to disregard parental objections to this form of control of the behavior of their children. Justice Powell said this for the Court: "Although the early cases viewed the authority of the teacher as deriving from the parents, the concept of parental delegation has been replaced by the view—more consonant with compulsory education laws—that the State itself may impose such corporal punishment as is reasonably necessary for the proper education of the child and for the maintenance of group discipline." So much for the American tradition—paraded in *Parham* as well as in "the early cases"—that "governmental power should [not] supersede parental authority."

The conservative nucleus of *Parham* also spoke quite differently in 1971 about placing the evidentiary presumption between "governmental power" and "parental authority" in judging the best interests of children. In *Wyman v. James*,[15] the Court ruled that state officials could demand home entry as a condition for welfare eligibility without submitting that demand to judicial scrutiny. Justice Blackmun for the Court[16] observed that the purpose of the home inspection was to protect children: "There is no more worthy object of the public's concern. The dependent child's needs are paramount, and only with hesitancy would we relegate those needs, in the scale of comparative values, to a position secondary to what the mother claims as her rights." The Court here assumed a conflict of interest between parent and child without any showing that the parent might be acting harmfully. In *Parham*, Chief Justice Burger appeared to reject this position by requiring a specific showing of "the likelihood of parental abuse" before the "traditional rights of parents" might be limited by some governmental official purporting to protect the child. He stated: "Simply because the decision of a parent . . . involves risks [of harm to a child] does not automatically transfer the power to make that decision from the parents to some agency or officer of the state."[17] In *Wyman,* the Court characterized the mother as claiming "her rights" without acknowledging that those rights could be understood to include authority to rear her child without inappropriate state interference, and that her privacy claim was not simply individualistic but encompassed both her own and her child's right to privacy in their familial relationship.

In *Wyman,* of course, the mother was inviting some state participation in her child-rearing conduct; she was requesting state financial assistance. The Court construed this supplicant posture as a general waiver of the mother's ordinary claims to personal or family privacy.[18] But in *Parham* the parents were also requesting state assistance in their child rearing by seeking admission of their children to state institutions. The Court did not construe this request as a waiver of individual or parental prerogatives; it characterized this parental wish in the high rhetoric of "Western Civilization concepts of the family as a unit with broad parental authority over minor children." The Court saw no irony in its invocation of this rhetoric to vindicate the parents' decision to relinquish their authority to a state psychiatrist.

A deeper consistency can be seen, however, in comparing *Parham* with *Wyman* and the school corporal punishment case. In each case, state-employed behavioral professionals—psychiatrists, teachers, and welfare workers—had opinions regarding proper techniques of child rearing. In *Parham* the parents agreed with those opinions; in the other cases, the parents disagreed. The Court—or, that is, the conservative bloc constituting the majority nucleus in those cases—supported the parents' decision only in *Parham.* In all three cases, irrespective of the parents' views, the professionals' opinions prevailed.

These three cases are not the whole of the Court's or its conservative bloc's family jurisprudence. Neither the Court nor this bloc consistently defers to professionals' child-rearing views any more than they give consistent deference to parental views. The Court's deference to behavioral experts in these cases does, however, point toward a unifying attitude that can be seen in other decisions.

The Court's (including its conservative bloc's) ruling in *Wisconsin v. Yoder*[19] appears a clear victory for parents' opposition to the views of state child-rearing professionals. The Court in *Yoder* upheld the religiously based claims of Amish parents to resist state demands that their children attend school beyond the eighth grade. Chief Justice Burger for the Court rested this decision on both notions of religious freedom and the "enduring American tradition" of the "primary role of the parents in the upbringing of their children." Justice Douglas dissented alone on the ground that the Court should protect only the child's right, and not his parents' rights as such, against state compulsion. The Chief Justice responded that the case record showed no conflict between the children and parents in their resistance to state demands; Justices Stewart and Brennan concurred in the Court's opinion on this understanding. But the Chief Justice spoke further for the Court on this point:

> Recognition of the claim of the State [to support children's opposition to their parents' wishes] . . . would, of course, call into question traditional concepts of parental control over the religious upbringing and education of their minor children recognized in this Court's past decisions. It is clear that such an intrusion by a State into family decisions in the area of religious training would give rise to grave questions of religious freedom. . . . On this record we neither reach nor decide those issues.

Unlike *Yoder,* the record in *Parham* did reveal explicit opposition between parents and children. The Court in *Parham* did not hold, however, that state officials were obliged to honor the parents' wishes in this conflict or even to give special weight to those wishes. The Court ruled only that deference was required from *judges*. The state physicians in *Parham* were not only free, in the Court's view, to take the child's side against his parents' wishes for hospitalization; the Court ruled that constitutional due process norms required the psychiatrists to "evaluate independently" the propriety of the child's hospitalization, to be "neutral and detached trier[s] of fact" in this parent-child dispute. Does this then mean that if the Court had seen explicit opposition between the Amish parents and children regarding school attendance the parents' wishes could have been overridden? It seems clear from the tone of the Court's opinions in the two cases that this result would not have followed, at least for the Chief Justice who wrote both opinions. But if not, why not?

The cases might appear different because the Amish parents' wishes were clearly rooted in religious beliefs while the parents' choice for psychiatric hospitalization carried only secular implications. But here we must take account of another recent Court decision adjudicating conflict between parents and children—the ruling in *Planned Parenthood v. Danforth*[20] that state law cannot withhold an abortion from a pregnant minor solely because of her parents' wishes. Justice Blackmun wrote for the Court with only Justices White and Stevens dissenting; thus the conservative nucleus was prepared here to override parental authority on a question that clearly implicates passionately held religious convictions for some parents. Many parents might oppose abortion on secular grounds, but many parents might oppose compulsory education on such grounds. The Court in *Yoder* took care to restrict its dispensation to parental objections based explicitly on religious belief; in *Danforth* no such exemption was given.

Withholding a requested abortion would seem to have more profound and irreversible consequences for a child than withholding attendance at a public secondary school. The differential severity of consequences might thus give a consistent explanation for the conservative bloc's willingness to defer to parental authority in one case but not the other. Reliance on this difference does appear to underlie the positions of the liberal bloc members, Justices Brennan and Marshall, who joined the Court majority in both *Yoder* and *Danforth*. But if the conservatives also relied on this difference, they would have joined with the dissenting liberals in *Parham* to honor the child's objection to his parents' wish for his psychiatric hospitalization. The psychological trauma of this forced confinement and its potentially life-long stigma are surely more analogous to the potential harm of forced child-bearing for an objecting minor than to the harmfulness of barring a student from public high school in deference to his parents' wishes.

Chief Justice Burger distinguished *Danforth* in his *Parham* opinion, however, on the ground that state law gave an "absolute parental veto" over the child's abortion, while parents could commit their child to mental institutions only when physicians "exercise independent [concurring] judgment as to the child's need for confinement." This distinction points to the underlying decisional principle for the conservative bloc—a principle whose visibility is only occasionally clouded by the rhetoric of deference to parental authority. The clouds clearly part, however, in a case decided just twelve days after *Parham*.

Massachusetts law provided that a pregnant child whose parents would not allow an abortion could obtain permission from a state judge. The Court, in *Bellotti v. Baird*,[21] ruled that the state law was unconstitutional only because it required the child to inform her parents of her wishes and to solicit their consent before asking the judge for his permission. Justice Powell, in a plurality opinion joined by the chief justice and Justices Rehnquist and Stewart, wrote that state law could constitutionally provide that a pregnant minor who wanted an abortion without her parents' consent or knowledge must persuade a judge (or some other state officer) that her wishes were "mature and well-informed" or if immature and ignorant were "nevertheless . . . in her best interest."[22] The Court had invalidated the parental consent law in *Danforth* on the ground that the state might not "give a third party [the parents] an absolute, and possibly arbitrary, veto over the decision of the physician and his patient [the pregnant child] to terminate the patient's pregnancy."[23] Justice Powell was, however, clearly prepared to give this veto power to a state official while withholding it from parents. Does he assume that parents are "possibly arbitrary" but that judges or other state officials are not? That judges can discern a child's maturity or best interest, while her parents cannot? That judges' possible arbitrariness can be constrained, while parents' cannot, by the crystalline clarity of the "maturity" and "best interest" standard that he posits?

These assumptions may inform Justice Powell's position. But there is a consistent principle that unites the conservative bloc justices' positions in these family cases that does not rest on these patently questionable assumptions. The principle is not that parental authority as such warrants respect. Rather, the only authority over children that commands constitutionally mandated respect is authority backed by force that clearly promises effective control over children's disruptive impulses. On this view, parents occasionally embody such force. But when parents in fact fail to control their child, then their authority no longer commands respect in principle. Parents whose effective authority has failed can rehabilitate themselves and their claim to constitutionally mandated respect only by invoking some extrafamilial authority to buttress their weakened force—a psychiatrist who will institutionalize their child, a teacher who will paddle their child, a judge who will rule their child.

When one of the conservative justices extols the American tradition of respect for parental authority, he is not commanding deference for the status of parenthood. The operative principle that gives consistency to this bloc's various decisions is rather that only parental authority exercised in a traditional authoritarian format requires constitutional deference. This principle dominates the *Yoder* decision. As noted, the strength of Amish parents' religious conviction does not adequately explain why their child-rearing wishes command state deference; otherwise, the minors' abortion cases are inexplicable. Nor can the case be explained by the intensity of the Amish parents' belief in the psychic damage inflicted on their children by the public school teachers; otherwise, the school corporal punishment cases are inexplicable. The Amish parents do not command respect from the conservative justices for the strength of any of their beliefs. They command respect because of their effective strength in imposing those beliefs on their children and by obtaining apparently conforming conduct from them. Throughout his opinion for the Court, Chief Justice Burger repeatedly and lavishly praises Amish parents' child-rearing techniques on this score:

> The testimony . . . showed that the Amish succeed in preparing their high school age children to be productive members of the Amish community. [One expert witness] described their system of learning through doing the skills directly relevant to their adult roles in the Amish community as "ideal" and perhaps superior to ordinary high school education. The evidence also showed that the Amish have an excellent record as law-abiding and generally self-sufficient members of society.
>
> The State attacks [the parents'] position as one fostering "ignorance" from which the child must be protected by the State. No one can question the State's duty to protect children from ignorance but this argument does not square with the facts disclosed in the record. Whatever their idiosyncrasies as seen by the majority, this record strongly shows that the Amish community has been a highly successful social unit within our society, even if apart from the conventional "main-stream." Its members are productive and very law-

abiding members of society; they reject public welfare in any of its usual modern forms. . . .

To be sure, the power of the parent, even when linked to a free exercise claim, may be subject to limitation . . . if it appears that parental decisions will jeopardize the health or safety of the child, or have a potential for significant social burdens. But in this case, the Amish have introduced persuasive evidence undermining the arguments the State has advanced to support its claims in terms of the welfare of the child and society as a whole. The record strongly indicates that . . . [upholding Amish parents' claims here] will not impair the physical or mental health of the child, or result in an inability to be self-supporting or to discharge the duties and responsibilities of citizenship, or in any other way materially detract from the welfare of society.[24]

If parental authority warrants deference only when the parents are "productive and . . . reject public welfare in any of its usual modern forms," then it is obvious why the claims to family and personal privacy of the welfare applicant mother in *Wyman v. James* were overridden. If parental child-rearing decisions forfeit respect as a matter of constitutional principle when those decisions would "result in [the child's] inability to be self-supporting," then no deference is owed parents' refusal to authorize an abortion for their pregnant unmarried daughter. (The state laws in *Danforth* and *Baird* provided that, if she were married, the pregnant minor would be deemed an adult and thus could reach her abortion decision without parental or judicial supervision.) And if parental authority must be honored only when parents succeed (as the Court found that "the Amish succeed") in bringing obedient social conformance from their children, then no honor is due to parents who have failed to keep their child from premarital intercourse and pregnancy.[25]

This is the thread that can be traced into a coherent pattern among the votes of the conservative bloc justices in the cases discussed thus far—that a specific, authoritarian style of parenting rather than the status of parent itself warrants constitutional deference. Justice Powell espoused this position with virtual explicitness in an opinion, joined only by the other conservative justices, dissenting from the Court's imposition of some procedural formality on school suspensions in *Goss v. Lopez.*[26] Justice Powell stated:

Education in any meaningful sense includes the inculcation of an understanding in each pupil of the necessity of rules and obedience thereto. This understanding is no less important than learning to read or write. One who does not comprehend the meaning and necessity of discipline is handicapped not merely in his education but throughout his subsequent life. In an age when the home and church play a diminishing role in shaping the character and value judgments of the young, a heavier responsibility falls upon the schools.

This "heavier responsibility" appears to fall not merely on school officials, in Justice Powell's view, but equally on other public officers including

Supreme Court justices. The Court in his view should not limit application of any "of the traditional means . . . used to maintain discipline in the schools" but rather should preach their propriety and necessity from the pulpit of the Court.

Propounding a rule that the Supreme Court must, in common with other state officials, defer to any parent's choice regarding child rearing would not accomplish this purpose because, it appears in Justice Powell's view, many modern parents themselves must be taught this lesson. He observed in his *Goss* dissent: "There is, no doubt, a school of modern psychological or psychiatric persuasion that maintains that *any* discipline of the young is detrimental. Whatever one may think of the wisdom of this unproved theory, it hardly affords dependable support for a *constitutional* decision." Justice Powell obviously thinks very little of the wisdom of this imagined theory, and he finds "support for a *constitutional* decision" in an opposed theory of child rearing.

That theory, as the Justice describes it, has one central attribute that applies equally to children and to Supreme Court justices: that discipline administered by traditional authorities should not be questioned. Thus for students, Justice Powell prescribes:

When an immature student merits censure for his conduct, he is rendered a disservice if appropriate sanctions are not applied or if procedures for their application are so formalized as to invite a challenge to the teacher's authority— an invitation which rebellious or even merely spirited teenagers are likely to accept.

For his brethren, Justice Powell prescribes:

In mandating due process procedures [in school disciplinary suspensions] the Court misapprehends the reality of the normal teacher-pupil relationship. There is an ongoing relationship, one in which the teacher must occupy many roles— educator, adviser, friend, and, at times, parent-substitute. It is rarely adversary in nature except with respect to the chronically disruptive or insubordinate pupil whom the teacher must be free to discipline without frustrating formalities.

In a subsequent opinion, *Ingraham v. Wright,*[27] Justice Powell identified a problem of central concern to him that could come from such "frustrating formalities": "If a prior hearing, with the inevitable attendant publicity within the school, resulted in rejection of the teacher's recommendation, the consequent impairment of the teacher's ability to maintain discipline in the classroom would not be insubstantial." Justice Powell's concern here was not limited to the ability of teachers to maintain discipline. In the penultimate footnote in his *Ingraham* opinion he observed: "The need to maintain order in a trial courtroom raises similar problems. In that context, this Court has recognized the power of the trial judge 'to punish summarily and without notice or hearing contemptuous conduct committed in his presence and observed by him.' . . . This punishment so imposed may be as severe as six months in prison."

Justice Powell wrote for the Court in *Ingraham*. As in *Goss v. Lopez*, he was joined by his three conservative colleagues, but Justice Stewart deserted the *Goss* majority here to make Powell's opinion the Court's result. In *Ingraham* the Court refused to require even an informal prior notice or hearing opportunity before administration of corporal punishment, unlike in the *Goss* ruling for school suspensions, and further refused to impose Eighth Amendment constraints on corporal punishment no matter how cruel, unusual, or punitive those beatings might appear to an untutored eye.[28]

It would be unfair, however, to portray the Court in *Ingraham* or its conservative nucleus generally as intending to condone or encourage brutality by teachers, parents, or judges. This nucleus in particular intends to encourage an unquestioning attitude toward, and a reciprocally firm and self-confident attitude by, constituted authority. An idealized image of conflict-free interpersonal relations appears to lie beneath this intention. Justice Powell reveals this in his *Goss v. Lopez* dissent: "The role of the teacher in our society historically has been an honored and respected one, rooted in the experience of decades that has left for most of us warm memories of our teachers, especially those of the formative years of primary and secondary education."[29] It might thus appear an insult to these honored memories if the Supreme Court were now to abandon what Justice Powell describes as "[our reliance] for generations upon the experience, good faith and dedication of those who staff our public schools."

Justice Blackmun in his opinion for the Court in *Wyman v. James* offers the same romantic vision of the relationship between authority (there the social worker) and dependent (the welfare applicant) in that case:

> The [challenged home] visit is not one by police or uniformed authority. It is made by a caseworker of some training whose primary objective is, or should be, the welfare, not the prosecution, of the aid recipient for whom the worker has profound responsibility. . . . [T]he program concerns dependent children and the needy families of those children. It does not deal with crime or with the actual or suspected perpetrators of crime. The caseworker is not a sleuth but rather, we trust, is a friend to one in need.[30]

Justice Blackmun's invocation of "trust" here has many meanings. The caseworker must be a trusting "friend" and "not a sleuth" to the welfare recipient. The welfare applicant qualifies as a worthy recipient of aid only if she is willing to trust the worker's good intentions. And "we trust"—the Court, that is, trusts—that the caseworker will deserve trust.[31] Justice Blackmun appears to assume that if the Court sees conflict between caseworker and welfare recipient and mandates adversarial process based on that perception, that this Court perception will itself create, or at least exacerbate, conflict and thus in itself defeat the ideal of conflict-free relations.

Chief Justice Burger in *Parham* expresses the same vision regarding parent-child relations: "[The law] historically . . . has recognized that natural bonds of affection lead parents to act in the best interest of their children [citing Blackstone and Kent]. . . . That some parents 'may at times be acting against the interests of their child' . . . creates a basis for caution, but is hardly a reason to discard wholesale those pages of human experience that teach that parents generally do act in the child's best interests."[32] The chief justice is not denying the possibility of conflict between parent and child, any more than his conservative colleagues are denying that possibility between teacher and student or welfare worker and recipient. These justices are, however, united in the belief that the Court must view these relations as if they were conflict-free in order to encourage a trusting, even childlike deference without which—as they see it—no wholesome relationship is possible between children and parents or among their social surrogates. The Court, in the eyes of these justices, has a special role in holding this ideal aloft, in legitimizing authority by teaching the populace to ignore—as they would have the Court ignore—the conflict-ridden aspects of their contemporary social relations.

In his paean to the Amish way of life, Chief Justice Burger appears to see Amish success in leading children into law-abiding, productive, and self-reliant adulthood as arising from their achievement of this heavenly goal: "Old Order Amish communities [have] devotion to a life in harmony with nature and the soil, as exemplified by the simple life of the early Christian era which continued in America during much of our early national life."[33] The chief justice may have an inaccurate vision of conditions in contemporary Amish communities;[34] he certainly has a historically inaccurate conception of the successful achievement of this simple, harmonious life in early American history.[35] He is correct, however, to see this ideal for community and for family life as a normative goal espoused throughout our national history, a goal that is sometimes more and sometimes less emphasized.

The chief justice and his conservative colleagues clearly believe that our contemporary national life is riddled with profound and socially harmful divisions. Justice Powell, in the school discipline cases, repeatedly notes "the seriousness of the disciplinary problems in the Nation's public schools"— problems which, he states, have "increased significantly in magnitude in recent years."[36] Our recent years have been marked not simply by conflict in particular classrooms. Students have seized and barricaded universities; many public secondary schools resemble armed camps, with violence common among students and between teachers and students. These recent years have seen bloody urban riots and assassinations of national political leaders.

The Court inevitably acts against the background of these transfixing events, attempting to place them in proper perspective and to evaluate its institutional role in responding to them. In the family cases, the conservative nucleus has set its agenda with reference to these larger social events. These justices have concluded that our contemporary national life is so fractionated that any challenge to constituted authority excessively undermines the legitimacy of all authority, that we must recapture an earlier social attitude of unquestioning deference to authority which alone can create a stable precondition for belief in the legitimacy of any authority.

But like any lost faith, unquestioning belief cannot be revived simply by exhortation. There are other possible techniques for resolving doubts about the good faith or legitimacy of authorities—whether parents or judges— beyond suppressing those doubts, pretending that we have none. The liberal justices offer an apparently different technique to this end in the family cases and more generally in their jurisprudence. On ultimate analysis, however, their technique depends on an uncomfortably transparent pretense that has more in common with their conservative brethrens' stance than either bloc likes to admit.

THE LIBERAL JUSTICES:
SUPPRESSING CONFLICT BY REASON'S FORCE

The modern Court's concern for a jurisprudence of the family can be clearly dated from *In re Gault,* decided in 1967.[37] This was only the second juvenile court case to reach Supreme Court adjudication,[38] though such courts had been established for some fifty years in virtually every state.[39] The central characteristic of these courts was informality: no clearly defined offenses, no clear separation of prosecutorial and adjudicatory roles, no defense attorneys adversarially committed to a juvenile client. The juvenile court was instead conceived as if it were a Victorian family with the juvenile as rebellious lad moved to repentence and reformation by the imprecation and example of the stern but kindly paterfamilias.

In *Gault* the Court ruled that the procedural informality that had marked the juvenile court from its inception would not satisfy constitutional norms— that juveniles must be given clear notice of the offense charged, opportunity to defend themselves against state intervention, and the right to an attorney who could be adversarially committed to protect them against interventions. The Court majority—then in its most confidently liberal heyday—rejected the vision of social fact and norm on which the juvenile court's informality had rested; it ruled that actual or potential conflict between child and state must not be ignored but rather must be structurally expressed in the procedures of the court.

In *Gault* the Court saw the juvenile court judge as an umpire presiding over a clash of views regarding the propriety of state intervention for the child. The juvenile court judge was not the reflexive embodiment of state power or a representative of adult authority indistinguishable from all other adults who control children. He was to stand outside the conflict between state or adult authority and children, to serve as neutral adjudicator of the claims of each. In effect the *Gault* majority mandated that the juvenile court judge must act as the majority justices conceived themselves in confronting more general social conflict: as umpireal adjudicators committed to protect minority rights (or, in this case, the rights of minors) against impositions by state authority.

The readiness with which the majority in the *Gault* case portrayed children in the same conceptual mold as other minority groups warranting judicial protection against majoritarian state power was evident in the presentational rhetoric of its opinion. The Court spoke consistently of vindicating children's rights, though the facts of the *Gault* case made clear that both the child and his parents were united in resisting juvenile court jurisdiction.[40] The Court's failure to seize on these facts, and to portray the dispute as between state and family unit, was not an oversight; this failure was a central aspect of the liberal majority's vision of the case.

This choice of characterization—children's rights rather than family rights—assumed even greater significance in a case decided two years after *Gault*, with the liberal majority of the Warren years still the dominant voice of the Court. In *Tinker v. Des Moines Independent School District*,[41] the Court ruled that school authorities violated constitutional norms by forbidding students to wear black armbands in class to protest the Vietnam War. The Court, in an opinion written by Justice Fortas (who also wrote the *Gault* opinion), perceived the state authorities as violators of the First Amendment expression rights of the schoolchildren and wholly ignored the question of whether the school's imposition of an ideological orthodoxy on the children transgressed their parents' child-rearing rights.

This analytic omission had more direct significance than in *Gault*. Justice Black dissented in *Tinker* on the explicit ground that the children's black armbands reflected their parents' antiwar views more than their own; he noted, among other things, that one of the children originally expelled from the Des Moines school for demonstrating was only eight years old.[42] Even assuming with Justice Black that the children had no discernible or "maturely" independent views, it does not necessarily follow that the school's imposition is to be preferred to the parents'.[43] The *Tinker* majority could have used Justice Black's facts characterization to posit a "family right" against state-imposed ideological conformity. But the liberal majority in *Tinker* was not interested in the family unit as such; they saw the family as an aggregation of discrete individuals with traditionally individualistic rights against state authority to be vindicated by umpireal judges who stood apart from the state.

Just as family unity was not relevant for the liberal majority in *Gault* and *Tinker*, family discord was not analytically significant for the liberal remnant in *Parham*. Justice Brennan's dissent argued that adversarial process, presided over by a judgelike officer, should protect children's rights against unjustified psychiatric hospitalization whether or not parents joined with state officials in such imposition. For the liberal dissenters in *Parham*, the familial guise of authority over chidren was not significant in principle. Authority required a judicialized process to assure its legitimacy for the liberal justices whether that authority was exercised by parents, teachers, psychiatrists, or police.

The liberals thus share with their conservative brethren an essentially unitary conception of authority in society. While the conservatives assess the legitimacy of particular claims to authority by reference to traditional conceptions of social order, the liberals see legitimacy only for authority that can justify itself by giving reasons, prodded by adversarial questioning. The conservative has no answer to those who challenge the legitimacy of the very social order used as the reference point for supporting claims to authority. The liberal vision has a comparable vulnerability. Its reliance on reason as the legitimizing touchstone for all authority tends to challenge the very idea of social order. The liberal justices cannot answer these central questions within the terms of their legitimizing schema: On what basis is one person's reasoning better than another's? Where reason rules, who is the ruling reasoner? The liberal's occasionally glib equation of rule by reason and rule by judges giving reasons attempts to mask the profoundly individualistic, destabilizing, and even antisocial, implications of their philosophic commitment to rationality.[44]

The critique of judicial activism that became widely current during the 1930s and in revised form again during the 1960s addressed the insufficiencies of judges as embodiments of right reason in solving social problems. Particular criticism of judicial capacities—pointing to the limited data provided by judicial process and the terse opaqueness of substantive standards independently available to judges through constitutional norms—rested against a more general vision of the courts' antidemocratic character. The courts' manifest unrepresentativeness created special tensions for the liberal justices' claim to rule by reason; if they could not persuade most people that their reasons were correct, what standard of rationality did these justices purport to rest their decision upon?

The liberals trap themselves in this problem because of their adherence to a further premise shared with their conservative brethren: that prolonged social conflict is in itself undesirable. I noted earlier the romantic visions of social harmony that Justice Blackmun invoked for welfare workers and recipients and that Chief Justice Burger invoked for general communal relations in his encomium to the Amish. The liberal justices have an equally idealized attachment to social harmony which they implicitly believe to be attainable by appeal to reason.

The liberals' habitual willingness to give judges specially active roles in resolving social conflict does not necessarily come from an assumption that judges are more honest or intelligent than others but rather from a belief that the judicial methodology of dispute resolution is most nearly synonomous with reasoned deliberation. The judge's commitment to an umpireal stance—to impartiality, to hearing all sides before deciding—is an important aspect of this methodology. But this stance alone might appear to put a premium on conflict as such; the conservative justices construe the liberal position in this way, accusing them, for example, of provoking conflict between parent and child (as in *Parham*) or student and teacher (as in *Goss, Ingraham,* and *Tinker*). The liberals have, however, a deeper commitment to a vision of social harmony beneath this apparent celebration of conflict. That commitment is revealed in a further aspect of the judicial methodology that most starkly differentiates it from the posture of other governmental or parental actors: the obligation to give reasons for decisions.

This obligation is not primarily directed toward the winning party, though it has its congratulatory aspects. The obligation is more fundamentally addressed to the loser. The judge is obliged to give reasons that in principle might persuade the loser that he should applaud, and not merely sullenly acquiesce in, his loss. In giving reasons, the judge attempts to show the loser how he should reconceive his own position and to convince him that he should abandon his initial claim of entitlement in the light of principles that dictate the decision for the winner—communal principles, that is, shared equally between loser and winner. The underlying premise of the methodological insistence on reasoned judicial opinions is that the initial conflict between plaintiff and defendant is thereby transformed into a shared celebration that justice has triumphed. The methodology posits that both parties can be persuaded to see themselves as sharers of victory in the judge's reassertion (or revelatory clarification) of the principles that bind plaintiff and defendant, that transcend their initial conflict and more fundamentally unite them in a harmonious community.

Justice Brennan's dissenting opinion in *Parham* is illustrative. It invokes a characteristically inflated vision of the commanding force of rationality and conflated view of reason's judicial embodiment. Judicialized adversarial hearings for institutionalized children, he observes, "may prove therapeutic. Children who feel that they have received a fair hearing may be more likely to accept the legitimacy of their confinement, acknowledge their illness and cooperate with those attempting to give treatment. This, in turn, would remove a significant impediment to successful therapy."[45] What leads Justice Brennan to believe that the child who protests the parents' decision to hospitalize and who resists the psychiatrists' custody will regard as "fair" and "legitimate" a proceeding that ends with a judge's ratification of the other adults' disposition? The majority opinion in *Parham* implicitly attacks this assumption. It cites studies of judicial civil commitment hearings for

adult psychiatric confinements that reveal a mean hearing time ranging
from 3.8 to 9.2 minutes. The chief justice concludes from this data that
"the supposed protections of an adversary proceeding . . . [regarding mental
hospitalization] may well be more illusory than real."[46]

The liberal dissenters in *Parham* may be correct that parents, psychiatrists, and child should be obliged to give reasoned accounts of their
decisions for or against psychiatric hospitalization. But certainly at the first
moments, or even after a "limited period," of hospitalization, reasoned
discourse is a scarce commodity between parents and child, the principal
participants in the controversy. The notion that an extrafamilial authority
can readily impose order on this controversy—whether that authority is a
psychiatrist or judge, whether the form of that imposition is shouted imprecation or cool reasonableness—is the fallacy that is shared by both liberal
and conservative justices. But in embracing this fallacy, the liberals—more
than their conservative brethren—are untrue to the basic underlying premises
of their ideology. Authoritative imposition is antithetical to reasoned discourse. Unless the liberal justices can dissociate reasoned discourse from the
idea of judge as the ultimate reasoner whose conclusion warrants special
respect apart from its persuasiveness to all its addressees, this liberal commitment to reason becomes a transparent mask for the conservative position that authority warrants deference simply as such.

THE COMMON GROUND:
THE AUTHORITARIAN CONCEPTION OF JUDICIAL REVIEW

Both the liberal and conservative blocs on the Court fail to see their proper
institutional role in leading fundamentally alienated combatants toward the
pursuit of mutual accommodation. The Court best serves that function when
it seeks only to provoke and structure rather than to resolve basic social
conflicts. The justices' failure in this regard—their willingness to demand
unanimity as unquestioning deference either generally to traditional authorities or specifically to judges as the supposed embodiment of right reason—
is the central error of the Court's contemporary jurisprudence.

This error equally afflicts cases where most of the conservative and liberal
justices have managed to find common ground. *Roe v. Wade*[47] is a particularly
striking instance. The Court's opinion, written by Justice Blackmun, gives
lengthy recitation of the history of social attitudes and conflict regarding
abortion, from early Greek to modern times. But this recitation is only a
prelude for the Court's claim to identify the correct answer for our time.
The opinion notes the dramatic recent shift in opinion, from a universal
regime of highly restrictive to increasing availability of abortions. Legislatures in some one-third of the states had, since the late 1950s, significantly
liberalized their abortion laws and during 1970, four states—New York,

Washington, Alaska, and Hawaii—wholly abolished restrictions. Because New York's legalized procedures were not limited to state residents, the more restrictive regimes of the heavily populated neighboring states appeared undermined, for practical purposes at least. However, since Washington required ninety days' prior residence, its law would most likely not have had a similar practical effect beyond its immediate borders. In any event, these legislative changes clearly affected the popular debate on the principled issues, giving visibility and enhanced legitimacy to proponents of free abortion and signaling that campaigns to educate and mobilize popular force directed at majoritarian institutions were not clearly doomed to failure anywhere.

At the same time that this legislative ferment was increasing in intensity, proponents of free abortion turned to the federal courts. *Roe v. Wade* reached the Supreme Court in 1971. It was the Court's first case involving direct constitutional challenge to state abortion restrictions.* The Court postponed decision and set the case for reargument in 1972. In 1973 the Court awarded victory to the plaintiffs, with such completeness and detail that (I suspect) even they were surprised.

Roe has not ended controversy regarding abortion. It was indeed the impetus for new forces of opposition to identify themselves and to mobilize political effort that has had considerable legislative success. The Court has reentered the dispute with some frequency, initially to defend its position in *Roe* but most recently to validate legislative restrictions aimed at poor women and minors.[48] Whatever their principled justifications, the Court's rulings in net result seem to echo, at least in rough facsimile, the wealth and race discriminations that held prior to *Roe*. The Court's decision in *Roe* has made it possible for middle-class women to obtain abortions in every state with greater convenience and easier consciences, at least for those women who were troubled at the prospect of traveling across state lines to avoid the laws of their resident state or of conspiring with a cooperative physician to exaggerate medical necessity or simply to flout state law. Poor women and minors are hampered in seeking abortions in the ways reminiscent of the disadvantages imposed by the pre-*Roe* statutory restrictions.

This apparently ironic result is an insufficient ground on which to argue that the Court was wrong in *Roe*. But the result raises a question nonetheless about what the Court expected to accomplish in its decision. If the Court meant to end dispute and to persuade most citizens of the moral propriety of freely available abortions, it has not accomplished that goal.

---

*In that same year, the Court had rejected a physician's claim that his criminal conviction should be overturned because the District of Columbia's abortion proscription was unconstitutionally vague. United States v. Vuitch, 402 U.S. 62 (1971).

If the Court meant to provoke a great national debate on this issue, to reopen the defeat of interests that had been unfairly disregarded in majoritarian institutions, its action was demonstrably unnecessary. The Court's action in *Roe* can be justified only if the principle at stake was so patently correct and important that its vindication could not depend on and would not be enhanced by the arduous effort of public persuasion and political organization that necessarily precedes legislative action. If there is no adequate public benefit from visible, prolonged, and legitimized conflict regarding the abortion issue, with its passionate psychological and moral significances, then the Court's swift proclamation in *Roe* was justified. But from these perspectives, there is no justification for *Roe*.

Roe v. Wade is perhaps the most egregious instance of the Court's desire to stifle conflict, and the one with the most far-reaching social consequences. But *Roe* does not stand alone. The Court's recent decision in *Moore v. City of East Cleveland*[49] is a particularly revealing example of the contemporary Court's authoritarian impulse in cases involving family relations.

The Court majority in *Moore* cut across the liberal and conservative blocs to invalidate a city housing ordinance that essentially limited residence within the municipality to nuclear families composed of parents and their children.[50] Mrs. Moore, the plaintiff, violated the ordinance by living with her two adult sons and their sons, in a so-called matrifocal extended family that is disproportionately characteristic of black lower-income households. Justice Powell, writing for the Court plurality, noted that the city ordinance was "unusual" and inconsistent with "the accumulated wisdom of civilization . . . that supports a larger conception of the family." Justice Brennan, in a concurring opinion joined by Justice Marshall, found the ordinance "senseless and arbitrary . . . eccentric . . . [reflecting] cultural myopia . . . in the light of the tradition of the American home that has been a feature of our society since our beginning as a nation"; he concluded that "this ordinance displays a depressing insensitivity toward the economic and emotional needs of a very large part of our society."

At first glance, the East Cleveland ordinance might appear antiblack and constitutionally suspect on that ground. But Justice Brennan observed that "the record . . . would not support [an] implication [of racially discriminatory purpose]." Justice Stewart, in a footnote to his dissenting opinion, explains why: "In point of fact, East Cleveland is a predominantly Negro community, with a Negro City Manager and City Commission." But though this fact was critical to a sympathetic understanding of the ordinance's purpose, the Court made nothing of it. The plurality viewed the ordinance as directed against "overcrowding, minimizing traffic and parking congestion, and avoiding an undue financial burden on [the] school system" and observed that these "legitimate goals" could be pursued by other means and were served "marginally, at best" by the ordinance itself. The plurality did not consider that the purpose of the ordinance was quite staightforward: to exclude from a middle-class, predominantly black community, which saw itself as socially and economically upwardly mobile, other black families whose life-style was most characteristic of the lower-class ghetto.

Perhaps the Court did not see this purpose or, if it did, considered this an "illegitimate goal," though in other cases the Court had been exceedingly solicitous of white middle-class communities' attempts to preserve a common social identity—"zones," as the Court had put the matter three years earlier, "where family values, youth values, and the blessings of quiet seclusion and clear air make the area a sanctuary for people."[51] Justice Brennan dissented in the earlier cases and cannot be charged with inconsistency. But even so, I find in his characterization of the East Cleveland ordinance as "senseless" and "eccentric" precisely what he alleges in it: "a depressing insensitivity toward the economic and emotional needs" of the current majority of residents in East Cleveland.[52]

There is a conflict between the current city majority, who purport to uphold middle-class nuclear family values, and other black families who prize extended family households. As this conflict was presented to the Court, there appeared to be diametric opposition between these two groups— the city alleging that it could not maintain its cherished associations among like-minded people if it were forced to accept Mrs. Moore's family, and Mrs. Moore equally alleging that she could not live with those she cherished if she complied with the city ordinance. But the city had a response to her complaint that she could not offer to theirs. The city, that is, could reasonably assert that she could preserve her preferred associations by moving to other communities in the metropolitan Cleveland area. She could not offer a similar accommodation to them. If Mrs. Moore and her family were forced to move, they would no doubt be considerably inconvenienced. But if Mrs. Moore succeeded in her argument that the city ordinance was unconstitutional, the nuclear families that had come together in East Cleveland could find nowhere to remain together as a self-consciously contained community.

The Court plurality saw Mrs. Moore as embodying the traditional American values of extended families—"uncles, aunts, cousins, and especially grandparents sharing a household along with parents and children." There is an equally powerful, and probably historically more prevalent, American tradition of nuclear family households that see themselves bonded in an extended communal group linked to a shared social identity that includes but is not limited to blood ties.[53] The city of East Cleveland sought to constitute itself as such an "extended kinship" network, perhaps to differentiate itself with particular clarity from the ghetto life-style that had greater salience and threat for them than for predominantly white middle-class communities which could more comfortably absorb multi-generational families without disturbing the nuclear families' sense of social solidarity.

From this perspective, victory for Mrs. Moore was total defeat for the other residents of East Cleveland, while victory for them was not total defeat for her, except insofar as she wished to remain in their community while transforming its membership to her taste. If Mrs. Moore were shut out from many different communities that were readily accessible to the other residents of East Cleveland—if, that is, the city ordinance was not "unusual" or even "eccentric" but was common throughout the Cleveland area and even the country—then the Court might properly have seen some role for itself in protecting her interests, in fomenting dispute on her behalf against the prevalent social forces that scorned and shut her out.[54] But the very oddity of the East Cleveland ordinance suggests that Mrs. Moore is not alone in her opposition to it, that the city residents are more the vulnerable, isolated dissenters than she in the broader society, that they more than she deserve special judicial solicitude as a "discrete and insular minority." The Court in *Moore* myopically saw the case as a dispute between "a family" and "the state" rather than as a dispute among citizens about the meaning of "family."

Mrs. Moore did not rest her argument solely on a claimed constitutional right to family integrity but further alleged that the city ordinance violated her right to privacy in the choice of associates.[55] This conjunction in her argument points to the general kinship in the Court's doctrine between the privacy and family integrity claims, and the way in which the privacy principle has been a vehicle for the justices to serve as final moral arbiters for everyone.

This use of the privacy idea reached its apotheosis in the abortion cases. The Court's doctrine in those cases reflects a basic misunderstanding of the legitimate judicial role. The Court's actions must be guided by this ideal: to provoke and to redefine disputes that might lead contending parties toward mutual accommodation, toward pursuit of unanimous consent. For this purpose, the Court's expansive, simplistic invocation of the privacy concept in the abortion dispute is fundamentally misleading.

Perhaps it is plausible to argue that the fetus is so clearly nonhuman that others generally cannot claim communal identification with it where its mother claims otherwise. But the Court's explicit assumption that the father of the fetus is as much a stranger to it as any other community member is not plausible.[56] The Court's apparent position that the mother always has the superior claim and interest, no matter how much the father might show that her burden in childbearing would be less than his burden in losing his child, appears to me an invidious sex discrimination.[57] Whether or not the Court should forbid all other institutions from engaging in such discrimination, it should not indulge in its own.

The Court's decision in the 1978 term to invalidate even a requirement of notification to parents when their child proposes an abortion is also flawed.[58] The Court would permit a judge to decide whether parents should be notified, thus rejecting the lower court's position that the child's privacy right mandates that her parents never be notified over her objections.[59] But both positions reflect and even reinforce the stark alienation of parent and child in this deeply contentious dispute. There is no easy way that any accommodation can be reached in this family conflict. But the justices too readily assume that a judge's opinion should supersede parents' wishes in these matters—either in making a case-by-case judgment for a particular child or in making a general judgment on the basis of constitutional doctrine for all children and parents.

This assumption reflects the same distaste for direct, prolonged conflict and the same failure to appreciate the importance of such conflict in forging communal bonds that marks the contemporary Court's general jurisprudence. There is no easy way to overcome the social alienation that afflicts many people in this society and that undermines the sense of mutual allegiance which alone can legitimate bonds of authority and community. The Court has an important, proper role to pursue in assuring these bonds, in continually renewing the constitution of our family feeling. But the Court's current authoritarian conception of itself is at war with that purpose.

• Six •

Race Discrimination

Paul Brest

THE LEGACY OF THE WARREN COURT

The Warren Court really had it pretty easy. By 1953, when the new chief justice assumed office, the overt racism of the deep South was no longer an American dilemma but was widely perceived as a national moral disaster. Indeed, the first Justice Harlan, a man not otherwise gifted with great insight, had recognized as much a half-century earlier in his biting dissent in *Plessy v. Ferguson.*[1] *Brown v. Board of Education*[2] was a decision whose time was long overdue.

The Court heard surprisingly few race discrimination cases in the fifteen years following *Brown.* A handful of decisions made clear that state-mandated discrimination was unconstitutional, not only in education but in every other sphere as well.[3] The issue of discrimination by private enterprises was more complex. The equal protection clause of the Fourteenth Amendment only provides that "no *state* shall . . . deny to any person within its jurisdiction the equal protection of the laws." However, in an important series of decisions, epitomized by the "sit-in" cases, the Court expanded the so-called state action doctrine to prohibit discrimination by some privately owned restaurants and other places of public accommodation.[4] In effect, it engaged in a holding action until 1964, when Congress enacted the first comprehensive modern civil rights statute. The Court easily sustained Congress's power to pass the Civil Rights Act of 1964,[5] which was soon supplemented by the Voting Rights Act of 1965 and the Fair Housing Act of 1968. And in a surprising decision toward the end of the Warren era, the Supreme Court revitalized the Civil Rights Act of 1866 to prohibit some private discrimination not reached by the modern statutes.[6]

It was the egregious nature of discrimination in the 1950s and 1960s that made life so easy for the Warren Court. The underlying claim in almost every case was that someone—an agency of the state or a large private enterprise—was currently and intentionally discriminating against blacks for no other reason than that they were black. Civil rights in the 1960s was a good guys/bad guys issue (perhaps the last one we shall be blessed with) and there was no doubt which side the Court was on. The legacy of this era—a bequest of the Court, Congress, and courageous civil rights workers and black schoolchildren—was the end of overt, garden-variety discrimination, whether practiced by school boards and voting registrars or private restauranteurs, landlords, and employers.

THE AGENDA FOR THE 1970S

By Warren Burger's second year as chief justice the Court had a new agenda. Two 1971 cases are illustrative. In *Swann v. Charlotte-Mecklenburg Board of Education,*[7] an urban southern school district, formerly segregated by mandate of state law, had begun assigning pupils to the schools nearest their homes. Although the schools remained heavily segregated, the board contended that this was due to residential segregation for which it bore no responsibility and over which it had no control. In *Griggs v. Duke Power Co.,*[8] black employees who were denied advancement because they lacked high school diplomas and had failed a "general intelligence" test given by the employer claimed that these requirements violated Title VII of the Civil Rights Act of 1964 because the adverse impact was felt much more heavily by blacks than whites—even if the employer had not used the test with any intention to discriminate.

These cases present two recurring issues of the first decade of the Burger Court: the desegregation of urban school districts, in the North as well as the South, and the legality of racially discriminatory effects in the absence of discriminatory purpose. A third issue, concerning affirmative action or "reverse" discrimination, emerged only toward the end of the decade and is still not fully resolved.

SCHOOL SEGREGATION

The Rural South

After reaffirming *Brown* in the face of massive southern resistance, the Warren Court left matters entirely to the lower courts to implement its mandate "with all deliberate speed."[9] Only toward the end of Earl Warren's tenure did the Court express its impatience with the pace of school desegregation.[10] And only then, assisted by the sanction (imposed by Title VI of the Civil Rights Act of 1964) of withholding federal funds, did the task of desegregation really get underway.

The last major school decision of the 1960s symbolized the transition from the agenda of the Warren Court to that of the Burger Court and set a tone that for the most part persisted during the following decade.

New Kent County's only two schools had always been segregated by mandate of state law. In 1965, after a desegregation suit was filed and the schools were threatened with the loss of federal funds, the school board adopted a so-called freedom of choice plan under which children could attend the school of their choice. Although blacks and whites were residentially dispersed throughout this small rural county, the schools remained as segregated after implementation of the freedom of choice plan as before. *Green v. New Kent County School Board*[11] unanimously held that the school system was unconstitutionally segregated. Justice Brennan wrote that *Brown* had charged school boards "then operating state-compelled dual systems . . . with the affirmative duty to take whatever steps might be necessary to convert to a unitary system in which racial discrimination would be eliminated root and branch."[12] This affirmative duty could not be met by an assignment scheme that perpetuated years of state-imposed segregation. Rather, the school board must "come forward with a [desegregation] plan that promises . . . realistically to work *now*."[13] The clear implication was that whether a plan "worked" depended on whether it in fact produced racially integrated schools.

Although Justice Rehnquist was later to charge that *Green* was a "drastic extension of *Brown*,"[14] it was hardly a radical decision on the facts of the case. The existing segregation could not plausibly be attributed to anything but the district's long history of de jure segregation, nor could the school board's tenacious adherence to so expensive and inefficient a method of pupil assignment as freedom of choice be explained by anything other than its desire to maintain segregation. In any case, it is fanciful to suppose that choices could have been entirely "free" under the circumstances in New Kent County.

Nonetheless, Justice Rehnquist's charge was not wholly unfounded. *Green* only required the school board to undo the present effects of past de jure segregation. By judging the adequacy of a desegregation plan in terms of its actual results, however, the Court exposed an inevitable tension between its commitment to remedying de jure segregation and its refusal to declare de facto segregation unconstitutional.

De Jure v. De Facto Segregation

Whether segregation is de jure or de facto depends, simply, on whether the state, through legislative action or the administrative decisions of school officials, has taken race into account in making decisions affecting the assignment of pupils to schools. Segregation is de jure to the extent that it is the result of race-conscious decisions, and de facto to the extent that it is not.

The most obvious form of de jure segregation, prevalent throughout the South when *Brown* was decided, was racial separation explicitly required by state statutes. But segregation brought about through *covert* race-conscious decisions, where, for example, a school board gerrymanders attendance zones, is also de jure. Segregation not the result of race-conscious decisions is, by definition, de facto or adventitious.

The Court's holding de jure but not de facto segregation unconstitutional is only a particular instance of the more general notion that the evil of discrimination inheres in the *prejudice* underlying a legislature's or an official's decision to classify people based on their race. Although citizens must bear the incidental burdens of all sorts of government decisions, no one must suffer the stigmatic and material injury inflicted by a decision based on racial prejudice. Though the opinion in *Brown* was couched in terms of educational opportunity, its central statement was not about education but about intentional racial segregation: "To separate [children] from others of similar age and qualifications solely because of their race generates a feeling of racial inferiority as to their status in the community that may affect their hearts and minds in a way unlikely ever to be undone."[15] This explains both why the Court so casually extended *Brown* beyond schools to prohibit de jure segregation of all sorts and why the Court has not read it to prohibit de facto school segregation.

The Burger Court Begins: The Urban South

In the Burger Court's first major school decision—and the Court's last unanimous one—the new chief justice applied the principle announced in *Green v. New Kent County School Board* to a large urban district in the South. Until well after *Brown* the Charlotte-Mecklenburg district had been de jure segregated. Now pupils were assigned to neighborhood schools, and the system was still segregated. The board of education claimed that this was wholly adventitious—the result of residential segregation—and not traceable to its past unconstitutional acts.

The Court disagreed. Writing for the majority in *Swann v. Charlotte-Mecklenburg Board of Education*,[16] the chief justice responded that because "[p]eople gravitate toward school facilities," present residential patterns might be the result of the school board's past decisions to build and locate segregated schools.[17] Creating a strong, practically irrebuttable presumption that existing segregation was the result of past misconduct, the Court affirmed the district court's order requiring the board to alter attendance zones and transport pupils throughout the district with the goal of achieving a racial mix at each school that approximated the composition of the district as a whole. The presumption was surely unrealistic. As Justice Powell later remarked:

> In imposing on metropolitan southern school districts an affirmative duty, entailing large-scale transportation of pupils to eliminate segregation in the schools, the Court required these districts to alleviate conditions which in large part did *not* result from historic, state-imposed *de jure* segregation. Rather, the familiar root cause of segregated schools in *all* the biracial metropolitan areas of our country is essentially the same: one of segregated residential and migratory patterns, the impact of which on the racial composition of the schools was

often perpetuated and rarely ameliorated by action of public school authorities. This is a national, not a southern, phenomenon. And it is largely unrelated to whether a particular State had or did not have segregative school laws.[18]

Swann was decided in the face of the Nixon administration's strong anti-busing views—views shared by Warren Burger. To understand the inconsistency of his supporting so strong a probusing decision, one need only consider (as he must have) the symbolism of the new chief justice breaking the Court's tradition of unanimity in school desegregation. He probably assigned the opinion to himself both to capture the image of leadership that Earl Warren had gained when he authored *Brown* seventeen years earlier and to exercise such control as he could over the result. He did not succeed in either respect.[19]

Desegregation Moves North

The Court's united position was precarious in 1971. It fell apart completely two years later in *Keyes v. Denver School District No. 1*,[20] where for the first time the Court confronted a claim that a school system, never segregated by statutory mandate, was nonetheless de jure segregated because of the school board's race-conscious decisions in constructing schools and drawing attendance zones. With Justice White not participating, Justice Brennan wrote for a majority including the Warren Court holdovers, Douglas, Stewart, and Marshall, and one new appointee, Harry Blackmun. Of the other Nixon appointees, Chief Justice Burger concurred in the result, Justice Powell both concurred and dissented in part, and Justice Rehnquist dissented outright.

There was nothing novel in the Court's recognition that covert acts of intentional segregation were unconstitutional. Quite striking, however, was its holding that proof of racial gerrymandering in one corner of the district justified systemwide desegregation.

The district court found that the defendants had deliberately contributed to the segregation of a handful of schools in the northeast Park Hill section of Denver but refused to order desegregation of the inner-city schools in the absence of any proof that they too were segregated because of the board's intentional actions rather than as a result of residential segregation.

Justice Brennan found the district court in error in two respects. First, it had not accounted for the possible spillover effects of intentional segregation in Park Hill on other sections of Denver: unless the school board could establish that the district's geography or natural boundaries divided it into separate and unrelated units, "proof of state-imposed segregation in a substantial portion of the district will suffice to support a finding by the trial court of the existence of a dual system."[21] Second, the district court ignored the evidentiary principle that "a finding of intentionally segregative school board actions in a meaningful portion of a school system . . . creates a presumption that other segregated schooling within the system is not adventitious. It establishes, in other words, a prima facie case of unlawful segregative design on the part of school authorities, and shifts to those authorities the burden of proving that other segregated schools within the system are not also the result of intentionally segregative actions."[22] The case was remanded to the trial court with instruction to desegregate the entire school system unless the board proved that segregation in Park Hill did not contribute to segregation elsewhere in the district and that other segregation was not brought about intentionally.

In the course of his opinion for the Court, Justice Brennan explained that "the differentiating factor between de jure segregation and so-called de facto segregation . . . is *purpose* or *intent* to segregate,"[23] and reasserted that only de jure segregation violates the Constitution. Nonetheless, the practical effect of the presumptions and his generous view of what constitutes a "substantial" or "meaningful" portion of a school district went a long way toward making the de jure/de facto distinction insubstantial and meaningless. With more or less effort one could probably uncover intentional segregatory acts in most American school districts. Thus, the main difference between districts that have been held unconstitutionally segregated and those that have not is the interest, energy, and resources of potential plaintiffs and the sympathies of the trial court.

It was partly out of concern for "uneven and unpredicatable results, . . . protracted and inconclusive litigation, . . . burdens on the federal courts, and . . . serious disruption of individual school systems,"[24] and partly to achieve national uniformity, that Justice Powell suggested that the Court abandon the de facto/de jure distinction entirely and impose a "constitutional obligation . . . [on] school districts throughout our country to operate *integrated school systems*."[25] In a separate opinion in *Keyes* he wrote:

> A system would be integrated in accord with constitutional standards if the responsible authorities had taken appropriate steps to (i) integrate faculties and administration; (ii) scrupulously assure equality of facilities, instruction, and curriculum opportunities throughout the district; (iii) utilize their authority to draw attendance zones to promote integration; and (iv) locate new schools, close old ones, and determine the size and grade categories with this same objective in mind.*[26]

Justice Powell's proposal did not attract any other justices, some of whom wanted more and others—most notably Justice Rehnquist—much less. Justice

---

*Justice Powell also devoted many pages to the charged issue of busing. He urged that courts respect the "legitimate community interests in neighborhood school systems" and that "transportation orders should be applied with special caution to any proposal as disruptive of family life and interests—and ultimately education itself—as extensive transportation of elementary-age children solely for desegregation purposes."[27]

Rehnquist dissented from the Court's most recent applications of the *Keyes* principles in *Columbus Board of Education v. Penick*[28] and *Dayton Board of Education v. Brinkman.*[29]

Although Ohio schools have not been segregated by statutory mandate in the twentieth century, the Court found that portions of the Columbus and Dayton systems were intentionally segregated when *Brown* was decided and held the school boards had not met their affirmative obligations to desegregate. Although there was no proof that the Dayton school board had engaged in any intentional segregation since *Brown*, Justice White wrote for the majority that "[t]he Court of Appeals was . . . justified in utilizing the Board's total failure to fulfill its affirmative duty—and indeed its conduct resulting in increased segregation—to trace the current, systemwide segregation back to the purposefully dual system of the 1950s and to the subsequent acts of intentional discrimination."[30] Justice Stewart, joined by Chief Justice Burger, concurred in the result in *Columbus* but dissented in *Dayton,* based on the district court's findings of continuing intentional segregation in the former but not the latter school system. Justices Powell and Rehnquist dissented in both cases, the latter noting that "the Court's cascade of presumptions . . . sweeps away the distinction between de facto and de jure segregation."[31]

Justice Rehnquist's observation seems accurate. For reasons mentioned above and that will become more apparent in the next section, one can readily understand why the Court has adhered to the doctrinal view that only de jure segregation violates the Constitution. It is more puzzling that a relatively conservative Court in a conservative political environment has continued to press so hard for integrated schools. With many black leaders supporting community control and white liberals wanting to keep their own children in safe middle-class schools, the Court's constituency is problematic. I imagine that an explanation lies partly in an institutional nostalgia for the Court's historical role in the civil rights struggle of the 1950s and 1960s and partly in the hope, for want of anything better, that integrated schools will promote a degree of racial equality.

The Problem of the Suburbs

Whether the Court is simply tilting at windmills depends partly on what alternatives remain open to families who wish to avoid the burdens of integration. The Court made one escape route more difficult by forbidding the states to aid private segregated schools and by construing an old civil rights statute to forbid discrimination by private schools.[32]

A rather different threat to the Court's strong desegregation doctrine is the movement of white middle-class families from the cities to the suburbs. In *Milliken v. Bradley,*[33] the Supreme Court, though not controverting the trial court's findings that the Detroit school system was unconstitutionally segregated and that desegregation of the 64 percent black district would precipitate white flight, nonetheless reversed the lower court's order that would have included the fifty-three surrounding suburban school districts in Detroit's desegregation plan. Chief Justice Burger wrote for the 5-to-4 majority that "the scope of the remedy is determined by the nature and extent of the constitutional violation"[34] and in the absence of proof that interdistrict segregation was the product of race-conscious gerrymandering, the judiciary had no power to cross district lines. Although it would have been easy to extend *Keyes* to create a series of practically irrebuttable presumptions of spillover and bad faith, the Court chose instead to emphasize that "[n]o single tradition in public education is more deeply rooted than local control over the operation of schools; local autonomy has long been thought essential both to the maintenance of community concern and support for public schools and to the quality of the educational process."[35] The issue is not dead, however, and when the Court eventually faces some proof of intentional gerrymandering of interdistrict lines it will have to choose between local autonomy and the *Keyes-Dayton* route.

DISCRIMINATORY INTENT V. DISPROPORTIONATE IMPACT

The de jure/de facto distinction has been a central issue in areas other than school segregation. The illegality of de jure discrimination, such as racially motivated decisions by employers not to hire, or voting officials not to register, minorities, has never been in doubt. But what of the use of employment and voting tests not adopted for discriminatory motives but which have a disproportionate adverse impact on minorities? Here, by contrast to school desegregation doctrine, the Burger Court has sharply distinguished between de jure discrimination and de facto effects, typically holding that while the *Constitution* only prohibits intentional discrimination, various civil rights *statutes* go further and prohibit discriminatory effects as well.

At first glance, *Griggs v. Duke Power Co.*[36] seems as surprising a decision as *Swann* to be authored by President Nixon's new chief justice. This was a suit brought under the employment discrimination provision, Title VII, of the Civil Rights Act of 1964, challenging the company's requirement that applicants for low-level jobs have high school diplomas and pass an intelligence test. The Court of Appeals had upheld the requirements, reading the act to prohibit only racially motivated discrimination and concluding that "there was no showing of a discriminatory purpose in the adoption of the diploma and test requirements."[37] In reversing, Chief Justice Burger wrote:

> [Congress's objective] was to achieve equality of employment opportunities and remove barriers that have operated in the past to favor an identifiable group of white employees over other employees. . . .

Congress directed the thrust of the Act to the *consequences* of employment practices, not simply the motivation. . . .

Nothing in the Act precludes the use of testing or measuring procedures; obviously they are useful. What Congress has forbidden is giving these devices and mechanisms controlling force unless they are demonstrably a reasonable measure of job performance. Congress has not commanded that the less qualified be preferred over the better qualified simply because of minority origins. Far from disparaging job qualifications as such, Congress has made such qualifications the controlling factor, so that race, religion, nationality, and sex become irrelevant.[38]

Griggs presented about as easy a case as one could imagine. The only blacks in the plant were employed as "laborers"—the company's lowest-paid classification. The plaintiffs had sought to advance one grade to the all-white "coal handling" department. The company admitted that it had not even considered the bearing of a high school diploma or intelligence test on these menial jobs. Furthermore, although the chief justice explicitly disclaimed any reliance on intentional discrimination, the plant in fact had a bad history in this respect.

The Court's unanimity in *Griggs* dissolved as it began addressing more subtle issues such as the relevant groups or populations for determining disproportionate racial impact and the burden of proof and standards for validating employment tests.[39] Justices Brennan and Marshall have complained that the standards have been insufficiently demanding.[40] Nonetheless, the basic principle of *Griggs* is alive and reasonably well today, not only in the courts but, of more practical importance, in the regulations of federal funding and contracting agencies.[41]

Griggs was an interpretation of a provision of the Civil Rights Act of 1964. Encouraged by the Court's emphasis on impact rather than intention, civil rights litigants attempted to expand the decision into a *constitutional* prohibition of a variety of governmental practices that disproportionately disadvantaged racial minorities. Ironically, the Court chose another case involving employment tests—one brought under the Constitution rather than under Title VII— to announce that *Griggs* had not changed the essentially intent-oriented character of constitutional antidiscrimination doctrine.

The case was *Washington v. Davis*,[42] in which black applicants challenged a verbal-ability test that had kept them off the District of Columbia police force. Since at the time Title VII did not apply to the federal government, the unsuccessful applicants invoked the Constitution itself. In an opinion by Justice White, the Court first refused to read *Griggs* into the Constitution, and then went on to state that the verbal-ability test was valid even under the Title VII standard.

Justice White reviewed the Court's precedents to conclude that "purpose" or "intent" to discriminate has always been the gravamen of unconstitutional

racial discrimination. He acknowledged that disproportionate impact was
sometimes significant evidence of a concealed discriminatory intent. For
example, the persistent absence of minorities from a government agency's
work force, combined with other evidence, might give rise to such a strong
inference of intentional discrimination as to require the agency to prove,
if it could, that its selection criteria were color-blind. But the ultimate issue
was discriminatory intent, which the Court was not prepared to infer from
the circumstances of this case, where the test was one developed by the
Civil Service Commission and widely used by government agencies; where
there was no evidence of intentional discrimination by the police department,
which, indeed had many black officers; and where the department was
"seeking modestly to upgrade the communicative abilities of its employees
. . . where the job requires special ability to communicate orally and in
writing."[43]

With respect to the underlying issue of doctrine, Justice White explained:

> [W]e have difficulty understanding how a law establishing a racially neutral
> qualification for employment is nevertheless racially discriminatory and denies
> "any person . . . equal protection of the laws" simply because a greater propor-
> tion of Negroes fail to qualify than members of other racial or ethnic groups. . . .
> Respondents, as Negroes, could no more successfully claim that the test denied
> them equal protection than could white applicants who also failed. The con-
> clusion would not be different in the face of proof that more Negroes than
> whites had been disqualified by Test 21. That other Negores also had failed to
> score well would, alone, not demonstrate that respondents individually were
> being denied equal protection of the laws by the application of an otherwise
> valid qualifying test being administered to prospective police recruits.[44]

Justices Brennan and Marshall dissented but only addressed the Court's
discussion of the Title VII standards.

The different results in *Griggs* and *Washington v. Davis* may respond
to several considerations. *Griggs* removed barriers to minority employment
while simultaneously affirming the meritocratic ideal of equal opportunity
for every individual to compete on the basis of ability. Between *Griggs*
and *Washington,* however, lower courts and federal agencies began invalidating employment criteria that seemed intuitively appropriate for the
job. Justice White's incredulous response to the plaintiff's attack on the
police department's verbal-ability test suggests his fear that the *Griggs* standard threatened to subordinate efficiency to the goal of race-conscious distribution of jobs—a program that would not have gained a majority even in
the heyday of the Warren Court.

But there is more than this to *Washington v. Davis*. However stringent
the *Griggs* standard might have been, it was based on a statute limited
to employment practices. The expansive language of the equal protection
clause implies no such limitations, and Justice White was concerned that to

read the *Griggs* principle into the Constitution would threaten every regulation and practice that disproportionately disadvantaged minorities: "A rule that a statute designed to serve neutral ends is nevertheless invalid, absent compelling justification, if in practice it benefits or burdens one race more than another would be far reaching and would raise serious questions about, and perhaps invalidate, a whole range of tax, welfare, public service, regulatory, and licensing statutes that may be more burdensome to the poor and to the average black than to the more affluent white."[45]

Justice White's reading of the constitutional precedents to require proof of discriminatory intent was accurate. The Court lacked a ready-made constitutional theory of discriminatory effects. There were alternatives to its resolution of the issue, but none was easy. The Court might have adopted the novel principle that no racial group may be appreciably worse off than the majority, so that any practice or regulation that contributes to the disparity must be specially justified.[46] This would have been a political statement of enormous magnitude, however, and one in tension with the widely held liberal notion that only individuals and not racial and ethnic groups have moral status.

Alternatively, without deviating from the idea that the Constitution prohibits only intentional discrimination, the Court might have presumed that disproportionate injuries inflicted on minorities even by seemingly "neutral" laws are the result of pervasive, if not specifically identifiable, discrimination against them and others of their race.[47] However, the Court may have sensed that the consequences of such a presumption would be very far-reaching and disruptive. Justice White made the consequences seem especially draconian by suggesting that any practice having a racially disproportionate impact could be upheld only if it had a "compelling justification"—the formidable test for racially motivated decisions. But nothing prevented the Court from fashioning a more modest and flexible standard for racially disproportionate impact. In the end, the Court may simply have boggled at the notion of undertaking the seemingly limitless task of redressing several centuries of discrimination.

The holdings in *Washington v. Davis* and *Griggs* are mirrored in the Court's different treatment of voting discrimination under the Constitution and the Voting Rights Act of 1965. Even within the strongly individualistic tradition of American law, it is generally acknowledged that racial minorities have strong collective political interests. Partly in recognition of this—and partly as a prophylactic against intentional discrimination—the Voting Rights Act of 1965 prohibits certain states and political subdivisions from engaging in practices that have the "effect" of "denying or abridging the right to vote on account of race or color."[48] The Court has vigorously enforced this standard even in the absence of any indication of discriminatory purpose. In *City of Rome v. United States*,[49] for example, it refused to allow the city

to annex some contiguous areas and make various changes in its electoral
system because that would have diluted the power of the black electorate.
On the same day a closely divided Court upheld Mobile, Alabama's at-large
election procedures in the face of evidence that it so diluted the power
of black voters that, though they constituted 35 percent of the population,
no black had ever been elected to the city commission.[50] The *Mobile* case
was brought not under the Voting Rights Act but directly under the Fourteenth and Fifteenth Amendments, and the Court held that in the absence
of proof of discriminatory intent, these facts did not state a constitutional
claim.

In *Washington v. Davis,* Justice White went out of his way to disapprove
of lower court decisions holding racially disproportionate impact unconstitutional in a variety of areas. The following year, in *Village of Arlington
Heights v. Metropolitan Housing Dev. Corp.,*[51] the Court found no constitutional problem with a Chicago suburb's single-family zoning requirement
that effectively excluded blacks. Thus, although the Burger Court remains
willing to construe some important federal statutes to prohibit disproportionate racial impact, the current doctrine is that only de jure discrimination violates the Constitution.

AFFIRMATIVE ACTION OR REVERSE DISCRIMINATION

It should not be surprising that there is no neutral title for this section:
it concerns an issue about which few people are neutral. The emotions
evoked by the topic explain, though hardly justify, the Court's unhelp-
ful, fragmented opinions in the *Regents of the University of California
v. Bakke.*[52]

The medical school at the University of California at Davis set aside
16 of the 100 places in each class for minorities, who were admitted with
lower scores than many rejected nonminority students. Alan Bakke, a white
applicant, had credentials that brought him close to admission as a regular
candidate and would easily have assured his admission as a black, Chicano,
Asian, or native American. In an action brought in state court, the Supreme
Court of California held that under the equal protection clause "no applicant
may be rejected because of his race, in favor of another who is less qualified, as measured by standards applied without regard to race."[53] It invalidated the preferential admission program, ordered the medical school to
admit Bakke, and prohibited the school from considering the race of any
applicant in the future. The United States Supreme Court heard and decided
the case, with the following results:

Justice Stevens, in an opinion joined by Chief Justice Burger and Justices
Stewart and Rehnquist, completely avoided discussing the constitutional
question and considered only the school's obligations under Title VI of the

Civil Rights Act of 1964, which provides that "No person in the United States shall, on the ground of race, color, or national origin, be excluded from participation in, be denied the benefits of, or be subjected to discrimination under any program or activity receiving Federal financial assistance." Without deciding whether Title VI precludes any consideration of race in the admissions process, Justice Stevens concluded that the Davis quota system violated the statute.

Justice Brennan, in an opinion joined by Justices White, Marshall, and Blackmun, concluded that Davis's admissions scheme did not violate either the equal protection clause or Title VI (which he believed "prohibits only those uses of racial criteria that would violate the Fourteenth Amendment."[54]).

Justice Powell held the swing vote. He agreed with Justice Brennan's equation of Title VI and the equal protection clause. Although he concluded that Davis's fixed quota system was unlawful, he explicitly stated that a school could take race into account as one factor bearing on admission.

This is not the place to undertake a detailed analysis of Title VI . My own reading of the provision comports with Justices Brennan's and Powell's: when Congress enacted the Civil Rights Act of 1964, judicial enforcement of the Fourteenth Amendment was the only game in town. The sanction of withholding funds was not designed to alter the judicially developed antidiscrimination standard but rather to enforce it more effectively and extend it to private discrimination. The really difficult question in *Bakke* was what the constitutional standard should be—and in particular whether reverse discrimination should be treated in the same way as discrimination against disadvantaged racial minorities.

Justice Powell noted that the Court's precedents condemned racial discrimination without qualification, and he repeatedly emphasized the *individual* nature of the right not to be discriminated against. He therefore invoked the traditional, almost impossibly demanding standard of so-called strict scrutiny: a racial classification is constitutionally permissible only if it is necessary to accomplish a compelling state purpose.

Justice Brennan, though conceding that even benignly motivated racial classifications might treat individuals unfairly based on immutable traits, argued that a preferential admissions program did not inflict the unique injury of traditional discrimination: it did not "stereotype and stigmatize politically powerless segments of society."[55] Therefore, he would have applied a more lenient standard of review than strict scrutiny: racial classifications designed to further remedial purposes "must serve important governmental objectives and must be substantially related to achievement of those objectives."[56]

Thus, one fundamental issue raised by *Bakke* is the underlying *purpose* of the constitutional prohibition of race discrimination. Justice Powell viewed the antidiscrimination principle as a kind of "merit" principle: every individual has the personal right to be treated based on her qualifications for a position, and an institution must define its qualifications so that, at least in theory, everyone has a chance to compete regardless of race. For Justice Brennan the equal protection clause is more narrowly concerned with the unique injuries that discrimination inflicts on its victim. While the stigma of being labeled inferior is not the only injury, it is an intrinsic and special evil of traditional racial discrimination and is largley absent from reverse discrimination. One may quibble about whether the minorities who gain from preferential admission also suffer some stigma as a consequence, but the real complaint against such programs arises from the frustration and anger of the nonpreferred applicants who lose out to a less "meritorious" minority applicant. This is quite different from racial stigma, however. Even when the nonpreferred "nonminority" is himself the member of an identifiable ethnic minority, he is not singled out because of his minority status but is, on the contrary, treated as part of the large undifferentiated majority of the nonpreferred.

Justice Brennan's position is supported by another consideration related to stigma and, in my view, even more fundamental. Every legislative and administrative decision imposes burdens unrelated to the individual's merit or desert. This is an inevitable cost of living in a complex modern society, and for the most part the Constitution leaves the allocation of benefits and burdens to policymakers. That, indeed, is what policymaking consists of. But in our moral and political system it is unacceptable for a policymaker to impose a burden on individuals simply because of *prejudice* against their racial or ethnic membership. The nearly impossible hurdle of "strict scrutiny" is designed to eliminate decisions based on prejudice. Where the group singled out for harmful treatment is inadequately represented in the legislature, the judiciary plays a special role in protecting it from injuries inflicted by a prejudicial or willfully indifferent majority. But so long as the legislature, or, in this case, the University Board of Regents, is not singling out particular minority groups for *disadvantageous* treatment, it is not clear why the standard of judicial review should be particularly high.

Ironically, although Justice Powell invoked the strictest standard of judicial scrutiny, he did not apply it. This becomes clear as we turn to his discussion of the rationales that might support a preferential admissions program.

One obvious rationale for preferential admissions is to remedy past discrimination against minorities. Justice Brennan would have upheld Davis's program on this ground. Justice Powell did not disagree with the rationale but asserted that only a court, legislature, or an agency with broader responsibilities than the regents of the University of California had authority to determine the extent of unlawful societal discrimination and to compensate for it. His view seems to reflect doubts about the responsiveness and perhaps the responsibleness of the university. Beginning with a somewhat exaggerated characterization of the precedents, Justice Powell wrote.

We have never approved a classification that aids persons perceived as members of relatively victimized groups at the expense of other innocent individuals in the absence of judicial, legislative, or administrative findings of constitutional or statutory violations. . . . After such findings have been made, the governmental interest in preferring members of the injured groups at the expense of others is substantial, since the legal rights of the victims must be vindicated. In such a case, the extent of the injury and the consquent remedy will have been judicially, legislatively, or administratively defined. Also, the remedial action usually remains subject to continuing oversight to assure that it will work the least harm possible to other innocent persons competing for the benefit. Without such findings of constitutional or statutory violations, it cannot be said that the government has any greater interest in helping one individual than in refraining from harming another. Thus, the government has no compelling justification for inflicting such harm.

Petitioner does not purport to have made, and is in no position to make, such findings. Its broad mission is education, not the formulation of any legislative policy or the adjudication of particular claims of illegality.[57]

The one rationale that appealed to Justice Powell was the university's asserted interest in promoting diversity for educational purposes—a matter about which it could reasonably claim some expertise. Justice Powell deemed "compelling" the medical school's concern that its students have diverse "experiences, outlooks and ideas that enrich the training of its student body and better equip its graduates to render with understanding their vital service to humanity."[58] But he thought the Davis plan, which focused "*solely* on ethnic diversity, would hinder rather than further the attainment of genuine diversity."[59] Although being a member of a minority race could be counted a "plus," an admissions program aimed at diversity must also consider such qualities as "exceptional personal talents, unique work or service experience, leadership potential, maturity, demonstrated compassion, a history of overcoming disadvantage, ability to communicate with the poor, or other qualifications deemed important."[60] A program of this sort, Justice Powell asserted, is not merely "a subtle and more sophisticated . . . means of according racial preference."[61] It differs from a quota because it

treats each applicant as an individual in the admissions process. The applicant who loses out on the last available seat to another candidate receiving a "plus" on the basis of ethnic background will not have been foreclosed from all consideration for that seat simply because he was not the right color or had the wrong surname. It would mean only that his combined qualifications, which may have included similar nonobjective factors, did not outweigh those of the other applicant. His qualifications would have been weighed fairly and competitively, and he would have no basis to complain of unequal treatment under the Fourteenth Amendment.[62]

All of this strikes me as nonsense. First of all, a university genuinely striving for diversity might properly conclude, on the basis of its experience, that its normal admissions process will produce a class sufficiently diverse in every respect except race. Second, and more troublesome, Justice Powell's supposed reconciliation of a race-conscious admissions policy with the notion that applicants must be treated as individuals is illusory. Admission to a medical school is a zero-sum game. If someone's race has played any role in his favor then someone else has been disadvantaged because she is not of that race. I do not believe this is unconstitutional. I do think that the Court—whose only justification for meddling in the affairs of other institutions is that its judgments are grounded in principle rather than political expediency—should have forthrightly confronted the central issue that the case presented. While the failure of principle or nerve or vision was not Justice Powell's alone, it is unfortunate that the Court allowed his ambivalent, obfuscatory, and inconclusive opinion to stand as the common denominator on such an important issue.

The status of benign race-consciousness thus remains unclear. It is *required* as a remedy for past de jure school segregation. It is sometimes permitted and sometimes required—even in the absence of intentional discrimination—to avoid diluting minority voting strength.[63] Like preferential admissions, the issue of preferential employment remains unresolved.

Shortly before *Bakke*, a divided Court held that the more or less identifiable victims of an employer's past discrimination were entitled to retroactive seniority under Title VII, even though this advanced them over incumbent employees with greater seniority.[64] Chief Justice Burger and Justices Powell and Rehnquist argued in dissent that the incumbents' legitimate expectations should be protected. One year after *Bakke,* in *Steelworkers Union v. Weber,*[65] Justice Brennan wrote for a 5-to-2 majority[66] upholding a controversial affirmative action plan adopted by the Kaiser Aluminum & Chemical Company and the United Steelworkers Union (USWA). The plan was designed to "eliminate conspicuous racial imbalance" in the company's 98 percent white craft work force by creating an in-plant craft training program and reserving 50 percent of its openings for blacks until the percentage of black workers was commensurate with their percentage in the local labor force. Brian Weber, a white worker whose application for the training program was passed over in favor of blacks with less seniority, sued to invalidate the racial quota, arguing that it violated Title VII of the Civil Rights Act of 1964. Sections 703(a) and (d) of the Act forbid employment "discrimination . . . because of . . . race." Moreover, section 703(j) states that the act does not "require any employer . . . to grant preferential treatment . . . because of race." Weber relied on these provisions and on a unanimous 1976 decision holding that the act prohibits discrimination against whites as well as blacks.[67]

"The only question before us," wrote Justice Brennan, "is the narrow statutory issue of whether Title VII *forbids* private employers and unions from voluntarily agreeing upon bona fide affirmative action plans that accord racial preferences in the manner and for the purpose provided in the Kaiser-USWA plan."[68] Reviewing the legislative history, he noted that Title VII was motivated by a concern for the unemployment and underemployment of blacks, which the Kaiser-USWA plan was designed to remedy. The voluntary plan was consistent with section 703(j), which did not forbid preferential treatment but only clarified that the act did not require it. "It would be ironic," he wrote, "if a law triggered by a Nation's concern over centuries of racial injustice and intended to improve the lot of those who had 'been excluded from the American dream for so long' . . . constituted the first legislative prohibition of all voluntary, private, race-conscious efforts to abolish traditional patterns of racial segregation and hierarchy."[69]

Justice Rehnquist wrote a passionate dissent, arguing that the decision flew in the face of both the language and legislative history of the act. He was joined by Chief Justice Burger, who also wrote a brief dissent of his own.

Weber is likely to have considerable impact on employment discrimination litigation and, equally important, on the "voluntary" adoption of affirmative action plans to avoid litigation. But it is a cautious decision. Justice Brennan emphasized that the Kaiser-USWA plan "does not unnecessarily trammel the interests of the white employees. The plan does not require the discharge of white workers, and their replacement with new black hirees. . . . Nor does the plan create an absolute bar to the advancement of white employees; half of those trained in the program will be white. Moreover, the plan is a temporary measure; it is not intended to maintain racial balance, but simply to eliminate a manifest racial imbalance."[70]

Because the plan at issue was voluntarily adopted by a private employer, *Weber* was decided solely on statutory grounds. Justice Powell was one of the five justices in *Bakke* to hold that Title VI of the Civil Rights Act of 1964 was no more restrictive of reverse discrimination than the Fourteenth Amendment, but he did not participate in *Weber*. Although his views in *Bakke* imply that he may be unenthusiastic about *Weber* as either statutory or constitutional law, his opinion in *Fullilove v. Klutznick*[71] makes it hazardous to predict his vote in future reverse discrimination cases.

Fullilove, decided on the last day of the Supreme Court's 1979 term, was a suit brought by various contractors' associations challenging the "minority business enterprise" (MBE) provision of the Public Works Employment Act of 1977, which requires that 10 percent of federal funds granted for local public works projects must be used to procure services or supplies from businesses owned by minorities. The legislative history evinced the concern that difficulties confronting minority contractors—such as lack of working capital, inability to meet bonding requirements, and unfamiliarity with bidding opportunities and procedures—were often the results of past discrimination. The MBE provision therefore contemplates that MBEs may be awarded subcontracts even when they are not the lowest bidder if the bids are reasonable and arguably inflated as a result of past discrimination.

The Court upheld the provision by a margin of 6 to 3, without a majority opinion. Chief Justice Burger wrote an opinion supporting the judgment, which was joined by Justices White and Powell. Without articulating the standard he was applying, he wrote that the objective of ameliorating past discrimination was legitimate, the Congress was not automatically forbidden to use racial criteria to achieve this end, that the burden on the complainants was "relatively light," and that "[w]hen effectuating a limited and properly tailored remedy to cure the effects of prior discrimination, such a 'sharing of the burden' by innocent parties is not impermissible." The chief justice cited *Bakke* only in the last paragaph, disclaiming any reliance on its "formulas of analysis" but asserting that the MBE provision "would survive judicial review under either 'test' articulated in the several *Bakke* opinions."

In a separate opinion, Justice Powell gently chided the chief justice for failing "to articulate judicial standards of review in conventional terms," and went on to apply the analysis set forth in his opinion in *Bakke*. Congress, in contrast to the Regents, was competent to make findings of unlawful discrimination and to pursue the "compelling" objective of remedying it. The only question remaining was whether the means chosen were necessary. Though the term "necessary," as applied to racial classifications, has denoted a very demanding standard, Justice Powell implicitly redefined it more leniently: "Congress' choice of a remedy should be upheld . . . if the means selected are equitable and reasonably necessary to the redress of identifiable discrimination."[72]

Justices Marshall, Brennan, and Blackmun, simply adopted their analysis in *Bakke*: The MBE provision was permissible because it substantially served important governmental objectives.

In a dissent joined by Justice Rehnquist, Justice Stewart initially suggested that the Constitution required governmental color blindness but later indicated that a race-conscious remedy was permissible if "its sole purpose is to eradicate the actual effects of illegal race discrimination." He thought that the MBE provision went beyond this because it sought "racial balance as a goal in and of itself" and "may have been enacted to compensate for the effects of social, educational, and economic 'disadvantage.'"

Justice Stevens wrote a separate dissent, taking a quite different approach. Noting that Congress had scarcely considered the MBE provision, he indicated that whatever deference he might accord a congressional judgment that reverse discrimination was necessary depended on Congress's having actually considered the issue and the possibility of achieving its objectives through less drastic means. The MBE provision "simply raises too many serious questions that Congress failed to answer or even to address in a responsible way."

At this writing, then, Justices Brennan and Marshall on the one side and Justice Rehnquist on the other have clearly articulated, opposed positions, while a majority of the Court continues to grope for intermediate grounds. The most interesting doctrinal development is the focus on the *process* by which affirmative action policies are made—Justice Powell's concern that the agency making the policy be competent and authorized to do so, and Justice Steven's demand for evidence that it have actually considered the interests at stake and the possibilities for accommodating them. We shall simply have to wait to see whether any position eventually gains a solid majority.

• Seven •

The Burger Court's Grapplings
with Sex Discrimination

Ruth Bader Ginsburg

THE OLD LINE BROKEN, SOME NEW LINES DRAWN

Evening up the rights, responsibilities, and opportunities of men and women
was not on the agenda of the Warren Court. Although that Court uncabined
the equal protection guarantee in diverse settings, sex discrimination was
an area in which no change occurred in the 1950s and 1960s. From the
1860s until 1971, the record remained unbroken: the Supreme Court rejected
virtually every effort to overturn sex lines in the law. Without offense to
the Constitution, women could be kept off juries,[1] and they could be barred
from a range of occupations, from law to bartending.[2]

The Court explained its position lucidly and without frills in a 1947
opinion, *Fay v. New York*.[3] Through ratification of the Nineteenth Amendment in 1920, the Court observed, women achieved the vote, but only that;
in other respects, the Constitution remained an empty cupboard for sex
equality claims. Justice Jackson wrote for the Court's majority: "The contention that women should be on the jury is not based on the Constitution,
it is based on a changing view of the rights and responsibilities of women
in our public life, which has progressed in all phases of life, including jury
duty, but has achieved constitutional compulsion on the states only in the
grant of the franchise by the nineteenth amendment."[4] Nearly a decade and
a half later, in *Hoyt v. Florida*,[5] a unanimous Warren Court reaffirmed
that jury service by women was a matter left largely to the states. As
the principal opinion reasoned, a volunteers-only system for females encountered no constitutional shoal, for it was rational to spare women from
the obligation to serve in recognition of their place at "the center of home
and family life."[6]

In contrast to the record of its predecessors, the Burger Court's performance has been striking. Although High Court decisions in this area
do not form an altogether even pattern, opinions in gender discrimination
cases were atypical of a Court sometimes typed as restrained or noninter-
ventionist. Sex, not unlike race, the Burger Court acknowledged, has traditionally been "the touchstone for pervasive and often subtle discrimination."[7] Hence, official resort to an explicit gender criterion ordinarily "would
require an exceedingly persuasive justification"[8] to withstand constitutional

challenge. Under the invigorated review standard evolved by the Burger Court, overt sex classifications were invalidated in a variety of contexts, from estate administration (*Reed v. Reed* in 1971)[9] to social welfare measures (*Califano v. Westcott* in 1979).[10]

Several of the cases women pressed in the 1970s involved less crystalline categorization: laws that placed women at a disadvantage, or restricted their choices, but did not explicitly invoke a sex criterion figured in some of the most difficult and turbulent controversies the Court entertained. In these cases, the Burger Court vacillated from bold stroke to deferential decision.[11]

EXPLICITLY GENDER-BASED CLASSIFICATION

Through the 1960s, the Supreme Court explained its equal protection rulings in terms of a two-tier model.[12] In the generality of cases, challenged legislation was ranked at the lower tier and survived judicial inspection if *rationally related* to a *permissible* governmental objective.[13] Exceptional cases, ranged on the upper tier, involved rights denominated *fundamental* (voting is a prime example)[14] or classifications labeled *suspect* (race is the paradigm).[15] Review in these exceptional cases was rigorous. To survive inspection, the legislative objective had to be *compelling,* and the classification *necessary* to its accomplishment.

Equal protection adjudication in fact is not so cleanly bifurcated, several commentators,[16] lower courts,[17] and even individual justices[18] observed at the start of the 1970s. Some decisions appeared to be governed by "in between" standards. Most notably, as the decade wore on, sex-based classification inched up to a place at or above the midpoint of the two tiers.[19]

The Turning Point: *Reed* and *Stanley*

Elevation of sex discrimination on the equal protection spectrum commenced with *Reed v. Reed* in 1971.[20] Chief Justice Burger announced for a unanimous Court that an Idaho estate administration statute, giving men preference over similarly situated women, denied would-be administrator Sally Reed the equal protection of the laws. The *Reed* decision attracted headlines; it marked the first solid break from the Supreme Court's consistent affirmation of governmental authority to classify by sex. The terse *Reed* opinion acknowledged no departure from precedent, but Court-watchers recognized that something new was in the wind.[21]

Two signals from Congress preceded the turning-point *Reed* decision: The Equal Pay Act (1963)[22] and Title VII of the Civil Rights Act of 1964,[23] the latter prohibiting discrimination on the basis of an individual's race, religion, national origin, or sex, in hiring, firing, and all terms and conditions of employment. Also in the background, the proposed equal rights amendment[24] was vibrant in Congress. These legislative developments

heightened public awareness of the adversely discriminatory conditions
women encountered in the job market. Attention to laws and practices that
limited women's opportunities made it difficult for jurists to repeat the
traditional supposition—that differential treatment of the sexes invariably
operated benignly in woman's favor, placing her not at the "back of the
bus," but on a pedestal.[25]

Several months before Sally Reed's appeal was heard, the first Title VII
gender discrimination case to reach the Supreme Court was decided in complainant's favor. In *Phillips v. Martin Marietta Corp.*,[26] the Court held that
an employer willing to hire fathers, but not mothers, of preschool children,
engaged in sex discrimination within the compass of Title VII. "Arguably,"
the Court said in dictum, a defense might be available to the employer
under the bona fide occupational qualification (bfoq) exception to Title
VII's sex discrimination ban. Perhaps Martin Marietta could prevail, the
per curiam opinion ventured, upon proof that "conflicting family obligations
[are] demonstrably more relevant to job performance for a woman than for
a man."[27] Six years later, however, as the Court's understanding evolved,
that dictum was effectively withdrawn. In *Dothard v. Rawlinson* (1977),[28]
the Court emphasized that, to assure effective application of Title VII's
nondiscrimination principle, the bfoq exception must be tightly contained.
(However, the Court found *Dothard* presented the rare situation in which
the exception applied. It held male gender a bfoq for "contact" guard positions in the "jungle atmosphere" of Alabama's violent, overcrowded, under-
staffed male maximum security penitentiaries.)

If *Phillips v. Martin Marietta Corp.* helped turn the Court in the direction
taken in *Reed*, a more problematic case, *Stanley v. Illinois*,[29] argued the same
day as *Reed*, clouded the way. It opened the question, does the equal
protection principle operate with the very same bite when men rather than
women complain of gender-based discrimination? *Stanley* raised this issue:
May a state deny to an unwed father, who had intermittently lived with
and supported his children, a presumed right to custody after the death of
the mother? Dividing 4 to 1 to 2, the Court ruled for the father, but
avoided the principal equal protection argument tendered by Stanley's counsel. Due process, the Court said, required a fair hearing for Peter Stanley
before the state could deny him parental status. The Court did not hold,
as Stanley invited it to, that unwed fathers stand even with mothers and
wed fathers when child custody is the issue.

In 1978, in *Quilloin v. Walcott*,[30] a unanimous Court held that an unwed
father who "has never exercised actual or legal custody over his child" had
no constitutional right to block adoption approved by the mother. But the
next year, in *Caban v. Mohammed*,[31] the Court ruled 5 to 4 that a state
statute discriminates on the basis of sex in violation of equal protection
when it permits adoption of a child born out of wedlock based solely

on the mother's consent, even when the father's parental relationship with the child is substantial. The same day, with Justice Powell casting the swing vote, the 5 to 4 lineup turned against an unwed father seeking to recover for the wrongful death of a child killed, along with the mother, in an automobile accident. The Court, in *Parham v. Hughes*,[32] held it permissible for the state to condition the unwed father's right upon his legitimation of the child by court order. The main theme of the opinion had been sounded in earlier Burger Court decisions: women and men were not similarly situated for the purpose at hand—maternity is rarely in doubt, but proof of paternity is often difficult, hence the state may erect safeguards against spurious filiation claims.[33]

A Near Great Leap Forward: *Frontiero v. Richardson*

In 1973, less than a year and a half after the laconic *Reed* decision, the Court came within one vote of declaring sex a suspect category. In *Frontiero v. Richardson*,[34] the justices held 8 to 1 that married women in the uniformed services were entitled the same fringe benefits as married men. Under the laws declared unconstitutional, men received a housing allowance and health care for their civilian wives automatically; women received these family benefits only if they supplied all their own support plus over half of their civilian husband's, in other words, over three-fourths of the couple's support.

Essentially, *Frontiero* was an equal pay case. A constitutional attack was mounted because the federal statutes prohibiting sex discrimination with respect to compensation, the Equal Pay Act and Title VII, do not apply to the military. Four of the justices, in a plurality opinion written by Justice Brennan, ranked sex a suspect criterion, entitled to the close review the Court gives above all to race discrimination, but also to discrimination based on national origin. Four, however, is one vote shy of a Supreme Court majority. Perhaps indicating that the plurality moved too swiftly too soon, no fifth vote has emerged for explicit placement of sex at the top tier of equal protection analysis.

Justice Powell, concurring in *Frontiero*,[35] identified a prime source of the reticence exhibited by five of the justices. It is unalterable historic fact that our eighteenth- and nineteenth-century Constitution-makers evidenced no concern at all about the equality of men and women before the law. The Court must tread lightly, Justice Powell cautioned, when it enters the gray zone between constitutional interpretation, a proper judicial task, and constitutional amendment, a job for the people's elected representatives.

Despite the absence of a majority opinion, the 8 to 1 *Frontiero* judgment was a notable way-paver. First, the Court did not invalidate the flawed legislation; it repaired the congressional product. Congress provided benefits for the military man's family. The Court evened out the arrangement; in effect, it extended the same benefits to families in which the service member was female. Second, in contrast to the obsolescent Idaho estate administration statute that figured in *Reed*, a nineteenth-century hangover repealed prospectively months before the Court heard Sally Reed's appeal, post–World War II legislation was at issue in *Frontiero*.

Most significantly, the statutes involved in *Frontiero* drew the gender line found more frequently than any other in federal and state legislation. Wives were deemed dependent regardless of their own economic circumstances. Husbands were ranked independent unless they contributed less than one-fourth of the couple's support. In disallowing resort to this particular stereotype in the context of military personnel benefits, where the cost of upward equalization was in fact minimal,[36] the Court set the stage for its subsequent disallowance of the stereotype in a setting—social security benefits[37]—where the price tag for upward equalization could run many hundreds of millions of dollars.

Backsliding or Best of Both Worlds: *Kahn* and *Ballard*

The *Reed-Frontiero* break from a century's precedent was not altogether clear and clean. The historic explanation for sex discrimination recaptured the Court in the next two confrontations, when men challenged laws that, at least on the surface, favored women: *Kahn v. Shevin* (1974),[38] and *Schlesinger v. Ballard* (1975).[39]

Kahn v. Shevin upheld a Florida real property tax exemption law, first enacted in 1885, providing what amounted to a $15.00 annual saving for widows, along with the blind and the totally disabled.[40] Mel Kahn, seeking the same tax break for widowed men, urged skepticism of the "benign preference" rationale Florida tendered for a provision passed decades before women achieved the franchise. The sex classification expressed the lawmakers' view that a wife's death is less significant to the family than the death of a husband, widower Kahn argued. The cumulative effect of laws of that age and genre, he said, was to reinforce practices and attitudes that restrict women's opportunities.

The afternoon following conclusion of oral argument in *Kahn,* the Court heard *DeFunis v. Odegaard*,[41] in which a white applicant to the University of Washington Law School claimed he had been denied the right to have his application considered in a racially neutral manner. The juxtaposition of *Kahn* and *DeFunis* may have influenced the votes of some of the justices in *Kahn*. It was not a propitious moment for acceptance of Sara Grimke's 1837 plea: "I ask no favors for my sex, I surrender not our claim to equality. All I ask of our brethren, is that they . . . take their feet . . . off our necks. . . ."[42] Only one of the justices (White) was prepared to declare any gender-based tax exemption unconstitutional. Two (Brennan and Marshall) would have upheld Florida's widows-only exemption, if only it had excluded affluent widows by including an income test. Six held the exemption a fair means of compensating lone women for the disadvantages they bear in economic endeavor. The exemption, as the Court appraised it, was genuinely "benign"—it helped some women and harmed none.

Following on the heels of *Kahn, Schlesinger v. Ballard*[43] was a tangled, idiosyncratic case. The Court ruled (5 to 4) that it was not a denial of equal protection to hold a male naval officer to a strict "up or out" system (out when twice passed over for promotion), while guaranteeing a female officer thirteen years before mandatory discharge for lack of promotion. Lt. Ballard had served seven years as an enlisted member. Tacking this period to a thirteen-year officer term, he would have qualified for a navy pension. Under the "up or out" system, his total service, some sixteen years, was insufficient to entitle him to a pension.

Lt. Ballard's case tendered a problem peculiarly resistent to judicial solution. The Court was asked to screen in isolation, and riveted to Lt. Ballard's special situation, a small piece of a large, complex puzzle. Well past 1975, sex-based differentials riddled the rules governing military service entrance, promotion, discharge, and retirement.[44] Many of these differentials favored men, providing them opportunities for education, training, experience, and advancement denied to women. Even the differential Lt. Ballard challenged had been viewed by some female officers as working in the typical case to the advantage of men and to the disadvantage of women.[45] The woman officer who wished to leave short of thirteen years would not be entitled to severance pay. And mandatory discharge at the thirteen-year mark would not bring her even close to the twenty years of service she needed to qualify for a navy pension. The male officer discharged, generally after nine years, under the "up or out" system would get severance pay and start up the ladder in a new career some four years earlier than his female counterpart.

Kahn and *Ballard* were greeted by some in a Panglossian manner. The decisions could be viewed as offering women the best of all possible worlds— a High Court ready to strike down classifications that discriminate against females, yet vigilant to preserve laws that prefer or favor them.[46] But the classification in *Kahn* was barely distinguishable from other products of paternalistic legislators who regarded the husband more as his wife's guardian than as her peer. And in *Ballard*, neither contender challenged the anterior discrimination responsible for promotion of men more rapidly than women— the drastically curtailed opportunities and assignments available to navy women. (Three and a half years later, in 1978, a federal district court held unconstitutional the law that prohibited assigning navy women to sea duty.[47] The government did not appeal that decision.)

Role Typing Spotlighted: *Taylor, Wiesenfeld,* and *Stanton*

Following retrenchment, or at least line-holding, in *Kahn* and *Ballard,* the Court moved forward again. First to fall in 1975 was Louisiana's former jury selection system, a system virtually identical to the scheme upheld by a unanimous Warren Court in 1961 in *Hoyt v. Florida.*[48] *Taylor v. Louisiana*[49] rejected as archaic and overbroad the exclusion of all women from jury duty save those who volunteered. "Weightier reasons" than those accepted in *Hoyt* were demanded by eight justices in *Taylor* because defendant's Sixth Amendment right (to a jury pool drawn from a fair cross section of the community) was implicated. Sixth Amendment incorporation into the Fourteenth Amendment's due process clause occurred in *Duncan v. Louisiana* in 1968,[50] seven years too late to aid Ms. Hoyt in her plea for women in the pool from which jurors would be selected to hear charges that she had murdered her husband.

Missouri misread *Taylor*'s message and had to be told again. In January 1979, in *Duren v. Missouri,*[51] the Supreme Court held unconstitutional that state's exemption of "any woman" from jury service. (The system invalidated in *Taylor* allowed women to opt in. The variant rejected in *Duren* permitted women to opt out.) *Taylor,* because it departed from prior holdings, was held not retroactive. *Duren,* because it followed from *Taylor,* was held applicable retroactively, giving Kansas City prosecutors, defense attorneys, and criminal court judges considerable business to be redone. In *Duren,* as in *Taylor* and *Frontiero,* Justice Rehnquist was the sole dissenter.

Two months after *Taylor v. Louisiana,* the Court announced a unanimous judgment invalidating the first of several social security sex lines removed by court decree. The case was *Weinberger v. Wiesenfeld,*[52] brought by a young widower whose wage-earning wife had died giving birth to the couple's son. *Wiesenfeld* declared unconstitutional the Social Security Act's provision of a mother's benefit for the caretaker of a deceased wage earner's child, but no corresponding father's benefit. As in *Frontiero,* the remedy was extension of the benefits in question to the entire class of similarly situated individuals, males as well as females. In effect, the *Wiesenfeld* judgment substitutes functional description (sole surviving parent) for the gender classification (widowed mother) employed in the statute.

Relying on *Kahn,* the Florida widower's real property tax exemption case, the government had urged that the sex differential in *Wiesenfeld* operated "to offset the adverse economic situation of women," "to compensate women . . . for the . . . difficulties" confronting them when they "seek to support themselves and their families."[53] But the Court read the legislative history closely and rejected that hindsight rationale. The justices declined to accept "the mere recitation of a benign, compensatory purpose" as "an automatic shield"[54] for laws in fact based on twin assumptions: (1) man's primary place is at work, woman's at home; (2) women who do work are secondary breadwinners whose employment is less valuable to and supportive of the family than the man's employment.

Wiesenfeld's focus on actual legislative purpose set a standard the Court continued to employ for sex classifications defended as "benign" or "compensatory." The Court's attention to actual purpose contrasts sharply with the once characteristic approach. Typical of the Court's former position is *Goesaert v. Cleary*,[55] a 1948 decision that upheld Michigan's exclusion of women from bartending, save only daughters and wives of bar owners. The Court cannot give ear, Justice Frankfurter asserted, to the alleged real impulse behind the law (to assure male bartenders a monopoly of the calling) so long as the Court could conceive an appropriate basis for the legislation.[56]

Also among the 1975 decisions, *Stanton v. Stanton*[57] declared inconsistent with equal protection a Utah statute that required a parent to support a son until the age of twenty-one, a daughter only until eighteen.

The 1971 to 1975 challengers, in *Reed, Frontiero, Kahn, Taylor, Wiesenfeld*, and *Stanton*, contended against gross assumptions that females are concerned primarily with "the home and the rearing of the family," males with "the marketplace and the world of ideas."[58] They did not assail the accuracy of these assumptions as generalizations. Rather, they questioned the law's treatment of men and women who do not fit the stereotype as if they did, and the fairness of gender pigeonholing in lieu of neutral, functional description. And the Court, although still holding back doctrinal development, displayed increasing awareness that the traditional legislative slotting had the earmarks of self-fulfilling prophecy. Thus, in *Stanton*, the Court said as to the age of majority differential: "To distinguish between [boy and girl] on educational grounds is to be self-serving: if the female is not to be supported so long as the male, she hardly can be expected to attend school as long as he does, and bringing her education to an end earlier coincides with the role-typing society has long imposed."[59]

The Court's movement away from the empty-cupboard interpretation of equal protection in relation to sex equality claims mirrored changes pervasively affecting society. An early indicator attracted scant attention. In the years 1947 to 1961, before the civil rights movement captured headlines, before Betty Friedan wrote *The Feminine Mystique* (1963), there was unprecedented growth in employment outside the home of women from ages forty-five to sixty-four.[60] A steep increase for younger women followed later, coinciding with, and shored up by, a revived feminist movement—a movement caused by, and in turn spotlighting, dramatic alterations in women's lives. Salient factors in the changing work and roles of women include a sharp decline in necessary home-centered activity; few goods we consume at home must be made there nowadays. Coupled with that, expansion of the economy's service sector opened places for women in traditional as well as new occupations. Curtailed population goals, facilitated by more effective means of controlling reproduction, count as well among important ingredients in this social dynamic. Also central to women's increasing opportunity is the phenomenon of vastly extended life spans. The combination of these last

two developments creates a setting in which the typical woman, for the first
time, is experiencing most of her adult years in a household not dominated
by childcare requirements. In addition, inflation has boosted attraction to
gainful employment for wife as well as husband. These conditions, along
with changing marriage patterns, account in significant measure for the
prevalence of the two-earner family, a unit increasingly more common
than the family in which a man is the sole breadwinner.[61] In fewer than
a dozen years, according to mid-1970s Bureau of Labor Statistics projec-
tions, two-thirds of all women between ages twenty-five and fifty-four would
be gainfully employed.[62]

Columbia economics professor Eli Ginzberg appraised the sum of these
changes as "the single most outstanding phenomenon of our century."[63] Automobiles, planes, nuclear power plants, all brought about by technology, he
called "infrastructural changes." "Important as they are, they do not go [as
directly and deeply] to the guts of a society, . . . how it works and how
it plays, how people relate to each other, whether they have children and
how they bring them up."

The 1976 term was particularly significant in the evolution of Burger
Court rulings on sex discrimination. In that term, the Court added doctrinal
underpinning to the precedent of the 1971-75 period. With the change Eli
Ginzberg called millennial prominent as the backdrop, the Court openly
acknowledged it was applying an elevated equal protection review standard
to gender-based classification, a standard more exacting than lower-tier
"rational basis," albeit less stringent than the "strictest scrutiny" applied
at the upper tier.

Heightened Review Openly Acknowledged: *Craig* and *Goldfarb*

Classification based upon gender, to withstand constitutional challenge, must
bear a "close and substantial relationship to important governmental objectives." Initial statement of this test occurred in December 1976 in *Craig
v. Boren*.[64] In *Craig* the Court held unconstitutional an Oklahoma "boy-
protective" law, a provision allowing girls to purchase 3.2 beer at age
eighteen, but requiring boys to wait until age twenty-one. There is a certain
irony in the Court's use of the thirsty boys case to disapprove *Goesaert
v. Cleary*,[65] the 1948 decision that upheld a prohibition on women serving
as bartenders, and to announce a heightened review standard for sex-based
classification. But reading *Craig v. Boren* together with the case argued
in tandem with it, *Califano v. Goldfarb*,[66] one senses the justices' evolving
appreciation that discrimination by gender generally cuts with two edges and
is seldom, if ever, a pure favor to women.

Califano v. Goldfarb might be described as *Frontiero* revisited with a
hefty price tag ($500 million annually was the government's estimate—
inflated, perhaps, but not totally off the mark), or *Wiesenfeld* without the

baby. Decided in March 1977, *Goldfarb* concerned social security provisions qualifying a widow for survivors' benefits automatically, a widower only upon proof that his wife supplied three-fourths of the couple's support (all of her own and one-half of his). The plurality opinion assiduously follows the pattern cut in *Wiesenfeld.* It concentrates on the discounted return on social security contributions made by the married female wage earner, on discrimination against women as breadwinners.

Justice Stevens, who cast the swing vote in favor of widower Goldfarb, approached the problem from a different entry point.[67] Social security, he pointed out, though requiring payments by employers and employees, is not an insurance scheme; it is a tax. (Benefits are loosely related to contributions, but they are neither contractual nor a form of compensation for services. Thus benefits currently distributed to workers and their survivors, often far in excess of the amount paid in, are not so sharply distinguishable from welfare benefits paid out of general revenues.) This starting place led Justice Stevens to focus initially on the discrimination against the surviving male spouse, not the alleged denigration of the gainfully employed woman. He next raised the question critical to his analysis: Why this discrimination against a class of men? Review of the legislative history indicated no congressional purpose to act affirmatively to improve women's status in economic endeavor. (Justice Stevens, in common with Justice Brennan, who wrote the *Goldfarb* plurality opinion, refused to accept the government's hindsight compensatory justification for the scheme.) Congress, the record suggested, ordered different treatment for widows and widowers out of longstanding "habit"; the discrimination encountered by widower Goldfarb was, in Justice Stevens's words, "merely the accidental by-product of [the legislators'] traditional way of thinking about females."[68] (Women are "the weaker sex," society's child rearers, men's dependents.)

While the Court stood 7 to 2 in *Craig,* the "near-beer" case, the judgment in the more immediately weighty *Goldfarb* case was a cliff-hanger. Four members of the Court, in dissent in *Goldfarb,* repeated a long-rehearsed argument: the sex-based classification accurately reflects the station in life of most women, it operates benignly in women's favor, and it is administratively convenient.[69] In 1980, however, the Court adhered to *Goldfarb* with a clearer (8 to 1) majority. The case, *Wengler v. Druggists Mutual Ins. Co.,*[70] presented a virtually identical question in the context of state workers' compensation death benefits for a surviving spouse.

A Synthesis Essayed: *Califano v. Webster*

Rulings in the social security cases, *Wiesenfeld*[71] and *Goldfarb,*[72] are not easily reconciled with the Court's decisions in *Kahn v. Shevin,*[73] the Florida widower's real property tax exemption case, and *Schlesinger v. Ballard,*[74] the male navy officer's tenure case, where sex classifications were upheld as "benign" or "compensatory." In *Califano v. Webster,*[75] a 1977 decision issued a few weeks after *Goldfarb,* the Court essayed a synthesis. The five justices responsible for the *Goldfarb* judgment subscribed to a per curiam opinion in *Webster* distinguishing from habitual categorization by sex a law designed, at least in part, to ameliorate disadvantages women experienced.

In *Webster* the Court upheld a classification, effective from 1956 to 1972, establishing a more favorable social security benefit calculation formula for retired female workers than for retired male workers. But the legislative history indicated that this scheme, unlike the one in *Goldfarb,* had been conceived as a response to discrimination commonly encountered by gainfully employed women, specifically, depressed wages for "women's work" and early retirement employers routinely forced on women but not on men.[76]

Congress phased out the differential in 1972. By then, the Equal Pay Act and Title VII were operative and had been extended to cover most sectors of the economy. Both acts directly prohibit the discriminatory employer practices that supplied a rationale for the 1956 sex-specific classification. Apparently for that reason, Congress dropped the classification. It did so by equalizing up—extending to men the more favorable calculation once reserved for women.

The *Webster* per curiam, following the line Justice Brennan developed in *Wiesenfeld* and *Goldfarb,* declares post hoc rationalization unacceptable to sustain laws in fact rooted in a "romantically paternalistic"[77] view of women as men's subordinates. While tilting toward a general rule of equal treatment, the *Webster* per curiam approves a corridor for genuinely compensatory classification—classification that is (1) in fact adopted for remedial reasons rather than out of prejudice about "the way women are," and (2) trimly tailored in scope and time to match the remedial end.

Unstable Returns: *Bakke* and *Vorchheimer*

The *Webster* problem and its resolution might have served as a pathmaker in *University of California Regents v. Bakke.*[78] The program assailed by Allan Bakke, aimed at increasing participation by minorities as medical students and in the medical profession, did not coincide with historic role typing nourished by race-based animus. Rather, its purpose was to redress society's longstanding disadvantageous, stigmatizing treatment of racial minorities. And the program did operate to remedy some part of the effect of past societal discrimination. Moreover, the arrangement was envisioned as transitional, a deliberate attempt to compensate during an interim period for economic and social disabilities with which blacks and other ghettoized minorities have been saddled.

But significant differences in the two cases, *Webster* and *Bakke,* and in the two forms of discrimination, sex and race, should not be papered over. The match between persons who had in fact experienced past discrimination and the benefited class was arguably closer in *Webster* than in *Bakke*. In the 1950s, when the provision challenged in *Webster* was enacted, unequal pay for women was in vogue and openly acknowledged by employers. The special admission program in *Bakke,* it was argued, encompassed some minority group applicants (Asian-Americans were cited) who had not recently suffered severe educational disadvantage and left out some Caucasians who had—poor whites from Appalachia figured prominently in amici briefs supporting Bakke's position.

Also, one would be hard put to justify a special admission program for women of the kind established by the Davis medical faculty for members of certain minority groups, for females have not been impeded to the degree ghettoized minorities have by the lingering effects of generations of segregation in housing and community life. Most nonminority females, although they have been shortchanged by some aspects of public school education (vocational and athletic training are salient examples), have not encountered, by reason of their sex, a formidable risk of "death at an early age."[79] Thus, on the Law School Aptitude Test, for example, the average for females at the start of the 1970s was at least as high as the average for males.[80] (And in fact the access difficulty the Allan Bakkes of the nation have confronted was much less the product of any minority admission program than it was the effect of the sharp increase in professional school applications in general, and in women's enrollment in particular.[81])

Nonetheless, the two-pronged inquiry in *Webster* framed questions relevant in *Bakke*: Was the challenged scheme rooted in traditional role typing; and if it was not, did it address and serve to counteract during a catch-up period longstanding disadvantageous treatment?

Justice Brennan, writing in partial dissent for four members of the Court in *Bakke,* cited *Webster* as a guide.[82] In contrast, Justice Powell, speaking only for himself although casting the deciding vote, regarded sex discrimination precedent as inapposite.[83] He made this initial point: It is easier to tell who is male and who is female than to decide who belongs in the category disadvantaged racial or ethnic minority. One might agree or at least demur on that issue and proceed to the second distinction, which Justice Powell considered more important: "[T]he perception of racial classifications as inherently odious," he wrote, "stems from a lengthy and tragic history that gender-based classifications do not share." "[T]he Court has never viewed [gender-based] classification as inherently suspect or as comparable to racial or ethnic classifications for the purpose of equal-protection analysis." The comment is reminiscent of Justice Powell's cautious concurring opinion in *Frontiero v. Richardson,*[84] but its implications are less than crystal clear.

Did Justice Powell mean preferential treatment for women ordered by a government agency should be less vulnerable to challenge in court than preferential treatment for racial and ethnic groups saddled with "a lengthy and tragic history"[85] of adverse discrimination? That seems an anomalous position. Did he mean, on the other hand, that courts should have a higher tolerance for official discrimination against women than for such discrimination against racial and ethnic minorities?

Along with the muddled *Bakke* return in 1978, *Vorchheimer v. School District of Philadelphia*[86] indicated a Court not yet fully secure in its grapplings with sex discrimination. *Vorchheimer* was the final joust in the Supreme Court's 1976 term encounter with officially prescribed male-female classification; it yielded a nondecision. Presented with the question whether Philadelphia could maintain sex-segregated secondary schools for academically gifted boys and girls, the Court was disarmed. Split 4 to 4, the justices wrote no opinion and set no precedent, but the even division meant automatic affirmance of the judgment of the Court of Appeals. That judgment, a 2 to 1 reversal of the district court's decision against the school district, remains the last word in the controversy.

Consolidation of the Decade's Development: *Orr* and *Westcott*

In two 1979 decisions, *Orr v. Orr*[87] and *Califano v. Westcott,*[88] the Burger Court made a clarion statement: explicit sex classification must fall whenever reflecting the "baggage of sexual stereotypes," particularly presumptions that men have "primary responsibility to provide a home and its essentials," women, a first duty at the center of "family life."[89] Traditional overt categorization by sex had not been officially stamped "suspect," but *Orr* and *Westcott* made it appear that all was in place save the seal.

Orr resolved an issue earlier deferred by the Court: may a state require husbands, but never wives, to pay alimony? *Wiesenfeld, Craig,* and *Goldfarb* had provided the framework. A heightened review standard applied, although the classification, on its face, discriminated against men rather than women. Sex as a proxy for need, or as an indicator of past discrimination in the marital unit, was a criterion too gross to survive vigorous equal protection measurement. Alabama held individualized hearings on alimony claims. Focus on the parties' relative financial circumstances in such hearings made the gender-based distinction "gratuitous," even "perverse," the Court reasoned, for the scheme gave "an advantage only to the financially secure wife whose husband is in need."[90]

Justice Brennan, principal 1970s builder of Burger Court precedent in this area (he wrote for the plurality in *Frontiero* and *Goldfarb,* and for the majority in *Wiesenfeld* and *Craig*), spoke for six justices in *Orr.* He closed the opinion on this note: "Legislative classifications which distribute benefits and burdens on the basis of gender carry the inherent risk of reinforcing stereotypes about the 'proper place' of women and their need for special protection. . . . Thus, even statutes purportedly designed to compensate for and ameliorate the effects of past discrimination must be carefully tailored."[91] The double edge of sex classification, "the baggage of sexual stereotypes," had been perceived by the 1979 Court in a case likely to have elicited a different response had it come up at the start of the 1970s.

Westcott[92] similarly indicated sharpened perception fostered by a decade of sex discrimination-equal protection litigation. At issue in that case, the constitutionality of the Aid to Families with Dependent Children, Unemployed Father (AFDC-UF) program. Congress had provided for public assistance benefits to families where dependent children have been deprived of parental support because of the father's unemployment; it had allowed no benefits when mother, rather than father, became unemployed. Complainants were two couples whose benefit applications were turned down because the father did not have a prior work history sufficient to qualify the family, although the mother did. Had Cindy Westcott (and Susan Westwood) been male, William Westcott (and John Westwood) female, the two families would have qualified for benefits.

Even after *Frontiero, Wiesenfeld,* and *Goldfarb,* the government had an argument. *Frontiero* involved compensation for employment, *Wiesenfeld* and *Goldfarb,* social security benefits Congress billed (and the administration publicized) as wage-earners' "insurance." *Westcott* entailed a noncontributory welfare program. In that area, perhaps more than any other, the Court had stressed the wide latitude accord the legislature—the lawmakers' option to deal with part but not all of a problem, their leeway to economize, pursue administrative convenience, take "one step at a time."[93] "But Congress may not legislate 'one step at a time' when that step is drawn along the line of gender, and the consequence is to exclude one group of families [those in which the female spouse is a wage earner] altogether from badly needed subsistence benefits."[94] Justice Blackmun so concluded for a Court unanimous on the constitutional issue. Although the justices divided 5 to 4 on the appropriate remedy (the majority extended the benefit to families of unemployed mothers, the dissenters would have invalidated the entire program),[95] all (even Justice Rehnquist) subscribed solidly to the equal protection ruling.[96]

DEFINING SEX DISCRIMINATION

Classification That Disproportionately Disadvantages Members of One Sex: *Feeney*'s Elaboration of the "Discriminatory Purpose" Test

"[G]ood intent or absence of discriminatory intent" does not immunize an employment practice from Title VII's equal opportunity requirement, the Court held in *Griggs v. Duke Power Co.,*[97] a notable 1971 Title VII decision. When a practice, although "fair in form," impacts more severely on blacks than on whites, the employer must show business necessity for it, Chief

Justice Burger wrote for a unanimous Court. In *Griggs* the Court declared inconsistent with Title VII certain preemployment requirements (a high school education and passing a standardized general intelligence test) that "render[ed] ineligible a markedly disproportionate number of Negroes" and were not "shown to be job related."[98]

The *Griggs* decision established precedent for all Title VII categories (race, religion, sex, and national origin). Lower courts applied its consequence-centered analysis in equal protection as well as in Title VII challenges to public sector employment practices.[99] But in 1976, in *Washington v. Davis*,[100] the Supreme Court ruled *Griggs* inapplicable to constitutional claims. Unsuccessful black candidates for District of Columbia police department positions alleged in *Washington v. Davis* that a written verbal-ability test, which blacks failed at a rate four times higher than whites, discriminated on the basis of race. Disproportionate impact alone, the Court said, was insufficient to establish a race-based denial of equal protection. When the constitutional guarantee is invoked, Justice White wrote, "the invidious quality of a law . . . must ultimately be traced to a racially discriminatory purpose."[101]

With discriminatory purpose a requirement in race discrimination–equal protection cases, a requirement of the same character could be expected in sex discrimination cases. *Personnel Administrator of Massachusetts v. Feeney* (1979)[102] applied *Washington v. Davis* to an assault on exorbitant veterans' preferences in civil service as impermissibly gender-biased. The Court clarified that discriminatory purpose "implies more than intent as volition or intent as awareness of consequences."[103] Rather, the lawmaker must *want* the consequences.

Feeney challenged the nation's most extreme veterans' preference—an absolute lifetime preference Massachusetts accorded to veterans in a range of civil service positions. The preference had "a devastating impact on the employment opportunities of women."[104] It operated to reserve top jobs for a class composed almost entirely of men. The purpose? Purely to aid veterans, surely not to harm women, Massachusetts, and the United States as amicus curiae, maintained. Helen Feeney attempted to distinguish *Washington v. Davis* based on the nonneutral selection criterion at work. To become a veteran one must be allowed to serve the country in the military. But the military had maintained highly restrictive quotas and more exacting qualification standards for females.[105] When litigation in *Feeney* commenced, over 98 percent of Massachusetts veterans were male; only 1.8 percent were female.[106]

Helen Feeney urged a judicial solution similar to the one Justice Powell advanced in *Bakke*.[107] She sought accommodation of the conflicting interests: aiding veterans and opening to women civil service employment beyond the "pink collar" ghetto. The typical points-added preference, she said, was not at issue, only the extreme arrangement Massachusetts had legislated, which placed a veteran with a minimum pass ahead of a woman with a perfect score, and did so for each promotion as well as for initial hire. A preference so large, she argued, took too much from Pauline to pay Paul.

The Court viewed the proffered distinction between moderate and exorbitant preferences as a difference in degree, not in kind. The "discriminatory purpose" hurdle could not be surmounted, Justice Stewart wrote for the majority, absent proof that the Massachusetts preference "was originally devised or subsequently re-enacted because it would accomplish the collateral goal of keeping women in a stereotypic and predefined place in the Massachusetts Civil Service."[108]

Laws based explicitly on sex, and "covert" sex classifications (those "ostensibly neutral" but "an obvious pretext for [sex-based] discrimination"[109]) are vulnerable to equal protection attack, Justice Stewart explained. But disparate impact on one sex, however "devastating" and "inevitable,"[110] does not constitute gender-based discrimination in violation of equal protection if the lopsided result is not affirmatively desired by the decision-maker. The forum for redress in such a case is the legislature, not a court sitting as constitutional adjudicator.

The discriminatory purpose requirement, as elaborated in *Feeney,* leaves a slack rein for legislative choices with foreseeable "adverse effects upon an identifiable group."[111] Suppose, for example, the social security payments at issue in *Wiesenfeld* or *Goldfarb* turned not on sex, but on the deceased wage earner's status as the family's principal breadwinner. In most families, husbands would fit that neutrally phrased description, wives would not. May Congress, without violating equal protection, resort to a principal breadwinner standard in social welfare legislation in the interest of fiscal economy? Would use of a principal breadwinner criterion survive constitutional review as a measure enacted "in spite of," rather than "because of" its practical effect—its reduction of the value to the family of the wife's earnings?[112]

Doctrine Boldly Pronounced, Then Notably Curtailed: The Reproductive Freedom Decisions

In two bold January 1973 rulings, *Roe v. Wade*[113] and *Doe v. Bolton,*[114] the Court struck down antiabortion laws as unwarranted state intrusions into the decision of a woman and her doctor to terminate a pregnancy. Most commentators, whether they applauded or deplored the decisions, remarked that in no other area had the Burger Court (or perhaps any Court) acted more intrepidly.[115]

The 1973 abortion decisions have been typed aberrational: extraordinarily activist decisions issued from a bench reputedly deferential to legislative judgments. But it bears emphasis that the Court bypassed the equal protection argument presented for the female plaintiffs. Rather, the Court anchored stringent review to a concept of personal autonomy derived from the due process guarantee. Two decisions, particularly, had paved the way: *Griswold v. Connecticut* (1965),[116] a Warren Court product holding inconsistent with due process Connecticut's ban on use of contraceptives even by married couples, and *Eisenstadt v. Baird* (1972),[117] a Burger Court ruling extending *Griswold* to strike down the Massachusetts prohibition on sales of contraceptives except by a licensed pharmacist to a married person on a doctor's prescription.

Some speculated that the 7 to 2 judgments in the 1973 abortion cases were motivated, at least in part, by population concerns and the specter of unwanted children born into impoverished families. But in three decisions announced in June 1977, the main one, *Maher v. Roe*,[118] the Court indicated that speculation was not altogether on target. The justices lined up 6 to 3 against extending the 1973 rulings to require state support for an indigent woman's elective abortion.

The impoverished women, on whose behalf constitutional claims to public assistance for abortion were pursued, relied primarily on the equal protection principle. They maintained that, so long as government covered the cost of childbirth, it could not withhold coverage for abortion, a far less expensive procedure and one that, at least in the first trimester, entailed fewer risks to the patient's life and health. The substantive due process analysis employed in the 1973 decisions figured in argument of the 1977 cases to this extent: if government pays for childbirth but not abortion, then government is intruding upon a choice *Roe v. Wade* seemed to say the state must leave to doctor and patient.

The Court's majority, however, distinguished government prohibition from government support. It said the state could not bar access to a woman able to pay for an abortion, but was not required to buy an admission ticket for the poor woman. Rather, government could pursue a policy of encouraging childbirth (even if that policy would affect only the poor) by refusing Medicaid reimbursement for nontherapeutic abortions and by banning such abortions in public hospitals.

Legal analysts who recognized that the 1973 decisions were difficult to explain viewed the route to decision for the indigent women in the 1977 public funding cases as shoal-free by comparison.[119] A prominent journalist commented that leaving "the poor alone ineligible for abortion defies justice, common sense, rational policy and the Federal budget."[120] Although criticized as particularly inappropriate in the reproductive choice context, the distinction between government carrot and government stick had been made in other settings to which the Court referred in its 1977 ruling.

Sex-Based Classification and Classification Based on Pregnancy

Burger Court decisions relating to pregnancy in the employment context display less than perfect logic and consistency. School teachers may not be dismissed or placed on forced leave arbitrarily at a fixed stage in pregnancy well in advance of term. That conflicts with due process, the Court ruled in 1974 in *Cleveland Board of Education v. LaFleur*.[121] Forcing every pregnant woman out of the classroom at an early date conclusively presumed, contrary to fact, that pregnancy per se disables, Justice Stewart reasoned for the majority. The due process-conclusive presumption line had not been argued by the *LaFleur* complainant (she relied upon equal protection analysis), and the Court's resort to it seemed a storm warning for a case in the wings. That case, *Geduldig v. Aiello*,[122] decided some weeks after *LaFleur*, held that a state-operated disability income protection plan could exclude pregnancy without offense to the equal protection principle.

Consistent with Title VII too, the Court ruled in *General Electric Co. v. Gilbert* in December 1976,[123] an employer may exclude from disability coverage women unable to work due to pregnancy or childbirth. Exclusion of pregnant women, the Court explained in *Aiello* and *General Electric*, was not gender-based on its face, and was not shown to have any sex-discriminatory effect. All "nonpregnant persons," women along with men, the Court pointed out, were treated alike.

But exactly one year later, in December 1977, in *Nashville Gas Co. v. Satty*,[124] the Court distinguished benefits for the pregnant woman from burdens placed upon her, a distinction resembling the one it had drawn some months earlier in *Maher v. Roe*,[125] dealing with public assistance for abortion. The Court held unlawful under Title VII an employer's practice of stripping women disabled by pregnancy of accumulated job-bidding seniority. Two years before *Nashville Gas*, and one year before *General Electric*, the Court had ruled on a state benefit program alleged to exclude pregnant women in violation of the Fourteenth Amendment. In 1975, in *Turner v. Department of Employment Security*,[126] the Court announced that, consistent with due process, pregnant women ready, willing, and able to work may not be denied unemployment compensation when jobs are closed to them.

When does disadvantageous treatment of pregnant workers operate to discriminate on the basis of sex? Justice Stevens offered a summary in his *Nashville Gas* concurring opinion: Justice Stevens thought the Court's answer should be "always," the 1976 *General Electric* decision appeared to say "never," but *Nashville Gas* made the correct response "sometimes."[127]

Lawyers may attempt to square the constitutional decisions by referring to the different principles pressed into service—equal protection in *Aiello*, the disability case, due process in both *LaFleur*, the school teacher's forced-leave case, and *Turner*, the unemployment compensation case. But the due process theory—the irrebuttable or conclusive presumption rubric employed in *LaFleur* and *Turner*—has lost favor with the Court in other contexts.[128] Few statutory classifications could stand if that analysis applied across the board.[129] It may be that a factor not fully acknowledged in the written opinions, and based more on the justices' life experiences than legal analysis, accounts for the divergent responses in *LaFleur*, *Turner*, and *Nashville Gas* on the one hand, *Aiello* and *General Electric* on the other. Perhaps the able pregnant woman seeking only to do a day's work for a day's pay, or the woman seeking to return to her job relatively soon after childbirth, is a credible figure to the Court, while the woman who asserts she is disabled by pregnancy is viewed with suspicion. (Is she really incapacitated physically or is she malingering so that she may stay "where [some think] she belongs"—at home tending baby?)

With respect to Title VII, Congress, in October 1978, simplified the judicial task by prospectively overruling *General Electric*. It amended the statute to say explicitly that classification on the basis of sex includes ("always," not "sometimes") classification on the basis of pregnancy.[130] This congressional definition is not controlling in constitutional as distinguished from statutory (Title VII) adjudication, but it is possible that the Court may be stimulated by the congressional understanding to think again about the notion that singling out "pregnant persons" is not a sex-based action.

Kenneth Karst has commented that not only the overt sex discrimination cases, but the cases on contraception, abortion, and illegitimacy as well, present various faces of a single issue—the roles women are to play in society.[131] Are they to have the opportunity to participate in full partnership with men in the nation's social, political, and economic life? This is a constitutional issue, Karst wrote, surely one of prime importance in the final quarter of the twentieth century. Karst suggested that the Court may someday remove from the separate cubbyholes in which they now rest cases on explicitly gender-based discrimination, out-of-wedlock birth, and reproductive choice; acknowledge the practical interrelationships; and treat these matters as part and parcel of a single, large, sex equality issue. That synthesis may well depend on clearer directions from the political arena, but it is a likely candidate for attention in the 1980s.

Actuarial Differences: The *Manhart* Case

The Court's treatment of actuarial differences in the Title VII case, *Los Angeles Dep't of Water and Power v. Manhart*,[132] contrasts with the difficulty a majority encountered in categorizing pregnancy-related regulation as sex-based. *Manhart* raised the question whether women could be required to pay more currently in order to receive monthly benefits on retirement equal to benefits received by men. The majority held that exacting higher payments from women was inconsistent with the statute's prohibition of sex-based classification. All recognized in *Manhart* that the statement, "on the average, women live longer than men," is accurate as a generalization. It is also an accurate statement that, on the average, women score better than men on verbal-ability tests. But there are highly verbal men (the legal profession, once typed male, provides a generous sample), and substantial numbers of women are destined to die young.

Actions based on sex averaging (men are more substantial breadwinners than women, physically stronger, poorer drivers, heavier drinkers) have not fared well in current constitutional and Title VII litigation for two reasons: they reinforce traditional restrictive conceptions of the social roles of men and women; and they burden members of one sex by employing gender as a proxy for a characteristic susceptible to individual testing or at least capable of sex-neutral description. The dissenters in *Manhart* emphasized that longevity is not testable in advance the way that capacity to do a job is.[133] But the majority refused to countenance a break from the general Title VII rule against sex (or race or national origin) averaging. Unquestionably, for pension purposes women destined to die young are burdened by placement in an all-female class, and men destined to live long are benefited by placement in an all-male class. Moreover, Justice Stevens suggested for the majority, the group insurance context may not be an ideal setting for urging a distinction other than age: "To insure the flabby and the fit as though they were equivalent risks may be more common than treating men and women alike; but nothing more than habit makes one 'subsidy' seem less fair than the other."[134]

CONCLUSION

Developments in the 1970s in gender discrimination cases reflect a combination of changes in social and economic conditions that influence and exert pressure on decisionmakers (small family norms, effective birth control, increasing life spans, inflation, decreasing incidence of a single life partner). Burger Court adjudication in sex discrimination cases has been "interventionist." Yet women could not be regarded as a constituency of the Burger Court to the same extent that blacks were of the Warren Court. Nonetheless, the gender classification decisions of the 1970s have a spectacular aspect. The race cases that trooped before the Warren Court were easier in this sense. The Reconstruction Congress had provided the foundation; the post–Civil War Court declined to build on it and instead trimmed parts of the structure. The Warren Court, in its race discrimination precedent, could be viewed simply as moving the federal judiciary onto the course set for it by Congress a century earlier.[135] As to gender-based classification, however, no foundation had been set deliberately by actors in the political arena. Hence, the Burger Court was exposed to charges not only of "legislating," but of imperially acting in contempt of the prescribed democratic processes for constitutional amendment.[136]

Also noteworthy in appraising gender discrimination decisions of the 1970s is the comparatively cold reception the Burger Court has accorded to other constituencies seeking to advance their positions on the equal protection spectrum. For the aging[137] and the poor,[138] equal protection remains a lean cupboard. Aliens did well in the early years of the Burger Court,[139] but later the majority backtracked a considerable way.[140] In contrast, apart from the slight slump in *Kahn v. Shevin*,[141] claims challenging explicit sex classifications inched steadily along. The *Frontiero-Wiesenfeld-Goldfarb* line, solidified in *Orr* and *Westcott*, suggested that stringent review for explicitly gender-based laws was here to stay.

Two of the Court's returns, *Schlesinger v. Ballard*[142] and *Califano v. Webster*,[143] are probably best explained on the basis of institutional constraints. The Court could not seize on Lt. Ballard's idiosyncratic case to right the wrongs responsible for women's limited promotion opportunities in the military; no litigant in *Ballard* even placed that issue in controversy. *Webster*, brought by a *pro se* litigant, involved a large price tag ($1.2 billion, the government estimated), and a prospective, equalizing legislative change. In contrast to the *Webster* situation, Congress was hardly on the brink of initiating the social security law alteration effected by *Wiesenfeld* and *Goldfarb*, and the Court's majority apparently appreciated that reality. The *Webster* per curiam, moreover, ends with an approving nod to the nonretroactive congressional adjustment, noting its consistency with the contemporary view that equal treatment is preferable to "romantic paternalism."[144]

The *Vorchheimer*[145] disposition does not constitute High Court precedent. Nor is it crystal clear that had Justice Rehnquist participated, the 4 to 4 nondecision inevitably would have become a 5 to 4 ruling condoning "separate but equal" public school education in the context of sex. It is conceivable that the Court settled on an even division to put off the issue. (Justices on the fence may have been uneasy about the absence of building blocks—*Brown v. Board of Education*,[146] holding separate education of the races inherently unequal, had been preceded by a parade of litigation[147] in which decisions turned on the markedly inferior opportunities afforded blacks, on inequalities solidly demonstrated at trial.) In any event, the Fifth Circuit has taken care of the most egregious situation—systemwide substitution of sex separation for race separation—by holding that the Equal Educational Opportunities Act of 1974 (ironically, an antibusing measure) prohibits assignment to public schools on the basis of sex.[148]

Following the Burger Court's boldest stroke, the 1973 abortion decisions,[149] the 1977 public funding of abortion rulings[150] may appear incongruous. The 1973 decisions were not easy to reach or write. Social and economic conditions that seem irreversible, however, suggest that the results

in those cases will remain with us in the long run, while the 1977 disposi-
tions may eventually succumb to a different view, expressed by legislators,
of state and national policy.

POSTSCRIPT

This article was completed in the spring of 1980.* High court gender
discrimination precedent since that time does not form a coherent pattern.
Burger Court judgments in 1980 and 1981 appear more immediately responsive to the political or social sensitivity of particular cases than to the
reasoned application, elaboration, or qualification of doctrine established in
the 1970s. However, at the end of the 1981 term, the Court issued a decision that consolidates and reaffirms precedent set in the 1970s regarding
explicitly gender-based classification.

The abortion funding question returned to the Court in 1980 in *Harris
v. McRae*[151] with this difference. *Maher v. Roe*,[152] in 1977, had sustained,
6 to 3, the constitutionality of a state's exclusion of nontherapeutic abortions
from Medicaid; *Harris v. McRae* involved a federal measure, the Hyde
Amendment, which excluded even therapeutic (medically needed) abortions
from that medical benefits program. In holding, 5 to 4, that the Hyde
Amendment violated neither the right to abortion recognized in *Roe v.
Wade*[153] nor the equal protection clause, the Court relied heavily on the distinction drawn three years earlier in *Maher*. While *Roe v. Wade* precluded
government from proscribing abortion, *Maher* explained that government
need not act affirmatively to assure a poor woman's access to the procedure.

Justice Stevens, who had joined the majority in *Maher*, switched sides
in *McRae* based on the critical difference he discerned, in the context of
the Medicaid program, between an abortion that is not a necessary medical
procedure, and one that is.[154] Congress had established two neutral criteria
for Medicaid benefits, he pointed out—financial need and medical need.
The pregnant women who challenged the Hyde Amendment met both criteria. By creating an exception to the neutral medical need criterion for the
sole purpose of thwarting the exercise of the fundamental constitutional
right declared in *Roe v. Wade,* Justice Stevens reasoned, the sovereign had
violated its "duty to govern impartially."[155]

Three explicitly gender-based cases were decided in the 1980 term. The
first, *Michael M. v. Superior Court,*[156] upheld, 5 to 4, California's "statutory
rape" law, which defined unlawful sexual intercourse as "an act of sexual
intercourse accomplished with a female not the wife of the perpetrator,

*The postscript to this chapter was written after the author was appointed to the United
States Court of Appeals for the District of Columbia Circuit.

where the female is under the age of 18 years." Under this statute, a male who engages in sexual intercourse with an underage female who is not his wife commits a crime; a female who engages in sexual intercourse with an underage male does not. Both participants in the act that precipitated the prosecution in *Michael M*. were underage; the male was seventeen and a half years old, the female, sixteen and a half.

There was no majority opinion in *Michael M*. Justice Rehnquist wrote for the Court's plurality. He postulated as the statute's purpose, as California had argued, the prevention of teenage pregnancy and reasoned that males and females are not similarly situated in this setting. Nature inhibited the female, for she would suffer the consequences. The law could legitimately take into account this fact of life by punishing the male, who lacked a biological deterrent. Moreover, the plurality found persuasive California's further contention that sparing the female from criminal liability might encourage her to report the unlawful activity.

The *Michael M*. plurality opinion waffled on the standard of review. Remarkably, in light of doctrine established in the 1970s, particularly in *Craig v. Boren*[157] and *Orr v. Orr,*[158] the plurality opinion suggested that statutes burdening males but not females do not attract "the special solicitude of the courts."[159] Given the ancient roots of the California law, Justice Brennan pointed out in dissent,[160] it was difficult to avoid recognition that the sex classification "was initially designed to further . . . outmoded sexual stereotypes" (young women are not capable of consenting to an act of sexual intercourse, young men can make such decisions for themselves).[161]

For Justice Stevens, who dissented separately,[162] the critical question in *Michael M*. was whether "the sovereign . . . govern[s] impartially" under a statute that authorizes punishment of the male, but not the female, even "when they are equally responsible" for the disfavored conduct, indeed even "when the female is the more responsible of the two."[163] The answer, it seemed to Justice Stevens, was clearly "no."

Although by 1980 many states had amended all of their sex crimes laws to render them equally applicable to males and females, *Michael M*. touched a sensitive nerve. The California Supreme Court had upheld the statute,[164] purporting to apply the "strict scrutiny" standard it had adopted in 1971 for sex discrimination cases.[165] In view of the 4 to 1 to 4 Burger Court division (Justice Blackmun concurred in the judgment),[166] the decision may well remain an isolated instance.

In contrast to the extralegal freight *Michael M*. carried, no emotion-laden question appeared in the Court's next encounter, *Kirchberg v. Feenstra*.[167] A unanimous bench declared inconsistent with the equal protection principle Louisiana's former "head and master" law, which gave the husband alone the unilateral right to dispose of property jointly owned with his wife. The Court's opinion by Justice Marshall[168] is solidly tied to precedent that evolved in the 1970s; it reiterated: "[T]he burden remains on the party seeking to uphold a statute that expressly discriminates on the basis of sex to advance an 'exceedingly persuasive justification' for the challenged classification."[169]

Kirchberg was an easy case. Louisiana had abandoned the "head and master" rule, but not retroactively, before the matter was argued in the Supreme Court. By that time, all eight United States community property states had extended marital property management and control rights to wives. In sharp contrast, the case decided last in the 1980 term, *Rostker v. Goldberg*,[170] presented the politically loaded question whether Congress could confine draft registration to males.

Congress had thought about the matter and decided it in 1980. It considered, on the administration's recommendation, authorizing the president to require registration by both sexes. But it decided on registration for males only. The Court's 6 to 3 decision upheld the sex classification. The opinion, written by Justice Rehnquist, boldfaced the special deference due congressional judgments in the area of national defense and military affairs.

The *Rostker v. Goldberg* opinion acknowledged, albeit in a half-hearted way, that gender-based discrimination generally attracts "heightened scrutiny."[171] It also asserted that men and women are not similarly situated for the purpose at hand because women are excluded from combat service, an exclusion "Congress specifically recognized and endorsed . . . in exempting women from registration."[172] (In contrast to the fact of life or anatomy Justice Rehnquist relied upon to explain why men and women were not similarly situated in relation to the issue presented in *Michael M.*, the combat exclusion that figured in *Rostker v. Goldberg* was not the work of the Creator, it was man-made policy.)

Reminiscent of *Schlesinger v. Ballard*,[173] where no party challenged the dissimilar promotion opportunities for male and female naval officers, no party challenged the combat exclusion in *Rostker v. Goldberg*. Even so, it was "the serious view of the Executive Branch including the responsible military services," a view communicated to Congress, that in the event of a major mobilization there would be a substantial number of positions in the armed services that conscripted women could fill, beyond those filled by women volunteers, despite women's ineligibility for combat.[174] *Rostker v. Goldberg* has been explained as a "war powers case," a case much like the "Japanese relocation" case,[175] a decision based on reasoning not likely to have a significant impact in future sex discrimination cases.[176]

No justice referred to *Michael M.* or *Rostker v. Goldberg* in the only equal protection challenge to a gender-based classification heard in the 1981 term. On July 1, 1982, just one day after expiration of the extended deadline for ratification of the proposed equal rights amendment, the Court announced its 5 to 4 decision in *Mississippi University for Women v. Ho-*

gan.[177] The case featured a male plaintiff who sought to enroll in a professional nursing school that offered degree-granting programs to women only.[178] Vigorously recapitulating the main themes of the 1970s, the Court held that Mississippi's single-sex admissions policy for the nursing school failed to meet the heightened standard of review applicable to gender-based classification.[179]

Justice O'Connor's opinion for the Court restated "several firmly-established principles." Prime among these:

> Our decisions . . . establish that the party seeking to uphold a statute that classifies individuals on the basis of their gender must carry the burden of showing an "exceedingly persuasive justification" for the classification. . . . The burden is met only by showing at least that the classification serves "important governmental objectives and that the discriminatory means employed" are "substantially related to the achievement of those objectives."[180]

Contradicting the suggestion Justice Rehnquist essayed in *Michael M.*,[181] Justice O'Connor crisply stated as settled: "That this statute discriminates against males rather than against females does not exempt it from scrutiny or reduce the standard of review."[182]

Most tellingly, the Court again spotlighted, as it did in most of its 1975–80 decisions,[183] the role typing that generally underlies gender-based classification, even when billed as "benign." The *Mississippi University for Women* opinion cautions lower courts to apply "the test for determining the validity of a gender-based classification . . . free of fixed notions concerning the roles and abilities of males and females"; to take "[c]are . . . in ascertaining whether the statutory objective itself reflects archaic and stereotypic notions"; and to engage in "reasoned analysis," not "mechanical application of traditional, often inaccurate, assumptions about the proper roles of men and women."[184]

Because Joe Hogan's exclusion from degree-granting programs at Mississippi University for Women's School of Nursing failed "the test previously relied upon by the Court to measure the constitutionality of gender-based discrimination," the -majority noted that it was unnecessary to "decide whether classifications based upon gender are inherently suspect."[185] Thus, the Court's majority, albeit a slim one, indicated that designating sex a "suspect" category remains an open question. If the Court continues to review categorization by gender as rigorously and incisively as it did in *Mississippi University for Women*,[186] the "suspect" seal may be placed on accumulated precedent in the 1980s.[187] Or, differently expressed but perhaps capturing the same idea, the Court may conclude that whenever recourse may be had to "more germane bases of classification,"[188] line drawing by gender must be rejected as inconsistent with the sovereign's "duty to govern impartially."[189]

· Eight ·

Individual Rights in the Work Place:
The Burger Court and Labor Law

Theodore J. St. Antoine

The Supreme Court, like other institutions, must play the part that the times demand, often with small regard for the personal predilections of its membership. The Warren Court and the Burger Court, in their respective contributions to the law of union-employer-employee relations, almost reversed the roles they might have been expected to assume. The major accomplishment of the Court in the labor area during the Warren era was a fundamental restructuring of intergovernmental relationships,[1] while the Court's overriding concern throughout the Burger decade of the 1970s and beyond has been the defining of individual rights in the work place.

During its first thirteen years the Burger Court averaged about a dozen noteworthy labor decisions a term. Over half of these, or eighty-six by my count, dealt with the rights of employees vis-à-vis their employers or unions, as distinguished from the more conventional competing claims of employers and labor organizations. By far the largest single category consisted of sixty-five cases of alleged discrimination on the basis of race, sex, religion, national origin or age. Twenty-one other decisions covered employees' rights to fair representation by their bargaining agents or their rights as union members. By contrast, the Warren legacy contains about five times as many leading cases dealing with traditional labor-management disputes as with individual rights in employment.[2]

The changing pattern of the Supreme Court's labor agenda over the past three decades was entirely natural. When Warren Burger became chief justice in 1969, the National Labor Relations Act (NLRA) was almost thirty-five years old, and the main interpretive lines of union-management law had already been laid down. Title VII of the Civil Rights Act of 1964, covering equal employment opportunity, had been in effect for only four years, however, and the first cases arising under it were just beginning to reach the Supreme Court. Race and sex discrimination are covered extensively elsewhere in this volume.[3] But one category of Title VII decision so dramatically juxtaposes traditional labor relations values and the new values of equal employment opportunity that it calls for discussion here.

157

EMPLOYMENT DISCRIMINATION AND SENIORITY

Aside from affirmative action or "reverse discrimination," the most painful and persistent clash of worthy interests resulting from antidiscrimination legislation has been presented by the problem of seniority. The essence of seniority, of course, is to give preference to more experienced workers in such employment decisions as layoffs, recalls, and promotions and also in such benefits as step increases in pay, length of vacations, and amount of pension. In part the notion is that the veteran employee is entitled as a matter of equity to greater job security than newer recruits. In part the aim is to remove a source of worker discontent by substituting an objective standard for job priorities in place of what might otherwise be arbitrariness or favoritism by employer or union.

The leaders of the AFL-CIO and several major international unions were among the prime movers for the inclusion of an equal employment opportunity title in the 1964 Civil Rights Act.[4] Opponents sought to rally grassroots union opposition by flooding thousands of locals with warnings that the enactment of Title VII would "destroy" the hard-earned seniority rights of many workers. The AFL-CIO and legislators backing the bill responded by assuring union members and the Congress that Title VII would have no adverse impact on acquired seniority. The principle of "last hired, first fired" would apply "even in the case where owing to discrimination prior to the effective date of the title, white workers had more seniority than Negroes."[5] Further to allay concerns, section 703(h) was added to the bill, providing that it would not be an unfair employment practice for an employer to differentiate in terms of employment "pursuant to a bona fide seniority . . . system, provided that such differences are not the result of an intention to discriminate."[6]

Since disinterested observers of the 1964 civil rights debate in Congress believed AFL-CIO support was crucial to success, these reassurances were probably the price that had to be paid for the enactment of Title VII. Yet the continuation of seniority systems without any change would leave black workers severely handicapped. A black employee moving into a formerly lily-white department or line of progression would start with zero seniority. He would be the first laid off, the last recalled, and the last promoted. The racial discrimination of the past prevented the black worker from earning seniority credits in jobs traditionally held by whites, and now lack of them would hobble his efforts to step into better positions even after the racial bars were removed.

This "perpetuation of the effects of past discrimination" proved too much to swallow for most of the federal trial and appellate courts that first encountered it.[7] The initial cases arose in plants or shops where "departmental" or "job" seniority prevailed, rather than seniority based on total time in the plant. Almost invariably the courts found that making post-act determinations regarding such matters as layoffs, recalls, or promotions on the basis of pre-act seniority credits acquired under discriminatory job conditions constituted violations of Title VII. Even though the act was not retroactive, Congress could not have meant to "freeze an entire generation of Negro employees into discriminatory patterns that existed before the Act."[8] Section 703(h) was disposed of by saying that a "racially discriminatory seniority system" existing prior to the act was not "bona fide." Concededly, the victims of pre-act discrimination who were never hired at all could not later claim credit for the time they might otherwise have worked. But blacks who were actually employed in a plant in a segregated department or line of progression could demand that the seniority they had acquired in their black jobs be accorded "equal status with time worked in white jobs."[9] In short, Congress was viewed as preserving only "plant" seniority, not "job" or "departmental" seniority when the latter would carry forward credits obtained under pre-act discriminatory conditions.

This distinction makes much sense as a matter of policy. Unfortunately, there is not a hint in the legislative history that Congress ever entertained such a distinction. The function of seniority to protect the equity of veteran workers in their jobs and to provide an objective standard for employment preferences is essentially the same whether the seniority is linked to a particular job, or a given department, or a whole plant. Be that as it may, by the early 1970s the battle over seniority under Title VII seemed finished. The vast majority of federal rulings had struck down seniority systems that "perpetuated the effects" of pre-act discrimination. The Supreme Court had denied certiorari. In 1972 Congress undertook a comprehensive revision of Title VII[10] and did nothing to overturn the seniority decisions. Eventually, the view that Title VII reached seniority systems perpetuating pre-act discrimination was accepted by six courts of appeals in the holdings of thirty cases and by two other courts of appeals in dicta, all without dissent.[11] Understandably, most sensible lawyers counselled their clients to settle claims, even with million-dollar price tags. Only the diehards fought on.

Then, in 1977, the Supreme Court dropped its bombshell. In *Teamsters v. United States* [*T.I.M.E.–D.C.*],[12] the Court broke with the long line of lower court precedent and held, 7 to 2, that section 703(h) does indeed sustain "bona fide" seniority plans, regardless of their perpetuation of the effects of prior discrimination. Speaking for the majority, Justice Stewart began by agreeing that Title VII reached practices "fair in form, but discriminatory in operation," and acknowledged the perpetuation of the effects of pre-act discrimination fitted that prescription. He added: "Were it not for § 703(h), the seniority system in this case would seem to fall."[13] "But," he proceeded, "both the literal terms of § 703(h) and the legislative history of Title VII demonstrate that Congress considered this very effect of many seniority systems and extended a measure of immunity to them." Justice Stewart found no support in the legislative history and "no rational basis" for distinguishing between discriminatees employed in less desirable jobs and those denied employment entirely. He recognized that only "bona fide" seniority plans are immunized by section 703(h), but pointed out that the plan challenged in *Teamsters* applied equally to all races and ethnic groups. Whites as well as blacks and Hispanics were "locked" into jobs as city drivers and servicemen and were discouraged from transferring to superior highway jobs. The employer's separate seniority units for highway drivers and for others was in accord with rational industry practice, did not have its "genesis in racial discrimination," and had been "maintained free from any illegal purpose."[14]

Justice Stewart's opinion was a sound, lawyerly product, the opinion that should have been written in 1970. The question is whether it was wise judicial statesmanship in 1977. There is little doubt that he reflected the thinking (and perhaps the nonthinking) of the Congress of 1964. But time had passed. Unions, employers, and white employees had endured their defeats and vented their rage. The more accommodating had bowed to the seemingly inevitable and worked out the apparently necessary adjustments. Neither the Supreme Court nor Congress had intervened. Now, a half dozen years after the tumult had begun to die down, the Supreme Court reopened the whole roiling controversy in a way that tended both to mock conciliatory unions and employers and to revive antagonisms among black and white employees. It is understandable that a legal craftsman like Justice Stewart may have felt driven to the result he reached by the legislative history of Title VII. There is ample precedent, however, for construing an earlier statute in light of subsequent legislation dealing with the same subject.[15] Had it wished, the Court could easily have justified a different decision by relying on the discreet yet suggestive silence of Congress in enacting the 1972 amendments.

Having set the clock back to 1964, the Court was then forced to confront an even closer legal question regarding seniority systems. Suppose an employer adopted a facially neutral seniority plan *after* the effective date of Title VII, but with a resulting discriminatory impact on black workers. Arguably, section 703(h) should not immunize such an arrangement, because that provision was primarily designed to preserve the established expectations of white workers concerning the seniority rights they had acquired before Title VII went into effect. Nonetheless, in *American Tobacco Co. v. Patterson*,[16] a 5 to 4 majority of the Court concluded that 703(h) was not so limited, and that it applied to sustain post-act as well as pre-act seniority systems. The dissent properly objected that the specific reason given in the legislative debates for the adoption of section 703(h) was the desire to protect pre-act seniority credits. Yet the majority could correctly respond that 703(h) itself "makes no distinction between pre- and post-act seniority systems," and none of its proponents explicitly indicated such a distinction was intended. *Patterson* quite reasonably could have gone either way, and it might well have been decided differently had Justice O'Connor not replaced Justice Stewart at the beginning of the 1981 term.

The upshot of *Teamsters* [*T.I.M.E.–D.C.*] and *Patterson* is to place a strong judicial imprimatur on the concept of seniority, one of the most hallowed values of organized labor, even against the competing claims of adversely affected minority groups. Discriminatory impact alone is not enough to invalidate a seniority system; an actual intent to discriminate must be proved. Moreover, the finding of intent or motive is a pure question of fact to be determined by the trial court, reversible only for clear error.[17] This of course does not mean that a court may not consider disparate effects on minorities in resolving the factual issue of discriminatory intent. An illustration would be an employer's continued use of separate seniority lists for two separate lines of progression which were segregated by race but are now desegregated, in a situation where all the jobs are functionally related and the normal pattern would call for a single line of progression with "line of progression" seniority. Absent such a distortion of customary arrangements, however, all traditional and legitimately grounded seniority systems now appear immune to challenge under Title VII. To that extent the long-term, organized, predominantly white worker has won out over the black newcomer to the work place.

FAIR REPRESENTATION

In the midst of World War II the Supreme Court for the first time declared that labor organizations have an obligation to represent all the employees in a bargaining unit fairly and without discrimination. *Steele v. Louisville & Nashville R.R.*[18] arose under the Railway Labor Act (RLA) and involved racial discrimination by a union and a cooperative employer. Neither the RLA nor the National Labor Relations Act expressly imposes any duty of fair representation. But each act does make a majority union in any bargaining unit the exclusive representative of all the employees, dissenters and adherents alike. In *Steele* the Court concluded that Congress had not intended to confer (and under the Constitution probably could not have conferred) this extraordinary power without imposing the concomitant obligation to protect minority as well as majority interests. The duty of fair representation was later extended to the National Labor Relations Act[19] and to arbitrary treatment on grounds other than race.[20] As soon as judicial review of union judgments went beyond such plainly invidious classifications as race, different problems of legal definition and of factual assessment could have been anticipated. The Burger Court had to confront one of the more troublesome.

A trucking company discharged several drivers for dishonesty, charging that they had sought reimbursement of motel expenses greater than those actually incurred. Motel receipts submitted by the drivers were in excess of the charges listed on motel records, whose accuracy was verified by affidavits from the motel clerk and the motel owner. The drivers suggested the motel be investigated, but the union told them "there was nothing to worry about." At an arbitration hearing before a joint union-management area committee, the employees denied any dishonesty but presented no other evidence to contradict the company's documents. The committee upheld the discharge. Subsequently the employees sued the employer for unjust discharge in violation of the collective agreement and sued the union for unfair representation. In a deposition the motel clerk at last admitted he had falsified the motel records and kept the difference between the amounts shown there and on the drivers' receipts. The Supreme Court held, in *Hines v. Anchor Motor Freight, Inc.,*[21] that the employer could not rely on the finality of the arbitral award as a defense against the employees' suit "if the contractual processes have been seriously flawed by the union's breach of its duty to represent employees honestly and in good faith and without invidious discrimination or arbitrary conduct."

The standard of representation enunciated in *Hines* can hardly be faulted in the abstract. Yet with the Supreme Court moving beyond the more clear-cut instances of discrimination and bad faith to reach "arbitrariness" and "perfunctoriness,"[22] the lower courts may be tempted to go on to negligence, or at least gross negligence. This would undoubtedly mean greater justice for individual employees in given cases, as in *Hines*. But union business agents, not learned in the niceties of due process, must often act quickly under pressure, and their customary aim has been the maximization of group interests, not the furthest pursuit of every individual claim. Moreover, decisions like *Hines* mean an employer cannot work out a grievance settlement with its employees' statutory bargaining representative which will have the same finality as an adjustment reached with a party's lawyer or other personally chosen agent. An undue extension of *Hines* could thus impair a union's flexibility and effectiveness in grievance handling and undercut its status as the employees' officially designated spokesman in dealing with their employer. One might reasonably question whether an increasing judicial scrutiny of union decisions involving matters of judgment and discretion bodes well for the total collective bargaining process.

INTERNAL UNION AFFAIRS

In the Labor-Management Reporting and Disclosure (Landrum-Griffin) Act of 1959[23] the federal government undertook for the first time a comprehensive regulation of internal union affairs. By 1969 and the advent of the Burger era, the federal courts of appeals, with an occasional emendation by the Supreme Court, had disposed of many of the most pressing issues raised by the new statute. Still, a number of significant questions remained unanswered. In addition, a few important decisions of the Burger Court interpreting the older National Labor Relations Act dealt more with union-member relationships than with traditional union-employer relationships. In several of these sensitive intraunion areas the Court struck a sound and practical, if not always totally satisfying, balance between individual claims and institutional interests.

Free Speech and Union Politics

Union members are guaranteed a broad right of free speech under the Landrum-Griffin Act. They may not be disciplined by their union, for example, even for libeling the organization's officers.[24] Despite this far-reaching protection, the Supreme Court held that a newly elected union president could lawfully discharge union-appointed business agents who had supported the opposing candidate for the presidency.[25] The Court emphasized that the safeguards of the statute apply to rank-and-file members of a labor organization and not to union officers or employees as such. Removal as a business agent does not affect one's membership status.

This result is supported by the need for a union president, like any other elected politician, to be free to choose those members of his staff who will exercise significant responsibility in the day-to-day operations of the organization. The Court expressly left open the question of whether it would be different if the employees occupied nonpolicymaking and nonconfidential positions. Even so, some nagging concerns are left that the analogy to civil government may not be entirely congruent. In the one-party system that prevails in nearly all labor unions, effective political action often requires the inside access that only an ongoing role in the administration can provide. While the Supreme Court's analysis makes good sense under the language of the statute, the Court might have been more troubled if it had dealt with a successful *incumbent* who had ousted his own dissenting business agents.

A much more difficult free-speech issue arose in *Steelworkers v. Sadlowski*.[26] In the hotly contested 1977 Steelworkers' election, Edward Sadlowski relied heavily on financial contributions from outside the union to offset the support his opponent, Lloyd McBride, received from the incumbent leadership and staff. McBride won handily and thereafter the Steelworkers' Convention forbade any candidate for union office to accept "financial support, or any other direct or indirect support of any kind" from a nonmember. In an opinion written by Justice Marshall, a 5 to 4 Supreme Court majority found this outsider rule to be a "reasonable" qualification on free speech within the meaning of the proviso to section 101(a)(2) of Landrum-Griffin. Declared the Court: "Although it may limit somewhat the ability of insurgent union members to wage an effective campaign, an interest deserving some protection under the statute, it is rationally related to the union's legitimate interest in reducing outsider interference with union affairs."[27] Justice White, joined by Chief Justice Burger and Justices Brennan and Blackmun in dissent, insisted that an absolute ban on nonmember contributions was unnecessary to prevent outsider control and would thwart the efforts of challengers in union elections. One may speculate that Justice Marshall veered away in this instance from his usual allies in cases involving individual rights because of his acquaintance with the special needs of mass movements to maintain their autonomy and avoid alien subversion.

Curiously, neither majority nor dissent seemed aware that the proviso of section 101(a)(2) does not authorize all "reasonable" limitations on free speech but only such as relate "to the responsibility of every member toward the organization as an institution and to his refraining from conduct that would interfere with its performance of its legal or contractual obligations." The standard examples have been the advocacy of dual unionism, "schism," or wildcat strikes; otherwise, the proviso has been tightly confined by the lower courts. An unfortunate by-product of Justice Marshall's sweeping generalization that the protections of free speech in section 101(a)(2) are not equivalent to those in the First Amendment, and his apparent acceptance of a "rational basis" test for justifying the outsider rule in *Sadlowski*, could be a reexamination of the scope of union members' freedom of expression under Landrum-Griffin. Union administrations may be entitled to considerable deference in the handling of most internal matters, but experience demonstrates that little latitude should be allowed in the restriction of dissidents' speech.

Union Elections

The Supreme Court has endorsed the secretary of labor's pragmatic approach toward determining what are "reasonable qualifications" for elective union office under Title IV of the Landrum-Griffin Act. If too many members (perhaps more than two-thirds) are disqualified by a particular rule or combination of rules, the provisions are presumed invalid. The Supreme Court agreed in *Steelworkers Local 3489 v. Usery*[28] that a requirement of attendance at one-half of a local's meetings during the three years preceding an election was unreasonable, where the result was that 96.5 percent of the local's 660 members were ineligible. The rule in the abstract may have had the legitimate purpose of ensuring knowledgeable and dedicated union leaders, but in actual operation it had the antidemocratic effect of restricting eligibility too drastically. In order to afford unions an initial opportunity to police their own house, however, the Court ruled that the secretary of labor may not sue to challenge an election on a ground that the complaining member did not raise previously in an internal protest to the union itself.[29]

Exclusive Representation and Minority Factions

A labor organization's power of exclusive representation received a major boost in *Emporium Capwell Co. v. Western Addition Community Organization.*[30] Minority employees charged a company with racial discrimination in job assignments and the union filed a formal grievance on their behalf. Several employees thought the contract procedures were inadequate and sought unsuccessfully to have the union picket the store in protest. When the company president refused to deal directly with the employees, they began picketing on their own, denouncing the store as racist and urging a customer boycott. After written warnings failed to deter continued picketing, two ringleaders were discharged. In an opinion written by Justice Marshall, from which only Justice Douglas dissented, the Supreme Court held that the dismissals did not violate the employees' rights of "industrial self-determination" guaranteed by section 7 of the NLRA. Their attempts to bypass the established grievance machinery and engage in separate bargaining with their employer were in derogation of the union's exclusive representational authority under section 9(a) of the act and cost them the protection of section 7. Justice Marshall left open the question of whether the discharges might have violated Title VII of the Civil Rights Act.

Black employees' distrust of predominantly white union representatives reached a peak in the late 1960s and early 1970s. Blacks formed separate caucuses within a number of major unions and often demanded separate representation in contract negotiations and grievance arbitrations. Such actions were understandable. But they constituted a grave threat to the whole structure of American collective bargaining and to its linchpin, the union's power of exclusive representation. Speaking with the special weight lent by the voice of Justice Marshall, the Court in *Emporium* set itself athwart these fractionating forces. Whether or not *Emporium* was the turning point, the assault on exclusive representation receded with the passing of the 1970s.

Union Security and Political Action

In *Abood v. Detroit Board of Education,*[31] the Burger Court finally confronted and resolved a constitutional issue that the Warren Court had avoided only through strained statutory interpretation sixteen years earlier.[32] *Abood,* in line with private sector precedents, sustained the constitutionality of a Michigan statute authorizing the negotiation of "agency shop" agreements under which public employees had to pay a service fee to the union, to the extent the service charges were used to finance collective bargaining, contract administration, and grievance adjustment. Then, reaching the long-mooted question, the Court held it would be unconstitutional to require a person "to contribute to the support of an ideological cause he may oppose as a condition of holding a job" under a union security arrangement. Justice

Powell, joined by the chief justice and Justice Blackmun, asserted that
there was no basis here for distinguishing "collective bargaining activities"
from "political activities" for First Amendment purposes. They contended
that collective bargaining in the public sector is always political in any
meaningful sense of the word, and the state should have to prove that
any union dues or fees required of nonunion employees are needed to
serve paramount governmental interests.

Neither in *Abood* nor in other related cases has the Supreme Court ever
addressed the point that unions, in both public and private employment,
are apparently being held to stricter constitutional and statutory limitations
than government itself. The union member can prevent the use of his compulsory dues for political purposes he opposes. The citizen cannot similarly
prevent the use of his tax money by government officials. If the answer to
this is that the legitimate governmental functions of civic personnel are
far broader than the legitimate collective bargaining functions of union
personnel, we are merely led to the more important practical question that
so far the Supreme Court has managed to sidestep: How are a union's
"collective bargaining" activities to be distinguished from its "political"
activities? How does one classify the congressional testimony of the Agri-
cultural Workers' president in support of federal bargaining rights for farm
labor? A union gift to the local United Fund in an effort to gain community
sympathy in forthcoming contract negotiations? A union's expenses in attempting to organize a neighboring plant whose substandard wage scale is
a threat to an existing bargaining unit? Although the protection of dissenters' rights in such cases as *Abood* can be applauded, sophisticated
judgment will have to be exercised in fixing the boundaries of activities
"germane to collective bargaining," or else a union could be unrealistically
restricted in the use of compulsory dues.

UNION-MANAGEMENT RELATIONS

Despite the focus of the Burger Court's labor cases on individual rights
in the work place, it has made almost as many decisions that are significant
to the more traditional law of union-management relations. It is in this
more conventional area that the greater solicitude of the Burger Court for
conservative values, such as an employer's property rights and managerial
prerogatives, becomes most pronounced. In the landmark cases of the Warren
era dealing with direct union-management confrontations, organized labor
had a victory record on the order of three to one. In such head-on union-
employer clashes before the Burger Court, management won 55 percent of
the cases. In addition, the Burger Court expressly overruled two of the
Warren Court's major prounion decisions[33] and significantly cut back or
undermined three others.[34] For all that, however, it would be a gross over-

simplification to characterize the Burger Court's record as a sharp reversal of a legal trend favoring unionism. It is natural that some of the closer, harder cases have arisen as the NLRA has matured; a 55 to 45 division is hardly a sign of overwhelming partisanship; and in the early 1980s unions actually prevailed more often than employers.

Union Organizing

The Burger Court has preserved and even extended the rights of employees to engage in union solicitation and the distribution of union literature on company premises during nonworking time, although the results have not always pleased the chief justice and other Nixon appointees. An employer may not forbid such activity even though the incumbent union has entered an agreement purporting to waive the employees' solicitation rights.[35] It makes no difference whether the employees are opposing or supporting the incumbent union. It also makes no difference whether the union literature is more political than organizational in nature, such as a pamphlet opposing a right-to-work law and supporting a higher minimum wage.[36]

The Burger Court awarded employers one notable victory, 5 to 4, in *Linden Lumber Div., Summer & Co. v. NLRB.*[37] Unless a company has engaged in unfair labor practices that would preclude a fair election, the majority held, the company is entitled to insist that a union file a petition for an election with the National Labor Relations Board (NLRB), and is not obliged to recognize the union on the basis of cards signed by a majority of the employees authorizing the union to represent them. The justices did not vote simplistically by blocs. There was an unusual, but in these circumstances understandable, alliance of some of the most liberal and some of the most conservative members of the Court. The employees' interest in the freest and best informed choice coalesced with the employer's interest in not having to recognize the union until it had an opportunity to dissuade the employees from their allegiance to the organization. Justice Douglas wrote the majority opinion and was joined by Justice Brennan along with three Nixon appointees. On the other hand, Justice Powell joined Justices Stewart, White, and Marshall in dissent.

Union Collective Action

Constitutional Protections

In *Food Employees Local 590 v. Logan Valley Plaza, Inc.,*[38] the Warren Court likened a large commercial shopping center to a normal municipal business block and held that union picketing of a nonunion retailer there was protected under the First Amendment. Ordinarily, of course, constitutional guarantees apply only against governmental action, not private action. In *Central Hardware Co. v. NLRB,*[39] the Burger Court refused to extend this

constitutional analysis to union solicitation on the privately owned parking
lots of a retail establishment. Instead, the proper inquiry was whether the
nonemployee solicitors had a statutory right of access under the NLRA on
the theory there were no reasonably available alternative channels of communication. Then, in *Hudgens v. NLRB*,[40] the Court declared that statutory
analysis rather than constitutional analysis was also the correct approach
to union picketing of a retail store in a privately owned, enclosed shopping
mall. Justice Stewart, for the majority, declared that "the constitutional
guarantee of free expression has no part to play in a case such as this."[41]
Logan Valley Plaza was expressly overruled.

The Court seems to have gone out of its way to lay *Logan Valley* to
rest, without its "ever having been accorded a proper burial," as dissenting
Justices Marshall and Brennan put it. *Hudgens* had to be remanded for a
determination of the picketers' rights under the NLRA, anyway, and the
resolution of the statutory question might have mooted the constitutional
issue. There is merit in the dissenters' complaint that the majority acted
precipitately in deciding such a "far-reaching constitutional question." Pru-
dence would have counseled waiting for more experience to verify or refute
the dissenters' claim that "the owner of the modern shopping center complex, by dedicating his property to public use as a business district, to
some extent displaces the 'State' from control of historical First Amendment forums, and may acquire a virtual monopoly of places suitable for
effective communication."[42] In any event, *Logan Valley* and *Hudgens* are
as good a pair of guides as we have to the respective attitudes of the
Warren and Burger Courts in balancing free speech and property rights.

The overruling of *Logan Valley Plaza* left open a question about the
continuing vitality of a significant dictum in Justice Marshall's majority
opinion in that case. After making the obvious point that the patrolling
element in picketing permits it to be regulated as a form of physical conduct, Justice Marshall went on to stress the "purpose" or "objective" of the
picketing as the crucial factor in determining whether its message may
constitutionally be prohibited or restricted. The cases where bans on picketing
have been upheld, he stated, "involved picketing that was found either
to have been directed at an illegal end . . . or to have been directed to
coercing a decision by an employer which, although in itself legal, could
validly be required by the State to be left to the employer's free choice."[43]
That test would still leave formidable questions for resolution. But it would
have the great virtue of focusing attention, as in other free speech inquiries,
on the content of the communication, and not on the form it takes. It seems
regrettable if the overruling of *Logan Valley*'s balancing of free speech
and property rights, when the *location* of the communicator was the issue,
should carry over to Justice Marshall's perceptive words on the wholly

different issue of the constitutional status of the picketers' message, regardless of their location.

In 1980, however, the Supreme Court so extended the "unlawful objectives" test for the constitutionality of picketing bans as to strip it of almost all practical meaning. In *NLRB v. Retail Store Employees Local 1001* [*Safeco*][44] it held that picketers asking customers not to buy a nonunion product being distributed by a second party was an unlawful boycott of the distributor where the distributor derived 90 percent of its income from sales of the picketed product. There was no indication that the picketing was intimidating in any way. Six justices considered the prohibition justified constitutionally by Congress's purpose of blocking the "coercing" or "embroiling" of neutrals in another party's labor dispute.

Justices Brennan, White, and Marshall dissented. But strangely they confined themselves to the statutory argument that the NLRA does not forbid consumer picketing aimed only at a particular nonunion product, as distinguished from the neutral distributor's business as such. The dissenters had nothing to say about what even concurring Justice Blackmun termed the "Court's cursory discussion of what for me are difficult First Amendment issues."[45] No justice dealt adequately with the question of how a union could constitutionally be prevented from asking individual members of the public not to purchase a designated nonunion product. Where was the "illegal end" within the meaning of Justice Marshall's *Logan Valley* formulation? Even if picketing addressed to an organized group like a union can be characterized as a "signal" calling for an "automatic response," rather than speech seeking a "reasoned response," is that also a proper characterization, as concurring Justice Stevens suggested, when the picketing is addressed to individual consumers exercising their own personal choice?[46] The Court has failed to provide a convincing rationale for distinguishing constitutionally between a "Do Not Purchase" appeal conveyed through a Nader-sponsored newspaper advertisement and a similar message conveyed through picketing, the working person's standard means of communication. Even the element of face-to-face confrontation (and arguable psychological coercion) cannot be the key if, as Justice Stevens maintains, distributing handbills is also to be placed in a different category from picketing because the former depends "entirely on the persuasive force of the idea."

Work Preservation and Changing Technology

If Local 100 calls a strike against Ace Manufacturing Co. to get better wages and working conditions, that is traditional, lawful "primary" activity. But if Local 100 asks the employees of Black Retailer to strike Black to force it to stop handling Ace's products until Ace settles with the union, that is a classic "secondary boycott" and forbidden by section 8(b)(4)(B) of the NLRA. So too, if Black agrees with Local 100 not to handle Ace's products until Ace settles, that is a contractual secondary boycott, a so-called hot goods clause, and forbidden by section 8(e) of the act. In each instance Local 100 is using its leverage against Black, a neutral, secondary party, to secure an objective elsewhere—at Ace, the primary party to the dispute. But suppose Ace agrees with Local 100 that it will keep within the plant all work traditionally done by Local 100 members and not sub-contract any to White Subcontractor. This "no-subcontracting" clause prevents employer dealings, just as the Local 100-Black agreement does. But here White is not the target; the objective is "work preservation" for Ace's own employees. This is also recognized as lawful primary activity, the Supreme Court's touchstone being that it is "addressed to the labor relations of the contracting employer *vis-à-vis* his own employees."[47]

The problem gets stickier if a "product boycott" is involved. Suppose the employer is a building contractor whose carpenters have traditionally cut and fitted doors for installation at the job site. The contractor has agreed with the carpenters union that it will not use "prefitted" doors, which have been prepared by the manufacturer for immediate installation without further cutting and fitting. Despite this agreement, the contractor goes ahead and orders prefitted doors. The union strikes to prevent their use. In *National Woodwork Manufacturers Ass'n v. NLRB*[48] the Warren Court held, 5 to 4, that such a strike was essentially concerned with "job preservation," the carpenters' traditional work of cutting and fitting doors at the construction site, and that it was therefore primary activity and not an unlawful secondary boycott. Four dissenting justices maintained that the union's conduct fell squarely within the language of section 8(b)(4)(B)—"forcing . . . any person to cease using . . . the products of any other producer"—and that product boycotts in particular have consistently been regarded as a proscribed secondary boycott.

The Burger Court had to handle a product boycott with an added wrinkle. After agreeing to a standard work preservation clause in a union contract that precluded the use of certain prefabricated climate controls, the contractor went ahead and entered into a construction subcontract that specified the use of prefabricated units. The union refused to install the units. The Supreme Court held that this refusal violated section 8(b)(4)(B) in *NLRB v. Enterprise Ass'n of Pipefitters Local 638.*[49] The majority reasoned that the product specifications contained in the employer's subcontract withdrew its "right of control" over the work in dispute, and thus the union's action was not directed at the contractor's labor relations "vis-à-vis his own employees," the accepted test for primary activity. The majority apparently regarded the general contractor that had imposed the specifications as the real target of the union pressure. Justices Brennan, Stewart, and

Marshall dissented on the quite forceful ground that the *Enterprise* result could not be squared with *National Woodwork*. Certainly it is hard to see how an employer's voluntary surrender of its "right of control" could metamorphose a union's lawful primary pressure into an illegal secondary boycott. Justices as sensitive to property rights as the majority in *Enterprise* should have remembered that the farmer who sells a cow to one buyer usually cannot turn around and sell the same cow to someone else. One might have suspected that the majority in *Enterprise* was basically at odds with *National Woodwork* itself. *Enterprise* gave priority to technological change and the flexibility of business arrangements over the capacity of unions to protect their members' jobs. That may be entirely supportable as a matter of economics, but it hardly squares with secondary boycott concepts. In any event the Supreme Court has long professed that such basic policy choices are the peculiar province of Congress.

Three years after *Enterprise,* a 5 to 4 majority of the Supreme Court somewhat surprisingly took a step back toward *National Woodwork*. In *NLRB v. International Longshoremen's Ass'n,*[50] the Court had to deal with work preservation in a situation where, as frequently happens, the work the union was trying to "preserve" had undergone a transformation because of technological innovation—here, containerized shipping. The ILA had agreed with a shippers association that ILA labor would have the job of "stuffing" or "stripping" all containers within a fifty-mile radius of a port, and that a royalty would be paid on any containers passing over the piers intact. The NLRB concluded that since the ILA's members had never performed off-pier stuffing or stripping, it was engaged in illegal work acquisition rather than permissible preservation of work within its traditional jurisdiction. The chief justice and Justices Stewart, Rehnquist, and Stevens accepted this view. But the majority disagreed that the determination that the work of the longshoremen had historically been the loading and unloading of ships was dispositive.

Writing for the Court, Justice Marshall declared the question was how the parties "sought to preserve that work, to the extent possible, in the face of a massive technological change."[51] The case was remanded to the labor board for initial consideration of whether "the stuffing and stripping reserved for the ILA . . . is functionally equivalent to their former work," or whether "containerization has worked such fundamental changes in the industry that the work formerly done at the pier . . . has been completely eliminated." Although insisting the board's answer was not preordained, Justice Marshall added pointedly: "This determination will, of course, be informed by an awareness of the congressional preference for collective bargaining as the method for resolving disputes over dislocations caused by the introduction of technological innovations in the workplace." A bare majority of the Court

was once again prepared to allow a union to defend the humane value
of job security even at the risk of some loss in industrial efficiency and
economic progress.

Federal Preemption and State Trespass Laws

During the Burger era the Supreme Court has alternately advanced and
retreated from the preemption line drawn by the Warren Court to exclude
state substantive law from areas regulated by Congress. The chief justice
and other Nixon appointees have generally tended to favor retrenchment,
opening the field to more extensive state regulation. The classic formulation of the Warren Court in the landmark *Garmon* case[52] was that conduct
"arguably protected" or "arguably prohibited" under the NLRA was subject
to the exclusive jurisdiction of the NLRB. States could act only if vital
local interests, such as the maintenance of public order, were at stake.

What some commentators viewed as a major departure from *Garmon*'s
preemption teachings came in *Sears, Roebuck & Co. v. San Diego County
District Council of Carpenters*.[53] A store sued a union for trespass in state
court for picketing on its property. No objection was made to the picketing
as such, but only to its location. Under federal law, such peaceful picketing on private property was both arguably protected and arguably prohibited.
The Supreme Court held the arguably prohibited nature of the conduct here
did not support preemption because the state was not regulating the picketing qua picketing but only as trespassory action affecting vital local interests. The Court also held that in the peculiar circumstances of this case,
even the arguably protected element did not justify preemption. The employer
could not get a ruling from the NLRB on actual protection (it could not
file charges against itself); only the union could, and it had declined to
file charges despite the employer's demand that the picketers leave. This
left the employer defenseless unless it resorted to force or could invoke
the state's trespass law. After pointing out that under the NLRA an employer may bar nonemployee union organizers from his property as a "general
rule," the majority concluded that the "risk of an erroneous state court
adjudication . . . is outweighed by the anomalous consequence of a rule
which would deny the employer access to any forum in which to litigate
either the trespass issue or the protection issue in those cases in which
the disputed conduct is least likely to be protected by § 7."[54]

Justices Brennan, Stewart, and Marshall dissented, emphasizing that the
Garmon test "has provided stability and predictability to a particularly complex area of law for nearly 20 years."[55] That practical point is the dissenter's
strong suit. The majority has all the theoretical trumps, especially if concurring Justice Blackmun's view that a union's filing of unfair labor practice
charges with the NLRB displaces state court jurisdiction is eventually ac-

cepted. Then, only a union bereft of hope of prevailing before the board would be consigned to the sometimes dubious mercies of state court judges.

Collective Bargaining

Duty to Bargain

Employers are required by the NLRA to bargain with the representative of their employees concerning "wages, hours, and other terms and conditions of employment."[56] Over the last two decades, the most controversial issue concerning the duty to bargain has been the extent to which employers must negotiate about managerial decisions that result in a shrinkage of employee job opportunities. Examples include subcontracting, automation, and plant relocations. Under established precedent, the crucial question is whether a subject is classified as a "condition of employment" or as a management right.[57] In *Fibreboard Paper Products Corp. v. NLRB,*[58] the Warren Court gave limited approval to the labor board's expansion of the range of so-called mandatory bargaining. It sustained a board order that a manufacturer bargain over subcontracting out its maintenance work within a plant. The Court emphasized that this did not alter the company's "basic operation" or require any "capital investment." There was simply a replacement of one group of employees with another to do the same work in the same place under the same general supervision. Negotiating would not "significantly abridge" the employer's "freedom to manage the business." That narrow approach did not reach the issue of subcontracting in general, and certainly not the issue of more fundamental structural or technological changes.

The Burger Court revisited the problem, with puzzling results, in *First National Maintenance Corp. v. NLRB.*[59] It was held that a maintenance firm did not have to bargain when it decided to terminate an unprofitable contract to provide janitorial services to a nursing home. The Court first stated broadly that an employer has no duty to bargain about a decision "to shut down part of its business purely for economic reasons."[60] But it then pointed out that in this particular case the operation was not being moved elsewhere and the laid-off employees were not going to be replaced, the employer's dispute with the nursing home concerned the size of a management fee over which the union had no control, and the union had just recently been installed and thus there was no disruption of an ongoing relationship. The Court consequently left unanswered many questions regarding the more typical instance of a partial closing or the removal of a plant to a new location.

Imposing a duty to bargain about managerial decisions such as subcontracting, plant removals, and technological innovation would obviously delay transactions, reduce business adaptability, and perhaps interfere with the confidentiality of negotiations with third parties. In some instances bargaining would be doomed in advance as a futile exercise. Nonetheless, the closer we move toward recognizing that employees may have something akin to a property interest in their jobs, the more apparent it may become that not even the employer's legitimate regard for profit making or the public's justified concern for a productive economy should totally override the workers' claim to a voice in the decisions of ongoing enterprises that will vitally affect their future employment opportunities. A moral value is arguably at stake in determining whether employees may be treated as pawns in management decisions. Often negotiations may benefit both parties by producing a less drastic solution than a shutdown or a relocation. At the very least, bargaining may serve a therapeutic purpose. As the Supreme Court put it in *Fibreboard*, in words that might sound platitudinous but for the grim historical reality behind them, the labor act "was framed with an awareness that refusals to confer and negotiate had been one of the most prolific causes of industrial strife."[61]

One of the persistent complaints about the National Labor Relations Act is the inadequacy of the remedy against an employer who unlawfully refuses to recognize or bargain with a majority union. Two or three years, and sometimes much longer, after the event, a recalcitrant employer will finally be subject to a judicially enforced order to bargain. Many critics insist that this is hardly more than a pious exhortation that the wrongdoer go and sin no more. Rarely will there be any financial repercussions. The employees receive nothing to make them whole for the losses they may have suffered by being denied the benefits of collective bargaining for several years. Apparently this situation will continue. In *H. K. Porter Co. v. NLRB*[62] an employer engaged in bad-faith bargaining over an eight-year period. The dispute mainly revolved around the company's unjustified refusal to agree to "check off" union membership dues from the employees' pay. Perhaps in exasperation, after several rounds of NLRB proceedings and court remands, the board at last ordered the employer to grant a checkoff provision. The Supreme Court held this was beyond the board's remedial powers.

The Court emphasized that a fundamental policy of the NLRA was "not to allow governmental regulation of the terms and conditions of employment, but rather to ensure that employers and their employees could work together to establish mutually satisfactory conditions."[63] Although the Court conceded that the congressional expression of this policy was contained in the section of the act *defining* the duty to bargain, it believed that the policy against imposing substantive contract terms should also extend to *remedying* proven violations. Its fingers thus burned, the NLRB has felt inhibited by the judgment in *H. K. Porter* from fashioning novel and potentially effective remedies for employer refusals to bargain, such as "make-whole" monetary relief for employees deprived of the fruits of collective bargaining. This has been true even though technically no continuing contract terms need be imposed, as occurred in *H. K. Porter*, and at most the putative contract that might have resulted from good-faith negotiations would simply be used as a measure of the employees' past losses.

Arbitration and Contract Enforcement

The Norris-LaGuardia Act generally prohibits the federal courts from issuing injunctions against peaceful strikes. When Congress in section 301 of the Taft-Hartley Act gave the federal courts jurisdiction over suits to enforce labor contracts, it deliberately rejected proposals to amend Norris-LaGuardia to take account of this new development. In *Sinclair Refining Co. v. Atkinson*,[64] the Warren Court made the obvious, logical deduction. Even strikes in breach of contract remained covered by Norris-LaGuardia's ban on federal injunctions. But there were evident policy deficiencies in this position. Most important, employers were deprived of what was often the most efficacious and sensible weapon against forbidden strikes. In the first year of the Burger era, the Supreme Court in *Boys Markets, Inc. v. Retail Clerks Local 770*[65] managed to confound the logic of *Sinclair* (and probably the intent of Congress) and do justice at last. A crafty opinion by Justice Brennan declared that Congress's refusal to amend Norris-LaGuardia when enacting Taft-Hartley did not mean the injunction ban was left intact. It merely meant Congress was prepared to leave to the federal judiciary the task of working out an appropriate "accommodation" between the two statutes. Justice Brennan's solution was to authorize federal injunctions against strikes where the underlying grievance is subject to a "mandatory grievance adjustment or arbitration procedure" in a collective bargaining agreement. While it may offend purists in statutory construction, this rule has much to commend it in elementary fairness. Norris-LaGuardia was designed to protect struggling unions against a biased and injunction-wielding judiciary, especially in organizing settings. When an established union has committed itself contractually not to strike and has been provided an effective alternative means of redress through arbitration, it is hardly a desecration of Norris-LaGuardia philosophy to grant the employer an injunction if the union goes back on its word and strikes.

The Burger Court has applied the *Boys Markets* test for injunctive relief with surprising literalness in favor of labor organizations. Thus, in *Buffalo Forge Co. v. Steelworkers*,[66] the Court held no injunction was available against a sympathy strike that was arguably a violation of the union's no-strike pledge. The key was that the strike was in support of other unions negotiating with the employer. The strike was not triggered by a dispute between the employer and the striking union, and hence the union had no grievance it could resolve through arbitration under its own contract.

Remedies other than an immediate injunction were of course available to the employer, including here resort to arbitration. The Supreme Court's continuing endorsement of arbitration as a centerpiece of national labor policy was further underscored in *Nolde Bros. v. Bakery Workers Local 358*.[67] In an opinion by Chief Justice Burger, the Court held arbitrable "a dispute which arises under the contract," even though "based on events that occur after its termination."[68] The dispute arose over severance pay called for in a contract that had expired four days before the company decided to close its plant permanently.

In two decisions involving "successor" employers, the Burger Court blurred, if it did not eradicate, major Warren Court teachings on the nature of the collective bargaining agreement. The earlier view was that it was "not an ordinary contract," but a "generalized code" setting forth "the common law of a particular industry or of a particular plant."[69] A predecessor's labor contract, in the Warren period, could bind a successor employer where there was "substantial continuity of identity in the business enterprise," without regard to the existence of actual consent. In the *Burns International Security*[70] and *Howard Johnson*[71] cases, the Burger Court refocused attention on traditional common law notions of the need for "consent" under "normal contract principles," and on the question of whether certain rights and duties were "in fact" "assigned" or "assumed."

On their facts, *Burns* and *Howard Johnson* held a predecessor's labor contract not binding on a rival company that supplanted the predecessor through competitive bidding or on a purchaser who retained only a minority of the seller's employees. This left open the possibility that the Warren successorship doctrine might still apply where there was a genuine link between predecessor and successor *and* a majority of the former's employees remained with the latter. What was more likely reflected here, however, was a clash of fundamental values in the labor area. The Warren majority was concerned about protecting employees against a sudden and unforeseen loss of bargaining and contract rights. There was also a concern about maintaining industrial stability and labor peace, through reducing the number of representation elections and sustaining the life of labor agreements. On the other hand, the Burger majority laid stress on the freedom and voluntariness of the collective bargaining process, on the importance of saddling neither unions nor employers with substantive contract terms to which they have not agreed. Stress was further laid on providing maximum flexibility in business arrangements, so that employers may respond to changing market conditions without being straitjacketed by the bargaining or contractual obligations that may have been assumed by imprudent predecessors. The future development of successorship law undoubtedly depends far more on the way the members of the Supreme Court ultimately balance out these competing values than on any logical deductions from the decisions to date.

Antitrust

The leading candidate as the Burger Court's most mangled labor decision would have to be *Connell Construction Co. v. Plumbers Local 100.*[72] The fault was not entirely the Burger Court's. *Connell* was only the latest in a long line of cases in which the Supreme Court has essayed the well-nigh futile task of reconciling age-old union restrictive practices with the strictures of the antitrust laws. The two worlds are fundamentally at odds. The essence of antitrust philosophy is the promotion of competition; the essence of unionism is the elimination of competition, at least the elimination of wage competition among all employees doing the same job in the same industry. An uneasy truce has prevailed whenever the Supreme Court has recognized that the antitrust laws have little if any place in dealing with restraints in the labor market, that is, the area of wages, hours, and working conditions, and that antitrust doctrines should largely be confined to restraints in the product market, the commercial sale of goods and services. Improper union restraints are more appropriately regulated through labor legislation, tailored to fit the peculiar characteristics and behavior of labor organizations.

In *Connell* a plumbers local picketed a general contractor and secured an agreement that the contractor would subcontract mechanical work only to firms that had a collective bargaining contract with the union. The contractor then sued the local for violating the Sherman Antitrust Act. In a 5 to 4 decision the Supreme Court sustained the cause of action. In the majority's view, the local had used direct restraints on the commercial market to achieve its concededly lawful organizational objective. As stated by Justice Powell, the restrictive agreement was designed to force nonunion subcontractors out of the market, "even if their competitive advantages were not derived from substandard wages and working conditions but rather from more efficient operating methods."[73] Viewed solely in antitrust terms this makes some sense, although it ignores long-standing precedent that the antitrust laws exempt agreements, whether primary or secondary, that are immediately aimed at promoting union organization[74] as well as agreements that are aimed at eliminating competition over wages and other labor standards. The principal vice of Justice Powell's majority opinion, however, is its total disregard of the necessary implications of applicable labor law.

When Congress outlawed "hot goods" agreements in section 8(e) of the amended NLRA, it recognized the special interrelationship of a general contractor and its subcontractors in the construction industry, and added a proviso excepting agreements regarding "work to be done" at a job site. The acknowledged purpose was to permit unions and employers in the building trades to enter "union-only" subcontracting arrangements. Indeed, the NLRB's general counsel has expressly declined to issue unfair labor practice complaints against contracts like the one at issue in *Connell*. Justice Powell evaded the force of the 8(e) proviso by engrafting two or three qualifications, none of which finds substantial support in the legislative history. The authorization for excluding nonunion contractors, he said, "extends only to [subcontracting] agreements in the context of collective bargaining relationships, and . . . possibly to common-situs relationships on particular jobsites as well."[75] The plumbers' clause barring nonunion subcontracting in *Connell* failed to meet this test, since the local did not seek to represent employees working directly for the general contractor but only the employees of plumbing subcontractors.[76]

The egregious failure of the *Connell* majority to take proper account of the policies of the labor laws in working out an accommodation with the antitrust laws was the principal focus of Justice Stewart's dissent. The plumbers' secondary activity at the Connell site was subject to comprehensive regulation under Taft-Hartley, and antitrust sanctions would necessarily upset the balance thus struck by Congress. True, section 303 of the Taft Act, providing for actual damages for secondary strikes in violation of section 8(b)(4), was not amended in 1959 to cover secondary agreements in violation of section 8(e). But that should not have meant, as Justice Powell inferred, that the omission of actual damages under Taft-Hartley for 8(e) violations made them liable to treble damages under Sherman. In the hierarchy of labor law values, coercive conduct is almost invariably subject to more severe sanctions than is an agreement having the same restrictive results.[77] It would therefore have been incongruous for Congress to prescribe actual damages under section 303 for secondary activity in violation of section 8(b)(4), but not for agreements in violation of section 8(e), all for the purpose of subjecting the latter alone to the much harsher remedy of treble damages under the antitrust laws.

Beyond that misreading of federal labor law, perhaps the most disquieting aspect of the majority's approach was its pronouncement that to permit subcontracting agreements with "stranger" contractors, without confinement to particular job sites, "would give construction unions an almost unlimited organizational weapon."[78] If any lesson should have been learned from a century of federal intervention in labor disputes, it is that the Congress and not the courts ought to have the primary responsibility for determining what economic weapons are allowable to either party in a labor dispute.

CONCLUSION

Organized labor is in decline in the United States. While the movement has grown to over twenty million, the labor force has expanded more rapidly, and union membership has fallen to only 19.7 percent of the total.[79] That is, proportionately, less than half the union population in Great Britain or Western Europe. And American unions today consistently lose over 50 percent of the representation elections in which they participate.[80] The principal cause of membership shrinkage and organizing failures is undoubtedly the shift of jobs from the blue-collar to the white-collar sectors. But it cannot be wholly coincidental that the period of organized labor's most dramatic growth began with the Wagner Act and practically ended with Taft-Hartley and that over the past quarter of a century unions have suffered an unbroken string of defeats in congressional battles concerning the balance of power between labor and management. At least psychologically, and presumably in much more tangible ways as well, the state of the law affects a union's capacity to organize and bargain.

Although the Burger Court's overall record has proved more moderate than the labor movement may have anticipated, the Court's secondary boycott and antitrust rulings in the construction industry, its ruling on shopping center picketing in retail settings, and its "successorship" rulings in industry generally, to mention a few noteworthy examples, tip the scales still further against union organizational efforts. Beside the stark statistics on union infirmity, the *Connell* majority's fear that unless section 8(e) of the NLRA is read to mean what it does not say, building trades unions would be given an "almost unlimited organizational weapon" seems an oddly misplaced concern. Federal labor law as written, without any stretching by the judiciary, appears more than adequate to suppress nearly any exercise of overweening union power.

The Burger Court's parsing of the statutory rights of individual workers has been more consistently defensible, even when controversial. Institutionalists may argue that the Court went too far in applying the duty of fair representation in *Hines*, the case of the altered motel receipts, and civil libertarians may contend that it sacrificed minority interests to outmoded notions of job seniority in cases like *Teamsters* and *Patterson*. But in weighing those and similar claims under the NLRA, Title VII, and Landrum-Griffin, the Court has constantly had to balance one person's grievance against the equities of fellow workers and the institutional needs of the collective representative of the entire group. All in all, the Court has responded sensibly in its handling of individual and minority rights. They have generally been accorded the high priority they deserve. At the same time, however, the Court has not forgotten that the mass of employees, too, have rights and that healthy, effective labor organizations are the best means yet devised for securing those rights in the work place.

• Nine •

The Burger Court, Antitrust, and Economic Analysis

R. S. Markovits

In my admittedly optimistic judgment, the Burger Court[1] has increasingly reached in recent years what I take to be correct conclusions[2] on the major antitrust issues it has addressed.[3] In so doing, it has departed not only from the actual decisions of the later Warren Court[4] but also from the positions taken by the Supreme Court when it was headed by Burger but still dominated, both numerically and intellectually, by Warren Court appointees.[5] In general, I would attribute the Burger Court's success in this area to its systematic replacement of the unjustified and usually unjustifiable social and economic assertions of the Warren Court with more sophisticated economic analyses of the relevant business practices.

I should admit at the outset that virtually all the evidence on which these conclusions are based is somewhat ambiguous. Since the Supreme Court hears only a few antitrust cases in any given term, since antitrust interpretations can gain little from doctrinal developments and decision patterns in other areas of the law, and since the recent Burger Court opinions on which I will primarily focus are far from clear, any attempt to generalize in this area must be subject to more than the usual quotient of scholarly qualifications. Nevertheless, I think that my evaluation of the Burger Court's antitrust performance is justified, for, as we shall see, since 1974 the Burger Court has (1) indicated that the test of antitrust legality is the effect of the acts in question on competition rather than their impact on populist democracy or the independence and survival of small businessmen; (2) insisted that it has both the responsibility and the ability to undertake the kind of particularized economic analysis necessary to implement a competitive impact test; (3) recognized that horizontal mergers may promote competition and that one cannot always predict the anticompetitive consequences of any such merger by defining the relevant market and computing its concentration and the market shares* of the merger partners; (4) refused to strike down ver-

---

*For antitrust purposes, a market consists of a product-geographic space within which a specifiable group of sellers competes. The market share of each such seller is then defined to be his percentage of the total sales in the market in question. Relatedly, the concentration of the relevant market is defined to equal the sum of the market shares of the market's leading four or eight firms.

tical territorial restrictions* that its predecessors would almost certainly have condemned on the ground that these arrangements may generate real efficiences that can increase competition and thus should not be held unlawful per se;† and (5) admitted that joint ventures between competitors can be lawful—that is, can benefit consumers by creating efficiencies of various kinds.[6]

THE ANTITRUST LAWS' TESTS OF LEGALITY

The most important provisions of the American antitrust laws respectively condemn "every contract, combination . . . or conspiracy in restraint of trade,"[7] acts of monopolization or attempts to monopolize,[8] and a number of specific types of conduct where their effect "may be to substantially lessen competition, or tend to create a monopoly."[9] Antitrust litigation has always been marked by a debate about whether these provisions create an essentially economic test of legality—roughly speaking, whether they condemn behavior that is designed to or is likely to injure buyers by reducing the competitive pressure their best-placed supplier faces‡—or whether the antitrust laws were also designed to further various noneconomic, usually "populist," goals such as protecting "viable, small, locally-owned businesses";[10] preserving "the freedom guaranteed each and every business, no matter how small"[11] "to dispose of the goods [it] own[s] as [it] see[s] fit";[12] and preventing the concentration of economic ownership across economic markets[13] even when no direct harm to economic competition seems likely to result.

I believe that the current American antitrust laws should be interpreted to contain a purely economic test of legality. In brief, I reach this conclusion because such a test is more compatible with (1) the acts' language ("attempts to monopolize," "lessen competition," "create a monopoly"); (2) the criminal provisions and tort antecedents of the Sherman Act; and (3) the general regulatory framework within which the American antitrust laws are set (a framework that includes patent and copyright laws that encourage innovation even when it leads to economic concentration). I reject

---

*A vertical territorial restraint is an arrangement in which a manufacturer restricts the areas within which each of his distributors can operate. Similar restraints are also sometimes imposed on a customer-by-customer or customer-type basis.

†A practice is unlawful per se if it is considered to violate the antitrust laws without regard to the particular circumstances in which it is employed or any countervailing values it may serve.

‡A buyer's "best-placed supplier" is that supplier who can profit from supplying the particular customer on terms that no one else could in the short run profit by beating. A best-placed supplier's advantage can reflect, among other things, the particular buyer's preference for the relevant seller's product or distributive variant, the seller's physical proximity to the particular buyer, or the seller's greater general technical efficiency (lower marginal cost).

the proposition that the antitrust laws should be used to serve goals relating to social or political organization in addition to economic efficiency. Not only is there little warrant in the texts or legislative histories of the antitrust statutes to support such a mode of interpretation but also there is good reason to question whether any important social and political goals would be served by restricting economically efficient arrangements and practices. Thus, I doubt that a local manager of a large corporation or an independent distributor who is subject to vertical constraints[14] will behave less well socially or politically than his independent or unrestricted counterpart. Indeed, local independent owners are likely to be less active and independent in local politics since they probably will have to spend more time in their businesses and may very well be more dependent on local financial and political support. Moreover, although large corporations may be well placed to lobby for economically undesirable legislation, one would have to limit internal growth as well as growth through mergers to prevent such distortions of the legislative process. Unfortunately, any such limitation would probably be very costly economically (though of course it would be desirable for economic reasons to reduce the artificial incentives for existing corporate growth created by the capital gains tax). In fact, such a policy might even be counterproductive politically, since large corporations may produce politically offsetting effects and no economically acceptable policy could eliminate all large organizations.

The later Warren Court reached the opposite conclusion. Led by Justices Douglas and Black, that Court sought to preserve the independence and freedom of small, locally owned businesses,[15] even at a cost to the consumers directly involved. Thus, according to the majority in the *Brown Shoe* case, Congress intended section 7 of the Clayton Act (which regulates mergers) to preserve locally owned businesses even where occasional higher costs and prices result.[16] Similarly, as Justices Stewart and Harlan admitted in a 1968 case, the Warren Court proceeded on the assumption that "one of the objectives of the Sherman Act was to preserve, for social rather than economic reasons, a high degree of independence, multiplicity and variety in the economic system."[17]

Although the mature Burger court has never explicitly addressed this issue, at least twice its majority has taken positions that imply its rejection of noneconomic criteria in antitrust adjudication. First, in *United States v. Marine Bancorporation*,[18] the Court defined the geographic area within which the impact of a merger is to be assessed as "the area in which the goods or services at issue are marketed to a significant degree by the acquired firm." This restrictive definition was selected so that assessments of market impact could be based on existing economic data rather than on speculation concerning possible future radiating effects. Again, in *Continental T.V. Inc. v. GTE Sylvania Inc.*,[19] the Court implied that the antitrust laws contain a purely economic test of legality by focusing its analysis of the legality of the vertical territorial restrictions under attack exclusively on the possibility that such provisions might reduce competition. Indeed, Mr. Justice White's concurring opinion in *Sylvania* explicitly objected to the Burger Court majority's conclusion on the ground that it failed to give cognizance to the value that "independent businessmen should have the freedom to dispose of the goods they own as they see fit." In short, although the tea leaves are admittedly scanty, the Burger Court appears to be preparing an antitrust brew with an exclusively economic flavor.

Given the Burger Court's apparent decision to give weight solely to economic values, it would not be surprising to see economic analysis play a greater role in the Burger Court's opinions than in the opinions of the Warren Court. In fact, the actual role of economic analysis in Burger Court opinions is even greater than this change in tests would suggest, for the mature Burger Court does not share its predecessor's belief that courts and judges are not competent to comprehend and make use of economic analysis.

The later Warren Court position on this issue is most clearly articulated by Justice Marshall's majority opinion in *United States v. Topco Assocs.*,[20] which declared unlawful per se territorial restraints that a joint-venture purchasing agent imposed on the grocery stores that were both its founders and its customers. In defending its refusal to examine the actual competitive significance of these restrictions, Marshall argued: "Courts are of limited utility in examining difficult economic problems. . . ."[21] [C]ourts are ill-equipped and ill-suited for such decision making [—that is, t]o analyze, interpret, and evaluate the myriad of competing interests and the endless data that would surely be brought to bear on such decisions, and to make the delicate judgment on the relative values to society of competitive areas of the economy."[22] Of course, if competition were the only value at stake, the Court's institutional incapacity could not justify its progovernment decisions, for, presumably, the fact that the Court was ignorant and noncomprehending would not shift the burden of persuasion from the government to the defendant. It is generally assumed that the later Warren Court did shift this burden to defendants by treating the legal judgments of the Justice Department's antitrust division, the prosecuting authority, as presumptively valid. However, I think that the Warren Court's decisional process can be better characterized in a significantly different way.

It seems more likely that the Court's apparent practice of requiring defendants to demonstrate the procompetitive impact of their conduct reflected a judgment that the antitrust laws also embody other, noneconomic values such as populism and business autonomy that it believed would be disserved by the business behavior in question. Since the Court assumed that the behavior in question would harm these noneconomic values sufficiently to establish its prima facie illegality, the justices could logically shift to defendants the burden of demonstrating that their conduct's competitive impact was sufficiently positive to outweigh its noneconomic negative consequences—a burden that defendants could rarely discharge before a court that was unwilling to try to comprehend or evaluate the relevant economic arguments.

Although the later Warren Court never articulated such a rationale for its approach to antitrust matters, and although it continued to require the government to come up with arguments relating to the supposed anticompetitive impact of the conduct in question, the Court's opinions seem more consistent with the approach just described. This explanation rationalizes the series of Court decisions in which the later Warren Court condemned horizontal mergers in the face of the government's failure to develop the kind of particularized analysis the Court had once deemed necessary.[23] This account is also consistent with the Warren Court's decision in *United States v. Schwinn*[24] to hold certain vertical territorial restraints per se unlawful in the face of its earlier conclusion that the actual business functions and competitive consequences of each such practice must be individually examined.[25]

As we have seen, the mature Burger Court rejected the Warren Court's noneconomic values. Hence, if the Burger Court shared its predecessor's self-doubts regarding its capacity to comprehend economic arguments, one would not expect the current justices to hold certain types of business behavior unlawful unless the government could establish that the type of conduct in question rarely produces any desirable efficiencies and normally reduces competition—that is, unless the government establishes the per se illegality of the conduct. However, the Burger Court does not believe that it is unable to comprehend or evaluate arguments on a case-by-case basis regarding the competitive impact of various business practices. Thus, as early as 1974,[26] in the *Marine Bancorporation* case, the Burger Court rejected certain unsubstantiated government assertions relating to market impact as "little more than speculation." The opinion appears—as Justice White noted critically in his dissent—to commit the courts to examine and make up their own minds about various relevant market conditions. The same increase in self-confidence is evident in the 1977 *Sylvania* case,[27] in which the court justified its abandonment of the per se rule, established previously in *United States v. Schwinn*, by arguing that it has an obligation to determine the possible efficiencies and competitive impact of such practices in varying circumstances.

In short, the mature Burger Court has brought economic analysis to the fore in antitrust litigation both by employing an exclusively economic test of legality and by insisting that courts must and can undertake particularized economic analyses.

HORIZONTAL MERGERS

Roughly speaking, horizontal mergers are mergers between companies that are, at least sometimes, well placed to compete for the patronage of the same buyers. Horizontal mergers can benefit buyers in two basic ways: (1) by generating efficiencies that increase the attractiveness of the sales offers the merger partners make to buyers they were not originally best placed to serve, offers which thereby increase the pressure the merger partners place on competitors who were originally better placed to serve the buyers in question, and (2) by making it profitable for the merged firm to make an investment in new product variants, distributive outlets, or production capacity that neither merger partner nor anyone else would have found attractive before the merger. Of course, horizontal mergers can also harm buyers in various ways: (1) by freeing the merger partners from each other's competition (for example, by taking away their incentive to undercut each other's prices and by inhibiting each from making investments that would reduce the profits the other realized on its established projects), and (2) by facilitating oligopolistic* interactions between the merger partners and their rivals or indeed among the rivals themselves, thus facilitating oligopolistic pricing by the merger partners and by their rivals.

In general, then, the net competitive effect of any horizontal merger will depend on the various factors that influence the strength of these offsetting tendencies. Ideally, the legality of any horizontal merger should depend on the answers to the following sorts of questions: (1) How large are the efficiencies generated by the merger, and how often was a merger partner the closest or almost the closest competitor of some remaining rival? In other words, to what extent will the merger benefit buyers by increasing the pressure the merger partners place on their rivals? (2) How often and by what margin were the merger partners each other's closest rivals? That is, to what extent will the merger harm buyers by freeing the merger partners from each other's competition? (3) To what extent did the merger partners face common potential rivals before the merger, and was one merger partner significantly better placed than the other to retaliate against such a common rival? That is, to what extent will the merger harm buyers by facilitating the merger partners' practice of oligopolistic pricing?[28]

Traditionally, however, the Justice Department and the courts have not based their predictions regarding the competitive impact of horizontal mergers on such specific inquiries. Instead, they have based their analysis on aggregate market data such as the concentration of the relevant market (the aggregate market share of the leading four or eight firms) and the market shares of the merger partners. To be precise, the courts typically have determined the legality of a horizontal merger by defining the relevant market and determining whether the merged firm's market share exceeded some critical percentage, which varied inversely with the market's overall concentration. The later Warren Court purported to use this approach, although the justices

---

*An interaction is said to be oligopolistic when one party's move is influenced by his realization that his rival knows that he can react to that rival's response.

defined the relevant markets in ways that resulted in the mergers in question being declared illegal.[29]

Unfortunately, even if applied faithfully, this method cannot produce an accurate or cost-effective* assessment of the economic consequences of a horizontal merger. The inadequacy of the traditional approach reflects three separate problems: (1) in a world in which product and locational differentiation abound, it will often be impossible to define the relevant markets nonarbitrarily since different, partially overlapping sets of firms will be competing for the patronage of different groups of affected buyers; (2) even where markets can be defined nonarbitrarily, market share and concentration data do not reveal (indeed have never been supposed to reveal) anything about many of the most important determinants of the competitive impact of a horizontal merger—for example, the size of the efficiencies the merger will generate; and (3) market share and concentration ratio data have little bearing on many of the determinants of a merger's impact to which these data are alleged to relate—for example, how often and by what margin were the merger partners each other's closest competitors, how often was one of the merger partners some rival's closest competitor, how often did the merger partners have common rivals, and so forth. For these reasons, I believe that the traditional approach is both less accurate and less cost-effective than the admittedly expensive, disaggregated approach I would recommend. The market-oriented approach spends a great deal of resources to establish market definitions that permit one to compute aggregated market share and concentration figures that have less predictive value than the disaggregated data from which the market definitions were derived.

Thus, there is little to be said not only for the later Warren Court's apparent conclusion that virtually all horizontal mergers are anticompetitive and hence unlawful but also for the traditional market-share–market-concentration approach the Court purportedly used to generate its specific outcomes. Concerning horizontal mergers the Burger Court had virtually nowhere to go but up. Although the only horizontal merger case the Burger Court has decided, *United States v. General Dynamics Corp.*,[30] involved a somewhat unique competitive situation, both the outcome in this case and the qualified rejection in the Court's opinion of the traditional market-oriented approach are enormously encouraging. Moreover, both the outcome of and the Court's opinion in a related conglomerate merger† case, *United States v. Marine Bancorporation*,[31] reinforces this optimism.

In *General Dynamics* the Court analyzed the legality of a horizontal merger

---

* An assessment is cost-effective if the knowledge resulting from it has more economic value (typically, because it can be used to generate efficiencies worth a certain amount) than the expense incurred in making the assessment.

† A conglomerate merger is a merger between two companies that do not compete for any common buyers and do not supply each other.

in the coal industry which raised the acquiring firm's market share from 7.6 to 12.4 percent in two geographic markets that were significantly and increasingly concentrated. Although these numbers would clearly have condemned the merger under the Warren Court's approach, Justice Stewart, joined by the four Burger Court appointees, upheld the merger primarily on the ground that the limited coal reserves possessed by one of the merging companies would have precluded its continuing as a strong competitive force in the future.

One could argue that the Court's partial rejection of the traditional approach in *General Dynamics* was limited to the special circumstances of that case.[32] The Court's opinion placed considerable emphasis on the special nature of the coal industry, particularly on the significance for the future strength of competition in the market of the fact that the relevant reserves of coal were diminishing. The opinion even suggested, by way of contrast, that for other industries, such as groceries and beer (both the subject of major Warren Court decisions),[33] market share statistics should still be controlling "since in most markets distribution systems and brand recognition are such significant factors that one may reasonably suppose that a company which has attracted a given number of sales will retain that competitive strength."[34]

Nevertheless, the *General Dynamics* decision represents a healthy appreciation by the Court of the fact that market share statistics do not always tell the complete, or even the most important, story. In this regard, it is noteworthy that in a dictum in his subsequent opinion for the Court in *United States v. Marine Bancorporation*, Justice Powell cited *General Dynamics* for the proposition that market share statistics "can be unreliable indicators of actual market behavior."[35]

This qualified skepticism is, of course, only a first step. But having once opened up the question of the probative value of market share statistics, and having forcefully reaffirmed the point that the ultimate measure of the permissibility of a horizontal merger is its actual impact on competitive behavior, the Court can be expected to pursue the logic of its insight in *General Dynamics* and eventually reject the traditional market share approach across-the-board. If the type of particularized assessment of competitive dynamics undertaken in *General Dynamics* becomes the rule rather than the exception in horizontal merger cases, the Burger Court will have ushered in a major advance in antitrust doctrine.

VERTICAL TERRITORIAL RESTRAINTS AND RESALE PRICE MAINTENANCE AGREEMENTS

A vertical territorial restraint restricts the territory within which a distributor can sell a product. Customer allocation clauses place similar restrictions on the customers with whom a distributor can deal. Resale price maintenance clauses restrict the price which the reseller can charge for the product in question, either by specifying a particular price or by establishing a minimum (maximum) price below (above) which the reseller cannot go.

All manufacturers must choose between distributing their products themselves, typically through separate marketing divisions of their companies, and marketing them through independent distributors. Regardless of which alternative a manufacturer selects, he is likely to realize lower profits than would be realized by a perfectly integrated concern combining both manufacturing and marketing operations, where all employees strive to maximize the overall organization's returns rather than the profits of the independent firm or the profits of the separate (at least for accounting purposes) marketing division of the integrated company. Sometimes manufacturers will lose profits because the decisions of its independent distributors or their marketing division counterparts affect the sales and returns that other distributors realize. And sometimes such firms' profits will be reduced because distributor and manufacturer decisions affect each other's joint and separate profits directly. Our analysis of vertical territorial restraints and resale price maintenance agreements must begin with an exploration of such problems since all of these devices function primarily by reducing the extent to which the use of an independent distributor system lowers profits in certain ways.

The economic functions of vertical restraints can be explained by examining the problems that can be caused by interdistributor spillovers. For illustrative purposes, I will focus on local advertising decisions that can best be made by local personnel, who know what sort of campaign is most likely to be effective in their area and what media are most likely to be cost-effective for them. Thus, where a manufacturer uses an independent local distributor, the manufacturer's profits will be reduced to the extent that that distributor is deterred from placing advertisements which would generate sales not only for himself but also for rival distributors of the manufacturer's product.[36] For example, assume that a manufacturer has two independent distributors in a given area and that each distributor could place a $100 advertisement that would increase its and the other distributor's sales sufficiently to yield for them additional profits of $90 and $20 respectively. Obviously, in such a case, neither distributor acting independently would place the advertisement, despite the fact that each advertisement would increase the profits of the manufacturing-sales network as a whole.[37]

Unfortunately, even if such a manufacturer could distribute his own products as efficiently as an independent distributor, such vertical integration would not necessarily solve the problem just described. Thus, if the salaries and promotions of local managers vary with the normal accounting profits that their outlet's books reveal, they would have no more incentive than independent distributors to place an advertisement that would increase the organization's overall profits by $10 but reduce their individual outlet's book profits by $10. Of course, in many circumstances it will be easier for a company to keep track of and respond to interdependencies among its own outlets and employees than to coordinate the behavior of independent distributors—that is, hierarchical data systems and controls will be superior to the capacity of market forces (such as the level of the franchise fees manufacturers charge independent distributors) to reflect these interdependencies. However, even when integration has such advantages, other factors may lead the manufacturer to use a system of independent distributors. For example, an independent distributor system will tend to be adopted when the manufacturer faces various barriers to expansion, or when individual attitudes toward being one's own boss rather than someone else's employee make it more cost-effective to contract out distribution than to hire distributional employees.

When circumstances such as these lead manufacturers to market their products by means of independent distributors, the performance of such a marketing system often can be improved by using vertical territorial restraints and resale price maintenance agreements. In particular, under certain conditions these restrictive devices can reduce or eliminate interdistributor spillover effects that sometimes make a particular marketing strategy unattractive to individual distributors even when it would be optimal from the standpoint of the manufacturer's overall marketing effort. Thus, by employing a series of vertical territorial restraints to assign each independent distributor the exclusive right to make sales within the territory covered by that distributor's advertising, the manufacturer can eliminate or at least significantly reduce the spillover effects that distort his individual distributors' advertising incentives.[38] Although resale price maintenance clauses, prohibiting all distributors from selling the product below a set price, are not quite so effective in this regard, they also reduce troublesome spillovers by precluding distant distributors from giving customers a price reason to abandon their local suppliers, whose advertising first interested the customers in the product.[39]

Although this explanation has focused on local advertising decisions, vertical territorial restraints and resale price maintenance agreements work in the same way to prevent interdistributor spillovers that can distort the incentives for independent distributors to provide customers with presale advice and postsale service. Such restraints promote presale advice by reducing the probability that buyers who are given such information by one distributor will purchase the relevant product from a second distributor who serves the same area or who gives the buyer a significant price discount. They promote postsale service by increasing the likelihood that distributors who give good service will thereby enable themselves to make new sales to the buyers they serve.[40] Vertical territorial restraints and resale price maintenance agreements can also provide distributors with incentives to exchange information about effective sales techniques, advertising layouts, store layouts, and so on by assuring them that their rival distributors will not use such information to steal their customers. Relatedly, such restraints may enable a manufacturer to prevent overall returns from being reduced by the kind of inter-distributor spillovers that result when one distributor of the manufacturer's product offers a lower price to capture a customer from another distributor who otherwise could have obtained the buyer's patronage at the higher price.

The early Warren Court appeared to recognize the possible procompetitive impact of vertical territorial restraints and argued that their legality should be determined on a case-by-case basis.[41] However, the later Warren Court partially rejected this position in its 1967 *Schwinn* opinion,[42] which held vertical territorial and customer allocations illegal per se where the manufacturer parted with dominion, risk, and control over the product. Admittedly, this decision brought the legal status of vertical territorial restraints more into line with the legal status of their functional equivalents, resale price maintenance agreements, since the latter have always been held per se unlawful under the Sherman Act. However, two wrongs do not make a right. Neither type of vertical restraint is inherently inefficient. Neither should be thought to violate the antitrust laws absent specific proof of its anticompetitive effect in the particular circumstances of each case.

In contrast, the Burger Court has consistently moved the law in appropriate directions. This tendency is most evident in *Continental T.V. v. GTE Sylvania Inc.*,[43] a 1977 decision which explicitly overruled the Warren Court's *Schwinn* decision. Justice Powell's majority opinion rejected *Schwinn*'s attempt to distinguish situations according to whether the manufacturer had parted with dominion, risk, and control of the relevant product. Instead, the Court held that vertical territorial restraints should be judged on a case-by-case basis, since there was no evidence that they usually have "a pernicious effect on competition" or that they "lack any redeeming virtue." In fact, Justice Powell's opinion, drawing heavily on the academic literature, acknowledges many of the legitimate functions such vertical restraints can perform:

> Economists have identified a number of ways in which manufacturers can use such restrictions to compete more effectively against other manufacturers. . . . For example, new manufacturers and manufacturers entering new markets can use the restrictions in order to induce competent and aggressive retailers to make the kind of investment of capital and labor that is often required in the distribution of products unknown to the consumer. Established manufacturers can use them to induce retailers to engage in promotional activities or to provide service and repair facilities necessary to the efficient marketing of their products. . . . Because of market imperfections such as the so-called "free

rider" effect, these services might not be provided by retailers in a purely competitive situation, despite the fact that each retailer's benefit would be greater if all provided the services than if none did.[44]

The Court still has a long way to go in this area. Justice Powell continues to employ a "paramutual approach," which permits small, less successful firms to use vertical restraints in circumstances in which large, more successful rivals cannot; fails to see that vertical territorial or customer restraints will seldom reduce competition in the relevant sense; and continues to insist that resale price maintenance agreements, which are functionally equivalent to vertical territorial restraints, are per se unlawful. Clearly, however, the opinion in *Sylvania* is a significant step in the right direction.

If space permitted, a similar argument could be made in relation to tying agreements—contracts by which a seller conditions his sale of one product on the buyer's agreement to purchase a second product from him as well at a stated price. Despite the fact that such agreements are almost never anticompetitive, the Warren Court held them to be virtually unlawful per se. Although the Burger Court has not yet explicitly acknowledged the various legitimate functions that tie-ins can perform, it has refused to condemn such agreements in two cases in which its predecessor clearly would have found antitrust violations.[45] The Court's new willingness to examine in some detail the economic functions served by all such vertical arrangements bodes well for the future development of doctrine regarding vertical restrictions.

JOINT VENTURES

Typically, a joint venture involves two companies that agree to form a third jointly owned concern in order to undertake some specific project. In addition to committing their participants to supplying various kinds of capital, personnel, and expertise, such arrangements often restrain the extent to which the two companies and their joint venture can compete against one another. Thus, when the Court is confronted with such a joint venture case, it must decide not only whether the full arrangement is likely to reduce competition but also whether the restraints it imposes are legitimately related to the venture. Unfortunately, it is not possible to make any general a priori predictions in this area.

On the one hand, a joint venture might permit the execution of a procompetitive and economically efficient new investment which neither company nor anyone else would have made in its absence. On the other hand, the joint venture might very well be a device to enable the two companies to prevent each other from making independent investments in the market in question. Similarly, although some competitive restrictions are essential for the viability of particular joint ventures, other restrictions perform purely anticompetitive functions. Regrettably, it is often very difficult to determine in a given case whether particular joint ventures and their associated restrictions are pro- or anticompetitive. Such predictions usually must be based on conjectures about whether (1) absent their cooperation either or both of the individual companies would have entered the market served by the joint venture, (2) the companies would have been able to enter each other's markets had they not learned from each other through their joint venture, or, alternatively, (3) the prospect of such entries would have induced someone else to deter their execution by introducing an additional product variant, opening up an additional distributive outlet or creating additional capacity in the market.

A mere recitation of this agenda for inquiry demonstrates that a court faced with a joint venture case needs a lot of detailed business knowledge in order to assess its likely economic impact. Of course, it is possible to develop some general guidelines. Auxiliary restraints agreed upon by the parties to a joint venture can be assumed not to be anticompetitive where the joint venturers are not and will not become uniquely well placed to enter into each other's markets. More generally, auxiliary restraints should not diminish competition in cases where there are and will always be enough other firms at least as well placed as the respective joint venturers to enter the relevant markets so that the restraints on the latter are likely to have no significant effect. However, a tremendous amount of knowledge and foresight will be required to apply even such general guidelines. In short, analysis of the competitive impact of joint ventures is inevitably a difficult and expensive task: accurate case-by-case determinations are extremely expensive and it does not seem possible to discover simplifying per se rules that can produce acceptably inexpensive and yet accurate predictions for significant categories of cases.

The major Warren Court decisions involving joint ventures are *United States v. Penn-Olin Chemical Co.*[46] and *United States v. Sealy, Inc.*[47] Penn-Olin was a joint venture of Pennsalt Chemical Corporation and Olin Mathieson Chemical Corporation, formed to produce and sell sodium chlorate in the southeastern United States. The District Court approved the joint venture, finding that (1) there was a possibility of individual entry by either Pennsalt or Olin before they executed their joint venture, but (2) there was no reasonable probability that both Pennsalt and Olin would have built plants in the Southeast had Penn-Olin not been created. No explicit additional restraint appears to have been involved in the joint venture, though Olin and Pennsalt were already in competition in various nonchlorate chemical markets.

The Warren Court majority accepted the district court's finding that both joint venturers would not have entered the market independently, did not inquire whether Penn-Olin might make a less (or more) effective competitor than either Pennsalt or Olin Mathieson, and did not suggest that the joint venture might reduce the extent to which its participants would compete against each other in other markets. Nevertheless, the Court reversed the district court's dismissal of the section 7 Clayton Act complaint and remanded the case on the theory that competition would have been more effective had one of the joint venturers entered the market and the other remained a significant potential competitor[48] whose presence under such circumstances might have induced the established firms in the market to lower their prices in order to deter further entry.

Unfortunately, this limit-price theory simply cannot bear scrutiny. In brief, I believe that such limit pricing would rarely succeed in deterring entry and would certainly be less profitable than various other methods established firms could employ to deter entry.[49] In any event, the majority's use of this theory in *Penn-Olin* was inconsistent with its assumption that the nonentering joint venturer did not have to be deterred—that is would not have entered the market even in the absence of limit pricing by the firms already in the market. *Penn-Olin* manifests the Warren Court's unreasoned and, I think, unjustified hostility to joint ventures.

This hostility was also manifest in the second major Warren Court joint-venture decision, *United States v. Sealy*.[50] Sealy was a joint venture undertaken by various local and regional mattress manufacturers. The Sealy company (1) licensed its founders to produce Sealy-brand mattresses of specified quality and (2) advertised the Sealy brand in the national media. The licensees were restricted to selling Sealy mattresses in territories that were not already served adequately by another licensee and were required to control the prices charged by the dealers through whom they distributed their products.

Once again, depending on the facts, such a joint venture could either be procompetitive or anticompetitive. In particular, for the Sealy arrangement to be purely procompetitive, two general conditions would have to be fulfilled. First, the joint venture and its ancillary restrictions would have to increase the attractiveness of the offers the joint venturers could make to the original customers of their remaining rivals by enabling the joint venturers to take advantage of economies of scale in research and national media advertising. Second, the joint venture could not, by precluding the participants in the venture from competing against each other, reduce the attractiveness of the offers against which each participant had to compete. This second condition could be fulfilled for any of three different reasons: (1) the joint venture may not have formally precluded its participants from selling non-Sealy brands in each other's territories *and* their production of Sealy mattresses may not have raised the cost the participants had to incur to produce non-Sealy mattresses; (2) the joint venturers may not in any case have found it attractive to enter each other's markets; and/or (3) other firms may have been equally well placed to make such entries. On the other hand, the Sealy joint venture may also have been purely anticompetitive. In particular, this result would obtain if the joint venture generated no relevant economies and none of the three conditions just listed was fulfilled. Obviously, mixed conclusions might also be justified.

Although not all the facts are available, my guess is that the Sealy joint venture and its associated restrictions were procompetitive on balance. In particular, the joint venture probably did generate significant economies. Thus, it was probably necessary to permit the participants to take advantage of national advertising, which appears to have been more cost-effective than its alternatives, and may also have permitted the company to take advantage of economies of scale in research. Similarly, the territorial restraints and price maintenance agreements probably generated closer-to-optimal incentives for the joint venturers and their dealers to promote their product regionally and locally and to give their customers closer-to-optimal presales advice and postsales service (by precluding any joint venturer or his distributor from offering price concessions to a customer whom another joint venturer or his distributor had originally interested in the Sealy product by means of advertising or presales advice). Moreover, the joint venture and its attendant restrictions probably did not benefit its participants by reducing the attractiveness of the offers the joint venturers made to each other's customers since the terms of the joint venture agreement did not prohibit participants from selling non-Sealy brands in each other's territories and since all the available evidence about the number of local mattress manufacturers suggests that the venturers would not be uniquely best placed to enter each other's markets.

Unfortunately, in holding that the Sealy joint venture violated section 1 of the Sherman Act, the Supreme Court did not address any of the relevant factual issues. Instead, it focused on the resale price maintenance restriction, which had been condemned by the district court in a mistaken, though precedentially consistent, ruling that Sealy had chosen not to appeal. In particular, the Court concluded that the territorial restraints were part of an unlawful "aggregation of trade restraints," whose anticompetitive effects were thought to be sufficiently apparent to require no further explanation. Basically, then, the *Sealy* opinion evidenced the Warren Court's continuing unreasoned hostility to joint ventures.

One might be tempted to qualify this conclusion in order to take account of the Court's effort in *Sealy* to distinguish the case of "a number of small grocers . . . [who] allocate territory among themselves on an exclusive basis as incident to the use of a common name and advertisements." However, the position taken by the Warren Court holdovers in the early Burger Court's only joint venture decision, *United States v. Topco Assocs.*,[51] demonstrates that the Warren Court majority did not take this suggestion very seriously. In fact, in *Topco* only Chief Justice Burger and his fellow recent appointee, Justice Blackmun, seemed to grasp the implications of the grocery store example.

Topco was a joint venture formed by twenty-five small and medium-size regional supermarket chains, allegedly to afford its members economies of scale in purchasing, quality control, and product design and to enable them to offer private-label (Topco) products and thereby achieve various economies in purchasing, transportation, warehousing, promotion, and advertising. Although Topco members were free to expand into each other's territories, Topco did restrict the territories within which its members could distribute the Topco brand. In fact, almost all Topco companies were given exclusive distribution rights within designated territories. As we have seen, such restraints may have been necessary to induce Topco members to engage in the amount of advertising and promotion that was optimal from the perspective of the group as a whole.

With a majority dominated by Warren Court holdovers, the Court held the Topco territorial restrictions to be horizontal and hence illegal per se. No economic analysis was attempted. The Court's effort to justify its decision was restricted to an assertion of its ignorance and incapacity regarding economics. However, Burger Court developments were foreshadowed when Justice Blackmun based his concurrence on the skeptical ground that the per se rule was too firmly established to overturn, and Chief Justice Burger dissented on the ground that the joint venture as a whole was efficiency-related while the restraint was designed to enable the participants to advertise more effectively.

Chief Justice Burger's realization that joint ventures may be efficient and procompetitive proved decisive several years later in *Broadcast Music, Inc. v. Columbia Broadcasting System.*[52] At issue was the "blanket license" employed by ASCAP and BMI, the two major organizations through which holders of copyrights in musical compositions sell performers and broadcast outlets the right to use their copyrighted music. This joint sales agency device is in effect a joint venture among all the members of the respective organizations. Under the blanket-license arrangement, the joint venture charges purchasers a fixed fee for its "product" consisting of the performance rights in any copyrighted musical composition owned by any member of the organization (participant in the joint venture). The fixed fee aspect of the blank license was challenged as an exercise in technical "price fixing," which is per se illegal under the antitrust laws.

The Supreme Court upheld the practice. The justices refused to characterize the fixed-fee blanket license as price fixing in the technical (illegal) sense on the ground that this particular licensing arrangement was necessary to the success of the joint sales agency strategy for exploiting and protecting copyrights. In effect, therefore, the Court approved the ASCAP and BMI joint ventures, indicating that such an arrangement is lawful unless "the practice facially appears to be one that would always or almost always restrict competition and decrease output" rather than "increase economic efficiency and render markets more rather than less competitive."

Thus, the Burger Court's treatment of joint ventures reveals its greater willingness, as compared with the Warren Court, to consider the legitimate functions such associations can perform and to engage in the type of economic analysis necessary to make discriminating judgments regarding the competitive effect of business practices.

ECONOMICS AND ANTITRUST ANALYSIS: THE BURGER COURT AND THE FUTURE

If we compare the antitrust performance of the Burger Court with that of the later Warren Court, a clear pattern emerges. The Burger Court has distinguished itself not only by insisting that the antitrust laws contain an exclusively economic test of legality but also by rejecting its predecessor's assumptions about the functions and likely competitive impact of the various types of business conduct the Court has been required to scrutinize. More affirmatively, the Burger Court has been far more sensitive to the possible efficiencies such practices may yield, far more skeptical about the reliability of various rules and presumptions that had previously been employed to make competitive-impact predictions, and far more confident of its own ability to undertake the kind of case-by-case analysis necessary for a proper evaluation of the legality of conduct under the American antitrust laws.

Undoubtedly, a large number of factors contributed to this development. As a group, the Burger Court's members are less sympathetic to the populist values of their Warren Court counterparts and are therefore less likely to find these values embedded in particular statutes. Similarly, as a group the Burger Court members are less suspicious of business motivation and are therefore likely to be less sympathetic to various antibusiness presumptions.

I would like to think, however, that part of the recent change in antitrust law can be attributed to the increasingly important role that economic analysis has come to play in legal scholarship and legal education in the antitrust area. The Court can now rely on a considerable body of research that uses economic theory to analyze the business functions and competitive impact of the various kinds of behavior regulated by the American antitrust laws. Equally important, the Court can now profit from the greater economic sophistication of its law clerks and of the antitrust lawyers who practice before it; virtually every antitrust course taught in leading American law schools is now substantially influenced by economic analysis.

What of the future? Given reasonable longevity, I expect that the Burger Court will (1) reject outright the market-share approach to merger analysis in favor of an approach that encourages firms to explain the business efficiencies they believe their merger will generate, (2) extend the case-by-case approach it now applies to vertical territorial restraints to resale price maintenance agreements as well, and perhaps eventually (3) reject this case-by-case approach to such vertical practices for a strong presumption in favor of the legality of these contractual devices.

Less concretely, I believe that there is a substantial chance that the trends I have described will continue—even if the Burger Court's members are replaced with less "conservative" personnel. The Court's responsiveness to sophisticated economic arguments has already led to an increase in the quantity and the quality of the economic arguments it hears. As lawyers become increasingly convinced of the effectiveness of such arguments, they will spend more time developing the relevant expertise and using it in their briefs and oral arguments. Thus, the Burger Court's approach to antitrust may produce a change in legal method that will outlast the judges themselves—a change that may eventually affect other areas of the law as well.

• Ten •

The Rootless Activism of the Burger Court

Vincent Blasi

In the American judicial tradition, debate about how a particular provision of the Constitution should be interpreted almost inevitably implicates the question of the role the Supreme Court should play in the system of government. One school of thought favors what is called an "activist" approach. Despite considerable disagreement over questions of application and ultimate rationale, activists are united by the belief that judicial enforcement of controversial as well as consensual norms should be a regular feature of American constitutional democracy, not merely a deviant phenomenon reserved for the most exceptional situations.

Judicial "restraintists," on the other hand, regard the exercise of judicial authority in the name of the Constitution as worrisome. Virtually all restraintists concede that courts must, on occasion, hold state and federal laws unconstitutional. But restraintists differ vigorously among themselves regarding what special circumstances justify judicial review and how that power should be exercised on those occasions when it can be justified.

These labels describe polar tendencies, not clearly demarcated positions. A restraintist who frequently finds "special" circumstances to justify the exercise of judical review could well be considered an activist. That the activist-restraintist division is a matter of tendency and degree does not imply, however, that it is amorphous or unimportant. To the contrary, this division has been at the heart of constitutional discourse for at least the last fifty years. There is little to indicate that the next era will witness a reformulation of the way people think about the Constitution that would make the activist-restraintist division unimportant.

In the future, the 1970s and early 1980s may well be looked upon as the period during which the activist approach to judicial review solidified its position in American judicial practice. If so, this development has not been a matter of professed ideology; the opinions of the last thirteen years abound with essays on the virtues of judicial self-restraint. Nevertheless, by almost any measure the Burger Court has been an activist court. And if a court with the make-up and mandate of this one has chosen not to resist the temptations of activism, that fact says something important about the practical

198

imperatives of the judicial process, if not the legitimacy of the activist philosophy.

MEASURES OF JUDICIAL ACTIVISM

Perhaps the most significant way in which the Burger Court has helped to solidify judicial activism has been, ironically, by means of a passive course of decision-making. The much anticipated—by some with hope, by others with dread—reversals and undercuttings of activist Warren Court precedents have not materialized. The great activist trilogy of the Warren years—*Brown v. Board of Education* (school desegregation),[1] *Reynolds v. Sims* (reapportionment),[2] and *Miranda v. Arizona* (confessions)[3]—remains intact. The central premises of those decisions, embodying the liberal ideal of human dignity and an activist conception of the Court's proper role in promoting that ideal, have not been challenged in the least as the Burger Court has elaborated doctrine regarding school desegregation, reapportionment, and the rights of criminal suspects under interrogation. The Nixon, Ford, and Reagan appointees have almost surely exerted a moderating influence on the growth of doctrine in these areas. But if, as was commonly supposed when the Warren Court was being eulogized, the core principles of *Brown, Reynolds*, and *Miranda* epitomize the activist philosophy of judicial review, that philosophy is even more securely rooted in American law today than it was in 1969. Constitutional principles that were once innovative and controversial are now familiar, even basic.

This point holds even when the focus shifts to what might be termed the "second line" landmark precedents of the Warren era, activist decisions such as *New York Times v. Sullivan* (radically altering the law of libel to the benefit of news organizations),[4] *Mapp v. Ohio* (prohibiting state courts from admitting into evidence proof obtained by unreasonable searches and seizures),[5] *Griswold v. Connecticut* (recognizing a constitutional right to use birth control devices),[6] *Engel v. Vitale* (prohibiting organized prayer sessions in public schools),[7] and *Baker v. Carr* (limiting the scope of the "political question" doctrine so as not to preclude the courts from adjudicating reapportionment cases).[8] Those decisions were highly controversial in their day, in large part because they were viewed as examples of the Court arrogating to itself too much decision-making authority. With the possible exception of *Mapp*, those precedents are now secure so far as judicial interpretation of the Constitution is concerned; they form a part of the enduring doctrinal heritage.

Much more than the failure to overrule the precedents of the Warren era marks the Burger Court as activist. One indication of a court's activism is its willingness to declare acts of Congress unconstitutional. It is today hardly controversial, in terms of political theory, for the Supreme Court to invalidate a *state* statute or practice in order to vindicate national values. But when the statute at issue has been passed by the *national* legislature, particularly after due deliberation of the constitutional implications, the basis for the court's authority to exercise the power of judicial review is at its weakest. In sixteen terms, the Warren Court invalidated nineteen provisions of federal statutes; in thirteen terms the Burger Court has struck down twenty-four.[9] Raw numbers can be misleading, but in terms of either social impact or doctrinal innovation few, if any, of the Warren Court decisions striking down federal laws match the significance of such Burger Court holdings as *Buckley v. Valeo* (striking down some major sections of the 1974 Campaign Finance Act),[10] *National League of Cities v. Usery* (invalidating the extension of the federal minimum wage requirement to large numbers of state and municipal employees,[11] *Oregon v. Mitchell* (invalidating Congress's attempt to grant the right to vote in state elections to eighteen-year-olds, a result ultimately achieved only by constitutional amendment),[12] *Northern Pipeline Construction Co. v. Marathon Pipeline Co.* (holding unconstitutional the special bankruptcy courts created by Congress as a key part of its comprehensive reform of the bankruptcy laws in 1978),[13] and the series of decisions prohibiting sex-based classifications in the military and in various social security programs.[14] If deference to Congress be the acid test of judicial restraint, the litmus of the Burger Court comes out much the same color as that of its predecessor.

A somewhat different measure of judicial activism is the willingness of a court to assume a prominent role in the resolution of constitutional crises, those rare disputes that shake the body politic to its foundations. Some theorists of judicial restraint have maintained that courts must be especially careful to assume a low profile on these occasions because controversies of such cosmic proportions can only be resolved by the branches of government that are directly responsible to the electorate. The Warren Court can be viewed as grasping the nettle in defiance of this restraintist credo in the school desegregation decisions and, more dubiously (the constitutional "crisis" was a time bomb), in the reapportionment cases. The other constitutional crisis of the Warren era, over the legality of the Vietnam War, was "resolved" without benefit of significant judicial participation.

With respect to the constitutional-crisis-resolving perspective on judicial activism, the Burger Court's headlong rush into the Watergate tapes controversy is extremely significant. The timing of the Court's decision in *United States v. Nixon*,[15] so crucial to its impact, was a result of the Justices' unusual action expediting the appeal from Judge Sirica's order, thereby permitting the parties to bypass the intermediate United States Court of Appeals. Had the Court of Appeals considered the case under its normal timetable, the impeachment process in the House and Senate would probably have run its course before the Supreme Court could have ruled on President

Nixon's claims of executive privilege. At the time the Court decided to hear the tapes case on an expedited basis, the impeachment process was proceeding apace, and indeed the House Judiciary Committee was performing so impressively that many citizens were reexamining their previous low regard for the Congress as an institution. Yet the Burger Court jumped in on its own initiative, and with a swift stroke essentially resolved the crisis, risking in the process a good deal of its institutional stature had Nixon decided to defy the order to turn over the tapes. *United States v. Nixon* represents nothing less than a bold and stunningly successful instance of judicial activism. Centuries from now, if the republic endures, the case will be one of the first cited by proponents of judicial review when challenged to give examples of how occasional rule by judges can benefit a democracy.

So far we have considered three dimensions of the judicial activism of the Burger Court: its preservation of the activist landmark precedents of the Warren era, its willingness to invalidate acts of Congress, and its willingness to step into the breach of a constitutional crisis. Another test of activism might be how comprehensive is the range of issues for which a court is willing to develop constitutional standards that help to shape the political landscape. The Warren Court, for example, had a great influence regarding civil liberties, but did less than many of its predecessors to influence the separation of powers between the branches of the federal government and the structure of the federal system (except insofar as the power of the states to restrict civil liberties, a power the Warren Court severely limited, is viewed as an issue of federalism). In this regard, the Burger Court shows signs of broadening the impact of judicial review.

So far as the separation of powers is concerned, *United States v. Nixon* is, of course, the centerpiece of the Burger Court's work. But that decision by no means stands alone. In the much-publicized *Pentagon Papers* case,[16] the Court held that under all but the most extraordinary circumstances the president does not have inherent power to enjoin the publication by news organizations of classified information. Because two of the six justices in the majority based their decision on the absence of congressional authorization for the injunction, the *Pentagon Papers* holding has as much to do with the division of authority between the president and Congress as with the First Amendment. The Burger Court further confined the scope of inherent executive power in *United States v. United States District Court*.[17] Absent congressional authorization, the justices ruled, the executive branch must secure a search warrant from a judicial officer in order to engage in electronic surveillance of persons or organizations that are considered to be threats to the national security but that are not shown to be directly involved with foreign powers. Finally, in the second *Nixon Tapes* case,[18] the Court held that a former president can be required by Congress to turn over his presidential papers to an executive agency for screening to facilitate eventual scrutiny by the general public. All told, the Burger Court has done at least as much as any of its predecessors to develop constitutional checks against the imperial presidency.

The development of doctrine regarding the separation of powers has not been exclusively in one direction, however. One of the many holdings in *Buckley v. Valeo*,[19] the campaign finance decision, protected the president's power of appointment by invalidating a statutory provision that provided for appoinment of a majority of members of the Federal Election Commission by the president pro tem of the Senate and the Speaker of the House. In *Nixon v. Fitzgerald*,[20] the Court held that the president enjoys an unqualified immunity from damage actions for any acts performed within the outer perimeter of his duties of office. And in *Schick v. Reed*[21] the Court affirmed the president's power to grant conditional pardons, such as lowering a death sentence to life imprisonment without possibility of parole.

Interestingly, the separation of powers issue that has generated the greatest number of cases during Chief Justice Burger's tenure does not concern presidential powers at all, but rather the immunity granted members of Congress in Article 1, section 6 from being "questioned in any other Place" for "any Speech or Debate in either House." It is one indication of the willingness of the Burger Court to fashion constitutional standards in diverse and untraditional areas that in the last decade it decided more cases under this clause than had been adjudicated by all its predecessors combined.[22]

For much of the nation's history, the Supreme Court's principal function has been to "umpire" the federal system by enforcing constitutional limitations on the power of Congress to regulate commerce and to tax and spend for the general welfare and on the power of the states to burden interstate commerce by means of regulatory or revenue laws designed to serve social or economic ends. The much maligned activism of the Court in the 1930s was in the discharge of this function. Since that time, the Court has almost totally eschewed the role of umpire of the federal system. What little effort there has been to fashion judicial standards governing the nation-state relationship has come largely from the Burger Court.

The most significant decision in this regard is *National League of Cities v. Usery*,[23] in which the Court held that Congress does not have authority under the commerce clause to require state and municipal governments to pay a minimum wage to employees engaged in "traditional governmental functions." The result is startling enough, representing as it does the first time since the constitutional crisis of the 1930s that the Court has held that Congress had exceeded its commerce clause power. Even more surprising, however, is the underlying theory adopted by the Court. For Justice Rehnquist's majority opinion treats the concept of state sovereignty embodied in the Tenth Amendment as a source of operational constitutional doctrine to be enforced by courts, not simply, as had been supposed for the previous thirty-nine years, an abstract ideal to guide federal executive officials and legislators in their discretion.

National League of Cities may be an aberration, destined to be confined as a precedent to its narrow facts.[24] But the state-sovereignty theory articulated by Justice Rehnquist could serve as the foundation for a radical expansion of judicial doctrine in the area of nation-state relations, perhaps even to the point of constraining the practice by which the federal government herds state governments into line by attaching conditions to federal grants. Such an expansion of doctrine would amount to nothing short of an activist revolution.

More subtle but probably no less significant has been the Burger Court's enhanced willingness to invalidate state regulatory laws that it regards as too burdensome to the flow of commerce among the states. For years there has been a debate concerning whether the Court ought to enforce the "dormant commerce clause" only against state laws that discriminate against out-of-state goods, or whether the federal commerce clause should also be considered to preclude state laws that serve purposes the justices regard as unimportant or cast burdens on interstate business the justices regard as undesirable. During the Warren era, the Court took very few cases raising the "dormant commerce clause" issue, and in those few cases exhibited an extreme reluctance to invalidate state legislation. A striking example of this attitude is *Brotherhood of Locomotive Firemen v. Chicago, Rock Island, & Pacific R.R. Co.*,[25] in which the Court upheld a state "featherbedding" law which required interstate railroads to employ statutorily defined "full crews" while passing through the state. In contrast, since 1969 the Court has chosen to hear twice as many cases in this area as were decided during all of the Warren years,[26] has struck down state laws in eight of the cases[27] (as compared to two such invalidations for the Warren Court),[28] and has developed a constitutional standard for dormant commerce clause disputes that, at least in abstract formulation,[29] provides for the invalidation of state laws that are unduly inefficient as well as those that are discriminatory. In virtually every relevant respect, the Burger Court has been a more active umpire of the federal system than was its predecessor.

As should be apparent by now, there are several indices by which one might measure the extent of a court's activism. I have tried to demonstrate that according to a number of meaningful criteria, the 1970s was one of the more activist decades in the Court's history. Those who would argue that the Warren years were even more activist, however, would probably emphasize three measures that have not yet been discussed: (1) the number and importance of new rights (or types of rights) recognized; (2) the extent to which the Court is willing to intrude its value judgments into the heart of the electoral process, the bedrock of any democratic system of government; and (3) how broadly the Court construes the statutes and doctrines that define the jurisdiction and remedial powers of the federal courts. In these important respects, the Burger Court to date may not have been as activist as its predecessor. Even here, however, the similarities between the two courts are at least as striking as the differences.

No one can accuse the Burger Court of failing to recognize important new rights. *Roe v. Wade*,[30] the abortion decision, is an innovative decision by any standard. So, too, is *Furman v. Georgia*,[31] the first Supreme Court case to hold unconstitutional a state capital punishment law. Virtually the entire panoply of constitutional protection against sex discrimination is of 1970s vintage. Resident aliens were routinely excluded from occupations and disadvantaged in other respects until the Burger Court recognized in the Fourteenth Amendment some important limitations on such discrimination.[32] The First Amendment right to engage in speech on commercial topics traces almost entirely to the decisions of the last decade;[33] the social consequences of this doctrinal innovation, such as the advent of advertising in the legal and medical professions, have been considerable.

In the area of criminal procedure, it is true, the Burger Court has not approached the level of innovation of the Warren Court. But with regard to civil and administrative procedure, probably the reverse is the case. For example, in *Shaffer v. Heitner*,[34] decided in 1976, the Court recognized a major federal constitutional limitation on the traditional exercise of jurisdiction by state courts in cases involving intangible assets. And today one of the most frequently litigated constitutional issues in the lower courts concerns when, and in what form, a person who is disadvantaged by an administrative decision (a job dismissal for example, or a denial of government financial benefits) is entitled to "procedural due process." The doctrinal basis for claims of this sort stems almost entirely from holdings of the last dozen years.[35] In addition, much of the standard commercial law and practice of the nation has had to be modified to incorporate formal notice and hearing requirements read into the Constitution by the Burger Court.[36]

Many journalists are chagrined by the recent failure of the Supreme Court to grant them certain rights, such as not to disclose the identity of a confidential source.[37] Yet in the last decade there have been many innovative decisions recognizing rights under the press clause of the First Amendment. The right to report to the public, free from prior restraint, evidence of guilt presented at open pretrial hearings was established for the first time, and in sweeping terms, in 1976.[38] The right of a newspaper to control its own pages, to be free from both legislative and judicial requirements of "balanced" news coverage, was first recognized in 1974.[39] The First Amendment right to have physical access to at least some newsworthy events such as trials, a major conceptual breakthrough, owes its existence to a Burger Court decision.[40]

Finally, a word should be said about that other pillar of the First Amendment, the guaranty of religious liberty. Certainly the most hotly debated, and in practical terms probably the most important, modern church-state issue is government financial aid to sectarian schools. Almost all the major precedents on this issue stem from the period of Chief Justice Burger's tenure, and the Court's results have been activist in nature, in the sense that the state political processes have been significantly constrained by the constitutional tests the Court has developed.[41] Similarly, with regard to the free exercise of religion by unorthodox sects, the Burger Court's decision in *Wisconsin v. Yoder*,[42] granting Amish high-school-age children a right to be exempt from compulsory public school attendance laws, is now the wellspring precedent.

All in all, the last thirteen years have been busy ones on the score of doctrinal innovation in the Supreme Court. Perhaps the Warren Court's pace was faster or its range broader. But if so, the differences can hardly be considered dramatic or fundamental. If its legacy of innovative constitutional doctrines is what made the Warren Court the paradigm of an activist court, no new paradigm is needed to comprehend the central tendency of its successor.

Another measure of activism is a court's willingness to render decisions that fundamentally alter the rules or practices of electoral politics. Certainly Justice Frankfurter, the high priest of judicial restraint, reserved a special place in his demonology for judicial decisions that attempt to structure the process by which public officials are elected, particularly decisions that affect, and thereby might be perceived by the public as influenced by, partisan party politics.[43]

No doctrinal development of the last decade can be said to have had the dramatic impact of the Warren Court's reapportionment decisions. Nonetheless, in *Buckley v. Valeo*[44] the Court invalidated the provision of the Federal Campaign Finance Act that prohibited independent expenditures over $1,000 per year by individuals and groups "relative to a clearly identified candidate." As a result, large private expenditures on behalf of certain election campaigns are still commonplace. Similarly, in *First National Bank of Boston v. Bellotti*[45] a narrow majority of the justices held unconstitutional a state law that prohibited business corporations from using company funds in an effort to influence the outcome of referendum elections. In addition, in 1970 the Court ruled that Congress does not have constitutional authority to enfranchise eighteen-year-olds in state elections.[46]

Finally, in a highly innovative doctrinal development of uncertain but potentially revolutionary impact, the Burger Court has in effect ruled the spoils system unconstitutional. In *Elrod v. Burns*[47] the Court held that neither process servers nor bailiffs can be dismissed from the public payroll to make room for other job-seekers more in tune with the party politics of the hiring official. In *Branti v. Finkel*[48] the Court applied the principle of *Elrod* to the job of assistant public defender, prompting Justice Powell in dissent to wonder whether even federal district attorneys must now be selected on a nonpartisan basis. Powell complained that the effect of the Court's "constitutionalized civil service" will be to undermine the party system as well as to force governments to fill more positions by election rather than appointment in order to maintain a politically responsive public work force.

Only time will tell whether the campaign spending and patronage decisions will turn out to be as important in terms of practical impact as the reapportionment cases. But no hindsight is needed to realize that in terms of willingness to intrude judicial review into the electoral process, the Burger Court has behaved very much in the activist spirit of its predecessor.

Only with regard to its interpretation of the technical doctrines and statutes that demarcate the jurisdiction of the federal courts can the Burger Court plausibly be said to have abided by the canons of judicial restraint. The Warren Court exhibited little faith in the state courts as forums for the vindication of federal constitutional rights. During the 1960s several doctrines were developed to ensure that civil rights organizations, prisoners challenging the propriety of their convictions, and other unpopular litigants could have their claims adjudicated by life-tenured federal judges.[49] In a series of notable decisions, the Burger Court has emasculated or severely restricted those doctrines, often sprinkling opinions with homilies about the comity that is owed the state courts. In other important respects, however, the reach of federal judicial authority has actually been extended in recent years.

In *Younger v. Harris*[50] and *Hicks v. Miranda*,[51] the Court established some major limitations on the power of federal judges to enjoin state court proceedings. As a result of those decisions, a private party who objects on constitutional grounds to a criminal or civil enforcement action by state officials cannot have his claims adjudicated in a federal forum unless a hearing on the merits is conducted by a federal court before the state court proceedings are commenced, the state proceedings can be shown to have been undertaken in bad faith, or the United States Supreme Court chooses the case as one of the few disputes worthy of its largely discretionary review. In places where and at times when federal constitutional doctrines are viewed critically by local authorities, this diminution in the role of the federal courts can have serious consequences.

In a similar vein, the Burger Court has gone even further than many of its critics feared it would in cutting back the habeas corpus jurisdiction of the federal courts to hear the grievances of state prisoners. Persons who claim to have been convicted on evidence obtained in violation of the Fourth Amendment were denied the right to raise that contention in habeas corpus proceedings.[52] That decision was based on the special nature of Fourth Amendment claims (when successful they result in the exclusion of reliable evidence), but a year later the court held that *no* constitutional claim can be raised on habeas corpus if the convicted person or his counsel had a fair opportunity to raise it at trial and failed to do so.[53] The ignorance or inadvertence of the often inexperienced and overburdened lawyers who represent indigent defendants now can result in valid constitutional claims never being adjudicated.

The "standing" doctrine, the traditional requirement that a litigant must have a personal, concrete interest at stake before his suit will be heard, has been the subject of many decisions in the last thirteen years. The Court has restricted the authority of courts to hear constitutional claims predicated on the plaintiff's status as a taxpayer allegedly injured by governmental expenditures or a citizen allegedly injured by governmental improprieties.[54] In addition, several times the justices have disallowed lawsuits by plaintiffs who postulated plausible but not incontrovertible scenarios to establish that challenged governmental action would ultimately affect their personal interests.[55] On the other hand, the Court has read the injury requirement for standing broadly enough to encompass the noneconomic harm suffered by persons who object on environmental grounds to the spoliation of the earth by industrial and recreational developers.[56] As was true in the Warren years, the Burger Court has manipulated the standing doctrine in an ad hoc fashion. However, no stable, coherent principles limiting the power of courts to hear lawsuits have been developed in the last thirteen years.

In several respects, moreover, the reach of the federal writ has actually been extended under Chief Justice Burger. Probably the most controversial exercise in history of comprehensive remedial authority by the federal courts has been the effort to desegregate the public schools by redrawing attendance zones and transporting students beyond neighborhood schools. It was the Burger Court, not the Warren Court, that validated compulsory busing as a remedial device.[57] It was the Burger Court, not the Warren Court, that first extended the program of comprehensive federal court remedial decrees to northern school districts that had not formally segregated students by race in the recent past.[58] For problems such as police brutality, the justices in recent years have invoked the precepts of judicial restraint in refusing to authorize comprehensive remedies that would attack patterns of constitutional violation at the systemic level.[59] In the area of school desegregation, however, the lower federal courts have been given considerable authority to restructure entire school systems in the quest for a racially unitary educational environment.

Another way in which the power of the federal courts has been expanded concerns the amenability of federal officials to suit. In *United States v. Nixon* the Court held for the first time that the president of the United States can be made a party defendant in a federal lawsuit. In *Butz v. Economou*[60] the Court held that federal officials, including cabinet officers, are not completely immune, as previously had been supposed, from money judgments for actions taken within the scope of their federal duties. In addition, on two important occasions the Burger Court held that Fourth and Fifth Amendment violations by federal officials can be the basis for damage actions by the injured parties even under circumstances that are not covered by the federal statutes that authorize such relief;[61] the justices implied legal causes of action directly from the constitutional provisions themselves, something the Warren Court never ventured to do.

Finally, the Court in recent years has greatly expanded the authority of the federal courts to award money judgments against municipal governments, which previously had been thought to possess an immunity from such judgments comparable to that enjoyed by state governments.[62] As a result of the innovative holdings of the Burger Court, local government officials can now be ordered by the federal courts to pay tax-generated funds to persons whose rights have been violated.

Thus, even in the technical but significant area of federal court jurisdiction and remedies, the Burger Court has occasionally displayed a penchant for doctrinal innovation and the expansion of federal court authority. It is true that in this area more than any other the work of the Warren Court has been attacked and to some extent undone. In this area, moreover, the philosophy of judicial restraint has been given much lip service. But the total product of the Burger Court regarding jurisdiction and remedies cannot be said to have reduced significantly the role of the federal courts in the American system of government. If a court's attitude toward federal court authority is regarded as the key test of its judicial philosophy, the Burger Court must be considered at least ambivalent if not tending somewhat toward the activist side of the spectrum.

THE REACTIVE NATURE OF JUDICIAL REVIEW

By virtually every meaningful measure, therefore, the Burger Court has been an activist court. That fact should come as no surprise, despite the lopsided predominance of Republican appointees. For a court is inevitably a product of its times, and in at least two important respects the 1970s was a period highly conducive to an activist conception of the judicial role.

First, the Burger Court inherited the Warren Court's legacy. Even though five new appointments in five years is far above the average rate of turnover, the continuing presence on the Court of several justices who served during the Warren years had to have an effect. Moreover, one element in the philosophy of judicial restraint is respect for precedent, even activist precedent. Had the Nixon appointees been far more restraintist by temperament than they are, it is still likely that the landmark decisions of the Warren Court would have continued to exert an influence. In addition, the heritage of the Warren Court helped to determine what lawsuits would be brought, how they would be argued, and how they would be decided in the lower courts. These all-important aspects of legal culture do not change overnight with each new judicial appointment, and they have a lot to do with how the Supreme Court, which is after all essentially a reactive institution, functions.

The 1970s was almost destined to be an activist decade for a second reason having to do with larger social phenomena. In some respects, judicial review can be seen not as a primary political process, but rather as a corrective, an antidote to other forces or tendencies that threaten the political system. In the last decade, two such destabilizing forces have come to dominate public perceptions, thereby engendering a yearning across most of the political spectrum for some sort of corrective.

One potentially destabilizing force is the rampant growth of government bureaucracy, at the state as well as the federal level. As the bureaucratic state expands its jurisdiction and increases its leverage, individual citizens often feel overwhelmed by the complexity, impersonality, indeed irrationality, of the political landscape on which they must operate. They yearn for a simpler, more manageable world where human choice seems to matter and where the relevant value judgments are within their comprehension.

Despite the mystique and technicality of the law, the phenomenon of constitutional interpretation by the Supreme Court goes far to answer this need. Although some of the political rhetoric of the day characterizes the Court as just another remote, impersonal institution, very much a part of the bureaucratic state, there are important ways in which the Court actually makes the process of government more accessible to the ordinary citizen by clarifying and sharpening political conflicts. Constitutional cases are between identifiable parties, one of whom typically is a lone individual with an interesting, legally relevant personal story. The issues are framed in human-scale terms. The trappings and rituals of the Supreme Court add a touch of drama. The cast of characters is neither so large nor so fluctuating as to discourage the casual observer. Ironically, in many ways the greatest contribution the Supreme Court makes to the political system is through its simplifying function, its role in preserving one arena in an otherwise incomprehensible political domain where the disputes are bilateral and rationally debatable and where the choices are intelligible and explainable. That is one reason why Supreme Court decisions frequently attract far more press coverage and engender more public debate than seems warranted by the social significance of the cases in purely practical terms.

The second destabilizing force that invites the corrective of judicial review is the tendency of the legislative process, seemingly augmented in the last decade, to be distorted by single-issue electoral politics. This tendency is not unrelated to the growth of the bureaucratic state. As government gets more complex and more unresponsive, individuals caught in the maze can less afford the luxury of concern for the public welfare; they must take care of themselves first. And as political behavior grows more parochial, inequities in the distribution of power come to matter more, giving rise in the minds of concerned democrats to the desire for a corrective to those inequities. In addition, one feature of parochial politics is the impoverishment of public debate as fewer people care seriously about arguments directed to matters other than their self-interest. Such a development must also lead good democrats to search for a corrective.

One possible function of judicial review is to counteract the inequities of the electoral process, both directly by fashioning constitutional principles governing the distribution of the franchise and of opportunities for political expression and indirectly by scrutinizing certain legislative outcomes more intensively than others. Another possible function of judicial review is to inject into the public debate the disinterested and structured musings of judges regarding the traditions and needs of the body politic. In both respects, an activist approach by the Supreme Court can be perceived as a possible corrective to unduly parochial patterns of political behavior.

Thus, the rapid growth of bureaucratic government and parochial politics in the 1970s may have had something to do with the activism of the Burger Court. Few justices of any political persuasion or judicial philosophy could be expected to observe the unfolding of those dangerous tendencies without feeling at least a powerful impulse to try to do something about them. But there are risks as well as imperatives associated with such an instrumental conception of the process of constitutional interpretation. Prominent among those risks is the possibility that constitutional law may lose its essential oracular quality, its claim to embody transcendent principles, when the Court conceives its function largely in pragmatic terms. This risk has been exacerbated by the somewhat peculiar personnel profile of the Burger Court.

THE CENTRIST ACTIVISM OF THE BURGER COURT

A common perception about the Court of recent years is that it represents one of the lower points in Supreme Court history so far as the quality of personnel is concerned. That perception is, I believe, quite mistaken. If one concentrates on the ideological center of the Court, the three or four or five justices who hold the balance of power on the most divisive constitutional issues of the era, the Burger Court measures up well compared with its predecessors. Seldom, if ever, in the Court's history has there been a period when the pivotal justices were as intelligent, open-minded, and dedicated as Potter Stewart, Byron White, Harry Blackmun, Lewis Powell, and John Paul Stevens. An advocate faced with the challenge of changing judicial minds with sound arguments would do better to attempt the task in front of that group than almost any other that has in the past held the balance of power on the Court.

Where the Burger Court has been weak compared with previous courts is at the ideological extremes. Neither William Brennan nor Thurgood Marshall is well suited for the role of dissenter on the left, articulating in pure and compelling form the liberal theory of the Constitution. Both are pragmatic men, more clever than profound. They lack the elemental force and vision of a Holmes, or Brandeis, or Black, or Douglas, or Warren.

The same holds true on the right. The chief justice is a man of limited capacity and no discernible coherent philosophy. Justice O'Connor has displayed in her brief tenure a sharp intellect and an unexpected tendency to think in ideological terms, but it is far too early to tell what role she will play on the Court. William Rehnquist has intelligence, energy, charm, and a very conservative judicial philosophy, but he is more a debater than a thinker, more a lawyer than a statesman. He has not even approached his predecessors Frankfurter, Jackson, and Harlan in articulating a conservative constitutional philosophy. In fact, Justices Rehnquist and Brennan can be viewed as twin aliens of the right and left, both men of considerable ability who are out of place on the extremes, who could serve much better as coalition builders operating at the center of the Court's divisions. Brennan performed that role to perfection during the heyday of the Warren Court. Rehnquist may have the chance to do so in the future.

Because the hallmark of the Burger Court has been strength in the center and weakness on the wings, a curious dynamic has governed the fashioning of constitutional doctrine. Normally, the intellectual leadership of a court comes from the extremes. The "swing" justices typically determine how the cases come out, but not what important new ideas emerge from those cases. The justices in the center usually moderate but do not generate the growth of constitutional principles. The Burger Court's activism, however, has been generated as well as moderated by the pragmatic men of the center. That activism has been inspired not by a commitment to fundamental constitutional principles or noble political ideals, but rather by the belief that modest injections of logic and compassion by disinterested, sensible judges can serve as a counterforce to some of the excesses and irrationalities of contemporary governmental decision-making. In other words, in the hands of the Burger Court judicial activism has become a centrist philosophy—dominant, transcending most ideological divisions, but essentially pragmatic in nature, lacking a central theme or an agenda.

The rootless quality of this new form of centrist activism can be appreciated by comparing some of the most important and controversial doctrinal innovations of the Burger Court with major counterparts from the Warren era. The landmark decisions of the last decade regarding abortion, capital punishment, and financial aid to sectarian schools opened up whole new areas of constitutional adjudication that have generated large numbers of cases in the Supreme Court and the lower courts. The Court's decisions in these areas are undeniably important and, to some minds, beneficial in their effects. But those decisions reflect no deep-seated vision of the constitutional scheme or of the specific constitutional clauses in dispute. In each area, the line-drawing aspect of the process of doctrinal formulation has come to dominate the endeavor. The justices have crafted some significant practical compromises, but have not exerted any kind of moral force either by legitimizing nascent aspirations or by reinvigorating dormant ideals.

In contrast, the Warren Court was fired by a vision of the equal dignity of man—the equal dignity of white student and black student, of urban voter and rural voter, of sophisticated, wealthy criminal suspect and ignorant, indigent suspect. The justices of the Warren era exhibited a pragmatic, compromising side on many occasions—the "all deliberate speed" principle for school desegregation[63] and the legitimation of anonymous informers[64] are only two examples—but the doctrinal compromises took place against a background in which the direction of constitutional development was both clear and, to many, inspiring.[65]

The closest the Burger Court has come to this style of committed, rooted activism has been in the area of abortion. Even there, however, the Court's work displays some features that distinguish it from the activism of the Warren Court. *Roe v. Wade* burst upon the constitutional scene with very little in the way of foreshadowing or preparation. In granting pregnant women the right to terminate undesired pregnancies in the early stages, the justices could not plausibly justify their decision as the working out of a theme implicit in several previous decisions, still less as the vindication of values deeply embedded in the nation's constitutional tradition. The Court's opinion in *Roe* is best characterized as an ad hoc comparison of material interests: the woman has an interest in avoiding the physical and psychological burdens of an unwanted pregnancy and childbirth; the state has an interest in protecting the woman's health and the potentiality of life represented by the fetus. Grounded not on principle but on contingent considerations, these interests either grow or diminish during the course of the pregnancy, and in fact change as technological developments alter the capacity to sustain a fetus outside the womb. No effort was made in the *Roe* opinion to relate the woman's burdens to more general conceptions of choice-making capacity, bodily integrity, nonsubordination to other human beings, or equality of treatment. Similarly, no effort was made to assess the state's claim to regulate in terms of the much mooted dispute over whether government is entitled to enforce moral precepts.

My point is not the familiar one that the Court's opinions have not been as candid or as thoroughly reasoned as would be desirable. That charge can be leveled, with justification, against the Warren Court as well. My point instead is that the peculiar nature of the Burger Court's activism can be seen from the fact that even so fundamental an issue as abortion was treated by this Court as a conflict of particularized, material interests—a conflict that could be resolved by accommodating those interests in the spirit of compromise. Thus, third trimester abortions can be prohibited but earlier abortions cannot.[66] The state cannot prohibit all abortions outright, but can refuse to fund them, even while funding the alternative of childbirth and thereby encouraging pregnant women to forgo the abortion option.[67] The woman's husband cannot veto her choice to have an abortion but a minor's parents can do so under certain limited circumstances.[68] These doctrinal lines are not necessarily incoherent. But each has in fact taken on a highly arbitrary character because in grappling with the issues that followed in *Roe's* wake, the justices were unable to draw upon any sort of theory, or vision, or even framework for determining the contours of the right they had recognized. Each variation on the abortion issue was treated by the Court as an isolated, practical problem.

That is not surprising. For even the progenitor, *Roe* itself, was inspired, I would speculate, by largely pragmatic considerations. Too many wealthy women were flouting the law to get abortions from respected physicians. Too many poor women were being injured by inadequately trained mass purveyors of illegal abortions. Concerns of that sort, rather than issues of high principle, are what appeal to the centrist activists of the Burger Court.

A similar pattern of judicial response can be discerned in the Court's decisions regarding capital punishment. Opposition to the death penalty typically is based on moral principle: the deliberate killing of a human being, even as retribution for or in deterrence of heinous acts, is a fundamentally barbaric practice that cannot be countenanced in a political community founded on the principle of the dignity of man. In *Furman v. Georgia* the Burger Court held unconstitutional the death penalty as then administered in all the states.[69] The Court's rationale, however, was context-bound and pragmatic: current systems of criminal justice operate in such a way that the decision as to who will die is made in an unpredictable and arbitrary manner. Some observers thought that the practical effect of the *Furman* decision would be the extinction of the death penalty. But the majority of state legislatures responded to the decision by reaffirming their commitment to capital punishment and devising systems for administering the death penalty in a more consistent fashion. The agonizing issue of capital punishment could not be put to rest by the Court's call for procedural regularity.

On the second round of death penalty cases, in 1976, the Court changed its emphasis. Three state systems for administering the ultimate sanction were upheld, even though none of the schemes, revised in light of *Furman*, could be said to have confined in a meaningful way the discretion to decide who should die that is exercised by judges and jurors, not to mention prosecutors and officials empowered to grant clemency.[70] The justices ascribed great significance to the fact that in each system the sentencing authority was required to find at least one statutorily defined aggravating circumstance as a precondition to imposing the penalty of death, and also was compelled to consider all possible mitigating circumstances. Yet the lists of aggravating circumstances that were approved were so encompassing (routine felony murders, for example, were treated as aggravated offenses in each of the systems that was upheld) that only a small percentage of those convicted of such aggravated crimes could be expected to be sentenced to death. This fact, combined with the Court's requirement that the sentencing authority's consideration of mitigating circumstances be completely unconfined, means that the decision for death remains largely a discretionary matter. The Court's effort to mitigate the unfairness of the death penalty by focusing on the tactic of controlling discretion turned out to be almost completely unavailing.

The Court has also attempted to constrain the use of the death penalty by developing standards for determining that certain offenses do not warrant such a brutal and final sanction. All mandatory death sentences, even for narrowly defined, exceptionally serious offenses, have been invalidated.[71] The rape of an adult woman was held an insufficient basis for imposing capital punishment.[72] The Court prohibited a state from executing a person convicted of felony murder for driving the getaway car in a robbery that unexpectedly led to a fatal shooting.[73] Some justices are willing to conclude outright on a case-by-case basis that a certain offense is not grave enough to warrant capital punishment. Others invalidate particular applications of the death penalty only on the ground that the sentencing authority did not fully consider all possible mitigating circumstances. The result has been a jurisprudence of death that is largely ad hoc in nature, rooted in common sense, and designed mainly to control egregious excesses.

The Burger Court's addiction to uneasy, middle-of-the-road doctrines is nowhere more apparent than in the series of judgments regarding the highly emotional issue of public assistance to religious schools.

The debate over whether such aid violates the establishment of religion clause of the First Amendment tends to polarize the participants. From one point of view, the expenditure of even one penny of taxpayers' funds for the benefit of sectarian schools raises an issue of principle. Whether the financial assistance takes the form of tax credits for tuition expenses borne by parents, loans of instructional materials, or direct grants to the educational institutions themselves, there can be no question that the viability and quality of the religious schools is thereby enhanced. Since one of the avowed missions of such schools is to inculcate its students with sectarian religious precepts, any tax funds that improve the quality of the schools inevitably contribute to the process of religious proselytizing. That the public funds are earmarked for the secular aspects of the school's enterprise only means that other funds are freed up to enrich sectarian endeavors.

Defenders of public aid to religious schools contend, on the other hand, that the enterprise of religious instruction is greatly burdened by the institution of public education, both because potential students are drawn away by the public schools and because parents who send their children to private schools can afford less for tuition because those parents are also taxed to support the public schools. The effect of public aid to parochial schools, these defenders assert, is only partially to counteract the discouraging impact the intervention of the state has on the inculcation of religious precepts.

These sharply contrasting perspectives, each in its own way plausible, present the adjudicator with a clear-cut, difficult choice. The Burger Court has never made that choice. Instead, the justices have charted a middle course demarcated by numerous fine, unconvincing distinctions. As a result of the Court's holdings of the last thirteen years, states are *not* permitted to: subsidize the salaries of lay teachers in sectarian elementary and secondary schools;[74] reimburse such schools for portions of the expenses they incur in maintaining their physical plants;[75] help religious schools finance field trips to public facilities;[76] lend those schools maps, charts, films, and instructional equipment;[77] or reimburse the parents of parochial school students for tuition expenses.[78] However, states *are* permitted to: finance the construction of buildings devoted solely to secular purposes on sectarian college campuses;[79] lend secular textbooks, approved by public authorities, to students in religious elementary and secondary schools;[80] and underwrite a portion of the general operating expenses of religious colleges.[81] The Court held that states may reimburse religious schools for the expenses they incur in administering achievement tests required by state law, but only if the instructors in such schools play no part in devising the test questions.[82] Similarly, the justices held that the costs of keeping records required by the state may be paid by the state only if the use made by the sectarian schools of such payments is carefully audited.[83] The personnel of a public school system may not offer therapeutic, guidance, or special education services to parochial school students in the religious schools themselves but may do so in public facilities or out of mobile units located off the property of the private schools.[84] On the other hand, diagnostic services to detect physical or psychological ailments may be administered by public employees on the premises of the religious schools.[85]

The justices have tried to rationalize these distinctions by claiming that some forms of public aid to parochial schools have more potential than others to advance the religious mission of the schools or to cause political divisions along religious lines. But these claims have seldom been persuasive. The fundamental issue posed by the phenomenon of public assistance to religious schools demands a more basic choice than the Court has been willing to make.

And in the last analysis, the distinctive hallmark of the new centrist activism has been the powerful aversion to making fundamental value choices. The Burger Court has been interventionist without question. Some of its decisions have had a profound impact on the political life of the nation. But the Court's efforts have been inspired almost exclusively by discrete, pragmatic judgments regarding how a moderate, sensible judicial accommodation might help to resolve a potentially divisive public controversy. The Court's handling of abortion, capital punishment, and aid to parochial schools is not atypical. In other areas such as affirmative action, campaign finance, the rights of aliens, commercial speech, press access to newsworthy places and events, and school desegregation remedies, the Burger Court has exhibited a notable determination to fashion tenuous doctrines that offer both sides of a social controversy something important.[86]

The Warren Court's activism was different. In that era the justices had a moral vision and an agenda. They could have confined the ambit of the "no-racial-classifications" principle, or they could have limited the state action doctrine so as to give racial bigots a meaningful sphere of operation, but the justices of the Warren Court did neither.[87] The issue of reapportionment could have been resolved by compromise, perhaps by requiring only one house of a bicameral legislature to be apportioned exclusively on a population basis, or by permitting the population principle to be overridden by popular referendum. Instead, the one person-one vote principle was fashioned and enforced in remarkably pure form.[88] Several different solutions to the problem of involuntary confessions can be imagined that would have offered law enforcement officials more solace and more room for maneuver than did *Miranda*. But the Warren Court was serious in its determination that the case the state builds against an accused person should not be a function of his lack of sophistication about his constitutional rights. The activist justices of the Warren era knew how to compromise and how to bide their time. But for the items at the top of their agenda, those justices also knew how to make fundamental choices.

The moderate, pragmatic men who have held the balance of power thus far in the Burger era have tried mightily to avoid making those choices. As a result, their doctrinal product, interesting and important as it may be, has none of the generative quality or moral force of the Warren Court's legacy. Ad hoc accommodations decreed by judges can reshape political conflicts for a time, but constitutional interpretation makes its most significant contribution to the governing process by legitimating or discrediting basic ideas that lie at the center of political dispute. In that one respect, but only in that respect, the Burger Court has kept a low profile.

This observation brings into question the thesis, defended earlier, that the Burger Court has been an activist court. Perhaps the true test of activism is not the generation of innovative doctrines or the willingness to intrude into constitutional crises, or any of the other measures canvassed above. Perhaps it is the willingness to make fundamental value judgments that truly marks a court as activist.

I think not. The labels "activist" and "restraintist" take on meaning only in the context of the effort to define the Court's proper role in a democratic system. The overriding enterprise is to determine which persons, which groups, which perspectives, which values shall control—in short, to allocate power. A court that reaffirms and enforces the activist precedents of its predecessor, invalidates the work of its co-equal branches, successfully aborts potential constitutional crises, umpires the systems of federalism and separation of powers, recognizes many new and important individual rights, structures the electoral process, and maintains and develops the jurisdictional and remedial potency of the federal courts is certainly wielding power. That a court's exercise of power seems inspired largely by pragmatic impulses says something about the quality, and possibly the durability, of that court's work. But even if a court's solutions are short-term and ad hoc, they are solutions that displace or reshape the solutions of other power centers that otherwise would prevail. The definition of judicial activism asserted at the beginning of this chapter thus seems appropriate: an activist court is one that regularly exercises the power of judicial review to enforce controversial as well as consensual norms.

By that standard, the Burger Court has been very much an activist court. Rootless activism is activism nonetheless.

• Eleven •

Fathers and Sons: The Court, The Commentators, and the Search for Values

Martin Shapiro

It is undoubtedly wrong to confuse what the Supreme Court does with what the commentators say about what it does. Yet, fashions in constitutional commentary obviously have a great deal to do with how we perceive the actions of the Court and particularly with the patterns we impute to what may appear to the justices as individual responses to particular cases. Whether the movements among the observers are ultimately reflected in the conduct of the observed is an open question. Here my concern is to draw some parallels and contrasts between the Burger Court's behavior and styles of contemporary commentary, without imputing causal relations in either direction.

NEW DEAL COURT AND NEW DEAL COMMENTATORS

For a time, noting the changes and continuities between the Warren and Burger Courts was a favorite sport of journalists and a sometime preoccupation of scholars.[1] The pleasures of this pastime fade as we have more than enough of the Burger Court on our plate without bothering to redigest the Warren Court's menu. Yet we have not been so conscious of the changing of the guard among commentators that occurred contemporaneously with the transposition of Warren to Burger.

Throughout the life of the Warren Court the commentary on that Court was produced almost exclusively by a generation of academic lawyers for whom the New Deal was a highly personal and often formative experience. Nearly every tentative sentence written about the Warren Court was subjected by the author and his rivals to a most peculiar test, which ran as follows: Pull the sentence from its contemporary Warren Court context. Pretend that it is being uttered between 1932 and 1937. In that context, does it favor the good guys or the bad guys, the New Deal or the nine old men? If it would have favored the latter then, it must be struck out of the commentary now. For the vindication of the New Deal was the principal task of the generation of commentators that dominated academic discourse between 1950 and 1970. Thus we heard endlessly about judicial self-restraint, that central theme of the Rooseveltian court crisis, long after the Warren Court had rendered the debate obsolescent by firmly choosing the path of activism.

Perhaps the most striking feature of the commentary of the 1950s and 1960s was that the participants battled so fiercely about whether the Court could or should act, while agreeing so fundamentally on the substantive goodness of what the Court was doing or would do if not restrained by its own modesty. To an outsider, it often seemed wondrous indeed that so much energy was expended in seeking to persuade a particular organ of government not to act to achieve a goal that the would-be persuader was so anxious that other parts of government achieve. To understand this highly artificial situation one must not only be aware that the New Deal commentators of the 1950s and 1960s remained fixated on events of the 1930s but must also appreciate the basic role of the Warren Court. Because the Warren Court was engaged in a consistent and comprehensive constitutionalization of the New Deal's fundamental vision of social justice, while violating its fundamental political theory of the strong presidency, the New Deal commentators loved what the Court was doing but hated the fact that it was doing it.

Even now, it may seem a little startling to associate the Warren Court with the New Deal. I have made the argument extensively in another place and will not repeat it at length here.[2] The point can be made in a number of ways. First, we may approach it at the purely political level. The New Deal coalition was built up of workers, the poor in general, racial minorities, intellectuals, and, once it had created them, masses of government workers. The Republicans were left with business and those who identified with business. The activism of the Warren Court served racial minorities, the poor, government workers, and, far more feebly, the intellectuals. It did not help the unions a great deal, but they did not need much help. The one group that the Court consistently refused to serve, and indeed occasionally even attacked, was the business community.

For those uncomfortable with this kind of bald counting of constituencies, the same thing can be said more acceptably in terms of the evolving welfare state. The welfare state implications of the New Deal were clear enough, but its legislative accomplishments were piecemeal and incomplete. A faction of the Warren Court led by Warren himself, but not constituting a clear majority, was slowly moving toward creating constitutional rights to at least minimum levels of subsistence, housing, and education and to the administrative fairness and legal services that would ensure access to welfare state services. The real landmark of the change from the Warren to the Burger Court is *San Antonio Indep. School District v. Rodriguez*,[3] in which a 5 to 4 majority declined to invoke the equal protection clause to prohibit school financing based on local property taxes, with all the attendant disparities between districts with rich tax bases and those without. In that pivotal case, the Burger Court dramatically called a halt to the Warren Court's translation of negative constitutional rights against government into positive constitutional claims to government services.

The fact that Warren was nominally a Republican and had been appointed by a Republican president somewhat obscured the reality that, at the very time the New Deal's welfarism had faltered in the legislative and executive arenas, it had moved forward persistently in the judicial arena. If some members of the Warren faction had had their way, Americans today would have a constitutional right to acquire the basic economic necessities from government. No wonder then that the New Dealer as court watcher could have been a happy man if the ghosts of 1937 had not prevented him from applauding the what because of the who.

Of course, not all New Deal commentators were uniformly wedded to an uncompromising judicial self-restraint. Differences among them, however, were simply a minor tactical quarrel within the New Deal itself. Again, I have made the argument at length elsewhere and will only summarize here.[4] When the New Deal overwhelmed the fortress of the Supreme Court and, in the persons of Justices Black, Frankfurter, and Douglas, took possession of the inner bastions, two alternatives were open. One was to dismantle the fortifications. The other was to rebuild and shift to new targets. After all, why destroy a weapon of political warfare that so much blood had been shed to capture? One New Deal faction, the judicial modesty school, opted for dismantling. The other invented the preferred position doctrine—singling out certain claims relating to speech, voting, and the criminal process for special judicial solicitude—to explain why it was virtue to use the fort to protect Democrats when it had been vice to use it to protect Republicans. And so among the keepers of the fortress the battle raged as to whether it should be blown up or put to new purposes of defending the various underdogs who were the New Deal's clients. One thing, of course, was agreed by all: the fortress should never be used to protect the economic "haves" who were the New Deal's enemies.

THE GENERATIONS CHANGE

All of these New Deal tactical disagreements now seem old hat, not because the Warren Court has turned into the Burger Court but for a far more fundamental reason—as fundamental as birth and death. The generations have changed.[5] In recent years there has emerged a new generation of Court commentators for whom the New Deal is history. Their consciousness-shaping crisis was not 1937 but 1954.[6] And, not surprisingly, their central problem is not whether the Court can or should act, but how it ought to act. They are developing a jurisprudence of values rather than institutional roles. While the immediate occasion of this preoccupation with values is their happy acceptance of the judicial activism that so troubled their immediate forebearers, its foundation is a broader movement in philosophy and legal theory. That movement can be summarized negatively as a rejection of "I like vanilla. You like chocolate." It rejects the notion that values are simply matters of individual preference that cannot be examined by logical discourse, hints that a reconstruction of values may be possible, and insists that both logical discourse and intuitions about values must be employed now in the practical world of affairs rather than deferred until such a reconstruction is completed. Because this movement is in many ways a reaction to utilitarianism and to positivism, it may appear perverse to label it a form of ethical positivism. I do so, however, because, at least in its current stage of development, each of the participants proceeds by insisting first that we must pursue values and then choosing some to pursue. While each of the participants may argue that the particular values he or she has chosen have somehow been demonstrated, those unpersuaded by the analysis must see those values as simply asserted or posited.[7]

The problem is, of course, that different value seekers will posit different values. The new generation of constitutional scholars has arrived at a working consensus as to the solution of that problem, a consensus that represents a development of, rather than a disjunction from, the New Deal solution. It rests on approving and urging extension of the Warren Court's tentative moves toward constitutionalization of the welfare state initiatives of the New Deal, largely without the qualms about judicial activism expressed by the earlier New Dealers.

At a slightly different level, the new commentators wholeheartedly accept the Warren Court's basic dynamic, judicial activism in the service of equality and use that dynamic as their critical criterion for analyzing the work of the Burger Court and making their own policy proposals. It is even easier for the new commentators to pour their economic and political theories of social democracy into the Constitution and the opinions of the Court than it was for their nineteenth-century laissez-faire counterparts. For their equivalent to the blessedly vague and all-encompassing due process clause that served the laissez-faire commentators is the equally vague and all-encompassing equal protection clause. At least the new favored clause contains the word equal, whereas the due process clause does not contain the word free. Moreover, the nineteenth-century constitutional theorists had to persuade the Court to move in their direction, while their modern counterparts need only follow after—the Warren Court having hit the equality trail long before the commentators arrived to applaud the trip.

It may be worth pausing to note another factor that makes the life of the new generation of commentators a bit easier than it otherwise might have been. The Warren Court, or at least the Warren faction of that Court, was reasonably consistent and positive in deciding issues of *equality*, running across voting, rights of the accused, race relations, welfare, and birth control. In the area of *freedom*, the Warren Court's record ran from ambivalence to disaster. Indeed, in the crisis of the mid-1950s, when the Court's racist and McCarthyite enemies formed a congressional coalition that came close to overwhelming it, the Warren Court quietly sacrificed freedom of speech, split the coalition, and saved itself and its racial equality policies. *Barenblatt v. United States*,[8] upholding an inquisition of the House Committee on Un-American Activities, is the monument to that choice of equality over freedom.

SONS OF PREFERRED POSITION

Intellectual life is not such that one can expect a total disjunction in constitutional thought when a change in generations occurs. For example, two members of the newer generation of constitutional commentators, Jesse Choper and John Hart Ely, have undertaken to preserve New Deal preferred position doctrines by grounding them in more sophisticated political analysis. Both continue to focus on the role of the Court problems so prominent in the 1950s. Both are anxious to approve much of the substantive performance of the Warren Court while somehow demonstrating its judicial self-restraint bona fides. In short, both want to do precisely what the inventors of the preferred position doctrine wanted to do—show that the commentator on justice can preserve a reputation for consistency as he both condemns the activism of the anti-New Deal justices and applauds activism in the cause of various interests he prefers to those of the business community.

Of the two, Choper's work[9] presents fewer problems for those bent on value analysis. He seeks to circumscribe and legitimate the role of the Supreme Court by concentrating on comparative institutional competence. The Court should do what it does best, leaving other matters to other branches. He undertakes an extensive analysis of the actual political workings of the legislative and executive branches and of the federal system in order to arrive at a more politically sophisticated version of the traditional New Deal doctrines. The Court should *not* interfere with the further dismantling of the federal system. It should *not* interfere with the growth of the imperial presidency. It should *not* protect economic rights. It should not do any of these things because they are best left to the political process in the legislative and executive branches. The Court *should* protect civil rights and liberties because that is the job best suited to its institutional capabilities.

Because Choper's approach is founded on delimiting spheres of action based on institutional capabilities, it does not predetermine his stance toward the judicial search for values. That is, while Choper may have some favorite values of his own, his theory does not dictate precisely what values the Court must pursue, but only that the justices confine their pursuit to the appropriate spheres of constitutional law. Within those spheres, he and others are free to give the Court good and bad marks for their particular value orderings, but the value issues are essentially independent of the role-of-the-Court issues. Thus Choper is free to describe the Court as pursuing values rather than simply interests and, if he chooses, to prescribe what values it should pursue.

Ely's work[10] presents more complex and far more value-constraining arguments. He is attempting the immensely challenging task of demonstrating that the very high levels of judicial activism represented by the Warren Court, and by his own ambitions for later courts, can be squared with traditional doctrines of judicial self-restraint. To do so he has elaborated the preferred position doctrine into what he calls the representation reenforcing doctrine. He argues that courts ought to intervene in ways that will strengthen the hands of groups not admitted to or not adequately represented in the particular interest coalitions that control the political branches at any given moment.

This approach is curiously anachronistic in the setting of the new commentators of the 1970s. It labors very hard, as did the writings of the postrealists, to demonstrate that an appropriate role for the Court can be derived solely from a procedural rather than a value-substantive theory of democracy. And its procedural theory is that of interest group pluralism, or polyarchy, which dominated the political theory of the 1950s and was explicitly based on the economist's definition of a value as something that someone valued. Politics was simply a kind of economic market in which whatever mix of goods and services the political process yielded was the correct one because it was obviously the one that the participants in the process wanted most.[11] The only problem was to assure that every interest had adequate access to the political marketplace. Otherwise an insufficient quantity of what the underrepresented interests valued would be produced. For Ely, the role of the Supreme Court is to render the market more efficient both by beefing up the capacity of certain groups to make demands on the market and by occasionally supplying what the market refuses to supply because these groups are not strong enough to make effective demands.

EQUALITY AS THE DOMINANT VALUE

There is a sense in which the cascade of recent writing by Ely is an elaborate attempt to deny the obvious, that the Warren Court was hell-bent on equality. No doubt we could construct some hypothetical cases in which the Ely formula did not yield egalitarian results. In practice, however, almost all of the real cases that the rest of the new generation of commentators can approve on equality grounds also will yield approval under the representation reenforcing formula. For Ely, of course, as for any constitutional lawyer worth his Harvard salt, it may not matter what the Warren Court was "really" doing so long as its decisions can be consistently rationalized under the formula proposed. In any event, while Ely rejects ethical positivism of the sort I have attributed to others of his generation,[12] and thus cannot move freely among values, it does turn out that his process-oriented constitutional criteria will usually yield just that substantive value that the others posit for first place in their value pantheon: equality.[13]

The new generation's dedication to equality is not, however, simply a latter-day approval of the work of the Warren Court justices for whom they clerked. It draws its intellectual sustenance, if not its political impact, from a deeper and more fundamental movement in constitutional law. After the assault of the realists, and in the heyday of political theories of interest group pluralism, balancing of interests became the dominant constitutional formula. That formula in effect denied the existence, or at least the legal and political relevance, of independent values. A value was whatever was valued by some recognizable segment of society. The task of constitutional law and constitutional courts was to contribute to the process of articulating and integrating those values.

At the same time that the commentators of the post–New Deal generation have moved beyond the political crisis of the 1930s, they have also attempted to move beyond the crisis described by Roberto Unger, a crisis that reached its peak in the philosophical movements of the previous generation: existentialism, logical positivism, consequentialism, and the work of the English analytics. The crisis is simply that mid-twentieth-century Western culture has no commonly agreed upon moral philosophy from which a set of nonsubjective constitutional values can be deduced. Faced with this discomforting reality, the commentators simply assert or posit certain values as ultimate or at least "higher"; their positings resting on various mixtures of the Judeo-Christian tradition, historical experience, personal conviction, social democratic political and economic theory, and ethical derivations from modern biology, linguistics, and other human "sciences."

This reconstruction of values has certainly not yet achieved the status of a fully articulated and agreed upon system or ideology. It contains many individual variations and internal tensions. Its general direction, nonetheless, is startlingly clear. The central value is equality. The moral philosopher John Rawls has given us a revived social contract theory that manages to render equality rather than freedom the central operating tenet of the contract. The legal philosopher Ronald Dworkin[14] is in the process of attempting to demonstrate that equality ought to be the central principle from which constitutional and other legal rules are to be deduced. My colleague John Coons, in an exercise typical of the current generation of constitutional theorists, has recently shown us why equality may be the one value that survives the Ungerian crisis.[15] He begins from three premises—not necessarily his own but ones he sees as dominant in contemporary thought. The first is that there is no authoritative, "objective" way of establishing core values. The second is that individuals exist. The third, which is heavily dependent on the first, is that we have no objective means of determining, for example, between two individuals, who is the more worthy in any ultimate sense. It follows, all other things being equal, that we ought to treat the two persons equally. In short, equality is the one value that can be logically derived from the contemporary combination of philosophic uncertainty and continued dedication to the worth of the individual human personality.

EQUALITY AND INDIVIDUALISM: THE *SUCCÈS D'ESTIME* OF THE WARREN COURT

At this point, then, the morality play of *Brown v. Board of Education*[16] and the play of morality of currently fashionable philosophers combine to give us a new firmness of purpose in constitutional commentary. It is assumed that the Court can and should act. It is posited that it should act for equality. All of the scholasticism of judicial activism versus judicial modesty and balancing of interests is past. We can move directly to the point: How much and how fast should the Court contribute to a more egalitarian American polity and society? And where equality is not a particularly relevant value to the constitutional dispute at hand, how much and how fast should the Court contribute to some other value posited as dominant in that situation?

As we have already noted, the Warren Court provides no particular difficulty for the new commentators because it did posit equality as its dominant value. It consistently pursued that value across an astounding range of its jurisprudence from obscenity to antitrust, even when it did not openly say so and even where the value was not the obviously dominant one.[17] Thus, the only real issue for the new commentators was whether the Warren Court was moving fast enough and far enough down the equality trail.

With the advent of the Burger Court the issues become more complex, for a number of reasons. The most important of these has to do with the equality value itself and its relation to individualism. Because of the precise stage of American social and political development in which the Warren Court operated, it could combine the quest for equality with individualistic values and so both build and profit from a value consensus. This alliance of egalitarianism with individualism is epitomized by that most popularly successful of all Warren Court slogans "one man-one vote." In both its reapportionment decisions and its desegregation decisions, the Warren Court could and did proclaim that the individual was the basic unit of social and political analysis and that the Constitution commanded that every *individual* be treated as an *equal* to every other.

In the same way, the Warren Court sought to *equalize* the treatment meted out by the criminal justice system to the rich and the poor, but it could do so through an emphasis on the individual rights guaranteed under the Fourth, Fifth, and Sixth Amendments without openly acknowledging its equality goals. Perhaps most importantly, the welfare state goals of the Warren Court appear, at least superficially, to combine equality and individualism because they purport to serve the goal of equality only by ensuring that every individual receives certain minimums of state support. In short, welfare statism in the mild New Deal form proposed to the Warren Court by many litigators and partially accepted by it finesses the potential conflict between equality and individual freedom by treating the problem as one of distribution, not redistribution. Needy individuals will be brought up to minimum subsistence, housing, education, and so forth, but the costs are to be borne only by the amorphous "government," not by individual taxpayers.

The American consensus of the 1950s which the Warren Court reflected was built on precisely this New Deal glossing of fundamental value problems. Subsequently, those problems dramatically reappeared because of a basic change in the way Americans viewed politics and social life, a change that was already occurring in the Warren Court years but which the Warren Court successfully ignored. The Warren Court's successes rested on treating the individual as the basic unit of analysis. Yet increasingly Americans also came to use groups as a basic unit of analysis, primarily of course racial groups but many others as well. The Warren Court managed to focus the last gleams of a twilight of individualism to muster support for its constitutional adventures.

The extent to which the Warren Court was already an anachronism can be seen in the chief justice's cavalier rejection of the by then standard political analysis of the varying influence of various constituencies, groups, and locales. In response to this essentially group analysis of electoral politics, he could respond that it was people (he meant individuals) not trees who voted. He could still cling to the earlier vision of politics as revolving about the individual choices of individual voters rather than admitting that politics was a matter of groups and constituencies of unequal strength. The eventual triumph of polyarchy as the orthodoxy of modern political analysis has made this kind of one man-one vote synthesis of equality and individualism intellectually untenable. The Warren Court exited just as this change in political theory became so strikingly clear that constitutional lawyers could no longer ignore it.[18]

EQUALITY VERSUS INDIVIDUALISM: THE DILEMMA
OF THE BURGER COURT AND ITS COMMENTATORS

Intellectual fashions alone, however, do not change the world. At the very time the Warren Court was passing into the Burger Court, real political struggles took up the basic themes of group theories of politics and made them an acknowledged part of public policy. The Warren Court began with

"Jim Crow," a vision of individuals deprived of their rights because they were Negroes. The Burger Court now faces "affirmative action," a vision of blacks as a disadvantaged class with an entitlement to wield advantages over whites as a class until equality between the two classes is achieved. A quick comparison of *Baker v. Carr*[19] with *United Jewish Organizations of Williamsburgh v. Carey*[20] and of *Brown v. Board* with the dissents in *Bakke*[21] will illustrate the fundamental changes in the political climate in which the Court operates. Perhaps Dworkin has put the change most brutally and thus most usefully when he argues that it is constitutionally justifiable to treat individuals very unequally on the basis of their race so long as the discrimination is aimed at achieving ultimate social equality.[22] When arguments such as this are part of the daily coin of constitutional dispute, we know that the apparent synthesis of individualism and equality achieved by the Warren Court has disintegrated.

In short, the new generation of value-oriented commentators can look back on the Warren era as a kind of golden age in comparison with that of the Burger Court because in the former era political rhetoric and political action still allowed the values of equality and individual freedom to march together in constitutional discourse. Brest, Michelman, Tribe, and Ely, to pick almost at random from among the new generation, can unite on many points in praise of the Warren Court, but that is because, at the stage of public policy development faced by the Warren Court, Brest's "anti-discrimination principle" was operationally equivalent to Ely's "representation reenforcing"[23] norm, and both appeared compatible with the social welfare goals of Michelman and Tribe. The Burger Court cannot, however, hope to do as well.

To illustrate why, we might briefly construct an equality-oriented direction that the Burger Court might take to achieve consistency in terms of the new value-oriented jurisprudence. I have composed this position from bits and pieces of the writings of Rawls, Dworkin, Ely, Michelman, Tribe, and Karst and from a number of remarkably frank opinions of Justice Marshall. It represents a development to a new stage of the egalitarian themes so favored by most of the younger commentators who have been nurtured by the Warren Court. It is built, moreover, on the two central ideas of contemporary American politics: (1) government is responsible for everything; (2) the underdog must be compensated. The position can be expressed in neutral principles, result orientation, or democratic process terms. I will not bother with such metaphysics or with all the nonsense about levels of scrutiny or "compellingness" of interest.

In brief, the Court's position would be first, to uphold the constitutionality of all legislative and executive initiatives whose purpose and effect was to decrease social, economic, and political inequalities in the society; second, to ignore constitutional challenges to measures against which the only constitutional claim was that they deprived members of favored classes or groups of political, social, or economic advantages; third, to create constitutional rights to government-provided subsistence, housing, education, and access to the political process for members of disadvantaged groups. As a corollary, any claim to individual freedom that did not conflict with any of the three equality standards might be entertained by the Court.

As I have said, I do not seek to work this position out systematically because personally I do not favor it. I do not set it up as a straw man, however, but rather as an illustration of a consistent value position that is available to the Court and as an indication of the contemporary value orientation among a large set of post–New Deal commentators—an orientation that provides the basis for much of the criticism of what the Burger Court actually does.

I am not claiming that the new generation of commentators is absolutely united or consistent in this orientation. Quite the contrary, the sketch I have offered is designed to make the point that in the Burger era the conflicts between individual autonomy and social justice that were suppressed in the Warren period come to the fore. If the Burger Court were to take a consistent egalitarian position, some of the progeny of the Warren Court would be pressed to hard choices over freedom versus equality.

The Burger Court has not chosen to move the egalitarian tendencies of the Warren Court on to this next stage. Only if it had done so could it have achieved a consistent value position, for, as I have tried to indicate, the only value position that appears to be compatible with recent developments in political and legal theory and popular ideology is that of compensating the underdog until equality is reached. If this value position is not adopted, only two other positions would seem available to the Burger Court. It might emphasize the value of autonomy *against* the contemporary winds of equality, or it might simply plunge into the ad hoc wars of day-to-day elite politics as practiced in the United States.[24]

AUTONOMY AS A CONSTITUTIONAL VALUE

In a very limited sense, and with many qualifications, the Burger Court might be said to have done the former. There is a certain strain of the autonomy value at work in the Court's decisions, and it is worth collecting some rather disparate cases to get a look at it. The word "autonomy" rather than "freedom" is used because the Court seems less concerned with individual freedom as such than with limiting the scope of government activity. At its most ambitious, the autonomy value would combine separation of powers, federalism, privacy, and individual freedom aspects into something close to a conservative political philosophy. It would seek to establish appropriate boundaries for each of the three branches of the central government, for the central government as a whole vis-à-vis both the states and individuals, and for all government vis-à-vis individuals, private organizations, families, and groups. Such a value orientation would run flatly against the assumption that all problems are the government's problems. It would seek to reassert the presumption against government action. It would challenge the strong presidency theory that was at the heart of New Deal political science and that sought to subordinate both Congress and the Supreme Court to the presidency. It would seek to place some ultimate limits on the invasions of state authority practiced by the central government. Borrowing not from liberal but conservative tenets, it would stress the integrity of groups and organizations such as unions and families that can provide a buffer between the individual and government. Finally, of course, it would stress both the privacy rights of individuals and their rights to self-determination.

The Burger Court's most striking activism has been exhibited over the abortion issue. And here, while the contemporary Court appears simply to be carrying the work of the Warren Court to its logical conclusion, a significant shift of values from equality to autonomy seems to have occurred. It is true that in starting down this road, the Warren Court, desperate to intervene, invented a constitutional right of privacy to justify its intervention. Seen in the context of the Warren Court's general jurisprudence, however, the fact situation in *Griswold v. Connecticut*,[25] striking down Connecticut's ban on the use of birth control devices, was crucial. The living law of Connecticut was that middle-class women received birth control information and purchased birth control supplies, and the Connecticut statute was enforced only to block the operation of birth control clinics that would bring these services to the poor. *Griswold* was an equality not a privacy decision just as *Gideon v. Wainwright*,[26] providing indigent criminal defendants a right to counsel at public expense, was an equality not a right-to-counsel decision.

As *Maher v. Roe*,[27] rejecting the contention that indigent women are entitled to state financed abortions, has instructed us, however, the fortuitous choice of a privacy rationale by the Warren Court has allowed the new Court to turn *Griswold* on its head. The evil is not government intervention that results in unequal distribution of services. The evil becomes government intervention per se—invasion of the autonomy of the individual woman. The Burger Court has been accused of creating a middle-class right to abortion. It has indeed insisted that the right to abortion is a negative right against government invasion of personal autonomy, not a Warren Court style positive claim to equal government services.

For those who have chosen either autonomy or equality as a master value, the foundering point is often the question of the appropriate recipient. Those who choose equality, for instance, are bedeviled with the question, Equality for whom—individuals or races? In the abortion area, the autonomy for whom issue has been acute. For in its concern for individual autonomy, the

Court has seriously breached the autonomy of the family in cases such as *Planned Parenthood v. Danforth*[28] and *Carey v. Population Services Int'l.*,[29] which vindicate the rights of children to have abortions and birth control services even over parental objection.

Yet in contexts where the issues can be seen as government power versus family autonomy rather than as a clash of individual autonomy and family authority, the Court has shown a certain sympathy for family autonomy. Illustrative are its decisions in *Moore v. City of East Cleveland*,[30] striking down a zoning ordinance that prohibited extended family households; *Village of Belle Terre v. Boraas*,[31] upholding an ordinance that prohibited cohabitation by three or more unrelated persons; *Wisconsin v. Yoder*,[32] upholding the right of Amish parents to keep their children out of public secondary schools; and *Smith v. Organization of Foster Families*,[33] holding that foster family relationships may be severed by the state pursuant to procedures of a more summary nature than would be required in the case of biological family relationships. When these cases are considered together, a value-oriented jurisprudence certainly emerges, although the value served is not quite that favored by most of the new value-oriented critics. The abortion decisions plus the decision in *Dept. of Agriculture v. Moreno*,[34] prohibiting the federal government from discriminating against households of unrelated persons in the award of food stamps, could be interpreted as creating a new constitutional right to choose one's own life-style. But *Moore* and company find the Burger Court reasserting traditional substantive due process in order to protect traditional family values. It is not that people are free to live any way they choose but that the family as a long-standing social institution has a certain autonomy as against governmental intervention.

As the citation of *Wisconsin v. Yoder* in conjunction with *Moore* suggests, this inclination toward recognizing the autonomy of the traditional family is related to a Burger Court concern for the autonomy of traditional religions. The chief justice himself waged a long campaign of building precedents that could ultimately be used to break an opening through the establishment clause to permit state aid to parochial schools. Although he lost by a vote or two, in the process the "no excessive entanglement" doctrine was erected. That doctrine strongly suggests that the state may act benevolently toward traditional organized religion so long as it does not breach its autonomy. The establishment clause is read far less as a bar to government aid to religion and far more as a barrier to government regulation of religion. *Wisconsin v. Yoder*, which permits a traditional religion, but not the newer life-style cults or groups, to violate a nondiscriminatory state compulsory education statute of general application, is a peak in the new value-oriented jurisprudence. The Court applauds the autonomy of a religious sect that sets itself against the modern world and condemns state interference with that autonomy even in pursuit of a highly worthy state interest. It carefully avoids considering the very real clash between the interests of the children and their religious elders that brings to the fore all the autonomy-for-whom questions that the Court prefers to avoid.

To the cases that suggest a certain autonomy for individuals, families, and traditional, organized religions may be added those that strive to assert a certain autonomy for traditional government units as against the sweep of central government authority. As we shall note presently, the autonomy value nearly always comes out second best in clashes with the equality value, even in the Burger Court. Nonetheless, it occasionally wins some minor victories. Thus the states have been told that they may deviate a bit from absolute voting equality in order to incorporate traditional city and county boundaries into their reapportionment schemes.[35] And *Milliken v. Bradley*,[36] prohibiting cross-district busing to achieve racial integration in public schools, contains a great deal of brave language and some real action in defense of the autonomy of local governments. The *Milliken* decision is, however, no more than a sign of the Court's attraction to autonomy, for the dynamic of school desegregation has now passed into such a totalitarian mode that it sweeps away all notions of individual, family, and governmental autonomy in its pursuit of forced equality. As the school busing cases of the 1978 and 1979 terms indicate, a little nostalgia for the autonomy of local government and local democratic processes is not likely to stem this tide of egalitarian coercion.[37]

Where equality is not involved, the Burger Court has become famous for its concern for governmental autonomy by virtue of its decision in *National League of Cities v. Usery*,[38] restricting the power of Congress to mandate minimum wage scales for state and local government employees. No one, least of all Justice Rehnquist who wrote the opinion, has been able to explain just where the boundary between state and central government authority lies. At least at the level of brave rhetoric the case does seem to express about all that can be said at this late date by those who preserve a certain affection for the states. It suggests that there must be some core of state autonomy that the federal government cannot breach if federalism is not to become a total sham. Just as the Court revives substantive due process to sing the praises of traditional family autonomy in *Moore*, it revives the Tenth Amendment in *Usery* to assert a constitutional basis for the traditional autonomy of the states. Neither of these revivals would have had much chance of making the Warren Court's production schedule.

This concern for autonomy rather than freedom, that is, for a reserve against outside interference rather than a capacity to act, helps to make some sense of the Court's rather tangled First Amendment jurisprudence. Let us begin from the premise that the media—and particularly that most traditional of the media, the press—are entitled to autonomy not so much because of the abstract pronouncement of freedom in the First Amendment as because

the media are significant private institutions whose autonomy serves as a
check on government.[39] The only creative push of the Burger Court in the
freedom of the press area has been the emphasis on editorial autonomy.
Editors must be free to mind their own business, to pick and choose what
they print, to make their own essentially private decisions.[40] But precisely
because the media are private, autonomous institutions, not public trusts of
some sort, they are entitled to no special privileges. Thus they may go only
where other private citizens may go,[41] like other private citizens are held
responsible for their own malice and negligence,[42] and like everyone else
must submit to lawful warrants,[43] subpoenas,[44] and pretrial discovery procedures.[45] Indeed, in the realm of newsman's privilege, many journalists have
seen the wisdom of denying themselves a privilege that would inevitably
carry with it the implication of government determination of just who is and
is not an "official" newsman. In this context, too, the growing differentiation of the print media from the electronic media[46] may be explained not in
terms of a special status for the print media resting on the specific wording
of the First Amendment but in terms of a clash of autonomies. When television intrudes directly on the autonomy of the family, it may be more
heavily regulated than the less intrusive print media. When there is no such
intrusion on a competing autonomy, however, even the broadcast media are
entitled to be treated as autonomous entities.[47]

Emphasis on the autonomy value may have some very real importance for
freedom of speech as the movement grows to transform the First Amendment
from a negative right against government into a positive egalitarian right in
the service of democracy. The modern fashion of turning all rights into
claims for government services, of subordinating all other values to equality, and of treating most rights as instrumental to the democratic process
rather than as ends in themselves, is far more than hinted at in *Buckley v.
Valeo*,[48] the decision upholding some sections of the Federal Campaign Finance Act and invalidating other sections. The overly ambitious inclusion
of commercial advertising under the freedom of speech umbrella will no
doubt generate a stream of decisions approving government limitations on
speech, which is allegedly constitutionally protected. Today the democratic
egalitarians demand the leveling down of freedom of speech à la *Buckley*
and the consumerites demand the purification of advertising à la the attacks
on children's commercials. The left is passing through one of those anti-
freedom-of-speech stages at which it alternates with the right. The bottom
line is—as always—that good speech should be encouraged, and now even
subsidized in the name of equality, and bad speech—that of the sugar Nazis
and the Warbucks—should be suppressed. The Burger Court is certainly not
sufficiently wedded to freedom of speech as an absolute or ultimate value
to do much against the growing movement to turn speech into a government-
regulated industry subservient to the "public interest." Against this move-

ment, the notion of the private autonomy of the media may be a weak reed, but about the only one available.

Of course, any treatment of a developing autonomy value in the Burger Court must run up against the reality of its search and seizure decisions— the very place where traditionally we would expect autonomy values to be most on display. And in a few cases like *Marshall v. Barlow's, Inc.,*[49] subjecting Labor Department regulatory work place searches to the warrant requirement, they are. More generally, of course, the Burger Court has whittled back the Warren Court's search and seizure holdings and has allowed the government new scope for searches of financial records.[50] To a degree it might be argued that what is involved here is respect for state autonomy. More persuasively it might be argued that the current Court believes that traditional warrant requirements set the proper boundary between individual autonomy and the needs of the criminal justice system, that it is prepared to uphold those requirements, but that it does not see the exclusionary rule as implicating autonomy values at all. Indeed the Court treats the rule as essentially an implementation or enforcement device and changes in it as a matter of pragmatic public administration rather than basic constitutional values.

AUTONOMY FOR SOME

In all candor, however, it must be admitted that the Court, like everyone else, seems to have an enemies list. It is far less interested in defending some people's autonomy than others. The bad guys include pornographers,[51] war protesters,[52] welfare recipients,[53] practitioners of nontraditional religions and life-styles,[54] and the business community. The last in this rogues' gallery may seem to be in odd company. But this is one area in which the Warren Court's constitutionalization of the New Deal's political victory has been sustained and reemphasized by the Burger Court. In *City of New Orleans v. Dukes*,[55] upholding a restriction on pushcart vendors in New Orleans' French Quarter, the Burger Court overruled the one post-1937 decision that offered business some constitutional equal protection.[56] The opinions in *Dukes* are disarmingly frank in announcing that the Court is supposed to protect the clients of the New Deal but not its enemies.

EQUALITY OVER AUTONOMY: RACIAL EQUAL PROTECTION AND THE END OF THE GOLDEN AGE

The crucial equal protection questions, however, involve race, and in this area all jurisprudences encounter grave problems, at least during the current stage of development. The constitutional prohibition of Jim Crow laws by the Warren Court was fully a New Deal step, serving one of the New Deal clients. Indeed the welfare state approach was particularly helpful in maintaining New Deal consensus because it aided blacks in the context of their shared interest with poor whites, who also voted Democratic.

The affirmative action stage of racial equal protection is, however, both a cause and an effect of the breakdown of the New Deal consensus. And that breakdown surely marks the post–New Deal generation of commentators, essentially because simple allegiance to equality as a value does not resolve the issue. The problem can be put a number of different ways. Affirmative action pits one member of the New Deal coalition, blacks, against two others, working class, unionized whites and Jews. So the allegiance to the New Deal shared by the post–New Deal commentators will not resolve the constitutional problem.

From another angle the crucial question of affirmative action is the choice of the relevant political unit. If the individual is the relevant unit, then all sorts of tough moral issues arise when we penalize individual whites who have not discriminated in order to benefit individual blacks who may not have been victims of discrimination. If the unit of analysis is the class, race, or group, then it can be more easily argued that a compensatory transfer of disadvantage from blacks to whites is justifiable until equality is achieved. By carefully thinking in "corporate" terms, all sorts of constitutional problems are avoided. Thus, Ely can arrive at the conclusion that a majority may disadvantage "itself" without violating the equal protection clause. That the "majority" may consist of middle-aged white males who have already achieved their career goals, while the disadvantaged may consist of young white males who have not, is submerged in the corporate identity of the white majority.

Thus it is not only individual versus group analysis that is at issue. Even within the context of group analysis, where do we draw the group boundaries, and who is vicariously represented in the legislature and who is not? Just as consulting the New Deal clients list leaves affirmative action problems unsolved, so does consulting the group theories of politics that percolated from political science into the constitutional law training of the post–New Deal commentators. First of all those theories never totally blotted out the traditional constitutional concern for the individual. Second, the problem of defining group boundaries just adverted to, and so central to Justice Powell's opinion in *Bakke*, is not easily solved. And third, there has been a reaction by political theorists to polyarchy notions, so that group-oriented constitutional theorists are finding that their intellectual bases are eroding.

If neither the New Deal nor group theory provides a firm basis for affirmative action, does the new jurisprudence of posited values? Even if all those in the value game posited equality as their dominant value, the answer would be no. An allegiance to equality does not, in and of itself, resolve the issue of whether inequalities should be visited by government action upon some individuals now in the hope that such visitations will result in equality for all later. Thus we can find that Ely,[57] by procedural twist, and Dworkin,[58] by direct substantive appeal to the equality value, justify governmental discrimination against whites, while Fiss[59] is greatly worried by such discrimination and Van Alstyne opposes it.[60]

The Court itself is in no better condition than the commentators. It has clearly decided that in its value scale the achievement of racial and sexual equality ranks far, far higher than autonomy. The Court persistently breaches the autonomy of political units, private organizations, and individuals in its quest for racial and sexual equality. Like the commentators, the Court is rendered uneasy by blatant discrimination against whites, but on the whole it manages to suppress those qualms in pursuit of an egalitarian social vision.[61]

In short, the young white male who is low on the career ladder has joined the pornographer and the businessman on the enemies list. To grant him or his school or employer autonomy would interfere with a value more important to the present Court and the new commentators, the value of racial and sexual equality. As a result, the Supreme Court and other courts have joined Congress and the executive in fostering pervasive and highly coercive government intervention in an astonishing range of private relationships in order to achieve precisely the desired pattern of discrimination and nondiscrimination. It must be frankly admitted that any allegiance to the autonomy value to be perceived in the Burger Court may, in historical perspective, seem minor compared to its approval of this massive government intervention in what had hitherto been autonomous educational and economic relationships. In this sense the Burger Court carries on the Warren Court's commitment to equality, but carries it beyond the New Deal consensus into areas in which the conflict between individual and group theories of equality is not easily resolved.

THE DEATH PENALTY

The Court's death penalty jurisprudence, like its body of decisions on race, is an area in which autonomy is subordinated to another value, although it is not quite clear what that value is. Earlier we noted that the Court had openly reverted to substantive due process in proclaiming the constitutional status of the autonomy of the traditional family. The other area in which it has most openly proclaimed a free jurisprudence of values is that of the death penalty. Initially that did not necessarily appear to be so. The early decisions[62] were very much in the mold of Warren Court criminal procedure decisions. While hooked to a specific clause of the Constitution that had nothing to do with equality, the early death penalty decisions might well have been defended on equality grounds. Death penalties were disproportionately levied on the black and the poor. Either abolishing the penalty altogether or demanding very strict procedures might cure this inequality. Curing inequality was worth massive federal interference in a policy area that had traditionally been at the very center of state authority. *Coker v. Georgia*,[63] striking down the death penalty as a punishment for rape, however, shows us that equality is not the value at play. Instead, the value appears to be some sort of Aristotelian proportionality. The Court dons the robes of the Mikado to decide when the punishment fits the crime. It feels in its bones that rape is not serious enough to warrant the death penalty.

Curiously, if the Warren Court had handed down *Coker*, it would have been uniformly applauded by liberals caught up in the intellectual fashions of a period dominated by psychological determinism, the demystification of sex, and the denigration of "traditional morality." The perpetrator was driven by forces beyond his control. The victim suffered a distasteful form of assault but not one that should be elevated into a particularly horrendous status because of old-fashioned notions of sex as defilement. Of course, what in the 1950s would have appeared progressive today sails against the winds of contemporary fashions of feminism. A jurisprudence of values administered by predominantly elderly judges may not be quite up to date. Yet if the Court is to constitutionalize its values, *Coker* seems sound enough. The death penalty for rape surely does derive from sexual taboos and attitudes toward sexual purity that have ceased to be primary in our pattern of values. And the question that would have appeared crucial to the commentators of the 1950s—whether the Court or the state legislatures ought to be the Mikado—no longer occupies center stage. The *Moore v. East Cleveland* and *Coker v. Georgia* decisions may tap different streams of value—one traditional, the other aging avant-garde—but both are landmarks in the jurisprudence of values.

CONCLUSION: THE GENERATION GAP

In the heyday of the Warren Court, the Court was activist and the commentators were not. In the day of the Burger Court, the Court is activist and so are the commentators. Yet this generation of commentators is no happier with the present Court than its predecessor was with the preceeding one. No doubt in part this is because of the tension that always exists between critic and playwright. This tension is further aggravated because each generation of critics is likely to be happier with the Court that shaped its intellectual adolescence than with the one it confronts when it reaches maturity. Beyond these structural phenomena, however, two factors seem to be particularly relevant.

First, the Warren Court was pursuing the equality value fairly consistently, and it was doing so along lines that had been clearly laid down by the New Deal. Indeed, the Warren Court showed promise of carrying the New Deal program to its ultimate conclusion in the welfare state and an egalitarian political process at a time when the legislative and executive branches were faltering. Both in terms of values and interests, the program toward which the Warren Court seemed to be moving was identical to that last great outbreak of the New Deal, Lyndon Johnson's "war on poverty" and "great society." That neither Warren nor Johnson was able to bring his program to total fruition makes them no less brothers in the New Deal.

The traumatic shock of the 1937 Court fight, however, resulted in the curious anomaly that the New Deal generation of commentators could not love the truly New Deal Court, that is, the Warren Court. The new generation of commentators, born late enough to inherit and build upon the New Deal's egalitarianism, *can* love the Warren Court. The new generation cannot love the Burger Court, because the Burger Court is responsive to, and a victim of, the breakdown of the New Deal consensus which the Warren Court pursued and in terms of which its achievements can be defended and rationalized. The new generation of commentators is retrospectively happy with the Warren Court for the same reasons it is retrospectively happy with the pre-Vietnam democracy of Lyndon Johnson, and it is unhappy with the Burger Court for the same reasons it is unhappy with the post-Vietnam democracy of Jimmy Carter and Ronald Reagan. In a world in which political goals are not clear and policy consensus is diminished, the Supreme Court is as unlikely as the rest of government to acquire a cheering section.

All of this leads to a second major factor in the new commentators' unhappiness with the Court. Once it is established either by the direct route or the preferred position detour that the Court should be active in defense of the values esteemed by the commentators, then the commentators face the same problem as the president when he appoints Supreme Court justices. If you want the Supreme Court to pursue equality, appoint a justice who believes in equality. In the real world, of course, big values like equality are too big to be certain guides to policy preferences. Instead of saluting a big value, the commentator or president must compose a policy agenda or an ordering of policy preferences. He will then prefer justices who have roughly the same agenda as he does. In the nature of things, it is hard to find a justice or even prospective justice who fills out his policy batting order exactly the same way as the justice evaluator. President Nixon found himself a chief justice who was tough on crooks, but then alas he turned out to be tough on presidents, too, and soft on abortion.

In other words, a jurisprudence of values must be translated into a jurisprudence of policies. And at the multiple, diffuse, and complex level of policy, neither an individual justice nor the Court as a whole is likely to produce precisely the mix of policies that any given commentator will favor. In this respect, the Warren Court experience is misleading. That Court was working out to its final conclusions a set of values and policy preferences that had achieved an overwhelming consensus produced by one of the few great crises and value reorderings in American political history. As a result, its policy agenda did happen to coincide rather well with those of large numbers of commentators whose own agendas had been shaped by that same consensus. In more normal periods of politics, it is far less likely that the Court's policy preferences will make a good fit with that of any other policy picker. Thus a group of commentators wedded to activism in pursuit of values, confronting a Court similarly committed, will nevertheless generate a highly critical commentary. The justices will simply not pick exactly the mix of policies that the commentators would prefer.

This uneasiness would exist even if the commentators and the justices had roughly the same values. They do not. With a few exceptions and differences in emphasis, the new generation of commentators takes equality as its key value. I have tried to show here that the Court, considered as a whole, does not. It is attracted by both equality and autonomy as base values. It has called at least a temporary halt in the constitutionalizing of the welfare state that was one of the central egalitarian pursuits of the Warren Court.[64] It wavers on the grand strategy question: Should the government intervene everywhere and in everything in order to achieve the equality of everybody in every respect? And it suffers from the same ambivalence as do the commentators as to whether a political theory of individualism or groups should serve as the bridge between the value of equality and the policy of nondiscrimination.

A jurisprudence of values is a poor one if the proper function of commentators and justices is to rationalize the case law—that is, to organize the Court's decisions into consistent patterns. For in the contemporary world, individual value systems are both internally inconsistent and inconsistent with those held by others. Moreover, the gap between generalized statements of value and actual policies is so great that two persons alleging the same values may come to conflicting policy conclusions. If, on the other hand, the job of commentators and justices is to arrive at good public policy, a jurisprudence of values does have one great advantage over its predecessor. At least so long as the Court is dedicated to action, it seems more sensible to argue about what the Court should do than about whether it should do it and to praise it when it does well rather than yearn for the good deeds to be done by someone else.

The post–New Deal generation of commentators is unlikely to achieve the elegance or the professional sense of superiority of the generation of judicial self-restraint, for it is going to be down with the rest of us in the dirty pit of public policy. It may, however, have more interesting things to say about what is really going on in the world and in the Court than did the generation that devoted itself to self-denial.

• Profiles of the Justices •

Hugo Black (1937–1971)
Born February 27, 1886, in Clay County, Alabama. Retired from the Court September 17, 1971. Died September 24, 1971. His father was a storekeeper and farmer. Black grew up in Ashland, Alabama, a town of 350. The family lived a comfortable existence. As a youth, he worked as a cotton picker and as a typesetter for a weekly newspaper. He attended public school. At the age of seventeen, Black enrolled in medical school but after a year abandoned that course in favor of the University of Alabama Law School. At the time, it was possible to bypass undergraduate education entirely, and Black chose that option. He received his law degree in 1906 with honors.

Upon graduation he returned to Ashland, where he practiced for a year. He then moved to Birmingham, began to build a general practice, and served part-time as a police court judge. In 1914 he became a prosecuting attorney, a position he held for three years. During that time he conducted a grand jury investigation that uncovered brutal police practices, including the obtaining of confessions by torture. After a year of service in the military during World War I, Black returned to private practice in Birmingham. He specialized in personal injury cases and the representation of labor unions. His eloquence before juries and in appellate argument earned him local renown.

In 1926 Black won election to the United States Senate. He served there until President Roosevelt appointed him to the Supreme Court in 1937. As a senator, Black was a committed liberal and a strong supporter of the New Deal. He argued against customs controls over obscene and subversive literature. He was instrumental in the passage of federal legislation restricting child labor and setting minimum wages and maximum hours. After the nomination of Black to the Supreme Court was confirmed by the Senate, a furor was caused by the rediscovery that for two years in the early 1920s he had been a member of the Ku Klux Klan. Black defused the controversy with a nationwide radio address explaining that he had resigned from the Klan, rejected its credo, and had had nothing further to do with the organization.

Of all the justices who have served during the years of the Burger Court, Black has the most secure place in history. By any measure, he is one of the towering figures of the American constitutional tradition. He served on the Court for thirty-four years and in that time was never far from the center of controversy. His judging combined the wisdom and breadth of vision of a learned student of history with the disingenuous certitude of a backwoods politician, both of which he was. His writing, particularly in his indignant dissents during the McCarthy era, has a clarity and power that has earned it a special place in the anthologies.

Black viewed the Constitution as a collection of bold, specific commitments designed to prevent the recurrence of historic evils. He reduced constitutional provisions to basic precepts and then insisted upon unyielding, unqualified adherence to those precepts. He claimed to be guided only by the literal meaning of the constitutional text and the intentions of the constitutional framers. He repeatedly criticized his brethren for writing their own views into the Constitution.

This philosophy led Black to take an expansive view of the constitutional clauses relating to freedom of speech, the separation of church and state, the privilege against self-incrimination, and trial by jury. He rejected limitations on those guarantees designed to make them "reasonable" or "balanced." On the other hand, the Fourth Amendment, which prohibits only "unreasonable" searches and seizures, he read more narrowly than most of his Warren Court brethren. Black was especially critical of the judicial practice of discovering innovative guarantees of liberty and equality in the broad, undefined Fourteenth Amendment concepts of equal protection and due process. Only for problems that concerned its framers, most notably racial discrimination, would he invoke the Fourteenth Amendment to invalidate arrangements adopted by state and local lawmaking bodies.

Black served under five chief justices. For twenty-five years he was the senior justice on the Court. After the first two years of Chief Justice Burger's tenure, Black was forced to resign because of ill health, disappointed that he fell short by less than a year of his goal of serving longer on the Court than any other justice in its history.

Harry Blackmun (1970–   )

Born November 12, 1908, in Nashville, Illinois. Grew up in St. Paul, Minnesota. His father owned a grocery and hardware store in St. Paul. The family lived in a working-class neighborhood and enjoyed a modest standard of living. Blackmun attended public schools, where one of his schoolmates was Warren Burger. They were friends; Blackmun was the best man at Burger's wedding.

Blackmun went to Harvard College on a scholarship and worked part-time to put himself through school. He majored in mathematics, was elected to Phi Beta Kappa, and graduated summa cum laude in 1929. He then enrolled in the Harvard Law School, where he compiled a good but not outstanding record. He received his law degree in 1932.

Following graduation, Blackmun clerked for a judge on the Eighth Circuit Court of Appeals, then joined a Minneapolis law firm. For sixteen years he remained in private practice, becoming a partner in his firm and specializing in taxation, estate planning, and civil litigation. During that time he taught part-time as an instructor at St. Paul College of Law and the University of Minnesota Law School. In 1950 Blackmun left his law firm to become resident counsel of the Mayo Clinic in Rochester, Minnesota.

In 1959 President Eisenhower appointed Blackmun a judge on the Eighth Circuit Court of Appeals. There he served for eleven years, establishing a reputation as a careful judge, somewhat progressive on civil rights matters and conservative regarding the rights of the accused. During the late 1960s his opinions sometimes contained gratuitous critical references to the permissiveness of modern society.

Blackmun was appointed to the Supreme Court in 1970 amidst a storm of controversy. Liberal Justice Abe Fortas had been forced to resign when some of his shady financial dealings came to light. Two Southern appeals court judges were successively nominated by President Nixon to fill the seat but were denied Senate confirmation in close, bitter struggles. Nixon then announced that he despaired of getting the Senate to approve a Southerner who shared his judicial philosophy and turned to the less controversial Blackmun, who quickly won enthusiastic Senate confirmation.

At first, Blackmun dismayed admirers of the Warren Court by joining consistently with his childhood friend, Chief Justice Burger, in a series of opinions criticizing the activist judicial philosophy of the previous era. One opinion by Blackmun in particular, in which he needlessly cast aspersions on a welfare recipient, aroused the ire of the liberal community. The disparaging epithet, "The Minnesota Twins," was coined to emphasize Blackmun's lack of independence from Burger.

Roe v. Wade, the 1973 abortion decision written by Blackmun, constituted a turning point in the justice's career on the bench. He brought to the issue the expertise and sympathies he acquired in his nine years representing the Mayo Clinic. He worked hard on the opinion for several months and was stung by the intemperate criticism the Court's decision evoked. Since *Roe v. Wade*, Blackmun has ruled in favor of women seeking abortions on a variety of different issues generated by the *Roe* precedent. In other areas as well, most notably racial discrimination, environmental law, and freedom of the press, Blackmun has shown an independence of mind and a respect for liberal values.

Blackmun is one of the hardest-working members of the Court. He is less inclined than any other justice to delegate research and writing chores to his law clerks. He agonizes over decisions to the point of indecisiveness. He is sometimes accused of lacking vision and of laboring too much over small points. By the same token, he has impressed Court observers with his diligence, open-mindedness, and capacity for growth.

William J. Brennan (1956–   )

Born April 25, 1906, in Newark, New Jersey. His father, an immigrant from Ireland, was a boiler worker, a labor leader, and eventually the elected commissioner of public safety of Newark. The future justice attended public high school in Newark and the Wharton School of Finance at the University of Pennsylvania, where he was an honor student. In 1931 he graduated from Harvard Law School, ranking in the top 10 percent of his class.

Upon graduation, Brennan joined a Newark law firm, became the resident expert in labor law, and was made a partner in 1937. During World War II he served on the staff of the undersecretary of war. In the mid-1940s he achieved statewide prominence for his work on reforming the judicial article of the New Jersey constitution.

In 1949 Brennan was appointed to the Superior Court of New Jersey and was later elevated to the appellate division and then the New Jersey Supreme Court. He was a highly respected judge and was generally considered a liberal. During the heyday of Senator Joseph McCarthy, Brennan publicly denounced the repressive tactics of the Senator's anti-Communist crusade.

In 1956 President Eisenhower nominated Brennan, a Democrat, to be an associate justice of the United States Supreme Court. Shortly after joining the high court, Brennan displayed a deep commitment to civil liberties and an activist philosophy of judicial review. He became a close friend and great admirer of Chief Justice Earl Warren. During the years of Warren's chief justiceship, when the liberal activists commanded a majority of the seats on the Court, Brennan wrote a large number of the Court's opinions. He exhibited great skill and ingenuity in writing opinions that could win the assent of several independent-minded and strong-willed justices.

Since the advent of Chief Justice Burger, Brennan has played a different role. Frequently he finds himself advocating a broader reading of the Bill of Rights or the Fourteenth Amendment than is acceptable to his more conservative or more moderate fellow justices. On these occasions, Brennan often writes long, thoroughly researched, sometimes angry, separate opinions lamenting the Court's failure to live up to the promise of the Warren Court's legacy.

Warren Earl Burger (1969–   )
Born September 17, 1907, in St. Paul, Minnesota. Grew up in a working-class neighborhood of St. Paul. His father was a rail cargo inspector and sometime traveling salesman. In high school, Burger was the editor of the weekly student newspaper and also did part-time reporting for metropolitan daily newspapers in St. Paul. He was a good student and a four-sport letterman. He earned a scholarship to Princeton University but was forced to decline it because he could not afford the remaining costs of such an education. Instead, Burger enrolled at the University of Minnesota for two years, then attended evening law classes for four years at St. Paul College of Law (now William Mitchell College of Law). He earned his law degree magna cum laude in 1931 and joined one of the leading law firms in St. Paul.

Burger rose quickly in law practice, making partner in five years and establishing himself as a civic leader. He became active in state politics as one of the leading supporters of Harold Stassen, then a progressive, youthful governor of Minnesota with national political aspirations. Throughout the 1940s, Burger worked hard for Stassen and in the process came to the attention of the leaders of the national Republican Party, including Richard Nixon. At the 1952 Republican Convention, Burger participated skillfully in the successful effort to deny the nomination to the conservative candidate, Robert Taft.

During the Eisenhower administration, Burger served in the Justice Department as the assistant attorney general in charge of the Civil Division. In that position, he gained notoriety among civil libertarians when during the height of the McCarthy era he defended before the Supreme Court the government's firing on loyalty grounds of a prominent physician. The solicitor general had refused to argue the case because he thought the government's action unjustified and offensive. In 1955 Burger was appointed to the United States Court of Appeals for the District of Columbia Circuit.

In his early years on the Court of Appeals, Burger adopted moderate positions on some of the controversial issues of criminal justice. Eventually, however, he developed a deep concern about the inefficiency and ineffectiveness of the criminal justice system and blamed much of the problem on expansive interpretation of the constitutional rights of the accused. In the late 1960s he emerged as a prominent public critic of the adversary system as it operates in the field of criminal law. In other areas of dispute, his opinions were occasionally innovative and did not in overall tenor display a markedly ideological orientation.

On the Supreme Court, Burger has not achieved success as a leader. Early in his tenure, he alienated some of his fellow justices with heavy-handed practices regarding the assignment of opinions. On occasion, his own opinions have been seriously deficient in craftsmanship. Within the Court, he appears to have remarkably little influence, even with justices who share his convictions on the issues that come before the Court.

In most areas of dispute, Burger tends to take a restrictive view of the liberties guaranteed by the Constitution and of the Supreme Court's role in the governmental scheme. He is almost invariably opposed to efforts to strengthen the rights of the accused or to extend the reach of the due process and equal protection clauses. On the other hand, when history provides support, he sometimes responds favorably to strong claims of liberty, as on such issues as freedom of the press and the separation of church and state. He also has taken a broad view of the power of Congress to legislate in the interest of racial equality and wrote the opinion that legitimated court-ordered comprehensive busing as a remedy for school desegregation.

William O. Douglas (1939–1975)

Born October 16, 1898, at Maine, Minnesota. Retired from the Supreme Court November 12, 1975. Died January 19, 1980. His father, who died when the future justice was six years old, was a home missionary for the Presbyterian Church in various communities of the Pacific Northwest. When his father died, his mother moved the family to Yakima, Washington, where Douglas grew up. The family was poor, and during his youth Douglas worked at a variety of jobs in stores, creameries, cold storage plants, packing houses, and orchards. Frail as a youngster, he developed a passion for vigorous hiking and backpacking in the mountains near his home. A lifelong devotion to natural beauty and the preservation of wilderness traces from this period.

Douglas attended Whitman College in Walla Walla, Washington, graduating in 1920. He then taught school for two years before enrolling in Columbia Law School, from which he graduated second in his class in 1925. Upon graduation, he worked for two years at the Wall Street firm of Cravath, de Gersdorff, Swaine and Wood, and then returned briefly to practice law in Yakima. In 1927 Douglas joined the faculty of Columbia Law School, then moved to Yale in 1929. As a law professor, his specialty was corporation law. He established a national reputation in that field by the age of 35. Douglas left law teaching in 1934 to work for the newly created Securities and Exchange Commission, becoming a commissioner in 1936 and its chairman in 1937. On March 20, 1939, President Franklin D. Roosevelt nominated Douglas to fill the seat on the Supreme Court previously held by the legendary Louis Brandeis. At the age of 40, Douglas was the youngest person appointed to the Court since 1811.

William O. Douglas served longer on the Court than any other person in its history. In his more than thirty-six years on the bench, he wrote over 1,200 opinions. His was a distinctive voice on the Court, strongly civil libertarian in outlook and often disrespectful of traditional canons of legal reasoning. Though widely acknowledged to have a brilliant mind, Douglas seldom produced opinions of great analytic power. His work on the Court was characterized by creativity, impatience with legal niceties, and a tendency to see disputes in the broadest terms.

During the years he served with Chief Justice Burger, Douglas was frequently cast in the role of an uncompromising dissenter lamenting the Court's complicity in the stifling of the individual spirit. In virtually all areas, Justice Douglas argued for broader and stronger interpretations of the Bill of Rights and the Civil War Amendments than were acceptable to his brethren. Never a congenial colleague on the Court, he established warmer personal relations with some of the Nixon appointees than he had enjoyed earlier with fellow justices who more closely shared his ideological orientation.

John Marshall Harlan (1955–1971)
Born May 20, 1899, in Chicago. Retired from the Supreme Court September 23, 1971. Died December 29, 1971. His father, grandfather, and great-grandfather were lawyers. The grandfather was a justice of the United States Supreme Court, the father, a Chicago alderman.

Harlan received his undergraduate degree from Princeton in 1920. He was class president and a good but not outstanding student. He then studied law for three years at Balliol College, Oxford, as a Rhodes scholar. Upon returning to the United States, Harlan joined a prominent Wall Street firm. For the first year of his practice he studied part-time at New York Law School in order to acquire an American law degree. Harlan practiced law on Wall Street for almost thirty years. During that time he became his firm's leading litigation partner, arguing several cases before the Supreme Court. He was also active in the New York bar. Throughout his career in private practice, Harlan devoted much of his time to public service, particularly to the investigation and prosecution of corrupt government officials.

In 1954 President Eisenhower appointed Harlan a judge of the United States Court of Appeals for the Second Circuit. Less than a year later, a vacancy occurred on the Supreme Court, and Eisenhower selected Harlan to fill the seat.

During his sixteen years on the Court, Harlan won the deep respect of his colleagues and of students of the Court for his remarkable intellectual integrity. He was a conservative and a frequent dissenter from the activist decisions of the Warren era. He was especially troubled by what he saw as the liberal majority's insensitivity to constitutional history and to the values of federalism. But unlike other conservatives who served on the Court before and after his time, Harlan never let his judicial philosophy prevent him from giving serious attention to specific arguments in favor of civil liberties claims. Harlan set a standard of open-mindedness, attention to detail, and balanced judgment that few justices in the history of the Supreme Court can match. For the last several years of his tenure, he was plagued by failing eyesight. Harlan served only two years under Chief Justice Burger before ill health forced his retirement.

Thurgood Marshall (1967–   )
Born July 2, 1908, in Baltimore, Maryland. His great-grandfather was a slave who was freed by his master. Marshall's father was the chief steward of an exclusive club on Chesapeake Bay. His mother was a schoolteacher in an all-black segregated primary school in Baltimore. Together his parents earned a decent living. Unlike some of his brethren, Marshall did not grow up in poverty.

He attended Lincoln University in Chester, Pennsylvania, considered in Marshall's day one of the best black colleges in the nation. He helped finance his education by working as a grocery clerk and waiter. Marshall was a successful undergraduate debater. He graduated cum laude in 1930.

Excluded because of his race from the University of Maryland Law School, Marshall enrolled to study law at Howard University in Washington, D.C., in 1931. He graduated first in his class from Howard, joined the Maryland bar, and established a private law practice. While in private practice from 1933 to 1936, Marshall served as counsel to the Baltimore branch of the National Association for the Advancement of Colored People.

He left Baltimore in 1936 to take a job with the NAACP's national office in New York and became special counsel to the NAACP in 1938. A year later, the NAACP Legal Defense Fund was formed, with Marshall as its head, to employ systematic litigation as a strategy for the achievement of civil rights for black people. Over the next twenty-five years, Marshall engineered the legal campaigns of the civil rights movement. He crisscrossed the South yearly, appearing in numerous courtrooms to lend support to beleaguered civil rights lawyers. He also argued many cases before the Supreme Court, including *Brown v. Board of Education*, in which the Supreme Court ruled school segregation unconstitutional.

In 1961 Marshall was appointed by President Kennedy to be a judge on the United States Court of Appeals for the Second Circuit in New York. He served on the federal bench until 1965, when he was appointed solicitor general of the United States. The solicitor general is the federal government's chief advocate before the Supreme Court, and in that capacity Marshall argued numerous times before his brethren-to-be. In 1967 President Lyndon Johnson nominated Marshall to be an associate justice of the Supreme Court.

To no one's surprise, Marshall's performance on the Court has been guided by the same dedication to racial justice and the rights of poor people that he displayed as an advocate. On almost all other issues of civil liberties, he consistently adopts broad readings of the Bill of Rights and the Fourteenth Amendment. In disputes between labor unions and their members, he has written some important majority opinions, finding the interest in organizational effectiveness to outweigh the claims of individual dissidence. He can be a stickler for strict, traditional procedures.

A raconteur of the first rank, Marshall draws heavily on his experiences as a litigator and his knowledge of the practical workings of the legal system, particularly in his questioning from the bench. His opinions tend to be scholarly and intellectually ambitious.

Sandra Day O'Connor (1981–   )
Born March 26, 1930, in El Paso, Texas. Her parents operated a cattle ranch in Arizona, not far from the New Mexico border. O'Connor attended a private secondary school in El Paso, then Stanford University, from which she received her B.A. degree magna cum laude in 1950. She then enrolled in Stanford Law School, where she was a member of the *Stanford Law Review*. She received her law degree in 1952.

O'Connor began her legal career as a deputy county attorney in San Mateo County, California, a position she held for two years. Next she worked for three years as a civilian attorney for the Quartermaster Market Center in Frankfurt, Germany, before returning to Arizona to engage in private practice in the town of Maryvale.

In 1969 she was appointed to fill a vacancy in the Arizona senate and was elected to two subsequent terms. She became the majority leader of the state senate in 1972. In 1975 she was elected a judge of the Maricopa County Superior Court in Phoenix and served on that bench for four years. O'Connor was appointed in 1979 to the Arizona Court of Appeals and two years later was nominated by President Reagan to be the first woman ever to sit on the United States Supreme Court.

O'Connor has not been on the Court long enough to permit a meaningful assessment of her judicial philosophy. At the time of her appointment, she was expected in light of her political and trial court experience to adopt a moderate, pragmatic approach to judging. In her first term, she surprised some observers by displaying a tendency in deciding cases to draw heavily upon elements of conservative ideology.

Lewis Powell (1972–   )
Born in 1907 in a suburb of Norfolk, Virginia. His father owned a box- and furniture-making business. Powell grew up in Richmond, Virginia, where he attended a private high school. He studied as an undergraduate at Washington and Lee College in Lexington, Virginia, from which he graduated in 1929. He was elected to Phi Beta Kappa and was president of the student body.

Powell then went to law school at Washington and Lee, graduating first in his class in 1931. After a year of graduate law study at Harvard, he returned to Richmond and began an eminently successful career as a corporate lawyer. During World War II he served as an air force intelligence officer in North Africa. After the war he returned to his Richmond firm, where he remained until his nomination by President Nixon to the Supreme Court in 1971.

While carrying on an active private practice and emerging as a leader in his rapidly growing firm, Powell managed to find time for an extraordinary range of outside activities. He served on the board of directors of eleven major companies. He was president of the American Bar Association, the American College of Trial Lawyers, and the American Bar Foundation. He was vice-president of the National Legal Aid and Defender Society and in that capacity was instrumental in persuading the organized bar to support the idea of publicly financed legal services for the poor. Powell was one of the most active members of President Johnson's Commission on Law Enforcement and the Administration of Justice. He also was a pillar of Richmond civic life, as chairman of the school board and a voice of moderation during the heated controversy over desegregation, as president of the Family Services Society, and in the reform of the city charter. In addition, he had a hand in drafting the revised Virginia constitution.

Justice Powell is a man of conservative instincts who does not let those instincts dominate his judging. He tends to think about cases in a particularistic fashion, carefully considering the arguments on both sides of an issue. Powell cares deeply about federalism and often favors doctrines that show respect for state government, especially state courts. In criminal procedure, his judgments tend to favor the prosecution. In labor law, his judgments tend to favor management. In most other areas, Powell seeks to fashion moderate doctrines that resist ideological classification. An unusually hardworking and conscientious person, Powell's considerateness and sense of civic responsibility have won him legions of personal admirers throughout his long and distinguished legal career.

William Rehnquist (1972–   )
Born October 1, 1924, in Milwaukee, Wisconsin. His father worked as a jobber selling paper. His mother was a commercial translator. Rehnquist grew up in Shoreham, Wisconsin, a suburb of Milwaukee, where he attended public elementary and secondary schools. He served in the air force weather service during World War II. Rehnquist received both his undergraduate degree and a master's in political science from Stanford University. He earned an additional master's degree in government from Harvard.

In 1949 he enrolled at Stanford Law School. He was a brilliant student, graduating first in his class and serving on the law review. One of his classmates was Sandra Day O'Connor. Upon receiving his law degree, Rehnquist clerked for a year for Associate Justice Robert Jackson of the United States Supreme Court. Then he entered private practice in Phoenix, Arizona, where he worked for several firms and eventually formed his own partnership. During that time he was active in public affairs. He was a member of the National Conference of Commissioners on Uniform State Laws. He worked in the presidential campaign of Barry Goldwater. He was a prominent and forceful public critic of many of the liberal political developments of the 1960s.

In 1968 Rehnquist moved to Washington to serve as assistant attorney general in charge of the Office of Legal Counsel. In that capacity he helped formulate and defend before Congress the legal positions of the Nixon administration on such issues as wiretapping, surveillance of allegedly subversive groups, executive privilege, and the war powers of the president. He also screened candidates for judicial appointments. In 1971 Nixon nominated Rehnquist to be an associate justice of the Supreme Court. Rehnquist's deep commitment to a conservative political ideology was well known at the time, and there was much discussion during his Senate confirmation hearings of whether a nominee of high professional ability could properly be denied a seat on the Court solely because of his political beliefs.

From the moment he joined the Court, Rehnquist has argued forcefully for an extremely conservative approach to constitutional interpretation. No other justice in modern times has favored so narrow a construction of the Bill of Rights and the Fourteenth Amendment. In case after case, Rehnquist has excoriated his brethren for injecting their own values into their readings of the Constitution. Rehnquist believes that the original understanding of the framers of particular constitutional clauses both can be discerned and can serve as the dominant guide for applying the provisions of the Constitution to modern, unforeseen problems. In most areas, this philosophy leads Rehnquist to be extremely reluctant to hold statutes unconstitutional. However, when federal laws displace the reserved powers of the states, which Rehnquist views as central to the constitutional scheme, he favors invalidating congressional enactments that other justices deferentially uphold.

Rehnquist is universally admired for his intelligence, sharp questioning from the bench, and friendliness. He is sometimes criticized as too political. His detractors claim that his ideological fervor makes him closed-minded as a judge and that he is too active within the Court in trying to influence the outcomes of cases.

John Paul Stevens (1975–   )
Born April 20, 1920, in Chicago. His
father owned and managed the Stevens
Hotel (now the Conrad Hilton), the largest
hotel in Chicago. His mother was a high
school English teacher. Stevens attended
the private elementary and secondary
schools operated by the University of
Chicago. He also received his undergraduate degree from the University of Chicago, graduating Phi Beta Kappa in 1941.
Stevens was a naval officer during World
War II. He attended Northwestern University Law School, graduating in 1947 first
in his class with one of the highest grade
averages in the history of the school.

During the 1947–48 term of court, Stevens served as a law clerk to
Supreme Court Justice Wiley Rutledge. With a year's interlude in Washington as associate counsel to the House Antitrust Subcommittee, Stevens
spent the next twenty-two years with a prominent Chicago law firm. His
specialty was antitrust, a field in which he earned a national reputation.
He wrote several law review articles on the subject and taught courses in
antitrust law at Northwestern and the University of Chicago.

In 1970 President Nixon appointed Stevens a judge of the United States
Court of Appeals for the Seventh Circuit. In his five years on the appeals
bench, Stevens attracted the attention and admiration of specialists in a
variety of fields with his lucid, insightful opinions. When he was nominated
in 1975 by President Ford for a seat on the Supreme Court, leaders of the
bar and the law schools hailed the choice as one of the finest in modern
times.

As Stevens began his service as a justice, knowledgeable observers expected him to become a leader on the Court by virtue of his powerful intellect and moderate instincts. That has not happened. Instead, Stevens has
tended to develop highly original, sometimes idiosyncratic theories that fail
to win the endorsement of his brethren. He is a formidable but unconven-
tional legal thinker. With Stevens operating as he has at the center of the
Court's divisions, the effect of his independence of mind often has been to
fragment potential majorities and leave the state of the law indeterminate.
His preferences are particularistic and difficult to categorize. He is the only
justice appointed in the last fifteen years who does not consistently rule
against an expansive view of the rights of persons accused of crime.

Potter Stewart (1958–1981)

Born January 23, 1915, in Cincinnati, Ohio. Retired from the Court July 3, 1981. Stewart was born into a prosperous family with a tradition of public service. His father was a mayor of Cincinnati and a justice of the Ohio Supreme Court. Stewart attended a private school in Cincinnati, an elite Eastern prep school, and Yale College. As an undergraduate, he served as the editor of the *Yale Daily News* and was class orator. Upon graduation in 1937, he studied for a year at Cambridge University, England, then enrolled at the Yale Law School. He was an outstanding law student, graduating high in his class and serving as comment editor of the *Yale Law Journal*.

After receiving his law degree in 1941 Stewart practiced for less than a year with a Wall Street firm, then joined the Navy as a deck officer on oil tankers serving in the Atlantic and Mediterranean. At the conclusion of the war, he returned briefly to New York but soon left to join one of Cincinnati's leading law firms. His practice consisted mainly of work for corporate clients, but he also served as court-appointed counsel for a number of indigent criminal defendants. During this period, Stewart was active in civic affairs, winning election to the city council and serving as vice-mayor of Cincinnati.

In 1954 Stewart was appointed by President Eisenhower to the United States Court of Appeals for the Sixth Circuit. In his four years on the Circuit Court, Stewart achieved high acclaim within the legal profession for his careful, technically competent, highly literate opinions. His appointment to the Supreme Court in 1958, at the unusually young age of 43, was widely praised as a choice made on the basis of professional merit.

During his twenty-three years on the Supreme Court, Stewart played a variety of roles. At first, he often found himself the swing vote on a Court deeply and closely divided by intense differences over the proper role of the Supreme Court in the governmental scheme. He resisted efforts to translate his judicial judgments into ideological terms, insisting that his duty was to decide cases according to the law. During the heyday of the Warren Court, Stewart was a frequent dissenter, especially in cases that rendered expansive interpretations of the rights of persons accused of crime, the clause of the First Amendment that prohibits the establishment of religion, the right of privacy, and the right to vote.

With regard to constitutional claims that are well grounded in the text of the Constitution or the history surrounding its adoption, however, Stewart was always one of the most receptive justices. He wrote several eloquent opinions extolling the importance of free expression. He interpreted the Fourteenth Amendment and the federal civil rights statutes broadly in cases challenging racial discrimination.

During the years of Warren Burger's tenure as chief justice, Stewart returned to his original position at the ideological center of the Court's divisions. This time, however, he was joined by several other justices who constituted a group of intelligent, moderate judges whose views on particular cases were not easily predictable.

Throughout his service on the Court, Stewart was a well-respected and well-liked colleague and probably the best writer among the justices.

Byron White (1962–   )
Born June 8, 1918, in Fort Collins, Colorado. Grew up in Wellington, Colorado, a community of approximately 350 persons. His father was the branch manager of a lumber supply company. As a child, White spent long hours working in sugar beet fields and on railroad section crews.

He won an academic scholarship to the University of Colorado, where he was elected to Phi Beta Kappa in his junior year, graduated first in his class, and achieved one of the highest grade averages in the history of the university. He also won ten varsity letters in three sports. White was a particularly outstanding football player, winning All-American honors as a tailback and leading a team that was undefeated and untied in regular season play.

Upon graduation in 1938, White accepted a Rhodes Scholarship to Oxford University in England but delayed his study there to play a season of professional football with the Pittsburgh Steelers. That season he led the National Football League in rushing. After a brief period at Oxford, White enrolled at the Yale Law School, where he ranked first in his class after his freshman year. His law study was interrupted, however, first for another season of professional football, this time with the Detroit Lions, and then for four years as a naval intelligence officer in the South Pacific.

After the war, White returned to Yale Law School and graduated magna cum laude in 1946. He then served for a year as law clerk to Chief Justice Fred Vinson. (When he was appointed to the Supreme Court, White became the first former law clerk to join the Court later as a justice.) Upon completion of his clerkship he returned to Colorado and joined a small but growing Denver firm. There he remained for fourteen years until he became a highly successful local organizer in the presidential campaign of John F. Kennedy.

With Kennedy's election as president, White was appointed deputy attorney general, the number two position in the Justice Department headed by Robert Kennedy. In that job, White's duties included the development of an innovative program for attracting exceptionally qualified lawyers to work for the Justice Department, supervision of federal marshals assigned to protect civil rights workers in the South, and the screening of candidates for judicial appointments. In 1962, White was nominated by President Kennedy to fill the position on the Supreme Court created by the resignation of Charles Whittaker.

White's years on the Court have been characterized by a rather consistent adherence to a few basic themes. He interprets narrowly the rights of persons accused of crime. He reads the First Amendment guarantees of freedom of speech and press less expansively than do most of his brethren. He worries about the proper role of the Supreme Court and prefers that social problems be solved by other branches of the federal government and by the states. However, in areas where political solutions are often unavailing and where the claims at issue relate to the material interests of disfavored groups and not symbolic notions of individual liberty, White can be one of the most activist justices on the Court. He has consistently favored constitutional claimants in cases involving racial discrimination, voting rights, and equal educational opportunity.

White's opinions tend to be austere in style, though argumentative in content. He prefers to keep the focus of dispute narrow. He is an active and often penetrating questioner from the bench during oral argument. He is an especially hard worker. Despite his keen intelligence, White has not left a strong mark on the development of legal doctrine. His judging is pragmatic, result-oriented, and skeptical of appeals to idealism.

• Chronology •

June 1969	Warren Burger appointed to be the fourteenth chief justice of the United States.
April 1970	*Dandridge* v. *Williams*. States permitted to disadvantage large families in computing per person allotments of welfare benefits.
May 1970	*Walz* v. *Tax Commission*. Property tax exemption for churches held not to violate the First Amendment.
	Harry A. Blackmun appointed to fill the seat previously held by Justice Abe Fortas.
December 1970	*Oregon* v. *Mitchell*. Congress held to have authority to require states to permit eighteen-year-olds to vote in elections for federal office but not in elections for state office.
February 1971	*Harris* v. *New York*. Prosecution permitted to use statement obtained from a suspect without *Miranda* warnings in order to impeach subsequent testimony of the suspect, even if the evidence would not be admissible as part of prosecution's case in chief.
April 1971	*Swann* v. *Charlotte-Mecklenburg Board of Education*. Federal district judges authorized to require substantial intradistrict busing as a remedy for past de jure school segregation.
June 1971	*Lemon* v. *Kurtzman*. Salary supplements paid out of public funds for teachers of secular subjects in religious schools held to violate the First Amendment.
	New York Times v. *United States*. Nixon administration's claim to enjoin publication of *The Pentagon Papers* denied.
September 1971	Hugo Black resigns from the Court.
	John Marshall Harlan resigns from the Court.
November 1971	*Reed* v. *Reed*. A gender-based classification held for the first time to be in violation of the Fourteenth Amendment.

December 1971	Lewis Powell appointed to fill the seat previously held by Justice Hugo Black.
	William Rehnquist appointed to fill the seat previously held by Justice John Marshall Harlan.
June 1972	*Moose Lodge* v. *Irvis*. The possession of a liquor license granted by the state held not by itself sufficient to make a private club subject to the Fourteenth Amendment prohibition on racial discrimination.
	Branzburg v. *Hayes*. First Amendment held not to immunize news reporters from being required in grand jury proceedings to identify confidential news sources.
	Furman v. *Georgia*. Capital punishment as administered in virtually all states held to violate the Eighth Amendment owing to the lack of regularity and consistency in selecting which offenders will receive the ultimate sanction.
January 1973	*Roe* v. *Wade*. The prohibition of abortion during the first and second trimesters of pregnancy held to violate the Fourteenth Amendment.
March 1973	*San Antonio School District* v. *Rodriguez*. School financing based on local property tax held not to violate the equal protection clause of the Fourteenth Amendment.
May 1973	*Schneckcloth* v. *Bustamonte*. Consent to a search given by a suspect who was unaware of his right to disallow the search held sufficient under some circumstances to justify use by the prosecution of evidence discovered during the search.
June 1973	*Paris Adult Theater* v. *Slaton*. Prohibition on the nonconspicuous exhibition of obscene films to willing adults held not to violate the First Amendment.
June 1974	*Miami Herald Publishing Co.* v. *Tornillo*. Legislation requiring newspapers to print replies to critical editorials and columns held to violate the First Amendment.
July 1974	*United States* v. *Nixon*. President of the United States required to submit to federal district judge tape recordings of conversations with aides for possible use in a criminal prosecution.
	Milliken v. *Bradley*. District judges held not to have authority to require the busing of school children

between different school districts as a remedy for segregative acts by one district.

November 1975   William O. Douglas resigns from the Court after serving longer than any other justice in its history.

December 1975   John Paul Stevens appointed to fill the seat on the Court previously held by Justice Douglas.

January 1976   *Buckley* v. *Valeo*. Most sections of the Campaign Finance Act of 1974 upheld, but Congress's prohibition on large independent expenditures in support of candidates for public office held to violate the First Amendment.

May 1976   *Virginia State Board of Pharmacy* v. *Virginia Citizens Consumer Council*. Commercial advertising of accurate price information by druggists held protected by the First Amendment.

June 1976   *Washington* v. *Davis*. Municipal hiring policies that display no intention to discriminate on the basis of race but that produce severely disparate results in racial terms held not to violate the Fourteenth Amendment.

                 National League of Cities v. *Usery*. Congress held not to have authority under the commerce clause to require that state and local employees be paid a federally prescribed minimum wage.

July 1976   *Gregg* v. *Georgia*. Death penalty held not to violate the Eighth Amendment prohibition on cruel and unusual punishment so long as special procedures are adopted to ensure regularity and consistency in the administration of the sanction.

                 Stone v. *Powell*. The availability of habeas corpus as a remedy to overturn convictions based on evidence obtained by illegal searches severely restricted.

May 1977   *Teamsters* v. *United States*. Seniority plans that have the effect of disadvantaging victims of past racial discrimination held not to violate the federal civil rights laws.

June 1977   *Maher* v. *Roe*. A state's refusal to subsidize abortions for poor women held not to violate the Fourteenth Amendment.

June 1978   *Regents of the University of California* v. *Bakke*. A university's use of a racial quota as a means of increasing black and Hispanic enrollment held to vio-

<table>
<tbody>
<tr><td></td><td>late federal law; more flexible consideration of race held permissible.</td></tr>
</tbody>
</table>

	Monell v. *Dep't of Social Services*. Municipal governments held not to be immune from suit under federal civil rights statutes for official actions that violate federally protected rights.
April 1980	*New York* v. *Payton*. Fourth Amendment interpreted to require the police absent exigent circumstances to obtain an arrest warrant before arresting a suspect in his home.
July 1980	*Richmond Newspapers* v. *Virginia*. First Amendment held to preclude the exclusion of news reporters from observing a criminal trial.
	Fullilove v. *Klutznick*. Congress held to have authority to require that a minimum percentage of federal funds expended under a public works program be used to purchase the services of business enterprises owned by members of a minority race.
June 1981	*Rostker* v. *Goldberg*. Male-only draft registration program held not to violate the Constitution.
July 1981	*Dames & Moore* v. *Regan*. President held authorized under the Constitution to suspend and provide for arbitration of various claims by private creditors against Iran as part of the settlement of the hostage crisis.
	Potter Stewart resigns from the Court.
September 1981	Sandra Day O'Connor appointed to fill the seat previously held by Justice Stewart. She becomes the first woman to serve as a justice of the Supreme Court.

• Bibliography •

BOOKS

T. BECKER & M. FEELEY, eds. THE IMPACT OF SUPREME COURT DECISIONS (2d. ed. 1973).

A. BICKEL THE CASELOAD OF THE SUPREME COURT AND WHAT, IF ANYTHING, TO DO ABOUT IT.

———, THE LEAST DANGEROUS BRANCH (1962).

C. BLACK, CAPITAL PUNISHMENT: THE INEVITABILITY OF CAPRICE AND MISTAKE (2d. ed. 1981).

———, DECISION ACCORDING TO LAW (1981).

———, THE PEOPLE AND THE COURT (1960).

H. BLACK, JR., MY FATHER: A REMEMBRANCE (1975).

G. CASPER & R. POSNER, THE WORKLOAD OF THE SUPREME COURT (1976).

J. CHOPER, JUDICIAL REVIEW AND THE NATIONAL POLITICAL PROCESS (1980).

A. COX, THE ROLE OF THE SUPREME COURT IN AMERICAN GOVERNMENT (1976).

W. DOUGLAS, GO EAST, YOUNG MAN: THE EARLY YEARS (1974).

———, THE COURT YEARS, 1939–1975 (1980).

J. ELY, DEMOCRACY AND DISTRUST (1980).

L. FRIEDMAN, ed., THE JUSTICES OF THE UNITED STATES SUPREME COURT: THEIR LIVES AND MAJOR OPINIONS, vol. 5 (1978).

L. FRIEDMAN & F. ISRAEL, eds., THE JUSTICES OF THE UNITED STATES SUPREME COURT: THEIR LIVES AND MAJOR OPINIONS, vol. 4 (1969).

R. FUNSTON, CONSTITUTIONAL COUNTERREVOLUTION? THE WARREN COURT AND THE BURGER COURT: JUDICIAL POLICY-MAKING IN MODERN AMERICA (1977).

S. HALPERN & C. LAMB, eds. SUPREME COURT ACTIVISM AND RESTRAINT (1982).

G. JACOBSOHN, PRAGMATISM, STATESMANSHIP, AND THE SUPREME COURT (1977).

R. KLUGER, SIMPLE JUSTICE (1976).

L. LEVY, AGAINST THE LAW: THE NIXON COURT AND CRIMINAL JUSTICE (1974).

L. LUSKY, BY WHAT RIGHT? (1975).

A. MASON, THE SUPREME COURT FROM TAFT TO BURGER (1979).

R. McCLOSKEY, THE MODERN SUPREME COURT (1972).

M. MELTSNER, CRUEL AND UNUSUAL: THE SUPREME COURT AND CAPITAL PUNISHMENT (1973).

W. MURPHY, ELEMENTS OF JUDICIAL STRATEGY (1964).

M. PERRY, THE CONSTITUTION, THE COURTS, AND HUMAN RIGHTS: AN INQUIRY INTO THE LEGITIMACY OF CONSTITUTIONAL POLICY-MAKING BY THE JUDICIARY (1982).

R. Saylor, B. Boyer & R. Gooding, eds., The Warren Court: A Critical Analysis (1969).

G. Schubert, The Judicial Mind Revisited: Psychometric Analysis of Supreme Court Ideology (1974).

J. Wilkinson, From Brown to Bakke: the Supreme Court and School Integration, 1954–1978 (1979).

B. Woodward & S. Armstrong, The Brethren: Inside the Supreme Court (1979).

ARTICLES

BeVier, *Justice Powell and the First Amendment's "Societal Function": A Preliminary Analysis*, 68 Va. L. Rev. 177 (1982).

Black, *The Unfinished Business of the Warren Court*, 46 Wash. L. Rev. 3 (1970).

Brennan, *State Constitutions and the Protection of Individual Rights*, 90 Harv. L. Rev. 489 (1977).

Brenner, *Ideological Voting on the Supreme Court: A Comparison of the Original Vote on the Merits with the Final Vote*, 22 Jurimetrics Journal 287 (1982).

Casper & Funston, *The Supreme Court and National Policy Making*, 70 Am. Pol. Sci. Rev. 50 (1976).

Chase, *The Burger Court, the Individual and the Criminal Process: Directions and Misdirections*, 52 N.Y.U. L. Rev. 518 (1977).

Cox, *Foreword: Freedom of Expression in the Burger Court*, 94 Harv. L. Rev. (1980)

Curry, *James Madison and the Burger Court: Converging Views of Church-State Separation*, 56 Ind. L. J. 615 (1981).

Dahl, *Decisionmaking in a Democracy: The Supreme Court as a National Policy Maker*, 6 J. of Public Law 279 (1957).

Emerson, *First Amendment Doctrine and the Burger Court*, 68 Calif L. Rev. 422 (1980).

Funston, *The Supreme Court and Critical Elections*, 69 Am. Pol. Sci. Rev. 795 (1975).

Galloway, *The First Decade of the Burger Court: Conservative Dominance (1969–1979)*, 21 Santa Clara L. Rev. 891 (1981).

Gunther, *In Search of Judicial Quality on a Changing Court: The Case of Justice Powell*, 24 Stan. L. Rev. 1001 (1972).

Haines, *Rolling Back the Top of Chief Justice Burger's Opinion Assignment Desk*, 38 U. Pitt. L. Rev. 631 (1977).

Harris, *Judicial Review: Vagaries and Varieties*, 38 J. of Politics 173 (1976).

Heck & Shull, *Political Preferences of Justice and Presidents: The Case of Civil Rights*, 4 Law & Policy Q. 327 (1982).

Hellman, *The Business of the Supreme Court under the Judiciary Act of 1925: The Plenary Docket in the 1970s*, 91 Harv. L. Rev. 1709 (1978).

Howard, *Mr. Justice Powell and the Emerging Nixon Majority*, 70 Mich. L. Rev. 445 (1972).

Israel, *Criminal Procedure, the Burger Court and the Legacy of the Warren Court*, 75 Mich. L. Rev. 1319 (1979).

Lamb, *Judicial Policy Making and Information Flow to the Supreme Court*, 29 VAND. L. REV. 45 (1976).

————, *The Making of a Chief Justice: Warren Burger on Criminal Procedure, 1956–1969*, 60 CORNELL L. REV. 743 (1975).

————, *Justice Stevens: The First Three Terms*, 32 VAND. L. REV. 671 (1979).

Mason, *Whence and Whither the Burger Court? Judicial Self-Restraint: A Beguiling Myth*, 41 REV. OF POLITICS 3 (1979).

Monaghan, *Taking Supreme Court Opinions Seriously*, 39 MD. L. REV. 1 (1979).

Nowark, *Evaluating the Work of the New Libertarian Supreme Court*, 7 HASTINGS CONST. LAW. Q. 263 (1980).

Peebles, *Mr. Justice Frankfurter and the Nixon Court: Some Reflections on Contemporary Judicial Conservatism*, 24 AMER. U. L. REV. 1 (1974).

Powell, *The Compleat Jeffersonian: Justice Rehnquist and Federalism*, 91 YALE L.J. 1317 (1982).

Rehnquist, *All Discord, Harmony Not Understood: The Performance of the Supreme Court of the United States*, 22 ARIZ. L. REV. 973 (1980).

————, *The Notion of a Living Constitution*, 54 TEX. L. REV. 693 (1976).

Saltzburg, *Foreword: The Flow and Ebb of Constitutional Criminal Procedure in the Warren and Burger Courts*, 69 GEO. L. J. 151 (1980).

Seidman, *Factual Guilt and the Burger Court: An Examination of Continuity and Change in Criminal Procedure*, 80 COLUM. L. REV. 456 (1980).

Shapiro, *Mr. Justice Rehnquist: A Preliminary View*, 90 HARV. L. REV. 293 (1976).

Slotnick, *Who Speaks for the Court? Majority Opinion Assignment from Taft to Burger*, 23 AMER. J. OF POL. SCI. 60 (1979).

Stewart, *"Or of the Press,"* 26 HASTINGS L.J. 631 (1975).

Stone, *The Miranda Doctrine in the Burger Court*, 1977 SUP. CT. REV. 99.

Swindler, *The Court, the Constitutional and Chief Justice Burger*, 27 VAND. L. REV. 443 (1974).

Whitman, *Individual and Community: An Appreciation of Mr. Justice Powell*, 68 VA. L. REV. 303 (1982).

Wilkinson, *Justice John M. Harlan and the Values of Federalism*, 57 VA. L. REV. 1185 (1971).

Comment, *The Emerging Constitutional Jurisprudence of Justice Stevens*, 46 U. CHI. L. REV. 155 (1978).

SYMPOSIA

The Burger Court: Nine Judges in Search of a Theme, NAT'L L.J., Feb. 18, 1980, pp. 17–28. (Profiles of the individual justices by Neuborne, Alschuler, Miller, Soifer, Aldave, Karst, Stone, Price, Tushnet.)

The Burger Court: Reflections on the First Decade, 43 LAW AND CONTEMP. PROB. 1 (1980) (Howard, Sandalow, Monaghan, Mishkin, Van Alstyne, Grey, Frank).

Constitutional Adjudication and Democratic Theory, 56 N.Y. L. REV. 259 (Gibbons, Perry, Monaghan, Ely, Michelman, Sager, Sandalow, Dworkin, Nagel, Estreicher).

Nebraska Press Association v. *Stuart*, 29 STAN. L. REV. 383 (1977) (Barnett, Erickson, Franklin, Freedman and Starwood, Garry and Riordan, Goodale, Isaacson,

Kaplan, Portman, Sack, Schmidt, Schmidt and Volner, Shellow, Simon, Younger).

Regents of the University of California v. *Bakke*, 67 CALIF. L. REV. 1 (1978) (Bell, Blasi, Dixon, Greenawalt, Henkin, O'Neil, Posner).

United States v. *Nixon*, 22 U.C.L.A. L. REV. 1 (1974) (Berger, Gunther, Henkin, Karst and Horowitz, Kurland, Mishkin, Ratner, Van Alstyne).

PERIODIC SURVEYS

HARVARD LAW REVIEW. The November issue each year is devoted to a survey of the preceding term of the Supreme Court. Approximately twenty-five of the leading cases of the term are assessed in student notes. A leading scholar contributes a foreword discussing a major theme in the Court's work or in the development of constitutional theory. Statistics on the term are compiled.

THE SUPREME COURT REVIEW. An annual volume, edited by Philip Kurland, Gerhard Casper, and Dennis Hutchinson, which contains articles by leading scholars on the work of the Supreme Court. Most of the articles follow a common format: a recent case is used as the occasion to identify and analyze a development of general significance in the Court's work.

THE SUPREME COURT: TRENDS AND DEVELOPMENTS. Three leading constitutional scholars, Jesse Choper, Yale Kamisar, and Laurence Tribe, participate annually in a symposium to assess the preceding term of the Supreme Court. The transcript of the proceedings is published.

• Notes •

CHAPTER 1

1. Near v. Minnesota, 283 U.S. 697 (1931); Grosjean v. American Press Co., 297 U.S. 233 (1936); Bridges v. California, 341 U.S. 252 (1941); Pennekamp v. Florida, 328 U.S. 331 (1946); Craig v. Harney, 331 U.S. 376 (1947); New York Times Co. v. Sullivan, 376 U.S. 254 (1964); National Broadcasting Co. v. U.S., 319 U.S. 190 (1943).

2. N.Y. Times, Apr. 25, 1979, at B5. *See also* JOHN HOHENBERG, A CRISIS FOR THE AMERICAN PRESS (1978).

3. Justice Stewart's Yale speech is reprinted in . . . *Or of the Press*, 26 HASTINGS L.J. 639 (1975). In support of the Stewart position, *see, e.g.,* Nimmer, *Is Freedom of the Press a Redundancy?* 26 HASTINGS L.J. 639 (1975); in opposition *see, e.g.,* Lange, *The Speech and Press Clauses*, 23 U.C.L.A. L. REV. 77 (1975). For a more recent discussion that cites the previous literature, *see Symposium on the Press Clause*, 7 HOFSTRA L. REV. 559 (1979). Supreme Court decisions in which the justices refused to make the distinction include Branzburg v. Hayes, 408 U.S. 665 (1972); Zurcher v. Stanford Daily, 436 U.S. 547 (1978); Houchins v. KQED, Inc., 438 U.S. 1 (1978); Gannett Co., Inc. v. DePasquale, 443 U.S. 368 (1979). Chief Justice Burger's discussion appears in First National Bank of Boston v. Bellotti, 435 U.S. 765, 797–802 (1978).

4. *See, e.g.,* Lange, *supra* note 3 at 107–13; Van Alstyne, *The Hazards to the Press of Claiming a "Preferred Position,"* 28 HASTINGS L.J. 761 (1977).

5. New York Times Co. v. Sullivan, 376 U.S. 254 (1964).

6. 376 U.S. at 270, 279, 280.

7. Extension of the "actual malice" rule to all matters of public or general interest took place in Rosenbloom v. Metromedia, 403 U.S. 29 (1971), which cites the earlier cases. Gertz v. Robert Welch, Inc., 418 U.S. 323 (1974); Time, Inc. v. Firestone, 424 U.S. 448 (1976); Hutchinson v. Proxmire, 443 U.S. 111 (1979); Wolston v. Reader's Digest Association, Inc., 443 U.S. 157 (1979).

8. Herbert v. Lando, 441 U.S. 153, 172, 176 (1979). For discussion of the problems raised by the *Herbert* case, *see* Oakes, *Proof of Actual Malice in Defamation Actions: An Unsolved Dilemma*, 7 HOFSTRA L. REV. 655 (1979).

9. Time, Inc. v. Hill, 385 U.S. 374 (1967); Cantrell v. Forest City Publishing Co., 419 U.S. 245 (1974); Cox Broadcasting Co. v. Cohn, 420 U.S. 469 (1975); Department of Air Force v. Rose, 425 U.S. 352 (1976). *See also* Smith v. Daily Mail Publishing Co., 443 U.S. 97 (1979); and Globe Newspaper Co. v. Superior Court, 102 S.Ct. 2613 (1982), discussed at note 49 *infra*.

10. *See e.g.,* Irvin v. Doud, 366 U.S. 717 (1961); Sheppard v. Maxwell, 384 U.S. 333 (1966); Estes v. Texas, 381 U.S. 532 (1965).

11. Nebraska Press Association v. Stuart, 427 U.S. 539 (1976).

12. 427 U.S. at 559, 562, 569.

13. Gannett Co., Inc. v. DePasquale, *supra* note 3.

14. 443 U.S. at 391, 440.

15. 443 U.S. at 392, 393, 447.

16. The debate among the justices is reported in *N.Y. Times*, Aug. 9, 11, and 14 and Sept. 4 and 9, 1979.

17. Richmond Newspapers, Inc. v. Virginia, 448 U.S. 555 (1980). Justice Rehnquist was the lone dissenter. Justice Powell did not participate.

18. 448 U.S. at 564, 569, 575, 579. The right-to-know cases are noted briefly *infra* at note 42.

19. 448 U.S. at 587 (italics in original), 585, 588, 589.

20. 448 U.S. at 580–81, 598.

21. Estes v. Texas, *supra* note 10; Chandler v. Florida, 449 U.S. 560 (1981). The fairness of a trial may also be affected by rulings on reporter's privilege, a matter discussed later in this chapter.

22. New York Times Co. v. United States, 403 U.S. 713, 714 (1971).

23. 403 U.S. at 718, 730, 757.

24. United States v. The Progressive, Inc., 467 F. Supp. 990 (W.D. Wis.), *request for writ of mandamus denied sub nom.* Morland v. Sprecher, 443 U.S. 709 (1979), *case dismissed*, Nos. 79-1428, 79-1664 (7th Cir. Oct. 1, 1979).

25. United States v. Marchetti, 466 F.2d 1309 (4th Cir. 1972), *cert. denied*, 409 U.S. 1063 (1972); Knopf v. Colby, 509 F.2d 1362 (4th Cir. 1975), *cert. denied*, 421 U.S. 992 (1975).

26. Snepp v. United States, 444 U.S. 507, 509 (1980).

27. *See also* Laird v. Tatum, 408 U.S. 1 (1972); United States v. Richardson, 418 U.S. 166 (1974).

28. Landmark Communications, Inc. v. Virginia, 435 U.S. 829, 841 (1978) (Justices Brennan and Powell not participating).

29. Smith v. Daily Mail Publishing Co., *supra* note 9, 443 U.S. at 103, 104 (Justice Powell not participating). *See also* Oklahoma Publishing Co. v. District Court, 430 U.S. 308 (1977).

30. Branzburg v. Hayes, 408 U.S. 665 (1972). On the significance of the pledge of confidentiality in newsgathering, *see* Blasi, *The Newsman's Privilege: An Empirical Study*, 70 MICH. L. REV. 229 (1971).

31. 408 U.S. at 680.

32. 408 U.S. at 681, 682, 690.

33. 408 U.S. at 710.

34. 408 U.S. at 725.

35. 408 U.S. at 738, 743.

36. New York Times Co. v. Jascalevich, 439 U.S. 1317, 1331 (1978). Cases where reporters are ordered to produce information are reported periodically in NEWS MEDIA AND THE LAW, published by the Reporters Committee for Freedom of the Press, Washington, D.C. *See also* JOHN HOHENBERG, A CRISIS FOR THE AMERICAN PRESS (1978), pp. 207–09. The *New York Times* cost figures appear in *New York Times*, Nov. 12, 1978, at E8. *See also* Herbert v. Lando, *supra* note 8.

37. Zurcher v. Stanford Daily, 436 U.S. 547 (1978).

38. 436 U.S. at 552 (italics in original).

39. 436 U.S. at 565, 566.

40. 436 U.S. at 571, 573–74.

41. Reporters Committee for Freedom of the Press v. American Telephone and Telegraph Co., 593 F.2d 1030 (D.C. Cir. 1978), *cert. denied*, 440 U.S. 949 (1979); Smith v. Maryland, 442 U.S. 735 (1979) (Justice Powell did not participate).

42. Lamont v. Postmaster General, 381 U.S. 301 (1965). Other cases upholding a right to know include Stanley v. Georgia, 394 U.S. 557 (1969); Red Lion Broadcasting Co., Inc. v. Federal Communications Commission, 395 U.S. 697 (1969); Virginia State Board of Pharmacy v. Virginia Citizens Consumer Council, 425 U.S. 748 (1976).

43. Pell v. Procunier, 417 U.S. 817 (1974); Saxbe v. Washington Post Co., 417 U.S. 843 (1974); Houchins v. KQED, Inc., 438 U.S. 1 (1978).

44. 438 U.S. at 15, 16.

45. 438 U.S. at 16, 17.

46. 438 U.S. at 32, 34, 35.

47. Gannett Co., Inc. v. DePasquale, *supra* note 3.

48. Richmond Newspapers, Inc. v. Virginia, *supra*, note 17, 448 U.S. at 582, 564.

49. Globe Newspaper Co. v. Superior Court, *supra* note 9, 102 S.Ct. at 2618, 2619, 2620. Chief Justice Burger and Justice Rehnquist, dissenting, would have upheld the statute; Justice O'Connor, concurring in the judgment, disavowed any intention to extend the *Richmond Newspapers* doctrine beyond access to criminal trials; Justice Stevens dissented on grounds of mootness.

50. 448 U.S. at 576, 581, 598.

51. For narrow interpretations of the Freedom of Information Act by the Burger Court, *see* Kissinger v. Reporters Committee for Freedom of the Press, 445 U.S. 136 (1980); Forsham v. Harris, 445 U.S. 169 (1980). *See also* Chandler v. Florida, *supra* note 21.

52. Federal Communications Commission v. National Citizens Committee for Broadcasting, 436 U.S. 775 (1978).

53. Red Lion Broadcasting Co., Inc. v. Federal Communications Commission, 395 U.S. 367 (1969); Columbia Broadcasting System v. Democratic National Committee, 412 U.S. 94 (1973). *See also* Columbia Broadcasting System v. Federal Communications Commission, 453 U.S. 367 (1981).

54. Miami Herald Publishing Co. v. Tornillo, 418 U.S. 241 (1974).

55. Federal Communications Commission v. Midwest Video Corporation, 440 U.S. 689 (1979).

CHAPTER 2

1. Cohen v. California, 403 U.S. 15, 25 (1971).

2. New York Times Co. v. United States, 403 U.S. 713, 717 (1971) (concurring opinion).

3. Brandenburg v. Ohio, 395 U.S. 444 (1969), overruling Whitney v. California, 274 U.S. 357 (1927).

4. Stanley v. Georgia, 394 U.S. 557 (1969).

5. Rosenbloom v. Metromedia, Inc., 403 U.S. 29, 44 (1971).

6. T. EMERSON, THE SYSTEM OF FREEDOM OF EXPRESSION 15–16 (1970).

7. Z. CHAFEE, FREE SPEECH IN THE UNITED STATES 18–21 (1941).

8. L. LEVY, LEGACY OF SUPPRESSION: FREEDOM OF SPEECH AND PRESS IN EARLY AMERICAN HISTORY 236–37 (1960).

9. L. TRIBE, AMERICAN CONSTITUTIONAL LAW § 12-2 (1978).

10. Shaman, *Revitalizing the Clear-and-Present Danger Test: Toward a Principled Interpretation of the First Amendment*, 22 VILL. L. REV. 60 (1976).

11. Bogen, *The Supreme Court's Interpretation of the Guarantee of Freedom of Speech*, 35 MD. L. REV. 555 (1976).

12. Karst, *Public Enterprise and the Public Forum: A Comment on* Southeastern Promotions, Ltd. v. Conrad, 37 OHIO ST. L.J. 247 (1976).

13. Meiklejohn, *Public Speech in the Burger Court: The Influence of Mr. Justice Black*, 8 TOLEDO L. REV. 301 (1977).

14. That our investigation is on the right track has been provocatively noted by Professor Van Alstyne of Duke Law School. *See* Van Alstyne, *The Recrudescence of Property Rights as the Foremost Principle of Civil Liberties: The First Decade of The Burger Court*, 43 LAW AND CONTEMP. PROBS. 66 (1980). Van Alstyne surveyed a wide range of Burger Court civil liberties decisions and observed a pattern of doctrinal development reminiscent of

. . . a different, tighter, more conservative view of liberty: liberty as security of private property; liberty as freedom of entrepreneurial skill; liberty from the impositions of government and of third parties from disposing of 'one's own.' Liberty, in brief, more in the mode of John Locke and of Adam Smith and somewhat less in the mode of John Mill (or of John Rawls). To that end, I shall speak briefly to what I think *does* represent the basic (albeit still very incomplete) change of direction that marks the "liberty" decisions of the preceding decade: the reemergence of the rights of property. *Id*. at 70 (footnotes omitted).

See also Nowak, *Foreword: Evaluating the Work of the New Libertarian Supreme Court*, 7 HASTINGS CONST. L.Q. 263 (1980).

15. 418 U.S. 405 (1974).

16. *Id*. at 408–09.

17. Wooley v. Maynard, 430 U.S. 705, 713 (1977).

18. 435 U.S. 765 (1978).

19. 431 U.S. 209 (1977).

20. 424 U.S. 1 (1976).

21. Consolidated Edison Co. of New York v. Public Service Comm'n of New York, 447 U.S. 530 (1980).

22. *Id*. at 539–40 (emphasis added).

23. Valentine v. Chrestensen, 316 U.S. 52, 54 (1942).

24. 421 U.S. 809 (1975).

25. Virginia State Bd. of Pharmacy v. Virginia Citizens Consumer Council, 425 U.S. 748 (1976).

26. Bates v. State Bar of Arizona, 433 U.S. 350 (1977). Just recently, the Court broadly applied *Bates* to invalidate a number of Missouri restrictions on the content and methods of lawyer advertising. *See In re* R__M.J.__, 102 S. Ct. 929 (1982).

27. 431 U.S. 85 (1977).

28. As the Court ventured further into the commercial speech area, it began to formulate distinctions between doctrines used to analyze restrictions on political speech and those identified to measure inhibitions on commercial speech. Such distinctions, initially suggested in the drug price advertising case, became the basis for differentiating the solicitation of clients for public interest litigation by ACLU lawyers from the solicitation of clients for pecuniary gain in commonplace personal injury cases. *Compare In re* Primus, 436 U.S. 412 (1978), *with* Ohralik v. Ohio State Bar Ass'n, 436 U.S. 447 (1978).

More recently, the notion that the nature of commercial speech entitles it to a lesser form of First Amendment protection was the basis for upholding a Texas statute that prohibited the practice of optometry under a trade name. Friedman v. Rogers, 440 U.S. 1 (1979). Although the Court relied on the potential deception of consumers made possible by the use of trade names, Justice Powell, in writing the majority opinion, expressed some concern about placing limits on the extent of First Amendment protection afforded to commercial speech. Additionally, in the context of distinguishing cases in which financial protection was given to well-established trade names, Justice Powell observed that "a property interest in a means of communication does not enlarge or diminish the First Amendment protection of that communication." 440 U.S. at 12, n. 11.

29. Central Hudson Gas & Electric Corp. v. Public Service Comm'n, 447 U.S. 557 (1980).

30. *Id*, at 591. By contrast, Justice Blackmun contended that the new tests did not adequately protect "truthful, nonmisleading, noncoercive commercial speech," while Justice Stevens believed that the promotional advertisements were not commercial speech at all, but rather advocacy speech subject to regulation only where a clear and present danger could be shown.

31. Zacchini v. Scripps-Howard Broadcasting Co., 433 U.S. 562 (1977).

32. Hynes v. Mayor and Council of Oradell, 425 U.S. 610 (1976).

33. *Id.* at 623. This was Justice Brennan's description of the Court's ruling.

34. Village of Schaumburg v. Citizens for a Better Environment, 444 U.S. 620 (1980).

35. Carey v. Brown, 447 U.S. 455 (1980).

36. Police Dep't of Chicago v. Mosley, 408 U.S. 92 (1972).

37. Carey v. Brown, *supra*, 447 U.S. at 459, n. 2.

38. *Id.* at 470, 471.

39. *Id.* at 477–78.

40. 326 U.S. 501 (1946).

41. Amalgamated Food Employees Union Local 590 v. Logan Valley Plaza, Inc., 391 U.S. 308 (1968).

42. Lloyd Corp. v. Tanner, 407 U.S. 551, 564–65, 568 (1972).

43. Hudgens v. NLRB, 424 U.S. 507 (1976).

44. PruneYard Shopping Center v. Robins, 447 U.S. 74 (1980).

45. *Id.* at 81.

46. Indeed, in the California case, Justice Marshall, the author of the 1968 Warren Court decision in *Amalgamated Food Employees Union Local 590 v. Logan Valley Plaza, Inc.,* and the principal critic of the 1976 decision that represented its formal demise, reiterated his concern that "[t]he Court's rejection of any role for the First Amendment in the privately owned shopping center complex stems . . . from an overly formalistic view of the relationship between the institution of private ownership of property and the First Amendment guarantee of freedom of speech." 447 U.S. at 91, quoting from his dissenting opinion in Hudgens v. NLRB, 424 U.S. at 542 (1976). As Justice White succinctly put it in his concurring opinion:

> [T]he First and Fourteenth Amendments do not prevent the property owner from excluding those who would demonstrate or communicate on his property. Insofar as the Federal Constitution is concerned, therefore, a State may decline to construe its own constitution so as to limit the property rights of the shopping center owner. 447 U.S. at 95–96.

The Court was able to avoid further consideration of these issues, in a difficult case that pitted a university's property and speech interests against a demonstrator's claim of access, by finding the controversy moot and dismissing the appeal. *See* State v. Schmid, 84 N.J. 535, 423 A.2d 615 (1980), *appeal dismissed sub nom.* Princeton University v. Schmid, 102 S.Ct. 867 (1982).

47. By the same token, New York might have been more successful in regulating utility company bill inserts, *see* Consolidated Edison Co. of New York v. Public Service Comm'n., 447 U.S. 530 (1980), if, instead of proscribing the messages a utility could put in "its own billing envelopes," *id.* at 540, the state had taken the approach suggested by Justice Blackmun in dissent:

> First, it appears that New York and other States might use their power to define property rights so that the billing envelope is the property of the ratepayers and not of the utility's shareholders. *Cf.* PruneYard Shopping Center v. Robins. . . . Since it is the ratepayers who pay for the billing packet, I doubt that the Court would find a law establishing their ownership of the packet violative of either the Takings Clause or the First and Fourteenth Amendments. If, under state law, the envelope belongs to the customers, I do not see how restricting the utility from using it could possibly be held to deprive the utility of its rights. 447 U.S. at 556.

48. 307 U.S. 496, 515 (1939).

49. Edwards v. South Carolina, 372 U.S. 229 (1963).

50. Gregory v. City of Chicago, 394 U.S. 111 (1969).

51. Bachellar v. Maryland, 397 U.S. 564 (1970).

52. Greer v. Spock, 424 U.S. 828 (1976).

53. Brown, Secretary of Defense v. Glines, 444 U.S. 348 (1980).

54. 418 U.S. 298 (1974).

55. Columbia Broadcasting System, Inc. v. Democratic National Comm., 412 U.S. 94 (1973). In a similar refusal to permit a right of access to the broadcast media, the Court held that the FCC had exceeded its statutory authority in promulgating "public access" rules that required cable television operators to set aside a number of cable channels for public use. FCC v. Midwest Video Corp., 440 U.S. 689 (1979). In CBS, Inc. v. FCC, 453 U.S. 367 (1982), however, the Court did uphold a limited statutory right of access for paid advertisements by federal political candidates.

56. With an occasional exception, the Court has declared prisons and military installations "off limits" to the normal application of First Amendment principles. *See, e.g.*, Parker v. Levy, 417 U.S. 733 (1974) (upholding court-martial conviction of an officer for antiwar speeches); Greer v. Spock, *supra* note 52; Brown, Secretary of Defense v. Glines, *supra* note 53; Pell v. Procunier, 417 U.S. 817 (1974) (upholding limits on press access to prisons); Jones v. North Carolina Prisoner's Union, 433 U.S. 119 (1977) (broadly rejecting inmates' rights to associate and to organize); Houchins v. KQED, Inc., 438 U.S. 1 (1978) (upholding restrictions on press access to prisons); Bell v. Wolfish, 441 U.S. 520 (1979) (upholding restrictions on mail to prisoners). *But see* Procunier v. Martinez, 416 U.S. 396 (1974) (invalidating some restrictions on prisoner correspondence with the outside world).

57. 453 U.S. 114 (1981).

58. 427 U.S. 50 (1976).

59. *Id.* at 53.

60. To be "obscene" in the constitutional sense, the material must appeal to the prurient interest, depict specific sexual conduct in a patently offensive way, and lack serious value. *See* Miller v. California, 413 U.S. 15, 24 (1973). Where minors are involved, the Court has given states even greater leeway to regulate. *See* New York v. Ferber, 102 S.Ct. 3348 (1982).

61. Erznoznick v. City of Jacksonville 422 U.S. 205 (1975).

62. Paris Adult Theatre I v. Slaton, District Attorney, 413 U.S. 49, 64 (1973); Miller v. California, 413 U.S. 15 (1973).

63. FCC v. Pacifica Found., 438 U.S. 726 (1978).

64. Metromedia, Inc. v. City of San Diego, 453 U.S. 490 (1981).

65. 102 S. Ct. 3164 (1982).

66. Whitney v. California, 274 U.S. 357, 375 (1927) (concurring opinion).

67. New York Times Co. v. Sullivan, 376 U.S. 254, 270 (1964).

68. Abrams v. United States, 250 U.S. 616, 630 (1919) (dissenting opinion).

69. T. EMERSON, THE SYSTEM OF FREEDOM OF EXPRESSION 7 (1970).

70. Blasi, *The Checking Value in First Amendment Theory*, A.B.F. RES. J. 521, 550–51 (1977).

71. Schenck v. United States, 249 U.S. 47 (1919).

72. Abrams v. United States, 250 U.S. 616 (1919).

73. Barenblatt v. United States, 360 U.S. 109 (1959).

74. 403 U.S. 15 (1971).

75. 274 U.S. at 375.

76. *Id.* at 377. *See* L. TRIBE, AMERICAN CONSTITUTIONAL LAW (1978) §§ 12-2, 12-8.

77. *See* Van Alstyne, *supra* note 14; Nowak, *supra* note 14.

78. *See generally* TRIBE, AMERICAN CONSTITUTIONAL LAW (1978), §§ 8-1 to 9-7.

79. Cohen v. California, 403 U.S. 15, 24 (1971).

CHAPTER 3

1. Gideon v. Wainwright, 372 U.S. 335 (1963); Griffin v. Illinois, 351 U.S. 12 (1956); Powell v. Alabama, 287 U.S. 45 (1932).

2. *See, e.g.*, Douglas v. California, 372 U.S. 353 (1963); Draper v. Washington, 372 U.S. 487 (1963); Lane v. Brown, 372 U.S. 477 (1963).

3. Harper v. Virginia Bd. of Elections, 383 U.S. 663, 668 (1966).

4. Economic Opportunity Act of 1964, Pub. L. No. 88-452, 78 Stat. 508 (codified at 42 U.S.C. §§ 2701 to 2996 (1976)).

5. *See* 42 U.S.C. § 2996 (1976).

6. Social Security Act of 1934, ch. 531, 49 Stat. 620 (codified at 42 U.S.C. §§ 301 to 1397 (1976)).

7. Califano v. Westcott, 443 U.S. 76 (1979); Miller v. Youakim, 440 U.S. 125 (1979); Quern v. Mandley, 436 U.S. 725 (1978); Batterton v. Francis, 432 U.S. 416 (1977); Philbrook, Comm'r, Dep't of Social Welfare v. Glodgett, 421 U.S. 707 (1975); Van Lare v. Hurley, 421 U.S. 338 (1975); Burns v. Alcala, 420 U.S. 575 (1975); Shea v. Vialpando, 416 U.S. 251 (1974); New York State Dep't of Social Servs. v. Dublino, 413 U.S. 405 (1973); Jefferson v. Hackney, 406 U.S. 535 (1972); Townsend v. Swank, 404 U.S. 282 (1971); Wyman v. James, 400 U.S. 309 (1971); Lewis v. Martin, 397 U.S. 552 (1970); Dandridge v. Williams, 397 U.S. 471 (1970); Rosado v. Wyman, 397 U.S. 397 (1970); Goldberg v. Kelly, 397 U.S. 254 (1970); Shapiro v. Thompson, 394 U.S. 618 (1969); King v. Smith, 392 U.S. 309 (1968). Another provision of the Social Security Act establishes a program of old-age, survivors, and disability insurance. In a 1979 decision under this provision, the Supreme Court noted fifteen previous cases that concerned the program. Califano, Secretary of Health, Education, and Welfare v. Boles, 443 U.S. 282 n.2 (1979). Fourteen of those cases were decided after 1970.

8. *See, e.g.,* Herweg v. Ray, 455 U.S. 265 (1982) (Medicaid); Schweiker v. Wilson, 450 U.S. 221 (1981) (Supplemental Security Income).

9. 394 U.S. 618 (1969).

10. 397 U.S. 471 (1970).

11. 394 U.S. at 627.

12. 397 U.S. 254 (1970).

13. *Id.* at 264 (footnote omitted).

14. 397 U.S. at 485.

15. *See id.* at 526 (Marshall, J., dissenting).

16. 394 U.S. at 637–38.

17. 397 U.S. at 487.

18. Goldberg v. Kelly, 397 U.S. 254, 262 (1970); Shapiro v. Thompson, 394 U.S. 618, 627 n.6 (1969).

19. 400 U.S. 309 (1971).

20. U.S. Const. amend. IV.

21. Camara v. Municipal Court, 387 U.S. 523 (1967).

22. *Id.* at 530–31.

23. *See* Marshall v. Barlow's, Inc., 436 U.S. 307 (1978).

24. 400 U.S. at 317–18.

25. *Id.* at 318–19.

26. *Id.* at 324.

27. *Id.* at 343 (Marshall, J., dissenting).

28. *Id.* at 322 n.9.

29. *Id.* at 323.

30. *Id.* at 317.

31. 443 U.S. 76 (1979).

32. *Id.* at 85.

33. *Id.*

34. 448 U.S. 297 (1980).

35. 410 U.S. 113 (1973).

36. I should perhaps acknowledge that I represented the plaintiffs in Williams v. Zbaraz, 448 U.S. 358 (1980), a companion case to *Harris*. For a fuller discussion of my thoughts on

the case, see Bennett, *Abortion and Judicial Review: Of Burdens and Benefits, Hard Cases and Some Bad Law*, 75 Nw. U.L. REV. 978 (1981).

37. 443 U.S. at 90.

38. New Jersey Welfare Rights Org. v. Cahill, Governor of New Jersey, 411 U.S. 619 (1973) (per curiam).

39. Memorial Hosp. v. Maricopa County, 415 U.S. 250 (1974).

40. Lassiter v. Dep't of Social Servs., 452 U.S. 18 (1981). The plaintiff in *Lassiter* lost her claim for appointed counsel.

41. Little v. Streater, 452 U.S. 1 (1981).

42. Ely, *Foreword: On Discovering Fundamental Values*, 92 HARV. L. REV. 5, 37–38 (1978); Karst, *Foreword: Equal Citizenship under the Fourteenth Amendment*, 91 HARV. L. REV. 1, 59 (1977); Tushnet, ". . . *And Only Wealth Will Buy You Justice"—Some Notes on the Supreme Court 1972 Term*, 1974 WIS. L. REV. 177, passim.

43. 411 U.S. 1 (1973).

44. The principal work is J. COONS, W. CLUNE, & S. SUGARMAN, PRIVATE WEALTH AND PUBLIC EDUCATION (1979).

45. Other factors such as the demand for noneducational public services obviously may affect a district's ability to finance education.

46. 411 U.S. at 28.

47. *Id*. at 33–34 (footnotes omitted).

48. 415 U.S. 250 (1974).

49. 410 U.S. 113 (1973).

50. *See* 411 U.S. at 34 n.76.

51. The interplay of Court decisions and legislative reaction in the welfare context is probably often more complex than the fixed welfare budget assumption suggests. The formerly disfavored group of recipients may have been disfavored because it lacked effective political power. When the Court forbids the discrimination, the disfavored group perforce becomes allied politically with the group that formerly obtained the benefit. This new coalition may be strong enough to require an increase in the total welfare budget to respond to the needs the Court has held cannot be disfavored.

52. The unanimous decision in Mills v. Habluetzel, 102 S. Ct. 1549 (1982), shows that the Court's activism on matters of illegitimacy is still very substantial.

53. Harris v. McRae, 448 U.S. 297 (1980); Williams v. Zbaraz, 448 U.S. 358 (1980). *See* Maher v. Roe, 432 U.S. 464 (1977); Beal v. Doe, 432 U.S. 438 (1977).

54. The ways in which the electoral process distorts the ideal are explored in A. DOWNS, AN ECONOMIC THEORY OF DEMOCRACY (1957).

55. *See* cases cited in note 7 *supra*, with the exceptions of Califano v. Westcott, 443 U.S. 76 (1979); Shapiro v. Thompson, 394 U.S. 618 (1969); and Goldberg v. Kelly, 397 U.S. 254 (1970), which were decided solely on constitutional grounds.

56. Miller v. Youakim, 440 U.S. 125 (1979); Philbrook, Comm'r, Dep't of Social Welfare v. Glodgett, 421 U.S. 707 (1975); Van Lare v. Hurley, 421 U.S. 338 (1975); Shea v. Vialpando, 416 U.S. 251 (1974); Townsend v. Swank, 404 U.S. 282 (1971); Lewis v. Martin, 397 U.S. 552 (1970); Rosado v. Wyman, 397 U.S. 397 (1970); King v. Smith, 392 U.S. 309 (1968).

57. Shea v. Vialpando, 416 U.S. 251 (1974). This decision was undone in part by 1981 amendments to the Social Security Act. *See* Pub. L. No. 97-35, 1981 U.S. CODE CONG. & AD. NEWS (95 Stat.) 843.

58. Van Lare v. Hurley, 421 U.S. 338 (1975).

59. Miller v. Youakim, 440 U.S. 125 (1979).

60. 415 U.S. 651 (1974).

61. U.S. CONST. amend. XI.

62. Hans v. Louisiana, 134 U.S. 1 (1889).

63. Ex parte Young, 209 U.S. 123 (1908).

64. 401 U.S. 371 (1971).

65. *Id.* at 376.

66. 409 U.S. 434 (1973).

67. *Id.* at 445.

68. *Id.* at 449.

69. *Id.* at 460 (Marshall, J., dissenting).

70. 410 U.S. 656 (1973).

71. 422 U.S. 490 (1975).

72. *Id.* at 495.

73. *Id.* at 504.

74. *Id.* at 505.

CHAPTER 4

1. 351 U.S. 12 (1956). Mayer v. Chicago, 404 U.S. 189 (1971), carried the *Griffin* principle quite far—further than the Court was to carry the *Gideon* principle (see note 2 *infra*).

2. 372 U.S. 335 (1963). Whether the Burger Court "expanded" or "contracted" *Gideon* is debatable. Rejecting the contention that *Gideon* should only apply in "nonpetty criminal offenses," i.e., those offenses *punishable* by more than six months' imprisonment, Argersinger v. Hamlin, 407 U.S. 25 (1972), applied *Gideon* to instances where a defendant is "*imprisoned for any offense,* whether classified as petty, misdemeanor, or felony" (emphasis added). But Scott v. Illinois, 440 U.S. 367 (1975), held that the Sixth and Fourteenth Amendments require only that no indigent misdemeanant be *incarcerated* unless he is afforded the right to counsel. A fairly generous reading of *Gideon*, the day after it was handed down, would have been that it applied to all "nonpetty" offenses. The Burger Court went beyond that generous interpretation of *Gideon* in one respect (*Argersinger*) but fell short in another (*Scott*).

3. 372 U.S. 353 (1963). Although a forceful argument can be made that the right to assigned counsel should apply to permissive review procedures as well as to appeals of right, the Court in *Douglas* stressed that it was dealing only with *the first appeal*, granted as a matter of right, and that is where the Burger Court, in Ross v. Moffitt, 417 U.S. 600 (1974), drew the line.

4. Allen, *The Judicial Quest for Penal Justice: The Warren Court and the Criminal Cases*, 1975 U. ILL. L. F. 518, 525.

5. Lopez v. United States, 373 U.S. 427, 448–51, 465–66 (1963) (Brennan, J., joined by Douglas and Goldberg, JJ., dissenting).
Even if this view had commanded a majority, and it never has, it would put no constitutional restrictions on the use of police spies *unequipped* with electronic transmitters or recorders, such as occurred in Hoffa v. United States, 385 U.S. 293 (1966). It would be better, I believe, to draw a constitutional distinction between a "trusted accomplice," who, absent prior arrangements with the police, *subsequently* provided them with evidence, and a "trusted accomplice" (whether or not equipped with an electronic device), who was a "police agent" all along—who was "planted" by the government to obtain incriminating evidence. But such a distinction was drawn only by Justice Douglas, who refused to join in the *Hoffa* opinion and who dissented in the companion cases of Lewis v. United States, 385 U.S. 206 (1966), and Osborn v. United States, 385 U.S. 323 (1966).

6. Lopez v. United States, 373 U.S. 427 (1963); United States v. White, 401 U.S. 745 (1971).

7. *See* Grano, *Foreword: Perplexing Questions about Three Basic Fourth Amendment Issues*, 69 J. CRIM. L.& C. 425, 432–33 (1978), discussing Hoffa v. United States, 385 U.S. 293 (1966); Lewis v. United States, 385 U.S. 206 (1966); United States v. White, 401 U.S. 745 (1971).

8. 389 U.S. 347 (1967).

9. 277 U.S. 438 (1928).

10. A. BEISEL, CONTROL OVER ILLEGAL ENFORCEMENT OF THE CRIMINAL LAW: ROLE OF THE SUPREME COURT 32 (1955).

11. 389 U.S. at 353. Dissenting in Desist v. United States, 394 U.S. 244, 273 (1969) (declining to give *Katz* retroactive effect), Justice Fortas described the matter even more forcefully. *Katz*, he observed, had only "administer[ed] the *coup de grâce*" to the "moribund doctrine" of *Olmstead*.

12. *See, e.g.*, L. B. Schwartz, *On Current Proposals to Legalize Wire Tapping*, 103 U. PA. L. REV. 157, 163 (1954).

13. 255 U.S. 298, 309–11 (1921). *See also, e.g.*, Abel v. United States, 362 U.S. 217, 237–38 (1960); Harris v. United States, 331 U.S. 145, 154 (1947); United States v. Lefkowitz, 285 U.S. 452, 464–66 (1932).

14. The manner in which the Court accomplished this left a good deal to be desired. Although Warden v. Hayden, 387 U.S. 294 (1967), did reject the distinction between the seizure of instrumentalities, fruits or contraband and the seizure of items of evidentiary value only, the evidence at issue in that case—items of clothing—"were not 'testimonial' or 'communicative' in nature, and their introduction therefore did not compel [a defendant] to become a witness against himself." *Id*. at 302–03. Thus the Court purported to leave open the question of "whether there are items of evidentiary value whose very nature precludes them from being the object of a reasonable search and seizure." *Id*. at 303. Moreover, two concurring justices explicitly disagreed with the *Hayden* decision's "broad" and "unnecessary" repudiation of the "mere evidence" rule. *Id*. at 310 (Fortas, J., joined by Warren, C.J.). A mere two weeks later, however, writing for the Court in Berger v. New York, 388 U.S. 41, 44 n.2 (1967), Justice Clark briskly dismissed the contention that court-ordered electronic surveillance "authorizes 'general searches' for 'mere evidence'" with a brief footnote announcing that this obstacle to the constitutional validity of law enforcement tapping and bugging had been "disposed of" in *Hayden*. When, later in the year, the Court made plain in *Katz* that at least some electronic surveillance, such as that involved in *Katz* itself, could be constitutionally authorized, nobody, not even Justice Douglas, invoked the "mere evidence" rule. *See generally* T. TAYLOR, TWO STUDIES IN CONSTITUTIONAL INTERPRETATION 95–102 (1969).

15. *See generally* H. Schwartz, *The Legitimation of Electronic Eavesdropping: The Politics of "Law and Order,"* 67 MICH. L. REV. 455 (1969).

16. Mapp v. Ohio, 367 U.S. 643 (1961), overruling Wolf v. Colorado, 338 U.S. 25 (1949).

17. Terry v. Ohio, 392 U.S. 1 (1968); Sibron v. New York and Peters v. New York, 392 U.S. 41 (1968).

18. 392 U.S. at 13.

19. *Cf*. Dershowitz & Ely, Harris v. New York: *Some Anxious Observations on the Candor and Logic of the Emerging Nixon Majority*, 80 YALE L.J. 1198, 1199 (1971).

20. *See generally* LaFave, *"Street Encounters" and the Fourth Amendment: Terry, Sibron, Peters, and Beyond*, 67 MICH. L. REV. 40, 47–54, 62–67, 88–91 (1968).

21. 392 U.S. at 30. At another point, the Court articulated an even vaguer standard and did so "negatively": "We cannot say [the officer's decision] to seize Terry and pat his clothing for weapons was the product of a volatile or inventive imagination, or was undertaken simply as an act of harassment; the record evidences the tempered act of a policeman who in the course of an investigation had to make a quick decision as to how to protect himself and others from possible danger, and took limited steps to do so." *Id*. at 28.

22. 386 U.S. 300 (1967).

23. 1 LaFave, Search and Seizure: A Treatise on the Fourth Amendment 577 (1978). For a discussion of various possibilities, see *id.* at 578–86; Grano, *A Dilemma for Defense Counsel,* U. Ill. L. F. 405, 445–47 (1971).

24. LaFave, *supra* note 23, at 586.

25. Project, *Interrogations in New Haven: The Impact of* Miranda, 76 Yale L.J. 1519, 1615 (1967). *See also* Israel, *Criminal Procedure, the Burger Court, and the Legacy of the Warren Court,* 75 Mich. L. Rev. 1320, 1384 (1977).

26. *See* Schaefer, *Symposium on Poverty, Equality, and the Administration of Criminal Justice,* 54 Ky. L.J. 464, 523 (1966). *See also* the comments by Justice Schaefer's fellow panelists, Edward Barrett and Richard Kuh, *id.* at 498–514.

27. *See, e.g.,* Stephens, The Supreme Court and Confessions of Guilt 165–200 (1973); Medalie, Zeitz, & Alexander, *Custodial Police Interrogation in Our Nation's Capital,* 66 Mich. L. Rev. 1347 (1968); Project, *supra* note 25.

28. F. Graham, The Self-Inflicted Wound 157 (1970).

29. Amsterdam, *Perspectives on the Fourth Amendment,* 58 Minn. L. Rev. 349, 353 (1974).

30. Allen, *The Judicial Quest for Penal Justice: The Warren Court and the Criminal Cases,* 1975 U. Ill. L.F. 539.

31. *Id.*

32. Massiah v. United States, 377 U.S. 201 (1964).

33. Israel, *Criminal Procedure, the Burger Court, and the Legacy of the Warren Court,* 75 Mich.L.Rev. 1319, 1425 (1977). *But compare, e.g.,* Levy, Against the Law 421–41 (1974); Hartman, *Foreword: The Burger Court—1973 Term: Leaving the Sixties Behind Us,* 65 J. Crim. L. & C. 437 (1974); Zion, *A Decade of Constitutional Revision,* N. Y. Times, Nov. 11, 1979 §6 (Magazine), p. 26.

34. Israel, *supra* note 33, at 1366.

35. United States v. Wade, 388 U.S. 218 (1967); Gilbert v. California, 388 U.S. 263 (1967); Stovall v. Denno, 388 U.S. 293 (1967). In *Stovall* the Court declined to give the *Wade-Gilbert* rule retroactive effect and held that the challenged identification was not "so unnecessarily suggestive and conducive to irreparable mistaken identification" as to violate due process.

36. United States v. Wade, 388 U.S. at 235–36.

37. *Id.* at 237.

38. *Id.* at 229.

39. *See* Kirby v. Illinois, 406 U.S. 682, 704 n.14 (1972) (Brennan, J., joined by Douglas and Marshall, JJ., dissenting).

40. 406 U.S. 682.

41. 390 U.S. 377, 384–85.

42. 461 F.2d 92 (D.C. Cir. 1972) (7 to 2, per Leventhal, J.).

43. Ash v. United States, 413 U.S. 300, 312–13, 317.

44. Defendants on appeal have the right to counsel but not the right to be present. Voluntary absence or contumacious conduct may cause defendants to lose the right to be present at their trials but not their right to counsel. *See* Grano, Kirby, Biggers, *and* Ash: *Do Any Constitutional Safeguards Remain against the Danger of Convicting the Innocent?* 72 Mich. L. Rev. 719, 764–66 (1974).

45. 413 U.S. at 314.

46. *See* Commentary to *Model Code of Pre-Arraignment Procedure* (Official Draft, 1975), at 428–33; Note, 64 J. Crim. L.C. & P.S. 428 (1973).

47. Note, 64 J. Crim. L.C. & P.S. 428, 433 (1973).

48. Neil v. Biggers, 409 U.S. 188, 198–201 (1972); Manson v. Brathwaite, 432 U.S. 98, 110–14, 117 (1977).

49. Manson v. Brathwaite, 432 U.S. 98, 110 (1977).

50. *See* Neil v. Biggers, 409 U.S. 188 (1972) (upholding identification on "totality of circumstances").

51. *See* Manson v. Brathwaite, 432 U.S. 98 (1977) (upholding identification on "totality of circumstances").

52. "Suggestive confrontations are disapproved because they increase the likelihood of misidentification, and unnecessarily suggestive ones are condemned for the further reason that the increased chance of misidentification is gratuitous." Neil v. Biggers, 409 U.S. at 198. But "weighing all the factors," such as the victim-witness's unusual opportunity to observe her assailant, the Court concluded that the one-man showup posed "no substantial likelihood of misidentification." *Id.* at 201.

53. The 1967 *Stovall* decision may be plausibly read, as Justice Marshall, joined by Brennan, J. (the author of *Stovall*), read it, dissenting in Manson v. Brathwaite, 432 U.S. at 120, as establishing a due process right of criminal suspects to be free from unnecessarily suggestive identifications. The *Stovall* showup, it seems, failed to violate due process only because the unusual necessity for the procedure was thought to outweigh the danger of suggestion. *See also* McGowan, *Constitutional Interpretation and Criminal Identification*, 12 WM. & MARY L. REV. 235, 240 (1970).

54. Manson v. Brathwaite, 432 U.S. at 110, quoting from a Seventh Circuit opinion by then Judge (now Justice) Stevens.

55. Grano, *supra* note 44, at 780.

56. *See* Commentary to *Model Code of Pre-Arraignment Procedure* (Official Draft, 1975), at 434–35; Eisenberg & Feustel, *Pretrial Identification: An Attempt to Articulate Constitutional Criteria*, 58 MARQ. L. REV. 659, 680 (1975); Note, 55 MINN. L. REV. 779 (1971).

57. *See* Allen, *The Judicial Quest for Penal Justice: The Warren Court and the Criminal Cases*, 1975 U. ILL. L. F. 518, 541–42; Grano, *supra* note 44, at 722; Zion, *A Decade of Constitutional Revision*, N. Y. Times, Nov. 11, 1979, § 6 (Magazine), pp. 26, 111.

58. P. WALL, EYE-WITNESS IDENTIFICATION IN CRIMINAL CASES 26 (1965), quoted in *Wade*, 388 U.S. at 228–29. *See also* Grano, *supra* note 44, at 723–24.

59. WHITEBREAD, CRIMINAL PROCEDURE 4 (1980). Of course, this point of view does not at all explain why the 1967 lineup decisions fared so badly in the 1970s. The 1970 pretrial identification cases suggest rather that "even the value of accuracy can be subordinated to the demands of the system for speed and finality." Chase, *The Burger Court, the Individual, and the Criminal Process: Directions and Misdirections*, 52 N.Y.U. L. REV. 518, 591 (1977).

60. 428 U.S. 465.

61. *Id.* at 489–91, 493.

62. *Id.* at 494. In the course of a long and powerful dissent, Justice Brennan, joined by Marshall, J., reminded the Court that *"the threat of habeas corpus serves as a necessary additional incentive for trial and appellate courts throughout the land to conduct their proceedings in a manner consistent with established standards."* 428 U.S. at 520–21 (emphasis supplied by Brennan, J.). "The Court," he observed, "does not, because it cannot, dispute that institutional constraints totally preclude any possibility that this Court can adequately oversee whether state courts have properly applied federal law, and does not controvert the fact that federal habeas jurisdiction is partially designed to ameliorate that inadequacy." *Id.* at 526. "There is no foundation in the language or history of the habeas statutes," he insisted, "for discriminating between types of constitutional transgressions, and efforts to relegate certain categories of claims to the status of 'second-class rights' by excluding them from that jurisdiction have [until today] been repulsed." *Id.* at 522. In a separate dissent, Justice White, for many of the reasons advanced by Brennan, J., stated his inability to distinguish between Fourth Amendment and other constitutional issues for purposes of federal habeas corpus relief but felt "constrained to say" that he "would join four or more other Justices in substantially limiting the reach of the exclusionary rule as presently administered." *Id.* at 537.

As to when, if ever, an erroneous state ruling may be said to deny a defendant "an opportunity for full and fair litigation" of a search and seizure claim, *see* KAMISAR, LAFAVE,
AND ISRAEL, MODERN CRIMINAL PROCEDURE 1571–72 (5th ed. 1980), and cases discussed
therein. As to whether, as dissenting Justice Brennan feared, *Stone* portends a withdrawal of
federal habeas corpus jurisdiction with regard to other (or all) claims that are not "guilt-
related," *see* Rose v. Mitchell, 443 U.S. 545 (1979) (state prisoners' claim of racial discrimination in selection of grand jury cognizable on federal habeas corpus), discussed at length in
Seidman, *Factual Guilt and the Burger Court: An Examination of Continuity and Change in
Criminal Procedure*, 80 COLUM. L. REV. 453–56 (1980).

63. Whitebread, *supra* note 59, at 20.

64. 414 U.S. 338, 349, 351–52 (Powell, J.).

65. *Id.* at 349. Justice Brennan, joined by Douglas and Marshall, JJ., dissented, maintaining, correctly I believe, that it was not the rule's possible deterrent effect, but "the twin goals of
enabling the judiciary to avoid the taint of partnership in official lawlessness" and of "assuring
the people [that] the government would not profit from its lawless behavior" that were "upper-
most in the minds" of the original framers of the exclusionary rule. *Id.* at 357.

66. 428 U.S. 433, 457–58 (Blackman, J.). Sixteen years earlier, Elkins v. United States,
364 U.S. 206 (1960), had overturned the "silver platter" doctrine and had held that illegal
state-gathered evidence could no longer be turned over to federal authorities for use in a federal
prosecution even though, so far as the record showed, the illegal evidence was being turned
over on a "silver platter," that is, without any state-federal collusion. The author of the *Elkins*
opinion, Justice Stewart, dissented in *Janis*, maintaining that the two cases could not be
reconciled. Justice Stewart argued, I think convincingly, that the majority's deterrence theory
compelled the opposite result in light of the fact that the relationship between federal officials
responsible for the enforcement of the wagering tax provisions and federal and local law
enforcement personnel combating gambling activities "is one of mutual cooperation and coor-
dination, with the federal wagering tax provisions buttressing state and federal criminal sanctions." *Id.* at 462. Brennan and Marshall, JJ., filed a separate dissent on the basis of their
dissenting views in *Calandra*.

67. Although in United States v. Ceccolini, 435 U.S. 268 (1978), the Court refused to
adopt a per se rule that the testimony of a witness identified or located as a result of police
misconduct should always be admissible, it did take the view that "the exclusionary rule should
be invoked with much greater reluctance" where the defense is seeking to suppress livewitness
testimony rather than an inanimate object. *But cf.* the *Brown-Dunaway-Taylor* line of cases,
discussed in text at notes 106–10 *infra*.

68. Alderman v. United States, 394 U.S. 165 (1969). But Justice Fortas, dissenting in part,
found "cogent and appealing" the views of many commentators that "the necessary implication
of the Fourth Amendment is that any defendant against whom illegally acquired evidence is
offered, whether or not it was obtained in violation of his right to privacy, may have the
evidence excluded." *Id.* at 205–06.

69. People v. Martin, 45 Cal.2d 755, 760, 290 P.2d 855, 857 (1955) (Traynor, J.) (abolishing the "standing" requirement as a matter of state constitutional law).

70. *See* Rakas v. Illinois, 439 U.S. 128 (1978) (car passengers lack "standing" to contest
the legality of the search of the car); United States v. Salvucci, 448 U.S. 83 (1980) (abolishing
"automatic standing" when defendants are charged with crimes of possession); Rawlings v.
Kentucky, 448 U.S. 98 (1980) (discussed later in the chapter). *Cf.* United States v. Payner, 447
U.S. 727 (1980) (supervisory power over federal criminal justice "does not authorize a federal
court" to exclude evidence obtained by "purposefully illegal" government conduct that did not
violate defendant's personal Fourth Amendment rights).

The decision in *Rawlings, supra*, the Court's latest major pronouncement on the subject,
evidently rejects the long-settled principle that an ownership or possessory interest in the things
seized is "quite enough to establish that the defendant's personal Fourth Amendment rights have

been invaded by the government's conduct." *See* Marshall, J., joined by Brennan, J., dissenting in *Rawlings*, 448 U.S. at 118. Moreover, the case suggests that one may invoke the protection of the Fourth Amendment "only if his expectation of privacy in the premises searched is so strong that he may exclude all others from that place" (*id.* at 119)—"a harsh threshold requirement [that] was not imposed even in the heyday of a property rights oriented Fourth Amendment." *Id.*

It may be, as the leading commentator on the subject hopes, that because Justice Rehnquist's opinion for the Court "is based upon a series of notions which, if taken seriously, would reduce the Fourth Amendment to nothing more than 'a form of words,'" *Rawlings* "will have a short life" or be limited to its peculiar facts. 3 LaFave, Search and Seizure § 11.3(c) (1982 Pocket Part) (hereinafter referred to as "LaFave" or "LaFave Pocket Part"). In the meantime, however, *Rawlings* has plunged the law of "standing" into chaos, a state of affairs not likely to eliminate significant incentives for police violations of the Fourth Amendment or prosecution use of such violations.

71. Burrows v. Superior Court, 13 Cal.3d 238, 247, 529 P.2d 590, 596 (1974) (Mosk, J.). Interpreting its state constitutional counterpart to the Fourth Amendment, the California Supreme Court held that a depositor has a "reasonable expectation of privacy" in his bank records. To the same effect is Commonwealth v. De John, 486 Pa. 32 403 A.2d 1283 (1979).

72. 425 U.S. 438, 442, 444 (1976).

73. *Id.* at 443. At this point, the Court in *Miller* relies on the so-called false friend cases (such as *Hoffa* and *White*, discussed in notes 5–7 *supra* and accompanying text)—those instances when the defendant confides in an apparent friend who actually is a secret government agent. However, as pointed out in 1 LaFave 415–17, the "false friend" cases provide a poor analogy.

First, the defendants in the false friend cases could have chosen their friends more carefully. A potential bank customer does not really have a "choice"—unless he wants to avoid taking part in the economic life of contemporary society. Second, in the false friend cases, the government obtains only what an individual reveals to a particular "friend." But when the government is allowed to scrutinize and sort a large quantity of banking data, it acquires a good deal more information than the bank depositor ever expected any particular bank employee to learn.

74. Justice Stewart (joined by Brennan, J.), dissenting in Smith v. Maryland, 442 U.S. 735, 748 (1979).

75. 442 U.S. 735, 742–44.

76. *Id.* at 744. In *Katz*, discussed at notes 8–11 *supra*, the Court held that the user of even a public telephone is entitled "to assume that the words he utters into the mouthpiece will not be broadcast to the world." 389 U.S. at 352. Dissenting in *Smith*, Justice Stewart, author of the *Katz* opinion, protested that the majority had forgotten the teachings of *Katz*:

> What the telephone company does or might do with [the numbers dialed] is no more relevant [than] it would be in a case involving the conversation itself. It is simply not enough to say, after *Katz*, that there is no legitimate expectation of privacy in the numbers dialed because the caller assumes the risk that the telephone company will disclose them to the public. 442 U.S. at 747.

77. *See* Amsterdam, *Perspectives on the Fourth Amendment*, 58 Minn. L.Rev. 349, 406 (1974).

78. *See* Stoner v. California, 376 U.S. 483 (1964). The current Supreme Court has furnished another example, and it did so, oddly, between the time it decided *Miller* and *Smith*. It recognized, in Marshall v. Barlow's, Inc., 436 U.S. 307, 315 (1978) (per White, J.), that although the owner of a business surrenders some privacy "by the necessary utilization of employees in his operation")"[w]hat [his employees] observe in their daily functions is undoubtedly beyond [his] reasonable expectation of privacy"—this does not mean that the owner

loses Fourth Amendment protection against "the warrantless scrutiny of Government agents." *Cf.* Walter v. United States, 447 U.S. 649, 659 (1980) (discussed at note 105 *infra*), holding, per Stevens, J., that the fact that cartons containing boxes of obscene film had been shipped to the wrong private party and opened by that party did not "alter the consignor's legitimate expectation of privacy" but "merely frustrated [it] in part. It did not simply strip the remaining unfrustrated portion of that expectation of all Fourth Amendment protection."

79. Zion, *supra* note 57, at 106. *See also* 2 LaFave 612.

80. 412 U.S. 218, 237–41, 242, 243 (per Stewart, J.)

81. *Id.* at 243. As dissenting Justice Marshall pointed out, however, "consent searches are permitted, not because such an exception . . . is essential to proper law enforcement, but because we permit our citizens to choose whether or not they wish to exercise their constitutional rights." *Id.* at 283. (Justices Douglas and Brennan also filed dissenting opinions.) For extensive discussion, and strong criticism, of *Schneckloth*, *see* Chase, *supra* note 59, at 525–40. Most commentators have been critical of the decision. *See* 2 LaFave at 612–20 and authorities discussed therein.

82. *See* 412 U.S. at 235–37, 241, 248.

83. *Id.* at 231–33, 248–49. Moreover, *Schneckloth* does not seem to offer much protection against loss of Fourth Amendment rights through coercion. The Court saw "no reason [to] depart in the area of consent searches, from the traditional definition of 'voluntariness,'" 412 U.S. 229, but there is no shortage of reasons for refusing to import this elusive standard into the consent area. The voluntariness test proved so ineffective and unworkable in the confession field that it was abandoned in favor of *Miranda*. There is no reason to expect it to prove more useful in the consent search setting. *See* 2 LaFave at 636–37; Weinreb, *Generalities of the Fourth Amendment*, 42 U. CHI. L. REV. 47, 57 (1974).

84. *Cf.* Escobedo v. Illinois, 378 U.S. 478, 490 (1964). *See also* Marshall, J., dissenting in *Schneckloth v. Bustamonte*, 412 U.S. at 288.

85. The genesis of the *Carroll* doctrine was Carroll v. United States, 267 U.S. 132 (1925). I share Judge Charles Moylan's view that "automobile exception" is a sloppy term for this doctrine, because many valid warrantless searches of automobiles are not based on the *Carroll* doctrine at all, but rather on some other exception to the warrant requirement, for example, "searches incident to arrest" or "inventory searches." *See* Moylan, *The Automobile Exception: What It Is and What It Is Not*, 27 MERCER L. REV. 987, 1012–15 (1976).

86. Chimel v. California, 395 U.S. 752 (1969), overruling United States v. Rabinowitz, 339 U.S. 56 (1950).

87. 414 U.S. 218 (1973). When "patting down" Robinson, who had been arrested for driving after the revocation of an operator's permit, the arresting officer felt an object in his pocket—"a crumpled up cigarette package"—pulled it out, opened it, and found heroin capsules inside. Although police regulations required the officer to take Robinson to the station house, in most jurisdictions and for most traffic offenses, the officer is free to effect a "full custody arrest" or merely issue a citation as he sees fit. *See* 2 LaFave 283. In Gustafson v. Florida, 414 U.S. 260 (1973), a companion case to *Robinson*, the officer had this customary discretion and he chose to arrest the defendant for driving without a license. A search of his person turned up a cigarette box that, when opened, revealed marijuana cigarettes.

88. 414 U.S. at 235. Thus in *Robinson* the Court made "the logically curious point that the authority to search, 'while based upon the need to disarm and to discover evidence,' does not require proof that either concern was in fact in the arresting officer's mind." Chase, *supra* note 59, at 544. For strong criticism of *Robinson*, *see id.* at 540–46.

89. 453 U.S. 454. *Belton* sustained the warrantless opening of a zippered pocket of a leather jacket found in the back seat of a car *after* the occupants, as directed by a police officer, had left the car and been placed under arrest. A search of the zippered pocket produced cocaine. "Our reading of the cases," observed the Court, per Stewart, J., *id.* at 460, "suggests the

generalization that articles inside the relatively narrow compass of the passenger compartment of an automobile are in fact generally, even if not inevitably, within 'the area into which an arrestee might reach in order to grab a weapon or evidentiary ite[m].' *Chimel.* In order to establish the workable rule this category of cases requires, we read *Chimel's* definition of the limits of the area that may be searched in light of that generalization." For a close examination of *Belton, see* Kamisar, *The "Automobile Search" Cases,* in CHOPER, KAMISAR, AND TRIBE, THE SUPREME COURT: TRENDS AND DEVELOPMENTS 1980–81 (1982) at 69, 87–100 (hereinafter referred to as "Kamisar"); 2 LaFave Pocket Part § 7.1.

90. 453 U.S. at 452 (concurring in the judgment in *Belton* and dissenting in Robbins v. California, *infra* note 94).

91. *See* Chambers v. Maroney, 399 U.S. 42 (1970); Cardwell v. Lewis, 417 U.S. 583 (1974); Texas v. White, 423 U.S. 67 (1975) (per curiam). *But see* Coolidge v. New Hampshire, 403 U.S. 433 (1971) (the car that was searched was parked in the driveway of the defendant's house, police had had probable cause for weeks to search the vehicle and other special circumstances). These cases are discussed extensively in Kamisar 72–85; 2 LaFave § 7.2; Moylan, *supra* note 85. For more recent analysis of these cases and of the lower court opinion in *United States v. Ross, infra* note 94, *see* Grano, *Rethinking the Fourth Amendment Warrant Requirement,* 19 AM. CRIM. L. REV. 603 (1982); Katz, *Automobile Searches and Diminished Expectations in the Warrant Clause,* 19 AM. CRIM. L. REV. 557 (1982).

92. *See* Kamisar 80–81 and cases discussed therein.

93. It hardly follows from the fact that the police may examine the license plates and headlights of a person's car that he has a reduced expectation of privacy with regard to the glove compartment or the trunk of his car. *See* Grano, *supra* note 91, at 638. Nor, for Fourth Amendment purposes, should an automobile be treated differently from a suitcase (protected by the warrant requirement when found outside a car) on the ground that a vehicle's function is transportation. No less than a suitcase, the automobile is a "container" that is commonly used as a temporary repository of personal effects. Automobiles "store [the] bank statement that should be brought inside the house, the library book that should be returned [and] the work one had planned to do overnight. . . . Any item that has been inside a suitcase undoubtedly has been inside an automobile. Moreover, many items most likely remain in automobiles, relatively safe and secure, far longer than they remain in suitcases." *Id.* at 637.

94. United States v. Ross, 102 S. Ct. 2157 (1982) (Stevens, J.), overruling Robbins v. California, 453 U.S. 420 (1981), although "there was no Court opinion supporting a single rationale for [the *Robbins*] judgment and the reasoning we adopt today was not presented by the parties in that case." 102 S. Ct. at 2172.

95. But the *Ross* Court reaffirmed the rule that despite probable cause to believe that they contain evidence of crime, movable closed containers located in a public place (for example, a bus depot) ordinarily may not be opened and searched without a warrant. *See* 102 S. Ct. at 2164–66.

96. 420 U.S. 103. *See generally* 2 LaFave 244–46. Although, over the objection of four justices, the Court, per Justice Powell, rejected the lower courts' conclusion that the determination of probable cause for detaining an arrestee pending further proceedings "must be accompanied by the full panoply of adversary safeguards—counsel, confrontation, cross-examination, and compulsory process for witnesses," 420 U.S. at 119—I believe the case still marks a significant net gain for Fourth Amendment protections. *But see* Chase, *supra* note 59, at 550 n.187.

97. 445 U.S. 573, 598–600 (Stevens, J.). *See id.* at 618 (Justice White, joined by the chief justice and Rehnquist, J., dissenting). The Court held that at least when the police "enter a dwelling in which the suspect lives when there is reason to believe the suspect is within," 445 U.S. at 603, an *arrest* warrant requirement "will suffice to interpose the magistrate's determination of probable cause between the zealous officer and the citizen." *Id* at 602.

Left for another day was the question when, if ever, a valid arrest warrant is sufficient justification for permitting the police to enter the home of the suspect's *friend* or *acquaintance* in order to make the arrest.

This issue was presented the following term, in Steagald v. United States, 451 U.S. 204 (1981). Writing for six members of the Court (the chief justice inexplicably concurred in the result without opinion; Rehnquist, J., joined by White, J., dissented), Justice Marshall concluded that, absent exigent circumstances, a valid warrant to arrest *A*, and naming only *A*, does not adequately protect the Fourth Amendment interests of *B* when *B*'s home is searched in an effort to locate *A*. Given *Payton*, the *Steagald* decision is not surprising. For an arrest warrant does not signify that the police have *any reason* to believe that the suspect may be found in somebody *else's* home, nor does it justify dispensing with a *search* warrant (where practical to obtain one) to search a third party's home.

98. 444 U.S. 85, 91–94 (Stewart, J.). *See id.* at 96–97 (Burger, C.J., joined by Blackmun and Rehnquist, JJ., dissenting); *id.* at 105 (Rehnquist, J., joined by the chief justice and Blackmun, J., dissenting). *But cf.* Michigan v. Summers, 452 U.S. 692 (1981), holding that the police could "detain" defendant and other occupants of his house before executing a warrant to search the house for narcotics. A valid warrant to search for contraband, held a 6 to 3 majority, per Stevens, J., "implicitly carries with it the limited authority to detain the occupants of the premises while a proper search is conducted." *Id.* at 705.

In *Ybarra*, before executing the warrant to search the public tavern, the police had detained *and* searched all of the persons who happened to be there. The validity of the detention itself was not challenged, only *the search* of those in the tavern. The police had no reason to believe that Ybarra had any special connection with the tavern or with the bartender. In *Summers*, on the other hand, the police knew the defendant lived in the house and they did not search his person until *after* a search of the house had turned up narcotics and they had probable cause to arrest the defendant and had done so. For a close examination of *Summers* and an effort to reconcile it with *Ybarra, see* Kamisar, *The* Steagald *and* Summers *Cases: What Is the Scope of the Authority Carried by Arrest and Search Warrants?* in CHOPER, KAMISAR, AND TRIBE, THE SUPREME COURT: TRENDS AND DEVELOPMENTS, 1980–81 (1982) at 121, 127–35.

99. 407 U.S. 297 (1972). Often called *Keith*, after then District Judge Damon Keith, the case involved a conspiracy to destroy federal government property.

100. *See* Saltzburg, *Foreword: The Flow and Ebb of Constitutional Criminal Procedure in the Warren and Burger Courts*, 69 GEO. L.J. 151, 163 (1980).

101. *Marshall v. Barlow's, Inc.* (1978), discussed in note 78 *supra.*

102. *Michigan v. Tyler*, 436 U.S. 499 (1978).

103. *Mincey v. Arizona*, 437 U.S. 385 (1978).

104. In United States v. Chadwick, 433 U.S. 1 (1977) (striking down the warrantless search of a locked footlocker taken from a person lawfully arrested in a public place), even the dissenters scolded the government for seeking to "vindicate an extreme view of the Fourth Amendment that would restrict the protection of the Warrant Clause to private dwellings and a few other 'high privacy' areas." Blackmun, J., joined by Rehnquist, J., dissenting, *id.* at 17. But language in the dissenting opinion of Justice White (joined by the chief justice) in Coolidge v. New Hampshire, 403 U.S. 443, 510 (1971), provided support for such an "extreme view."

Arkansas v. Sanders, 442 U.S. 753 (1979), invalidated the warrantless search of a suitcase, which had been removed from the trunk of a lawfully stopped motor vehicle. The Court, per Powell, J., pointed out that the warrant requirement "applies to personal luggage taken from an automobile to the same degree it applies to such luggage in other locations" and thus a warrantless search of such luggage must be justified under some exception to the warrant requirement other than the *Carroll* doctrine. *Id.* at 766. But because the police had been following the defendant and had probable cause to search the suitcase *before* it was placed in the vehicle, the chief justice, joined by Stevens, J., concurred on the narrow ground that *Sanders* was not an automobile search case at all, but a suitcase search case plainly controlled by *Chadwick*. *See id.* at 766–68. The Burger-Stevens interpretation of *Sanders* prevailed in United States v. Ross, 102 S. Ct. 2157, 2166–69, 2172 (1982) (Stevens, J.).

105. 447 U.S. 649, 658–59 (Stevens, J., announcing the judgment of the Court). In the lead opinion, *id.* at 651, Justice Stevens recounts what he calls "a few of the bizarre facts."

106. 422 U.S. 590.

107. "If *Miranda* warnings, by themselves, were held to attenuate the taint of an unconstitutional arrest, regardless of how wanton and purposeful the Fourth Amendment violation," observed the Court, per Blackmun, J., "the effect of the exclusionary rule would be substantially diluted. [Illegal arrests] would be encouraged by the knowledge that evidence derived therefrom could well be made admissible at trial by the simple expedient of giving *Miranda* warnings. Any incentive to avoid Fourth Amendment violations would be eviscerated by making the warnings, in effect, a 'cure-all,' and the constitutional guarantee against unlawful searches and seizures could be said to be reduced to 'a form of words.'" *Id.* at 602–03.

Although the Court rejected the per se rule urged by the state, it "also decline[d] to adopt any alternative per se or 'but for' rule." *Id.* at 603. Although "the *Miranda* warnings are an important factor [in] determining whether the confession is obtained by exploitation of an illegal arrest," other relevant factors are "[t]he temporal proximity of the arrest and the confession, the presence of intervening circumstances, and particularly, the purpose and flagrancy of the official misconduct." *Id.* at 603–04.

108. 442 U.S. 200.

109. 102 S. Ct. 2664 (1982). A 5 to 4 majority, per Marshall, J., held that the confession at issue was the impermissible fruit of the illegal arrest, although six hours had elapsed between the illegal arrest and the time petitioner confessed, petitioner had been advised of his *Miranda* rights three times and had been allowed to visit briefly with his girlfriend and neighbor shortly before he confessed. Dissenting Justice O'Connor, joined by the chief justice and Justices Powell and Rehnquist, did not challenge the *Brown-Dunaway* approach but maintained that those cases required a contrary result in *Taylor*.

110. "The detention of petitioner," pointed out the Court, per Brennan, J., "was in important respects indistinguishable from a traditional arrest. . . . [H]e was taken from a neighbor's home to a police car, transported to a police station, and placed in an interrogation room. . . . The mere facts that petitioner was not told he was under arrest, was not 'booked,' and would not have had an arrest record if the interrogation had proved fruitless, . . . obviously do not make petitioner's seizure even roughly analogous to the narrowly defined intrusions [upheld in the stop and frisk cases]. Indeed, any 'exception' that could cover a seizure as intrusive as that in this case would threaten to swallow the general rule that Fourth Amendment seizures are 'reasonable' only if based on probable cause." 442 U.S. at 212–13.

Pointing to the facts that no weapons were displayed and that Dunaway had not been handcuffed, nor had he been told he was under arrest or warned not to resist or flee, dissenting Justice Rehnquist, joined by the chief justice, maintained that Dunaway had not been "seized" within the meaning of the Fourth Amendment but had only "*voluntarily accompanied* the police to the station to answer their questions." *Id* at 222 (emphasis added). Since the police usually have little difficulty persuading people to accompany them to the station house *without* displaying their weapons, using handcuffs, issuing warnings not to resist or flee, or making formal announcements that the individual is under arrest, the Rehnquist-Burger view, if it had prevailed, would have had a devastating impact on Fourth Amendment protections. It would also have seriously undermined the rule that "*custodial* interrogation" (emphasis added) must be preceded by warning a suspect of his *Miranda* rights and obtaining a waiver of those rights.

111. 438 U.S. 154, 168.

112. 2 LaFave 60.

113. 438 U.S. at 169. To earn an evidentiary hearing, held the Court, the defendant must make "a substantial preliminary showing that a false statement knowingly and intentionally, or with reckless disregard for the truth, was included by the affiant" and that the statement was "necessary to the finding of probable cause." *Id.* at 155–56. Thus, as the *Franks* Court recognized, its holding left "a broad field where the magistrate is the sole protection of a citizen's Fourth Amendment rights." *Id.* at 170. If anything, the Court did not go far enough, *see* 2 LaFave 66–67, but it went too far for dissenting Justice Rehnquist, joined by the chief justice. *See id.* at 186.

114. 440 U.S. 648, 661 (White, J.). "Chance stops" or "haphazard stops" might be a better term, because "random" sometimes connotes some sort of systematic sampling.

115. *See* United States v. Calandra, 414 U.S. 338, 356, 365–66 (1974) (Brennan, J., joined by Douglas and Marshall, JJ., dissenting); United States v. Peltier, 422 U.S. 544, 545, 551, 561–62 (1975) (Brennan, J., joined by Marshall, J., dissenting); United States v. Janis, 428 U.S. 433, 460 (1976) (Brennan, J., joined by Marshall, J., dissenting).

116. Dissenting in Bivens v. Six Unknown Named Agents, 403 U.S. 388, 411, 415, 419, 420 (1971), the chief justice called the exclusionary rule, *inter alia*, "universal 'capital punishment,'" "unworkable and irrational," and "both conceptually sterile and practically ineffective in accomplishing its stated objective." But he did "hesitate to abandon [the rule] until some meaningful substitute is developed." *Id.* at 415. Five years later, however, in *Stone v. Powell*, the chief justice was no longer hesitant. It "now appear[ed] [to him] that the continued existence of the rule, as presently implemented, inhibits the development of natural alternatives. . . . It can no longer be assumed that other branches of government will act while judges cling to this Draconian, discredited device in its present absolutist form." 428 U.S. at 500 (concurring opinion). For criticism of this view, see Kamisar, *The Exclusionary Rule in Historical Perspective*, 62 JUDICATURE 337, 345–50 (1979).

117. Both in Michigan v. Tucker, 417 U.S. 433, 447 (1974), and in United States v. Peltier, 422 U.S. 531, 539 (1975), Justice Rehnquist observed, for the Court: "The deterrent purpose of the exclusionary rule necessarily assumes that the police have engaged in willful, or at the very least negligent, conduct. . . . Where the official action was pursued in complete good faith, . . . the deterrence rationale loses much of its force." Nor, in *Peltier*, did the Court, per Rehnquist, J., see how the "imperative of judicial integrity" would be offended if courts used evidence obtained by police who "reasonably believed in good faith" that they were acting lawfully, even if it turned out that they had violated the Fourth Amendment. 422 U.S. at 537–38. For criticism of this view, see Allen, *Foreword: Quiescence and Ferment: The 1974 Term in the Supreme Court*, 66 J. CRIM. L. & C. 391, 397–98 (1976).

In *Stone v. Powell*, dissenting Justice White also took the position that the exclusionary rule should not operate in those many instances where the officer "act[ed] in the good-faith belief that his conduct comported with existing law and [had] reasonable grounds for this belief." 428 U.S. at 538. Although he would not "wholly abolish" the exclusionary rule, Justice White did believe that, insofar as it was aimed at deterring police misconduct, the rule often "overshot" its mark. In "many of its applications," it was "a senseless obstacle to arriving at the truth." *Id.* at 537–38.

Concurring in Brewer v. Williams, 430 U.S. 387, 413–14 n.2 (1977), Justice Powell took a position similar to Justice White's. He, too, would draw a distinction between "flagrant" and "technical" or "inadvertent" Fourth Amendment violations and would not apply the exclusionary rule in the latter cases. *See also* Justice Powell's views in *Brown v. Illinois*, discussed in text at notes 106–07 *supra*. Concurring in *Brown*, Justice Powell, joined by Rehnquist, J., stressed the significance of the willfulness and flagrancy of the illegal arrest. 422 U.S. at 610–11. Where only "technical" Fourth Amendment violations were involved, for example, a "good faith arrest" on a warrant later invalidated, Powell would only require "proof that effective

Miranda warnings were given and that the ensuing statement was voluntary in the Fifth Amendment sense." *Id.* at 611–12. Justice White, who concurred separately in *Brown*, seemed to take an approach similar to Justice Powell's.

118. California v. Minjares, 443 U.S. 916, 928 (1979) (dissenting from denial of stay of mandate of the California Supreme Court).

119. In addition to the views of various members of the Court set forth in note 117 *supra, see, e.g.,* United States v. Williams, 622 F.2d 830 (5th Cir. 1980) (second *en banc* majority opinion); Attorney General's Task Force on Violent Crime, Final Report 55 (Aug. 17, 1981); Ball, *Good Faith and the Fourth Amendment: The "Reasonable" Exception to the Exclusionary Rule,* 69 J. Crim. L. & C. 635 (1978); Wright, *Must the Criminal Go Free if the Constable Blunders?* 50 Tex. L. Rev. 736 (1972). *Cf. Model Code of Pre-Arraignment Procedure* § 290.2(2) (1975). For a forceful criticism of the proposed "good faith" exception, see LaFave, *The Fourth Amendment in an Imperfect World: On Drawing "Bright Lines" and "Good Faith,"* 43 U. Pitt. L. Rev. 307, 335–59 (1982); Mertens & Wasserstrom, *The Good Faith Exception to the Exclusionary Rule: Deregulating the Police and Derailing the Law,* 70 Geo. L.J. 365 (1981); Comment, 15 Ga. L. Rev. 487 (1981).

120. 102 S. Ct. 2664, 2669. Justice Marshall spoke for himself and for Justices Brennan, Blackmun, Stevens, and—somewhat surprisingly—Justice White. Only two days earlier, dissenting from the Court's retroactive application of a search and seizure decision to all convictions not yet final at the time the decision was rendered, Justice White had maintained that neither of the two purposes traditionally understood to be served by the exclusionary rule— preserving "judicial integrity" and "deterring" unconstitutional police conduct—was furthered when the police "reasonably believed in good faith" that they were proceeding lawfully. United States v. Johnson, 102 S. Ct. 2579, 2595 (1982) (White, J., joined by the Burger, C.J. and Rehnquist and O'Connor, JJ., dissenting). For Justice White's earlier views to the same effect, see *supra* note 117.

Some months after this book went to press the Supreme Court restored *Illinois v. Gates* to the calendar for reargument and requested the parties to address the question whether the Fourth Amendment exclusionary rule "should to any extent be modified, so as, for example, not to require the exclusion of evidence obtained in the reasonable belief that the search and seizure at issue was consistent with the Fourth Amendment." 103 S. Ct. 436 (Nov. 1982). In *Gates,* 85 Ill.2d 376, 423 N.E.2d 887 (1981), a 5 to 2 majority of the Illinois Supreme Court held that a search warrant should not have issued on the basis of an anonymous letter describing defendant's alleged dealings, a letter corroborated to some extent by an independent police investigation.

Although I am not a proponent of a "good faith" or "reasonable, good faith" exception to the exclusionary rule, it must be said that *Gates* is an appealing case for adopting such an exception. The police did go through the desired procedure of obtaining a search warrant; did place the suspects under surveillance for several days before seeking the warrant, thereby corroborating various details of the unknown informant's letter (although the state supreme court regarded this verification as merely corroboration of "innocent" activity); and did not withhold any information or otherwise mislead the judicial officer. Now that the Court seems bent on addressing the issue, it would not be surprising if it rules that "close" counts not only in "horseshoes and grenades" but in some search and seizure contexts as well. *Cf.* LaFave, *supra* note 119, at 340. If so, however, the Court is likely to limit this modification of the exclusionary rule, at least for the near future to the *search warrant setting.*

121. Comptroller General of the United States, *Impact of the Exclusionary Rule on Federal Criminal Prosecutions* Washington, D.C.: U.S. Government Printing Office, Apr. 19, 1979), summarized in the first page of the 1982 pocket part to the LaFave treatise. An LEAA-sponsored empirical study of state felony cases in various jurisdictions, Brosi, A Cross-City

COMPARISON OF FELONY CASE PROCESSING 18–20 (1979), also summarized in LaFave, *supra*, produced similar findings.

The 1979 studies also cast serious doubt on the sufficiency and appropriateness of the data in two earlier studies that have furnished much aid and comfort to critics of the "exclusionary" rule: Oaks, *Studying the Exclusionary Rule in Search and Seizure*, 37 U. CHI. L. REV. 665 (1970); Spiotto, *Search and Seizure: An Empirical Study of the Exclusionary Rule and Its Alternatives*, 2 J. LEGAL STUD. 243 (1973). Oaks and Spiotto rely on the high frequency with which motions to suppress are granted in certain kinds of Chicago cases, for example, to conclude that, long after adoption of the exclusionary rule, illegal searches and seizures were commonplace in Chicago law enforcement. But the 1979 studies indicate, as maintained in Canon, *Is the Exclusionary Rule in Failing Health? Some New Data and a Plea against Precipitous Conclusion*, 62 KY. L.J. 681, 721 (1974), that Chicago is "a gross exception to the national norm of granting suppression motions."

122. The 1979 empirical studies suggest that most front-line courts are *already* limiting application of the exclusionary rule to "willful" or "bad-faith" police illegality and that "official" adoption of such a position may reduce the actual operation of the rule to the vanishing point.

123. LIEBERMAN, MILESTONES! *200 YEARS OF AMERICAN LAW* 326 (1976).

124. *Id. See generally* GRAHAM, THE SELF-INFLICTED WOUND 305–22 (1970); HARRIS, THE FEAR OF CRIME 22–29 (1969); LEVY, AGAINST THE LAW 1–6 (1974); Kamisar, *How to Use—Abuse—and Fight Back with—Crime Statistics*, 25 OKLA. L. REV. 239 (1972); Seidman, *Factual Guilt and the Burger Court: An Examination of Continuity and Change in Criminal Procedure*, 80 COLUM. L. REV. 436, 438–41 (1980).

125. 401 U.S. 222, 224 (1971) (Burger, C.J.). For the Brennan-Douglas-Marshall dissent, see *id.* at 226. Justice Black also dissented, without opinion. For extensive discussion, and strong criticism, of *Harris*, see LEVY, *supra* note 124, at 149–63; Dershowitz AND Ely, Harris v. New York: *Some Anxious Observations on the Candor and Logic of the Emerging Nixon Majority*, 80 YALE L.J. 1198 (1971); Stone, *The* Miranda *Doctrine in the Burger Court*, 1977 SUP. CT. REV. 99, 106–15 (hereinafter referred to as "Stone").

126. 420 U.S. 714 (1975) (Blackmun, J.), criticized in Stone at 125–29.

127. 447 U.S. 231 (1980), criticized in Bradley, Havens, Jenkins, *and* Salvucci, *and the Defendant's "Right" to Testify*, 18 AM. CRIM. L. REV. 419, 434–35 (1981); Saltzburg, *supra* note 100, at 204–05; Note 94, HARV. L. REV. 77, 82–85 (1980).

128. 102 S. Ct. 1309 (per curiam), summarily reversing 658 F.2d 1126 (6th Cir. 1981). Whatever one's views on the merits, the Court's summary disposition of this difficult question seems indefensible.

In both *Jenkins* and *Weir*, the Court distinguished Doyle v. Ohio, 426 U.S. 610 (1976), which held that impeachment by silence violates due process, but where defendant was silent *after* receiving the *Miranda* warnings. Because of the nature of the *Miranda* warnings (implicitly assuring a suspect that his silence will not be used against him), the Court deemed it "fundamentally unfair" in a case such as *Doyle* "to allow the arrested person's silence to be used to impeach an explanation subsequently offered at trial." *Id.* at 618.

But the use of *post*arrest silence for impeachment purposes also seems "fundamentally unfair." After all, the implied promise contained in the *Miranda* warnings that one's silence will not be used against him is derived not from the words of the *Miranda* opinion, but from the actual constitutional guarantees which they express. Many, if not most, people do associate the right to remain silent with an arrest—a view widely disseminated by the media. *Miranda* has become part of the popular culture. Why should it matter whether knowledge of the right to remain silent is imparted by the police or absorbed from our "common culture"?

129. An arrested person is not *entitled* to *Miranda* warnings. Only "custody" *plus* "inter-

rogation" must be preceded by the warnings. May silence in the face of improper "custodial interrogation," that is, custodial interrogation *not* preceded by the *Miranda* warnings, be used for impeachment purposes? At first blush, it would seem not. But if, as *Harris* and *Hass* make plain, incriminating statements induced by questioning in violation of *Miranda* may be used for impeachment purposes, why not *silence* preceded by interrogation in violation of *Miranda*?

130. 423 U.S. 96 (Stewart, J.)

131. Once an in-custody suspect "indicates in any manner, at any time prior to or during questioning, that he wishes to remain silent, the interrogation must cease." 384 U.S. at 473–74.

132. *See* 423 U.S. at 104–06. As dissenting Justice Brennan, joined by Marshall, J., pointed out, however, *id.* at 119, the other location "was merely a different floor of the same building."

133. It has been forcefully argued, Stone at 134, that the fact that the second interrogation of Mosley was restricted to a separate and "unrelated" crime "seems critical, for in its absence one is left only with a renewed effort to question by a different member of the same police force, in a different room in the same building, only two hours after Mosley's assertion of his right to be questioned." I wish *Mosley* would be limited in this manner, but I do not find much support for this interpretation in Justice Stewart's opinion for the Court. Some language in the *Mosley* opinion supports Stone, but at other places the opinion indicates that the essence of "scrupulously honoring" a suspect's "right to cut off questioning" is immediately ceasing the interrogation, suspending questioning entirely for a significant period, and giving another set of *Miranda* warnings at the outset of the second interrogation. *See* 423 U.S. at 105–07.

134. Stone at 133.

135. *See* 423 U.S. at 107–11 (concurring opinion).

136. *See* 423 U.S. at 115–18 (Brennan, J., joined by Marshall, J., dissenting).

137. Stone at 137.

138. By "custodial questioning," stated the *Miranda* Court, "we mean questioning initiated by law enforcement officers after a person has been taken into custody or otherwise deprived of his freedom of action in any significant way." 384 U.S. at 444. *See also id.* at 477: Warnings are required before a suspect "is first subjected to police interrogation while in custody at the station or otherwise deprived of his freedom of action in any significant way."

139. Mathis v. United States, 391 U.S. 1, 8 (1968) (White, J., joined by Harlan and Stewart, JJ., dissenting); Orozco v. Texas, 394 U.S. 324, 329 (1969) (White, J., joined by Stewart, J., dissenting).

140. 412 U.S. 218, 232, 247 (1973). *Schneckloth* is discussed in notes 80–84 *supra*.

141. 429 U.S. 492, 495, 498 (1977) (per curiam). Marshall, J., dissented on the merits. Brennan, J., dissented from the summary disposition without opinion. He "would set the case for oral argument." Stevens, J., also dissented from the summary disposition, believing the issues were of too much import for the case to be so decided. He noted that "the fact that the respondent was on parole at the time of the interrogation . . . lends support to inconsistent conclusions."

142. *Dunaway* is discussed in note 110 and in the text at notes 108–10.

143. Stone at 107. *See also* Dershowitz AND Ely, *supra* note 125, at 1210.

144. 412 U.S. 218, 224–25, 227, 229 (1973).

145. 417 U.S. 433, 444–46. *Tucker* dealt with the admissibility of the testimony of a witness whose identity had been learned by questioning defendant without giving him the full *Miranda* warnings. The questioning occurred before *Miranda* was decided, but defendant's trial took place afterward. Thus, *Miranda* was applicable to the case and, accordingly, the defendant's own statements to the police were excluded; but the Court held that under the circumstances the witness's testimony was admissible. Although the Court found it unnecessary to decide "the broad question" of whether the fruits of "statements taken in violation of the *Miranda*

rules must be excluded regardless of when the interrogation took place," it strongly indicated that it would answer that question in the negative, at least where the police acted in "complete good faith."

146. Harlan, J., joined by Stewart and White, JJ., dissenting in *Miranda*, 384 U.S. at 511. The *Miranda* opinion may contain some overstatements, but surely the observation that "[i]n these cases, we might not find the defendants' statements to have been involuntary in traditional terms" is not one of them. 384 U.S. at 457.

147. *Id.* at 455, 458.

148. 417 U.S. at 444.

149. *See* 384 U.S. at 444, 458, 467, 479.

150. *Id.* at 479.

151. Stone at 119.

152. 446 U.S. 291 (Stewart, J.).

153. *Cf.* Michigan v. Tucker, 417 U.S. at 444: "Certainly no one could contend that the interrogation faced [by Tucker] bore any resemblance to the historical practices at which the right against compulsory self-incrimination was aimed."

154. Grano, Rhode Island v. Innis: *A Need to Reconsider the Constitutional Premises Underlying the Law of Confessions,* 17 AM. CRIM. L. REV. 1 (1979).

155. A third officer and the suspect sat in the back. A screen separated those sitting in the front from those sitting in the back. All the occupants were aware that those in the back could hear the conversation in the front.

156. *See* cases discussed in White, *Interrogation without Questions*: Rhode Island v. Innis *and* United States v. Henry, 78 MICH. L. REV. 1209, 1223 n.106 (1980) (hereinafter referred to as "White").

157. 446 U.S. at 300–01.

158. *See* Y. KAMISAR, POLICE INTERROGATION AND CONFESSIONS: ESSAYS IN LAW AND POLICY 156–58 n.21 (1980) (hereinafter referred to as "Kamisar essays").

159. 446 U.S. at 302–03. Justice Marshall (joined by Brennan, J.) and Justice Stevens dissented on this point. Although I find the dissenters' arguments persuasive, I am not greatly disturbed by the Court's result. I do think there is a stronger basis for an objective listener's conclusion that the officers' remarks were made for a purpose *other than* that of eliciting an incriminating statement than there will be in the great bulk of cases. *See* White at 1234–35.

160. At one point, Justice Stewart seems to contrast "likelihood" of eliciting an incriminating response with "unforeseeability" that an incriminating response will result: "[S]ince the police surely cannot be held accountable for the *unforeseeable results* of their words or actions, the definition of interrogation can extend only to words or actions on the part of police officers that they *should have known* were reasonably likely to elicit an incriminating response." 446 U.S. at 301–02 (first emphasis added). Justice Stewart properly excluded "administrative questioning" (the routine questions asked of all arrestees who are booked or processed) from the definition of interrogation. "Administrative questioning" does not add "a measure of compulsion above and beyond that inherent in custody itself." *Id.* at 300. Moreover, an incriminating response is an *unforeseeable* consequence of such questioning. But when an incriminating response is foreseeable, the police conduct should generally be regarded as interrogation. "Foreseeable" is a better term than "reasonably likely," because the latter suggests "probable." But I think Justice Stewart only meant "foreseeable" when he used "reasonably likely."

I am quite reluctant to criticize Justice Stewart's wording because I suggested a similar definition in criticizing various lower courts' narrow definitions of interrogation. *See* Kamisar essays at 155–60. Indeed, so far as I can tell, all the commentators who urged an expansive interpretation of interrogation used wording very similar to Justice Stewart's. *See* authorities collected in White at 1229 n.106. I venture to say we were all focusing on the narrow definitions we were criticizing rather than thinking too much about the outer boundaries of the term.

After being educated by Justice Stevens's dissent in *Innis* and Professor White's insightful discussion of the case, I have revised my earlier suggested definitions of interrogation as indicated in the text. I think the new wording, based heavily on Justice Stevens's dissent, is substantially clearer and more helpful than the definitions I employed earlier. But this is what I meant to say in the first place. And I think this is what *Innis* means.

Thus, although I can see why Justice Stevens is concerned that the *Innis* test may turn on what might be called the "apparent probability" or "likelihood of success" that police speech or conduct will elicit an incriminating response, *see* 446 U.S. at 311–16, I do not share his fears. Such a view of the *Innis* test, as Professor White points out, would be inconsistent with the Court's professed aim of defining interrogation to include the functional equivalent of direct questioning (which, of course, need not satisfy any probability or likelihood of success test). *See* White at 1224–29. I also share Professor White's view that the *Innis* test will include "at least any police speech or conduct that an objective observer would perceive as 'designed' to elicit an incriminating response." *Id.* at 1236.

161. 430 U.S. 387, 415, 416, 419–20 (1977). Although *Brewer* was decided on the basis of *Massiah* (see text at notes 169–72 *infra*), not *Miranda*, the *Brewer* Court evidently thought it important, if not crucial, to establish that the challenged "Christian burial speech" constituted "interrogation"—and all four dissenters insisted that it did not. *See generally* Kamisar essays at 139–60.

162. The "speech" is discussed at great length in Kamisar essays at 113–60.

163. 446 U.S. at 304 (concurring opinion).

164. Edwards v. Arizona, 451 U.S. 477 (1981); Estelle v. Smith, 451 U.S. 454 (1981). *Miranda* fared less well, however, in California v. Prysock, 453 U.S. 355 (1981) (per curiam), where the Court upheld arguably defective *Miranda* warnings. The issue was not, as a majority of the Court seemed to think, whether "the warnings were inadequate *simply because* of *the order* in which they were given," *id* at 361 (emphasis added), but whether the substance of an important feature of the *Miranda* warnings—the right to have a lawyer provided free of charge prior to any questioning—had ever been effectively conveyed to the defendant. See the discussion in Kamisar, *Police Interrogation and Confessions: Will* California v. Prysock *Prove to Be a Substantial Setback for* Miranda?, in CHOPER, KAMISAR, and TRIBE, THE SUPREME COURT: TRENDS AND DEVELOPMENTS 1980–81 (1982) at 138, 143–47.

165. 451 U.S. at 462–63 (Burger, C.J.).

166. *Id.* at 468. Because the pretrial psychiatric examination had taken place after Smith had been indicted for murder and been appointed counsel, but occurred without notice to his lawyer, the Court had little difficulty concluding that the use of the examination at the penalty phase of the case also violated the *Massiah* doctrine (discussed in text at notes 169–73 *infra*). Justice Stewart, joined by Powell, J., concurred in the judgment on *Massiah* grounds without reaching the *Miranda* question. In a separate opinion, Justice Rehnquist also concurred in the result on *Massiah* grounds, but, in effect, dissented on the *Miranda* issue.

167. 451 U.S. at 484–85, 491–92.

168. A similar "standardized procedure" also seems appropriate for the resumption of questioning once a suspect has asserted his right to remain silent. Although the *Edwards* Court attempted to reconcile its opinion with *Mosley* (where the suspect had merely expressed a wish to remain silent), "it failed to do so convincingly," Note, 95 HARV. L. REV. 131 (1981), for *Miranda* seems to prohibit reinterrogation after an invocation of the right to remain silent just as unequivocally as after an assertion of the right to counsel.

169. 377 U.S. 201 (1964).

170. 430 U.S. 387 (1977). As pointed out in *Innis*, "the policies underlying the [*Miranda* and *Massiah*] constitutional protections are quite distinct." 446 U.S. at 300 n.4. *See generally* Kamisar essays at 160–201.

171. Grano, *supra* note 154, at 7.

172. Kamisar essays at xvi. *See also id.* at 160–64.

173. 447 U.S. 264, 271, 274, discussed at length in White at 1217–23, 1236–52. Although dissenting Justice Blackmun, joined by White, J., forcefully argued that the Court had significantly expanded the doctrine, "for purposes of this case" he saw "no need to abandon *Massiah*," 447 U.S. at 277 n.1. Justice Rehnquist, who dissented separately, did, but he was the only member of the Court to call for a reexamination of the *Massiah* doctrine.

174. Israel, *Criminal Procedure, the Burger Court, and the Legacy of the Warren Court*, 75 MICH. L. REV. 1319, 1408 (1977).

175. *Cf.* White, Rhode Island v. Innis: *The Significance of a Suspect's Assertion of His Right to Counsel*, 17 AM. CRIM.L. REV. 53, 69 (1979).

176. The chief justice did break sharply with Justice Rehnquist in *Henry*, did seem to "make peace" with *Miranda* in *Innis*, and did give *Miranda* a generous reading in *Estelle v. Smith*.

177. Unable to speak because of the tube in his mouth, the suspect responded to the detective's questions by writing answers on pieces of paper, at one point writing: "This is all I can say without a lawyer." Nevertheless, the trial court found "with unmistakable clarity" that the suspect's statements were "voluntary" and thus, despite being obtained in violation of *Miranda*, were admissible for impeachment purposes. The state supreme court unanimously affirmed. On the basis of its independent evaluation of the record, the Supreme Court per Stewart, J., reversed. Mincey v. Arizona, 437 U.S. 385 (1978). Only Justice Rehnquist dissented. As was true in so many of the pre-*Miranda* voluntariness cases, the dissent disputed the Court's reading of the record.

CHAPTER 5

1. Bellotti v. Baird, 443 U.S. 622 (1979).

2. Lalli v. Lalli, 439 U.S. 259 (1978).

3. Caban v. Mohammed, 441 U.S. 380 (1979).

4. Califano v. Boles, 443 U.S. 282 (1979).

5. Orr v. Orr, 440 U.S. 268 (1979).

6. *See, e.g.*, Roe v. Wade, 410 U.S. 113 (1973); Maher v. Roe, 432 U.S. 464 (1977); Bellotti v. Baird, 443 U.S. 622 (1979); Planned Parenthood v. Danforth, 428 U.S. 52 (1976); Harris v. McRae, 448 U.S. 297 (1980); Frontiero v. Richardson, 411 U.S. 677 (1973); Craig v. Boren, 429 U.S. 190 (1976); Califano v. Westcott, 443 U.S. 76 (1979). *See generally* Ginsburg, *The Burger Court's Grapplings with Sex Discrimination*, chapter 7 below.

7. *See, e.g.*, Stanley v. Illinois, 405 U.S. 645 (1971); Quilloin v. Wollcott, 434 U.S. 246 (1978); Caban v. Mohammed, 441 U.S. 380 (1979); Smith v. Offer, 431 U.S. 816 (1977).

8. *See e.g.*, Wisconsin v. Yoder, 406 U.S. 205 (1972); Goss v. Lopez, 419 U.S. 565 (1975); Ingraham v. Wright, 430 U.S. 651 (1977).

9. 442 U.S. 584, 600, 602, 607, 608, 633 (1979), decided in conjunction with Secretary of Public Welfare of Pa. v. Institutionalized Juveniles, 442 U.S. 640 (1979).

10. *Cf.* Addington v. Texas, 441 U.S. 418 (1979); O'Connor v. Donaldson, 422 U.S. 563 (1975).

11. *See* FISCHER, GROWING OLD IN AMERICA 230 (1978); Elder, *Approaches to Social Change and the Family*, in TURNING POINTS: HISTORICAL AND SOCIOLOGICAL ESSAYS ON THE FAMILY 57 (Demos and Boocock eds. 1978).

12. On the contemporary Court, the Nixon-appointed "conservatives" are Chief Justice Burger (appointed in 1969) and Justices Blackmun (1970), Powell (1972), and Rehnquist (1972); the "liberals" are Justices Brennan (appointed by President Eisenhower, 1956) and Marshall (appointed by President Johnson, 1967).

13. 442 U.S. at 603.

14. 430 U.S. 651, 662 (1977).

15. 400 U.S. 309, 318 (1971).

16. The Court's majority included Chief Justice Burger and Justices Black, Harlan, Stewart, and White; Justices Douglas, Brennan, and Marshall dissented.

17. 442 U.S. at 603.

18. The Court observed: "One who dispenses purely private charity naturally has an interest in and expects to know how his charitable funds are utilized and put to work. The public, when it is the provider, rightly expects the same." 400 U.S. at 319.

19. 406 U.S. 205, 231, 232, 237, 243 (1972).

20. 428 U.S. 52 (1976).

21. 443 U.S. 622 (1979).

22. *Id.* at 647–48. In *Baird,* alone among the cases discussed thus far, the four Nixon appointees were not united; Justice Blackmun voted to invalidate judicial supervision of the minor's abortion decision. He has, more than his conservative colleagues, been consistently opposed to any governmental restriction on abortions for adults or children. *See* Beal v. Doe, 432 U.S. 438 (1977); Maher v. Doe, 432 U.S. 464 (1977); Poelker v. Doe, 432 U.S. 519 (1977).

23. 428 U.S. at 74.

24. 406 U.S. at 212–13, 222, 233–34.

25. I owe this observation, and am generally indebted, to Anne Shere Wallwork (J.D. Yale University, 1979) and her unpublished paper, The Most Authoritarian Alternative: Parents, Children, and the State before the Burger Court.

26. 419 U.S. 565, 591, 593, 594, 598 n.19 (1975).

27. 430 U.S. 651, 681 n.50, 682 n.54 (1977).

28. *See* Burt, *Children as Victims,* in CHILDREN'S RIGHTS: CONTEMPORARY PERSPECTIVES 37–38 (P. Vardin and I. Brody eds. 1979).

29. 419 U.S. at 594 n.12.

30. 400 U.S. at 322–23.

31. *See* Burt, *Forcing Protection on Children and Their Parents: The Impact of Wyman v. James,* 69 MICH. L. REV. 1259, 1261–64 (1971).

32. 442 U.S. at 602–03.

33. 406 U.S. at 210.

34. Justice Douglas in his *Yoder* dissent pointed to evidence of defections from Amish communities and of high suicide rates, adolescent drinking, and "rowdyism and stress" in those communities. 406 U.S. at 245 n.2, 247 n.5.

35. *See* Fischer, *supra,* note 11 at pp. 66–76.

36. 430 U.S. at 681 n.53, 419 U.S. at 592.

37. 387 U.S. 1 (1967).

38. The first was Kent v. United States, 383 U.S. 541 (1966), a case originating in the District of Columbia Juvenile Court that the Supreme Court resolved on statutory grounds.

39. *See* PRESIDENTS COMM'N ON LAW ENFORCEMENT AND ADMINISTRATION OF JUSTICE, TASK FORCE REPORT: JUVENILE DELINQUENCY AND YOUTH CRIME 2–3 (1967).

40. 387 U.S. at 5–7.

41. 393 U.S. 503 (1969).

42. 393 U.S. at 516. Justice Black also observed that one parent was "paid a salary by the American Friends Service Committee" and another was "an official in the Women's International League for Peace and Freedom." *Ibid.*

43. This reflexive assumption was, as noted earlier (text at note 15), the conservative majority's position in the welfare home visit case, Wyman v. James, 400 U.S. 309 (1971), where Justice Black joined with the Court majority. *See* Burt, *Developing Constitutional Rights of, in, and for Children,* 39 LAW & CONTEMP. PROBS. 118, 123 (1975).

44. *See* K. ARROW, SOCIAL CHOICE AND INDIVIDUAL VALUES (2d ed. 1963).

45. 442 U.S. at 636 n.22.

46. *Id.* at 609 n.17.

47. 410 U.S. 133 (1973).

48. *See* Planned Parenthood v. Danforth, 428 U.S. 52 (1976); Maher v. Roe, 432 U.S. 464 (1977); Bellotti v. Baird, 443 U.S. 622 (1979).

49. 431 U.S. 494 (1977).

50. Justices Powell, Brennan, Marshall, Blackmun, and Stevens voted to invalidate the ordinance, though for differing reasons; Chief Justice Burger and Justices Stewart, White, and Rehnquist dissented, though for differing reasons.

51. Village of Belle Terre v. Boraas, 416 U.S. 1, 9 (1974). *See also* James v. Valtierra, 402 U.S. 137 (1971).

52. Compare Christopher Lasch's observation:

[B]lacks themselves regard the male-centered household as the most desirable form of the family. . . . The defenders of the matrifocal family, posing as critics of cultural parochialism, have unthinkingly absorbed the rising middle-class dissatisfaction with the isolated "privatized" suburban family, a dissatisfaction that has become especially pervasive in the very suburbs in which the "sentimental model of the family" is said to originate. Claiming to have liberated themselves from the assumptions of their own class, these writers share the fashionable concern with "alternatives to the nuclear family" and project the search for alternate life-styles onto the ghetto. They idealize the matrifocal family, exaggerate the degree to which it is embedded in a rich network of kinship relations, and ignore evidence which plainly shows that blacks themselves prefer a family in which the male earns the money and the mother rears the young. C. Lasch, Haven in a Heartless World 162–63 (1978).

53. *See* Demos, *The American Family in Past Times*, 43 The American Scholar 422, 425 (1974):

Scholars have long thought that premodern society was organized into "extended households"—large kin-groups, including several conjugal pairs, and spanning three or four generations. A corollary assumption has connected our own "nuclear" pattern with the coming of the Industrial Revolution little more than a century ago. But recent demographic research has shown these notions to be quite unfounded. It is now clear that nuclear households have been the norm in America since the time of the first settlements, and in England for as far back as evidence survives. The fundamental unit, then as now, was husband, wife, and their natural children.

54. Compare, by contrast, the application of local zoning laws that, in excluding small-group homes for mentally ill or retarded persons, perpetuate the pervasive state and local policies that have shut these people away in remote institutions. *See, e.g.,* Pennsylvania Ass'n for Retarded Children v. Pennsylvania, 343 F. Supp. 279 (E.D. Pa. 1972); Burt, *Helping Suspect Groups to Disappear*, in Psychology and the Law 33 (G. Berman, C. Nemeth and N. Vidmar eds. 1976); Burt, *Beyond the Right to Habilitation*, in The Mentally Retarded Citizen and the Law 417 (M. Kindred ed. 1976).

55. Justice Stevens, whose vote for invalidation made the Court majority, embraced a version of the privacy claim that he portrayed as Mrs. Moore's "right to use her own property as she sees fit." 431 U.S. at 513.

56. The Court reasoned that "[T]he State cannot 'delegate to a spouse a veto power which the state itself is absolutely and totally prohibited from exercising.'" Planned Parenthood v. Danforth, 428 U.S. 52, 69 (1976).

57. The discrimination is asserted with particular boldness as part of a feminist agenda by Carolyn G. Heilbrun:

Childbirth must be seen as the commitment of two people, and, especially because of past history, as the commitment of the *father*, who must devote himself equally with the mother to the infant he calls into being. From such a commitment will arise . . . the initiation of men into intimacy and nurturance of which they have been long deprived, and which follows from the care of wanted children. . . . Women must retain control of their bodies, including the decision of whether or not to carry a child within them. At the same time, men must acquire control of their fatherhood—and choose acts of procreation only when they intend to endow the resulting child with time and attention. C. HEILBRUN, REINVENTING WOMANHOOD 195–96 (1979).

58. Bellotti v. Baird, 443 U.S. 622 (1979).

59. Baird v. Bellotti, 450 F. Supp. 997, 1001–02 (D. Mass. 1978). *See also* H. L. v. Matheson, 450 U.S. 398 (1981).

CHAPTER 6

1. 163 U.S. 537 (1896).

2. 347 U.S. 483 (1954).

3. *E.g.*, Muir v. Louisville Park Theatrical Assn, 347 U.S. 971 (1954); Mayor of Baltimore v. Dawson, 350 U.S. 855 (1955); Gayle v. Browder, 352 U.S. 903 (1956).

4. *E.g.*, Burton v. Wilmington Parking Auth., 365 U.S. 715 (1961); Peterson v. City of Greenville, 373 U.S. 244 (1963); Robinson V. Florida, 378 U.S. 153 (1964); Lombard v. Louisiana, 373 U.S. 267 (1963).

5. Heart of Atlanta Motel v. United States, 379 U.S. 241 (1964); Katzenbach v. McClung, 379 U.S. 294 (1964).

6. Jones v. Alfred H. Mayer Co., 392 U.S. 409 (1968).

7. 402 U.S. 1 (1971).

8. 401 U.S. 424 (1971).

9. Brown v. Board of Education (II), 349 U.S. 294, 301 (1955).

10. *E.g.*, Alexander v. Holmes County Board of Education, 396 U.S. 19 (1969).

11. 391 U.S. 430 (1968).

12. *Id.* at 437–38.

13. Id. at 439.

14. Keyes v. Denver School District No. 1, 413 U.S. 189, 258 (1973) (dissenting opinion).

15. 347 U.S. at 494 (1954).

16. 402 U.S. 1 (1971).

17. *Id.* at 20–21.

18. Keyes v. Denver School District No. 1, 413 U.S. 189, 223 (1973) (separate opinion).

19. For a description of the Court's internal politics surrounding the decision, see B. WOODWARD AND S. ARMSTRONG, THE BRETHREN 95–112 (1979).

20. 413 U.S. 189 (1973).

21. *Id.* at 203.

22. *Id.* at 208.

23. *Id.*

24. *Id.* at 235 (separate opinion).

25. *Id.* at 236.

26. *Id.* at 226.

27. *Id.* at 251.

28. 99 S. Ct. 2941 (1979).

29. 99 S. Ct. 2971 (1979).

30. *Id.* at 2981.

31. *Id.*

32. *See* Norwood v. Harrison, 413 U.S. 455 (1973); Gilmore v. City of Montgomery, 417 U.S. 556 (1974); Runyon v. McCrary, 427 U.S. 160 (1976).

33. 418 U.S. 717 (1974).

34. *Id.* at 744.

35. *Id.* at 741–42.

36. 401 U.S. 424 (1971).

37. *Id.* at 428.

38. *Id.* at 429–30, 432, 436.

39. *See* Washington v. Davis, 426 U.S. 229 (1976); Furnco Constr. Corp. v. Waters, 438 U.S. 567 (1979). *Cf.* Dothard v. Rawlinson, 433 U.S. 321 (1977) (gender discrimination).

40. *Id.*

41. *See* Uniform Guidelines on Employee Selection Procedures, 41 C.F.R. Part 60-3 (1978).

42. 426 U.S. 229 (1976).

43. *Id.* at 246.

44. *Id.* at 245–46.

45. *Id.* at 248.

46. *See, e.g.,* Fiss, *Groups and the Equal Protection Clause*, 5 PHIL. & PUB. AFFAIRS 107 (1976). *Cf.* Freeman, *Legitimizing Racial Discrimination through Antidiscrimination Law: A Critical Review of Supreme Court Doctrine*, 62 MINN. L. REV. 1049 (1978).

47. *See generally* Brest, *Foreword: In Defense of the Antidiscrimination Principle*, 90 HARV. L. REV. 1, 31–43 (1976); Eisenberg, *Disproportionate Impact and Illicit Motive: Theories of Constitutional Adjudication*, 52 N.Y.U. L. REV. 36 (1977); Perry, *The Disproportionate Impact Theory of Racial Discrimination*, 125 U. PA. L. REV. 540 (1977).

48. 42 U.S.C. § 1973c (1976).

49. 100 S. Ct. 1548 (1980).

50. City of Mobile v. Bolden, 100 S. Ct. 1490 (1980).

51. 429 U.S. 252 (1977).

52. 438 U.S. 265 (1978).

53. 18 Cal.3d 34, 55, 553 P.2d 1152, 1166 (1976).

54. 438 U.S. at 328.

55. *Id.* at 360.

56. *Id.* at 359.

57. *Id.* at 307–09.

58. *Id.* at 314.

59. *Id.* at 315.

60. *Id.* at 317.

61. *Id.* at 318.

62. *Id.*

63. A year before *Bakke,* in United Jewish Organization of Williamsburg v. Carey, 430 U.S. 144 (1977), a divided Court approved of New York's race-conscious redistricting of a section of Kings County, done to comply with the Voting Rights Act of 1965. The redistricting, which was designed to increase minority voting power, had the unintended effect of diluting the political power of the Hasidic Jewish community by splitting it into two electoral districts. Although no opinion gained a majority of the Court, most of the justices agreed that racially conscious districting was not unconstitutional under the circumstances. Only Chief Justice Burger dissented on this issue.

64. Franks v. Bowman Transp. Co., 424 U.S. 747 (1976).

65. 443 U.S. 193 (1979).

66. Justices Powell and Stevens did not participate.

67. McDonald v. Santa Fe Trail Transp. Co., 427 U.S. 273 (1976).

68. 443 U.S. at 200.

69. *Id.* at 204. In a concurring opinion, Justice Blackmun explained that "this case arises from a practical problem in the administration of Title VII. The broad prohibition against discrimination places the employer and the union on . . . a 'high tightrope without a net beneath them.' . . . If Title VII is read literally, on the one hand they face liability for past

discrimination against blacks, and on the other they face liability to whites for any voluntary preferences adopted to mitigate the effects of prior discrimination against blacks" (443 U.S. at 209–10). To avoid this problem and yet facilitate voluntary compliance with Title VII, the company and the government argued that voluntary plans should be permissible if, but only if, they responded to an "arguable violation" of Title VII. Although this approach appealed to Justice Blackmun, he believed that it was unadministrable and also unduly narrow insofar as it prohibited an employer from voluntarily remedying discrimination not prohibited by the Act (for example, discrimination committed before 1964).

70. *Id.* at 208.

71. 448 U.S. 448 (1980).

72. This description is more evocative of Chief Justice Marshall's expansive interpretation of the "necessary and proper" clause in McCulloch v. Maryland, 17 U.S. (4 Wheat.) 316 (1819), than of the strict scrutiny test. Indeed, paralleling Marshall's failure to explain just why the Bank of the United States was necessary to implement the enumerated powers, Justice Powell did not explain in what sense the MBE provision remedied "identifiable" discrimination. There was no suggestion that the particular minority subcontractors who benefited were victims of prior discrimination.

CHAPTER 7

1. *See* Strauder v. West Virginia, 100 U.S. 303, 310 (1880); Fay v. New York, 332 U.S. 261, 290 (1947); Hoyt v. Florida, 368 U.S. 57 (1961).

2. Bradwell v. Illinois, 83 U.S. (16 Wall.) 130 (1873); Goesaert v. Cleary, 335 U.S. 464 (1948).

3. 332 U.S. 261.

4. *Id.* at 290.

5. 368 U.S. 57 (1961).

6. *Id.* at 62.

7. Personnel Adm'r of Massachusetts v. Feeney, 442 U.S. 256, 273 (1979).

8. *Id.*

9. 404 U.S. 71 (1971).

10. 443 U.S. 76 (1979).

11. *Compare* Roe v. Wade, 410 U.S. 113 (1973) (state antiabortion legislation held inconsistent with due process), *with* Personnel Adm'r of Massachusetts v. Feeney, 442 U.S. 256 (1979) (upholding absolute lifetime preference accorded veterans for state civil service positions); Maher v. Roe, 432 U.S. 464 (1977) (public funding need not be supplied for elective abortion); Geduldig v. Aiello, 417 U.S. 484 (1974) (classification on the basis of pregnancy is not sex-based classification).

12. *See generally* Gunther, *Foreword: In Search of Evolving Doctrine on a Changing Court: A Model for a Newer Equal Protection*, 86 HARV. L. REV. 1 (1972).

13. *E.g.,* McGowan v. Maryland, 366 U.S. 420 (1961).

14. Harper v. Virginia Bd. of Elections, 383 U.S. 663 (1966).

15. Loving v. Virginia, 388 U.S. 1 (1967).

16. *See* Gunther, *supra* note 12.

17. *E.g.,* Eslinger v. Thomas, 476 F.2d 225, 229 (4th Cir. 1973).

18. *E.g.,* Vlandis v. Kline, 412 U.S. 441, 458–59 (1973) (White, J., concurring); San Antonio Indep. School Dist. v. Rodriguez, 411 U.S. 1, 98 (1973) (Marshall, J., dissenting).

19. *See* L. TRIBE, AMERICAN CONSTITUTIONAL LAW 1060–77 (1978); Karst, *Foreword: Equal Citizenship under the Fourteenth Amendment*, 91 HARV. L. REV. 1, 53–59 (1977); Note, 91 HARV. L. REV. 70, 177 (1977); Note, 93 HARV. L. REV. 130 (1979).

20. 404 U.S. 71 (1971).

21. *E.g.*, Gunther, *supra* note 12, at 34.

22. 29 U.S.C. § 206(d).

23. 42 U.S.C. § 2000e-2.

24. H.R.J. Res. 208, 92d Cong., 2d Sess., 86 Stat. 1523 (1972).

25. *See* Eastwood, *The Double Standard of Justice: Women's Rights under the Constitution*, 5 VAL. U.L. REV. 281 (1971).

26. 400 U.S. 542 (1971) (per curiam).

27. *Id.* at 544.

28. 433 U.S. 321 (1977).

29. 405 U.S. 645 (1972).

30. 434 U.S. 246 (1978).

31. 441 U.S. 380 (1979).

32. 441 U.S. 347 (1979).

33. *See* Lalli v. Lalli, 439 U.S. 259 (1978).

34. 411 U.S. 677 (1973).

35. *Id.* at 691.

36. Relatively few women served in the military, in part the result of sex-based entrance and opportunity barriers. *See generally* M. BINKIN AND S. BACH, WOMEN AND THE MILITARY (1977); Note, *The Equal Rights Amendment and the Military*, 82 YALE L. J. 1533 (1973).

37. Weinberger v. Wiesenfeld, 420 U.S. 636 (1975); Califano v. Goldfarb, 430 U.S. 199 (1977).

38. 416 U.S. 351 (1974).

39. 419 U.S. 498 (1975).

40. *See* Fla. Stat. § 196.202 (Supp. 1974–75).

41. 416 U.S. 312 (1974).

42. S. GRIMKE, LETTERS ON THE EQUALITY OF THE SEXES AND THE CONDITION OF WOMEN 10 (1838).

43. 419 U.S. 498.

44. *See supra* note 36.

45. *See* Two v. United States, 471 F.2d 287 (9th Cir. 1972), *cert. denied*, 412 U.S. 931 (1973).

46. *Cf.* Harvard Law School Record, March 23, 1973, at 15 (reporting Justice Stewart's comment that "the female of the species has the best of both worlds." Under the equal protection clause she can "attack laws which unreasonably discriminate against [her] while saving some, such as exemption from conscription, which favor [her].").

47. Owens v. Brown, 455 F. Supp. 291 (D.D.C. 1978).

48. 368 U.S. 57 (1961).

49. 419 U.S. 522 (1975).

50. 391 U.S. 145 (1968).

51. 439 U.S. 357 (1979).

52. 420 U.S. 636 (1975). Although the judgment was unanimous, the Court divided 5–2–1 on the reasons in support of the decision. Four years later, Justice Rehnquist announced a change of mind. In Califano v. Boles, 443 U.S. 282, 294–95 n.12 (1979), he declared his vote in *Wiesenfeld* plain error, based on a misreading of legislative history.

53. 420 U.S. at 646, 648.

54. *Id.* at 648.

55. 335 U.S. 464 (1948).

56. *Id.* at 466–67.

57. 421 U.S. 7 (1975).

58. *Id.* at 14–15.

59. *Id.* at 15.

60. Labor force participation rates for women ages 45 to 54 were 24.5% in 1940, 49.5% in 1970, 54.9% in 1974; for women ages 55 to 64, participation rates were 18% in 1940, 37.4% in 1960, 41.7% in 1974. "By 1960, the rate for women 45 to 54 . . . had risen to such an extent that it was noticeably higher than the proportion for 20- to 24-year-old women . . . ." Women's Bureau, U.S. Dep't of Labor, Handbook on Women Workers 12 (1975).

61. By 1976, in 55 percent of families in which the husband was gainfully employed, the wife was also gainfully employed. U.S. Bureau of Labor Statistics, Dep't of Labor, U.S. Working Women: A Databook 37 (1977).

62. Fullerton and Flaim, *New Labor Force Predictions in 1990*, in U.S. Bureau of Labor Statistics, Dep't of Labor, Monthly Labor Review 3, 5 (Dec. 1976).

63. Quoted in Briggs, *How You Going to Get 'Em Back in the Kitchen? (You Aren't)*, Forbes, Nov. 15, 1977, at 177–78.

64. 429 U.S. 190, 197. The formulation, as quoted in the text, appears in Personnel Adm'r of Massachusetts v. Feeney, 442 U.S. 256, 273 (1979).

65. 335 U.S. 464 (1948).

66. 430 U.S. 199 (1977) (5 to 4 decision). Chief Justice Burger's dissenting vote in *Goldfarb* is difficult to reconcile with the concurring opinion (by Justice Powell) to which he subscribed in *Wiesenfeld*.

67. 430 U.S. at 217 (Stevens, J., concurring).

68. *Id.* at 222.

69. *Id.* at 224 (Rehnquist, J., dissenting).

70. 446 U.S. 142 (1980).

71. 420 U.S. 636 (1975); *see supra*, text at notes 52–56.

72. 430 U.S. 199 (1977); *see supra*, text at notes 66–69.

73. 416 U.S. 351 (1974); *see supra*, text at notes 40–42.

74. 419 U.S. 498 (1975); *see supra*, text at notes 43–45.

75. 430 U.S. 313 (1977).

76. *Id.* at 318.

77. *Cf.* Frontiero v. Richardson, 411 U.S. 677, 684 (1973) (characterizing as "romantic paternalism" certain legislation purporting to favor or protect women, but in practical effect confining their activity and opportunity).

78. 438 U.S. 265 (1978).

79. J. Kozol, Death at an Early Age (1967). In contrast, for most women, regardless of race, customary responsibility for household management and care of young children creates stubborn psychological and logistical barriers to achieving equal opportunity. *Cf.* Wasserstrom, *Racism, Sexism, and Preferential Treatment: An Approach to the Topics*, 24 U.C.L.A. L. Rev. 581 (1977).

80. H. Kay, Sex-Based Discrimination 875 (2d ed. 1981).

81. *See* Ruud, *That Burgeoning Law School Enrollment Is Portia*, 60 A.B.A.J. 182 (1974).

82. 438 U.S. at 359–60.

83. *Id.* at 302–03.

84. 411 U.S. at 691. *See supra*, text accompanying note 41.

85. 48 U.S. at 303. Earlier, in San Antonio Indept. School Dist. v. Rodriguez, 411 U.S. 1 (1973), Justice Powell wrote for the Court's majority that "the traditional indicia of suspectness" exist when a class is "saddled with such disabilities, or subjected to such a history of purposeful unequal treatment, or relegated to such a position of political powerlessness as to command extraordinary protection from the majoritarian political process." *Id.* at 28.

86. 430 U.S. 703 (1977), *affirming by an equally divided court*, 532 F.2d 880 (3d Cir. 1976) (2 to 1), *reversing* 400 F. Supp. 326 (E.D. Pa. 1975).

87. 440 U.S. 268 (1979).

88. 443 U.S. 76 (1979).

89. 440 U.S. at 283; 443 U.S. at 89.

90. 440 U.S. at 282.

91. *Id.* at 283. The three dissenting justices in *Orr* found procedural impediments to federal adjudication and did not reach the merits.

92. 443 U.S. 76 (1979).

93. *See, e.g.,* Dandridge v. Williams, 397 U.S. 471, 484–85 (1970). *But cf.* New Jersey Welfare Rights Organization v. Cahill, 411 U.S. 619 (1973) (per curiam).

94. 443 U.S. at 89.

95. *See* Ginsburg, *Some Thoughts on Judicial Authority to Repair Unconstitutional Legislation,* 28 CLEVE. ST. L. REV. 301 (1979).

96. *Cf.* Wengler v. Druggists Mut. Ins. Co., 446 U.S. 142 (1980) (8 to 1 decision) (equal protection precludes denying widowers workers' compensation death benefits on the same terms as widows).

97. 401 U.S. 424, 432 (1971).

98. *Id.* at 429, 431.

99. *E.g.,* Douglas v. Hampton, 512 F.2d 976, 981 (D.C. Cir. 1975).

100. 426 U.S. 229 (1976).

101. *Id.* at 240.

102. 442 U.S. 256 (1979).

103. *Id.* at 279.

104. *Id.* at 260.

105. *See supra* note 36.

106. 442 U.S. at 270.

107. 438 U.S. 265 (1978).

108. 442 U.S. at 279.

109. *Id.* at 272.

110. *Id.* at 260, 278.

111. *Id.* at 279.

112. *Compare* Califano v. Westcott, 443 U.S. 76, 91–93, 95 n.1 (1979) (assuming validity of a principal breadwinner criterion), *with* Equal Employment Opportunity Commission Sex Discrimination Guidelines, 29 C.F.R. § 1604.9(c) (conditioning fringe benefits on "principal wage earner" status violates Title VII's sex discrimination ban).

113. 410 U.S. 113 (1973).

114. 410 U.S. 179 (1973).

115. *Compare* L. TRIBE, *supra* note 19, at 924–33, *with* Ely, *The Wages of Crying Wolf: A Comment on Roe v. Wade,* 82 YALE L.J. 920 (1973).

116. 381 U.S. 479 (1965).

117. 405 U.S. 438 (1972).

118. 432 U.S. 464 (1977) (equal protection ruling); Beal v. Doe, 432 U.S. 438 (1977) (Social Security Act ruling); Poelker v. Doe, 432 U.S. 519 (1977) (public hospitals not required to perform elective abortions).

119. See L. TRIBE, *supra* note 19, at 934 n.77; Perry, *The Abortion Funding Cases: A Comment on the Supreme Court's Role in American Government,* 66 GEO. L.J. 1191 (1978).

120. T. Wicker, *Kitchen-Table Justice,* N. Y. Times, June 28, 1977, at 31.

121. 414 U.S. 632 (1974).

122. 417 U.S. 484 (1974).

123. 429 U.S. 125 (1976).

124. 434 U.S. 136 (1977).

125. 432 U.S. 464; *see supra,* text at notes 118–20.

126. 423 U.S. 44 (1975).

127. 434 U.S. at 153–54.

128. *See* Weinberger v. Salfi, 422 U.S. 749, 772 (1975).

129. *See* Bezanson, *Some Thoughts on the Emerging Irrebuttable Presumption Doctrine*, 7 IND. L. REV. 644 (1974). *But cf.* Ackerman, *The Conclusive Presumption Shuffle*, 125 U. PA. L. REV. 761 (1977).

130. Pub.L. No. 95–5551, Oct. 31, 1978, 92 Stat. 2076 (*amending* 42 U.S.C. 2000e (1976)).

131. Book Review, 89 HARV. L. REV. 1028, 1036 (1976). *See also* Karst, *Foreword: Equal Citizenship Under the Fourteenth Amendment*, 91 HARV. L. REV. 1, 57–58 and n.320 (1977).

132. 435 U.S. 702 (1978).

133. *Id.* at 728 (Burger, Ch. J., joined by Rehnquist, J.)

134. *Id.* at 710. On questions in *Manhart*'s wake, see Bernstein and Williams, *Sex Discrimination in Pensions:* Manhart's *Holding* v. Manhart's *Dictum*, 78 COLUM. L. REV. 1241 (1978).

135. See L. LUSKY, BY WHAT RIGHT? 179–242 (1975).

136. *Cf.* Frontiero v. Richardson, 411 U.S. 677, 692 (1973) (Powell, J., concurring); *supra*, text at note 35.

137. Massachusetts Bd. of Retirement v. Murgia, 427 U.S. 307 (1976).

138. San Antonio Indept. School Dist. v. Rodriguez, 411 U.S. 1 (1973); Jefferson v. Hackney, 406 U.S. 535 (1972); James v. Valtierra, 402 U.S. 137 (1971).

139. Graham v. Richardson, 403 U.S. 365 (1971); *In re* Griffiths, 413 U.S. 717 (1973).

140. Foley v. Connelie, 435 U.S. 291 (1978); Ambach v. Norwick, 441 U.S. 68 (1979).

141. 416 U.S. 351 (1974); *see supra*, text at notes 40–42.

142. 419 U.S. 498 (1975); *see supra*, text at notes 43–45.

143. 430 U.S. 313 (1977); *see supra*, text at notes 75–78.

144. *Id.* at 320.

145. 430 U.S. 703 (1977); *see supra*, text at note 86.

146. 347 U.S. 483 (1954).

147. The most immediate *Brown* predecessor was Sweatt v. Painter, 339 U.S. 629 (1950).

148. United States v. Hinds County School Bd., 560 F.2d 619 (5th Cir. 1977).

149. Roe v. Wade, 410 U.S. 113 (1973); Doe v. Bolton, 410 U.S. 179 (1973).

150. *See particularly* Maher v. Roe, 432 U.S. 464 (1977); *supra* notes 118–20 and accompanying text.

151. 448 U.S. 297 (1980).

152. 432 U.S. 464; *see supra*, text at notes 118–20.

153. 410 U.S. 103 (1973); *see supra*, text at notes 113–15.

154. 448 U.S. at 349.

155. *Id.* at 357.

156. 450 U.S. 464 (1981).

157. 429 U.S. 190 (1976); *see supra*, text at notes 64–66.

158. 440 U.S. 268 (1979); *see supra*, text at notes 87–91.

159. 450 U.S. at 476.

160. *Id.* at 488 (joined by Justices White and Marshall).

161. *Id.* at 494–96.

162. *Id.* at 496.

163. *Id.* at 500–02.

164. 25 Cal.3d 608, 601 P.2d 572 (1979).

165. Sail'er Inn, Inc. v. Kirby, 5 Cal.3d 1, 485 P.2d 529 (1971). This decision, which declared sex a "suspect classification," predated the Supreme Court's turning point decision in Reed v. Reed, 404 U.S. 71 (1971); *see supra*, text at notes 20–21.

166. 450 U.S. at 481, 483 (explicitly applying a heightened review test).

167. 450 U.S. 455 (1981). *Michael M.* was argued November 4, 1980, *Kirchberg*, December 10, 1980. Both were decided March 23, 1981.

168. Justice Marshall wrote for seven justices. Justice Stewart concurred in the result in a two-paragraph opinion joined by Justice Rehnquist. 450 U.S. at 463.

169. *Id.* at 461 (quoting Personnel Adm'r of Massachusetts v. Feeney, 442 U.S. 256, 273 (1979)). The *Kirchberg* opinion, 450 U.S. at 459, 461, prominently cites Wengler v. Druggists Mut. Ins. Co., 446 U.S. 142 (1980), in which the Court held, 8 to 1, that the heightened equal protection review standard applicable to sex-based classifications precludes denying widowers workers' compensation death benefits in circumstances in which widows would be entitled to such benefits.

170. 453 U.S. 57 (1981).

171. *Id.* at 69–70.

172. *Id.* at 76–77. Justice Rehnquist cited in support of the combat exclusion the legislative prohibition on assigning women to duty on (navy) vessels contained in 10 U.S.C. § 6015, a prohibition declared unconstitutional in 1978 in an unappealed district court decision, Owens v. Brown, 455 F. Supp. 291 (D.D.C.). No opinion in Rostker v. Goldberg mentions this decision.

173. 419 U.S. 598 (1975); *see supra*, text at notes 43–47.

174. 453 U.S. at 83–84 (White, J., dissenting) (citing a Defense Department estimate that approximately 80,000 women draftees could be used productively in the first six months).

175. Korematsu v. United States, 323 U.S. 214 (1944); *see* Hirabayashi v. United States, 320 U.S. 81 (1943). *See generally* Rostow, *The Japanese American Cases—A Disaster*, 54 YALE L. J. 489 (1945).

176. J. CHOPER, Y. KAMISAR AND L. TRIBE, THE SUPREME COURT: TRENDS AND DEVELOPMENTS, 1980–1981, at 37, 40, 191 (1982) (remarks of Professors Choper and Tribe).

177. 102 S. Ct. 3331 (1982).

178. Men were permitted to audit courses, but not to enroll for credit.

179. Citing Vorchheimer v. School Dist. of Philadelphia, 532 F.2d 880 (3d Cir. 1975), *aff'd by an equally divided Court*, 430 U.S. 703 (1977), *see supra*, text at notes 86 and 145–48, the Court noted that Mississippi maintained no single-sex public university or college other than Mississippi University for Women, therefore the question whether a state may maintain "separate but equal" undergraduate schools for males and females was not presented. 50 102 S. Ct. at 3334 n.1.

180. 102 S. Ct. at 3336 (citing and quoting from Kirchberg v. Feenstra, 450 U.S. 455, 461 (1981); Personnel Adm'r of Massachusetts v. Feeney, 442 U.S. 256, 273 (1979); and Wengler v. Druggists Mut. Ins. Co., 446 U.S. 142, 150 (1980)).

181. *See supra*, text at note 159.

182. 102 S. Ct. at 3336 (footnote omitted).

183. *See supra*, text at notes 48–77 and 87–96.

184. 102 S. Ct. at 3336–37. In the eyes of the dissenting justices (Chief Justice Burger and Justices Blackmun, Powell and Rehnquist), the case did not involve "genuine sexual stereotyping." *See* 50 U.S.L.W. at 5073 (Powell, J., dissenting). *But see id.* at 3339 and n.15 (admissions policy in question assured more openings for women than for men in state-supported nursing schools, thus "lend[ing] credibility to the old view" of nursing as a "woman's job," a view that nurses suggest has operated to depress their wages).

185. *Id.* at 3336.

186. Justice Blackmun, however, in a brief dissenting opinion, *Id.* at 3341, expressed concern about "go[ing] too far" in this area, and may have drifted some distance from the direction in which his prior analyses of role typing appeared to be heading. *See particularly* Califano v. Westcott, 443 U.S. 76 (1979), discussed *supra*, text at notes 92–96; and Stanton v. Stanton, 421 U.S. 7 (1975), discussed *supra*, text at notes 57–59.

187. *See supra,* text following note 89.

188. 102 S. Ct. at 3337 (quoting Craig v. Boren, 429 U.S. 190, 198 (1976)).

189. The expression is Justice Stevens's. *See supra*, text at notes 155, 162, and 163.

CHAPTER 8

1. The Warren Court established the primacy of federal over state law in the regulation of union organizing, collective bargaining, and the enforcement of labor contracts. St. Antoine, *Judicial Valour and the Warren Court's Labor Decisions*, 67 MICH. L. REV. 317 (1968).

2. One count is 39 to 7, based on the number of decisions reproduced in a standard labor law casebook. *See, e.g.,* R. SMITH, L. MERRIFIELD AND T. ST. ANTOINE, LABOR RELATIONS LAW: CASES AND MATERIALS (6th ed. 1979).

3. *See* Brest, *Race Discrimination*; Ginsburg, *The Burger Court's Grapplings with Sex Discrimination.*

4. R. MARSHALL, THE NEGRO WORKER 40–41 (1967); Rathbun, *Organized Labor: Changing of the Guard,* The Atlantic 6, 12 (Dec. 1979).

5. 110 CONG. REC. 7207 (1964) (Justice Dep't Memorandum submitted by Sen. Clark).

6. 42 U.S.C. § 2000e–2(h) (1976).

7. *See, e. g.,* Quarles v. Philip Morris, Inc., 279 F. Supp. 505 (E.D. Va. 1968); Paperworkers Local 189 v. United States, 416 F.2d 980 (5th Cir. 1969), *cert. denied*, 397 U.S. 919 (1970).

8. Paperworkers Local 189 v. United States, 416 F. 2d 980, 987–88 (5th Cir. 1969), *cert. denied*, 397 U.S. 919 (1970).

9. *Id.* at 995.

10. 86 Stat. 103 (1972).

11. Teamsters v. United States [T.I.M.E.–D.C.], 431 U.S. 324, 378 n.2 (1977) (dissenting opinion).

12. 431 U.S. 324 (1977).

13. *Id.* at 349.

14. *Id.* at 356.

15. *Id.* at 393–94, citing cases (dissenting opinion).

16. 102 S. Ct. 1534 (1982).

17. Pullman-Standard Div., Pullman, Inc. v. Swint, 102 S. Ct. 1781 (1982).

18. 323 U.S. 192 (1944).

19. Syres v. Oil Workers Local 23, 350 U.S. 892 (1955) (per curiam).

20. Humphrey v. Moore, 375 U.S. 334 (1964).

21. 424 U.S. 554, 570 (1976).

22. *See. e.g.,* Vaca v. Sipes, 386 U.S. 171, 191 (1967).

23. 29 U.S.C. § 401 *et seq.* (1976).

24. *See, e.g.,* Salzhandler v. Caputo, 316 F.2d 445 (2d Cir. 1963), *cert. denied*, 375 U.S. 946 (1963).

25. Finnegan v. Leu, 102 S. Ct. 1867 (U.S. 1982).

26. 102 S. Ct. 2339 (U.S. 1982).

27. *Id.* at 2346.

28. 429 U.S. 305 (1977).

29. Hodgson v. Steelworkers Local 6799, 403 U.S. 333 (1971).

30. 420 U.S. 50 (1975).

31. 431 U.S. 209 (1977).

32. Machinists v. Street, 367 U.S. 740 (1961).

33. Sinclair Refining Co. v. Atkinson, 370 U.S. 195 (1962), *overruled by* Boys Markets, Inc. v. Retail Clerks Local 770, 398 U.S. 235 (1970); Food Employees Local 590 v. Logan

Valley Plaza, Inc., 391 U.S. 308 (1968), *overruled by* Hudgens v. NLRB, 424 U.S. 507 (1976).

34. San Diego Building Trades Council v. Garmon, 359 U.S. 236 (1959); John Wiley & Sons, Inc. v. Livingston, 376 U.S. 543 (1964); National Woodwork Mfrs. Ass'n v. NLRB, 386 U.S. 612 (1967).

35. NLRB v. Magnavox Co., 415 U.S. 322 (1974).

36. Eastex, Inc. v. NLRB, 437 U.S. 556 (1978).

37. 419 U.S. 301 (1974).

38. 391 U.S. 308 (1968).

39. 407 U.S. 539 (1972).

40. 424 U.S. 507 (1976).

41. *Id.* at 521.

42. *Id.* at 539 (dissenting opinion).

43. Food Employees Local 590 v. Logan Valley Plaza, Inc., 391 U.S. 308, 314 (1968).

44. 447 U.S. 607 (1980).

45. *Id.* at 616 (concurring opinion).

46. *Id.* at 619 (concurring opinion).

47. National Woodwork Mfrs. Ass'n v. NLRB, 386 U.S. 612, 645 (1967).

48. 386 U.S. 612 (1967).

49. 429 U.S. 507 (1977).

50. 447 U.S. 490 (1980).

51. *Id.* at 509.

52. San Diego Bldg. Trades Council v. Garmon, 359 U.S. 236 (1959).

53. 436 U.S. 180 (1978). In an unusual case that found organized labor resisting an extension of federal preemption, the Burger Court sustained (6 to 3) the validity of the New York unemployment compensation statute, which grants benefits to strikers after eight weeks. New York Tel. Co. v. New York Dep't of Labor, 440 U.S. 519 (1979). In another decision the Court broadened the preemption doctrine in a way advantageous to unions. It held in Machininsts Lodge 76 v. WERC, 427 U.S. 132, 140 (1976), that certain concerted activity that was technically neither "protected" nor "prohibited" under the NLRA, and hence not covered by the usual formulation of the *Garmon* preemption test, was nonetheless intended by Congress "to be controlled by the free play of economic forces," and thus it too was immune to state regulation.

54. 436 U.S. at 206–07.

55. *Id.* at 216 (dissenting opinion).

56. NLRA §§ 8(a)(5), 8(d), 9(a), 29 U.S.C. §§ 158 (a)(5), 158(d), 159(a) (1976).

57. *Cf.* NLRB v. Wooster Div., Borg-Warner Corp., 356 U.S. 342 (1958).

58. 379 U.S. 203 (1964).

59. 452 U.S. 666 (1981).

60. *Id.* at 686.

61. 379 U.S. at 211.

62. 397 U.S. 99 (1970).

63. *Id.* at 103.

64. 370 U.S. 195 (1962).

65. 398 U.S. 235 (1970).

66. 428 U.S. 397 (1976).

67. 430 U.S. 243 (1977).

68. *Id.* at 253.

69. John Wiley & Sons, Inc. v. Livingston, 376 U.S. 543, 550 (1964).

70. NLRB v. Burns Int'l Security Serv., Inc., 406 U.S. 272 (1972).

71. Howard Johnson Co. v. Hotel & Restaurant Employees Detroit Local Joint Board, 417 U.S. 249 (1974).

72. 421 U.S. 616 (1975).

73. *Id.* at 623.

74. *E.g.,* Hunt v. Crumboch, 325 U.S. 821, 823 (1945).

75. 421 U.S. at 633.

76. The Court made partial amends for *Connell* in Woelke & Romero Framing, Inc. v. NLRB, 102 S. Ct. 2071 (1982). There it was held unanimously that "union-only" subcontracting clauses are protected by the 8(e) proviso if they are sought in the context of a collective bargaining relationship, even if they are not limited to particular job sites at which both union and nonunion workers are employed.

77. For example, the sort of "union-only" subcontracting clause permitted by the §8(e) proviso in the construction industry could not be enforced by strike action if an employer reneged on its agreement and employed a nonunion subcontractor. The union's strike would violate §8(b)(4)(B) of the NLRA. *Cf.* Carpenters Local 1976 v. NLRB [Sand Door], 357 U.S. 93 (1958).

78. 421 U.S. at 631.

79. N. Y. TIMES, July 13, 1980, §3, p. 1, col. 1. *See generally* U.S. BUR. LAB. STAT., DEP'T LAB. BULL. NO. 2000, HANDBOOK OF LABOR STATISTICS 1978 at 507 (1979); L. REYNOLDS, LABOR ECONOMICS AND LABOR RELATIONS 352–58 (7th ed. 1978).

80. 44 N.L.R.B. ANN. REP. 19 (1979).

CHAPTER 9

1. My use of the phrase "the Burger Court" is not intended to imply that Chief Justice Burger has taken a position of leadership in the antitrust area. In fact, Justice Powell has come closer to assuming such a position than any of his brethren.

2. Unlike most economist-lawyers, I do not believe that our current antitrust laws should be construed to condemn those practices and only those practices that it would be allocatively efficient to condemn. The correct judicial response to an antitrust question may therefore differ from the correct legislative response to the problem posed by the transaction in question.

3. Since doctrine has had much less predictive value in antitrust than in most other areas of our law, I will focus here as much on the outcomes of the major antitrust cases of the past decade as on their holdings. This focus reflects the fact that the complexity and uncertainty of many of the factual issues that dominate antitrust litigation gives courts that are so disposed the opportunity to surmount doctrinal obstacles to outcomes they find attractive by making findings that suit their purposes. Thus, regardless of the market share and concentration figures that are supposed to condemn a horizontal merger, a court wishing to prohibit horizontal mergers can rationalize such outcomes by defining the relevant markets to produce the required numbers.

4. I say the later Warren Court because the 1963–67 Warren Court's decisions are in many respects inconsistent with the earlier opinions of that Court. At least in part, then, the 1974–79 Burger Court might be said to be returning to and developing the positions first adumbrated by the earlier Warren Court.

5. Although Burger has been chief justice since 1969, post–Warren Court appointees did not achieve numerical superiority until 1975. Burger was appointed in 1969; Blackmun in 1970; Powell and Rehnquist in 1972; and Stevens in 1975. Thus, one could not expect a new majority to coalesce until 1973—that is, until at least four post–Warren Court appointees had an opportunity to think through various antitrust issues.

6. This essay will ignore the Burger Court's treatment of such practically important issues as the passing on, state action, and labor exemption doctrines. *See* Illinois Brick Co. v. Illinois, 431 U.S. 720 (1977); Goldfarb v. Virginia State Bar, 421 U.S. 773 (1975); Cantor v. Detroit Edison Co., 428 U.S. 579 (1976); and Connell Construction Co. v. Plumbers and Steamfitters Local 100, 421 U.S. 616 (1975).

7. Sherman Act § 1, 26 Stat. 209 (1890), *as amended by* 15 U.S.C. §§ 1–7 (1973).

8. Sherman Act § 2.

9. Clayton Act § 14, 38 Stat. 730 (1914), *as amended by* 15 U.S.C. §§ 12–27 (1973).

10. *See, e.g.,* Brown Shoe Co. v. United States, 370 U.S. 294 (1962).

11. United States v. Topco Assocs., Inc., 405 U.S. 596, 610 (1972).

12. Continental T.V., Inc. v. GTE Sylvania, Inc., 433 U.S. 36, 67 (1977) (concurring opinion).

13. One could argue that cross-market concentration of ownership may tend to produce anticompetitive results indirectly by facilitating lobbying that produces various kinds of protective legislative and executive decisions.

14. *See supra,* note at p. 181.

15. *Cf.* Brown Shoe v. United States, 370 U.S. 294 (1962); United States v. Von's Grocery Co., 384 U.S. 270 (1966); Federal Trade Commission v. Proctor & Gamble Co., 386 U.S. 568 (1967); and United States v. Arnold Schwinn & Co., 388 U.S. 365 (1967).

16. *Cf.* Brown Shoe v. United States, 370 U.S. at 316.

17. Albrecht v. The Herald Co., 390 U.S. 145, 158 (1968) (dissenting opinion).

18. 418 U.S. 602 (1974). Although the government argument rejected by the Court in *Marine Bancorporation* did not focus explicitly on the supposed noneconomic goals of antitrust, Justice Powell's majority opinion did explicitly reject as overbroad language in Justice Black's opinion in United States v. Pabst Brewing Co., 384 U.S. 546 (1966) that could have been used to support the introduction of such values.

19. 433 U.S. 36 (1977). In this case the Supreme Court overturned a Warren Court holding that it was per se illegal for a manufacturer who had parted with dominion over the relevant goods to restrict the areas his distributors served.

20. 405 U.S. 596 (1972).

21. *Id.* at 609.

22. *Id.* at 611–12.

23. *See, e.g.,* United States v. Von's Grocery, 384 U.S. 270 (1966); Brown Shoe v. United States, 370 U.S. 294 (1962).

24. 388 U.S. 365 (1967).

25. *Cf.* White Motor Co. v. United States, 372 U.S. 253 at 263 (1963).

26. United States v. Marine Bancorporation, 418 U.S. 602 (1974).

27. 433 U.S. 36 (1977).

28. For a complete analysis of these and other factors, *see* Markovits, *Predicting the Competitive Impact of Horizontal Mergers in a Monopolistically Competitive World*, 56 TEXAS L. REV. 587 (1978).

29. This practice led Justice Stewart to make the following comment in his dissent in United States v. Von's Grocery, 384 U.S. 270, 301 (1966): The "sole consistency . . . in litigation under [Clayton Act] § 7 . . . [is that] the Government always wins."

30. 415 U.S. 486 (1974).

31. *Supra* note 26 at 602.

32. Professor Bork has taken this pessimistic view in his book, THE ANTITRUST PARADOX 218 (1978).

33. United States v. Von's Grocery Co., 384 U.S. 270 (1966); United States v. Pabst Brewing Co., 384 U.S. 546 (1966).

34. *Supra* note 30 at 501.

35. *Supra* note 30 at 631.

36. A similar problem will arise where the local distributor's advertisements generate profits for the manufacturers as well as for himself—that is, where the per unit price the manufacturer charges this distributor for the extra goods the advertisement enables the latter to sell exceeds the marginal cost the manufacturer incurs to supply him with the units in question. Although the contractual devices discussed here will not take care of this problem, other con-

tractual solutions are available—for example, agreements which obligate the manufacturer to pay the proportion of the independent distributor's advertising budget that the manufacturer obtains of the joint profits generated on any resulting sales. Obviously, the same problem can arise when the "advertising" in question takes the form of plentiful and prominent shelf space. In this case, the manufacturer may overcome the problem by using his deliverymen to enforce a requirement that the distributor give his products adequate (that is, jointly optimal) shelf space and location.

37. Admittedly, where only two distributors are involved, transaction costs might not preclude them from working out a contract that committed both to placing such advertisements.

38. Although the examples here all deal with cases in which independent distributors will engage in too little advertising, interdistributor spillovers can also induce them to engage in too much advertising. Thus, one distributor may place an advertisement that costs $100 and increases his sales sufficiently to yield for him an additional $120 profits despite the fact that enough such sales are taken from other distributors of the manufacturer's product to reduce their profits by $50—that is, despite the fact that this advertisement would reduce all distributors' operating profits by $30. Once again, such an advertisement could be costly to the manufacturer since the lump-sum (franchise) fees he can charge his distributors increase with the operating profits they would anticipate realizing during their franchise period.

39. Some have argued that resale price maintenance agreements should be held to violate the Sherman Act because (1) most such agreements reflect an attempt by resellers to get manufacturers to police the resellers' own anticompetitive price fixing agreements and (2) it is not practicable or cost-effective to determine whether particular agreements are performing this function instead of one of the functions described in the text. I reject this position because I disagree with both of its premises. In fact, I suspect that almost no resale price maintenance agreements reflect reseller cartels: retail "market" structures are rarely more conducive to such price fixing than manufacturing markets. Others have based a parallel argument on the premise that most such arrangements are part of an attempt by manufacturers to enforce their own price fixing agreements. Admittedly, resale price maintenance is useful in this regard since manufacturers will have less of an incentive to break price fixing agreements if their resellers cannot pass on such price cuts to final consumers. However, the inability of resellers to pass such price cuts on does not make them pointless. Thus, although the resale price maintenance agreement will reduce the extent to which such price cuts will increase the manufacturer's sales, it will not eliminate such increases altogether since the price cuts will give the distributors a greater incentive to increase their sales-increasing advertising, presale advice, postsale service, and so forth. In any case, I doubt that many such agreements function in this way, and even if they did I see no obstacle to identifying them on a case-by-case basis.

40. In many cases, a manufacturer will be able to increase his returns by guaranteeing his product's performance, since he is better placed both to insure himself against the risk of such breakdowns and to obtain insurance coverage from independent sources. Manufacturers who wish to remove such risks from their customers basically have three different options: (1) they can do the necessary repairs themselves; (2) they can pay their distributors (or others) to do the necessary repairs; or (3) they can require their distributors to make such repairs at their own expense. All these solutions have certain advantages and disadvantages. The first may place the manufacturer in the position of having to expand his overall operations more rapidly than he wishes and preclude him from taking advantage of any available joint distribution-repair economies. The second gives the independent distributors an incentive to defraud the manufacturers by doing unnecessary repairs or making claims for work not actually done. And the third places the associated risk on parties (the distributors) who are probably poorer self- or external-insurers than the manufacturer and who have insufficient incentives to do the repair work well. In fact, the only economic incentive such distributors have is the prospect that a good repair reputation will induce their customers to continue to patronize them. This incentive problem is

likely to be particularly troublesome where a sufficient number of customers move (or travel) during the guarantee period to preclude the manufacturer from requiring his ultimate customers to obtain repairs from their supplying distributor. Obviously, in such cases, the success of a dealer-service program will depend on whether the manufacturer can assure his distributors that their service record will help them to retain the patronage of those buyers who stay in their area—that is, will depend on whether the manufacturer can prevent his other dealers from taking a free ride on the repairer's efforts by stealing his customers. As the text indicates, both vertical territorial restraints and resale price maintenance agreements will be useful in this connection.

41. White Motor Co. v. United States, 372 U.S. 253 (1963).

42. 388 U.S. 365 (1967).

43. 433 U.S. 36 (1977).

44. *Id.* at 54–55.

45. *See* United States Steel Corp. v. Fortner Enterprises, 429 U.S. 610 (1977); Broadcast Music Corp. v. Columbia Broadcasting System, 99 S. Ct. 1551 (1979).

46. 378 U.S. 158 (1964).

47. 388 U.S. 350 (1967). Although Sealy is normally analyzed as a case involving horizontal price fixing and market division, the distinguishing characteristics of the fact situation it involves make it more sensible to consider it as a joint venture.

48. The majority assumed that neither of the joint venturers would be perceived by Penn-Olin or anyone else as a significant potential competitor.

49. For a detailed discussion, *see* Markovits, *Potential Competition, Limit Price Theory, and the Legality of Horizontal and Conglomerate Mergers Under the American Antitrust Laws,* 1975 Wis. L. Rev. 658 (1975).

50. 388 U.S. 350 (1967).

51. 405 U.S. 596 (1972).

52. 441 U.S. 1 (1979).

CHAPTER 10

1. 347 U.S. 483 (1954).

2. 377 U.S. 533 (1964).

3. 384 U.S. 436 (1966).

4. 376 U.S. 254 (1964).

5. 367 U.S. 643 (1961).

6. 381 U.S. 479 (1965).

7. 370 U.S. 421 (1962).

8. 369 U.S. 186 (1962).

9. Federal statutes, or sections thereof, were held unconstitutional in the following Warren Court decisions: Trop v. Dulles, 356 U.S. 86 (1958); Kennedy v. Mendoza-Martinez, 372 U.S. 144 (1963); United States v. Jackson, 390 U.S. 570 (1968); Toth v. Quarles, 350 U.S. 11 (1955); Reid v. Covert, 354 U.S. 1 (1957), *see also* McElroy v. United States, 361 U.S. 281 (1960), Kinsella v. United States, 361 U.S. 234 (1960), and Grisham v. Hagan, 361 U.S. 278 (1960); United States v. Robel, 389 U.S. 258 (1967); Aptheker v. Secretary of State, 378 U.S. 500 (1974); Albertson v. Subversive Activities Control Board, 382 U.S. 80 (1965); Afroyim v. Rusk, 387 U.S. 253 (1967); Schneider v. Rusk, 377 U.S. 163 (1964); Marchetti v. United States, 390 U.S. 39 (1968), *see also* Grosso v. United States, 390 U.S. 62 (1968); Leary v. United States, 395 U.S. 6 (1969); Haynes v. United States, 390 U.S. 85 (1968); O'Callahan v. Parker, 395 U.S. 258 (1969); United States v. Brown, 381 U.S. 437 (1969); Lamont v. Postmaster General, 381 U.S. 301 (1965); Shapiro v. Thompson, 394 U.S. 618 (1969); and United States v. Romano, 382 U.S. 136 (1965).

The Burger Court invalidated federal statutory provisions in the following cases: Turner v. United States, 396 U.S. 398 (1970); Blount v. Rizzi, 400 U.S. 410 (1971); United States v. United States Coin & Currency, 401 U.S. 715 (1971); Schacht v. United States, 398 U.S. 58 (1970); Tilton v. Richardson, 403 U.S. 672 (1971); Oregon v. Mitchell, 400 U.S. 112 (1970); Weinberger v. Wiesenfeld, 420 U.S. 636 (1975); Chief of Capitol Police v. Jeanette Rankin Brigade, 409 U.S. 972 (1972); Califano v. Goldfarb, 430 U.S. 199 (1977); Railroad Retirement Bd. v. Kalina, 431 U.S. 909 (1977); Frontiero v. Richardson, 411 U.S. 677 (1973); Jiminez v. Weinberger, 417 U.S. 628 (1974); National League of Cities v. Usery, 426 U.S. 833 (1976); Richardson v. Davis, 409 U.S. 1069 (1972), *see also* Richardson v. Griffin, 409 U.S. 1069 (1972); Marshall v. Barlow's, Inc., 436 U.S. 307 (1978); Dept. of Agriculture v. Moreno, 413 U.S. 528 (1973); Dept. of Agriculture v. Murray, 413 U.S. 508 (1973); Buckley v. Valeo, 424 U.S. 1 (1976); Califano v. Westcott, 443 U.S. 76 (1979); Califano v. Jablon, 430 U.S. 924 (1977), *summarily aff'g* 399 F. Supp. 118 (Md. 1975); Califano v. Silbowitz, 430 U.S. 924 (1977), *summarily aff'g* 397 F. Supp. 862 (S.D. Fla. 1975); United States v. Will, 449 U.S. 200 (1980); Northern Pipeline Constr. Co. v. Marathon Pipe Line Co., 50 L.W. 4892 (1982); and Railway Labor Executive's Ass'n v. Gibbons, 50 L.W. 4258 (1982).

10. 424 U.S. 1 (1976).

11. 426 U.S. 833 (1976).

12. 400 U.S. 112 (1970).

13. 50 L.W. 4892.

14. Frontiero v. Richardson, 411 U.S. 677 (1973); Weinberger v. Wiesenfeld, 420 U.S. 636 (1975); Califano v. Goldfarb, 430 U.S. 199 (1977); Califano v. Jablon, 430 U.S. 924 (1977), *summarily aff'g* 399 F. Supp. 118 (Md. 1975); Califano v. Silowitz, 430 U.S. 924 (1977), *summarily aff'g* 397 F. Supp. 862 (S.D. Fla. 1975).

15. 418 U.S. 683 (1974).

16. New York Times Co. v. United States, 403 U.S. 713 (1971).

17. 407 U.S. 297 (1972).

18. Nixon v. Admin'r of General Services, 433 U.S. 425 (1977).

19. *Supra* at note 10.

20. 50 L.W. 4797 (1982).

21. 419 U.S. 256 (1974).

22. *See* Note, *The Supreme Court, 1974 Term*, 89 HARV. L. REV. 47 131 (1975).

23. *Supra* note 11.

24. In subsequent cases concerning the federal commerce power the Court has read *National League of Cities* narrowly. *See* Hodel v. Virginia Surface Min. & Recl. Ass'n, 452 U.S. 264 (1981); Transportation Union v. Long Island R. Co. 50 L.W. 4315 (1982); Federal Energy Regulatory Comm'n v. Mississippi, U.S. (1982).

25. 393 U.S. 129 (1968).

26. By my count, the Warren Court heard only seven cases in which a state regulatory provision was challenged in part on dormant commerce clause grounds. To date, the Burger Court has heard fourteen such cases. This computation does not include cases involving dormant commerce clause challenges to state taxing schemes. The Warren Court heard thirteen cases of that description, invalidating the state tax in six instances. The Burger Court thus far has heard thirteen dormant power tax cases, and has struck down the state tax in three of the cases. These figures also do not include cases in which state laws were challenged solely on the ground that they were preempted by federal legislation, nor cases in which state laws were held to be in conflict with constitutional provisions governing the federal system other than the dormant commerce clause.

27. Pike v. Bruce Church, 397 U.S. 137 (1970); Great A & P Tea Co. v. Cottrell, 424 U.S. 366 (1976); Raymond Motor Transp., Inc. v. Rice, 434 U.S. (1978); Hunt v. Washington

Apple Advertising Comm'n, 432 U.S. 333 (1977); Hughes v. Oklahoma, 441 U.S. 322 (1979); Lewis v. BT Investment Managers, Inc., 447 U.S. 27 (1980); Kassel v. Consolidated Freightways Corp., 450 U.S. 662 (1981); Allenberg Cotton Co. v. Pittman, 419 U.S. 20 (1974).

28. Polar Ice Cream & Creamery Co v. Andrews, 375 U.S. 361 (1964); Bibb v. Navajo Freight Lines, 379 U.S. 520 (1959).

29. *See* Pike v. Bruce Church, 397 U.S. 137 (1970).

30. 410 U.S. 113 (1973).

31. 408 U.S. 238 (1972).

32. *See, e.g.,* Graham v. Richardson, 403 U.S. 365 (1971); In re Griffiths, 413 U.S. 717 (1973).

33. *See, e.g.,* Virginia State Bd. of Pharmacy v. Virginia Citizens Consumer Council, 425 U.S. 748 (1976); Bates v. State Bar, 433 U.S. 350 (1977).

34. 433 U.S. 186 (1977).

35. Goldberg v. Kelly, 397 U.S. 254 (1970); Arnett v. Kennedy, 416 U.S. 134 (1974); Goss v. Lopez, 419 U.S. 565 (1975); Morrissey v. Brewster, 408 U.S. 471 (1972).

36. North Georgia Finishing, Inc. v. Di-Chem, Inc., 419 U.S. 601 (1975); Fuentes v. Shevin, 407 U.S. 67 (1972). The progenitor for this line of cases, Sniadach v. Family Finance Corp., 395 U.S. 337 (1969), was decided during Chief Justice Warren's final term.

37. *See* Branzburg v. Hayes, 408 U.S. 664 (1972).

38. Nebraska Press Ass'n v. Stuart, 427 U.S. 539 (1976).

39. Miami Herald Pub. Co. v. Tornillo, 418 U.S. 241 (1974).

40. Richmond Newspapers, Inc. v. Virginia, 448 U.S. 555 (1980).

41. See text accompanying notes 74–85 *infra*.

42. 406 U.S. 205 (1972).

43. See his livid dissent in Baker v. Carr, 369 U.S. 186 (1962).

44. 424 U.S. 1 (1976).

45. 435 U.S. 765 (1978).

46. Oregon v. Mitchell, *supra* at note 12.

47. 427 U.S. 347 (1976).

48. 445 U.S. 507 (1980).

49. *See, e.g.,* Dombrowski v. Pfister, 380 U.S. 479 (1965); Fay v. Noia, 372 U.S. 391 (1963); McNeese v. Bd. of Educ., 373 U.S. 668 (1963); Monroe v. Pape, 365 U.S. 167 (1961).

50. 401 U.S. 37 (1971).

51. 422 U.S. 332 (1975).

52. Stone v. Powell, 428 U.S. 465 (1976).

53. Wainwright v. Sykes, 433 U.S. 72 (1977).

54. United States v. Richardson, 418 U.S. 166 (1974); Schlesinger v. Reservists Committee to Stop the War, 418 U.S. 208 (1974).

55. *See, e.g.,* Warth v. Seldin, 422 U.S. 490 (1975); Simon v. Eastern Ky. Welfare Rights Org., 426 U.S. 26 (1976); Linda R.S. v. Richard D., 410 U.S. 614 (1972).

56. United States v. SCRAP, 412 U.S. 669 (1973); Duke Power Co. v. Carolina Environmental Study Group, 438 U.S. 59 (1978).

57. Swann v. Charlotte-Mecklenburg Bd. of Educ., 402 U.S. 1 (1971).

58. Keyes v. School District No. 1, Denver, Colo., 413 U.S. 189 (1973).

59. *See* Rizzo v. Goode, 423 U.S. 362 (1976); Shea v. Littleton, 414 U.S. 488 (1974).

60. 438 U.S. 478 (1978).

61. Bivins v. Six Unknown Agents, 403 U.S. 388 (1971); Davis v. Passman, 439 U.S. 1113 (1979).

62. *See* Monell v. Department of Social Services, 436 U.S. 658 (1978); Owen v. City of Independence, 445 U.S. 622 (1980).

63. Brown v. Bd. of Educ., 349 U.S. 294 (1955).

64. McCray v. Illinois, 386 U.S. 300 (1967).

65. I have developed this theme at greater length in Blasi, *A Requiem For the Warren Court*, 48 TEX L. REV. 608 (1970).

66. Roe v. Wade, 410 U.S. 113 (1973). Opponents of abortion have come to view this aspect of the *Roe* decision as small consolation, but the tone of the Court's opinion suggests that at the time the justices viewed their holding as a middle-of-the-road solution to the abortion controversy.

67. Maher v. Roe, 432 U.S. 464 (1977).

68. Bellotti v. Baird, 443 U.S. 622 (1979).

69. 408 U.S. 238 (1972).

70. *See* Gregg v. Georgia, 428 U.S. 153 (1976); Proffitt v. Florida, 428 U.S. 242 (1976); Jurek v. Texas, 428 U.S. 262 (1976). The cases are preceptively discussed in Black, *Due Process For Death*, 26 CATH. U. L. REV. 1 (1976).

71. Woodson v. North Carolina, 428 U.S. 280 (1976); Stanislaus Roberts v. Louisiana, 429 U.S. 325 (1976); Harry Roberts v. Louisiana, 431 U.S. 633 (1977).

72. Coker v. Georgia, 433 U.S. 584 (1977).

73. Enmund v. Florida 50 L.W. 5087 (1982); *see also* Lockett v. Ohio, 438 U.S. 586 (1978).

74. Lemon v. Kurtzman, 403 U.S. 602 (1971).

75. Committee For Public Educ. v. Nyquist, 413 U.S. 756 (1973).

76. Wolman v. Walter, 433 U.S. 229 (1977).

77. Meek v. Pittenger, 421 U.S. 349 (1975).

78. Committee For Public Educ. v. Nyquist, *supra* note 75.

79. Hunt v. McNair, 413 U.S. 734 (1973).

80. Meek v. Pittenger, *supra* note 77. This principle was first recognized in Board of Educ. v. Allen, 392 U.S. 236 (1968), decided when Earl Warren was still the chief justice.

81. Roemer v. Bd. of Public Works, 426 U.S. 736 (1976).

82. Wolman v. Walter, *supra* note 76; *compare* Levitt v. Comm. For Public Educ., 413 U.S. 472 (1973).

83. Comm. For Public Educ. v. Regan, 444 U.S. 646; *compare* Levitt v. Comm. For Public Educ., *supra* note 82.

84. Meek v. Pittenger, *supra* note 77; Wolman v. Walter, *supra* note 76.

85. Wolman v. Walter, *supra* note 76.

86. *See, e.g.,* Regents of the University of California v. Bakke, 438 U.S. 265 (1978); Buckley v. Valeo, 424 U.S. 1 (1976); Graham v. Richardson, 403 U.S. 365 (1971); Ambach v. Norwick, 441 U.S. 68 (1979); Bates v. State Bar, 433 U.S. 350 (1977); Friedman v. Rogers, 440 U.S. 1 (1979); Houchins v. KQED, 438 U.S. 1 (1978); Richmond Newspapers v. Virginia, 448 U.S. 555 (1980); Keyes v. School District No. 1, Denver, Colo., 413 U.S. 189 (1973); Milliken v. Bradley, 418 U.S. 717 (1974).

87. *See, e.g.,* Lee v. Washington, 390 U.S. 333 (1968); Hunter v. Erickson, 393 U.S. 385 (1969); Burton v. Wilmington Parking Authority, 365 U.S. 715 (1961); Reitman v. Mulkey, 387 U.S. 369 (1967).

88. *See, e.g.,* Lucas v. Forty-fourth General Assembly, 377 U.S. 713 (1964).

CHAPTER 11

1. *See, e.g.,* R. FUNSTON, CONSTITUTIONAL COUNTER-REVOLUTION? THE WARREN COURT AND THE BURGER COURT: JUDICIAL POLICY MAKING IN MODERN AMERICA (1977); S. WASBY, CONTINUITY AND CHANGE—FROM THE WARREN COURT TO THE BURGER COURT (1976).

2. See Shapiro, *The Supreme Court and Economic Rights*, in ESSAYS ON THE CONSTITUTION OF THE UNITED STATES (M. Harmon ed., 1978); Shapiro, *Judicial Activism*, in AMERICA IN THE TWENTY-FIRST CENTURY (S. Lipset ed. 1979); Shapiro, *The Supreme Court: From Warren to Burger*, in THE NEW AMERICAN POLITICAL SYSTEM (A. King ed. 1978).

3. 411 U.S. 1 (1973).

4. See *supra* note 2.

5. A representative list of the new generation with years of birth would be:

Vincent Blasi	1943
Paul Brest	1940
Jesse Choper	1935
John Ely	1938
Owen Fiss	1938
Thomas Grey	1941
Frank Michelman	1936
Henry Monaghan	1934
Lawrence Tribe	1941
William Van Alstyne	1934

Ronald Dworkin (1931) and Kenneth Karst (1929) are the elder statesmen of the group.

6. See particularly Karst, *Foreword: Equal Citizenship Under the Fourteenth Amendment*, 91 HARV. L. REV. 1 (1977).

7. The basic flavor of the movement can be caught in C. FRIED, RIGHT AND WRONG (1977), and the review of that book by Barry, 88 YALE L. J. 629 (1979). Its most explicit manifestation in the work of the new generation is Fiss, *Foreword: The Forms of Justice*, 93 HARV L. REV. 1 (1979).

8. 360 U.S. 109 (1959).

9. J. CHOPER, JUDICIAL REVIEW AND THE NATIONAL POLITICAL PROCESS (1980).

10. J. ELY, DEMOCRACY AND DISTRUST (1980).

11. Of course it was not quite "Pareto optimal," but it did "satisfice" in the language of Arrow and Simon.

12. See J. ELY, *supra* note 10, at 43–72.

13. Henry Monaghan is a third younger commentator who does continue to be preoccupied with the older role-of-the-Court questions. His formula of "constitutional common law" will not allow him to devote himself as completely to activism as Ely's "representation reenforcing" does, but it does allow him to make his peace with post–New Deal developments.

14. See R. DWORKIN, TAKING RIGHTS SERIOUSLY (1977).

15. Coons, *Compromise as Precise Justice*, in COMPROMISE (NOMOS XX) (J. Pennock and J. Chapman eds. 1979).

16. 347 U.S. 483 (1954).

17. Because this is a volume on the Burger not the Warren Court, it seems enough to repeat the obvious and frequently made points.

Quite apart from its obvious egalitarianism in the race and apportionment areas, the whole range of the Court's rights-of-accused decisions was aimed essentially at equaling up procedural guarantees for the poor and ignorant. Its birth control decisions were designed to provide services to poor women that were already enjoyed by the middle classes. Decisions like *Shapiro v. Thompson*, 394 U.S. 618 (1969), while supposedly resting on such esoteric bases as a "right to travel," were really aimed at welfare state goals. In antitrust the Warren Court fairly consistently favored small business over big, and even in such areas as obscenity, which admittedly is peripheral to the equality value, the standard was to be that of the average man and there was to be no elitist grading of the quality of literature, everything not utterly without redeeming social importance enjoying equal protection. See R. FUNSTON, note 1 *supra*; Kurland, *Foreword: "Equal in Origin and Equal in Title to the Legislative and Executive Branches of the Government,"* 78 HARV. L. REV. 143 (1964).

18. The point at which constitutional scholars decided they could no longer ignore modern political theory is marked by the flurry of citations to Deutsch, *Neutrality, Legitimacy, and the Supreme Court: Some Intersections between Law and Political Science*, 20 STAN. L. REV. 169 (1968).

19. 369 U.S. 186 (1962).

20. 420 U.S. 114 (1977).

21. Regents of the University of California v. Bakke, 438 U.S. 265 (1978).

22. R. DWORKIN, TAKING RIGHTS SERIOUSLY, 223 (1977).

23. See text at notes 61–64 *infra*.

24. For a description of that politics, see H. HECLO, A GOVERNMENT OF STRANGERS, (1977).

25. 381 U.S. 479 (1965).

26. 372 U.S. 335 (1963).

27. 432 U.S. 464 (1977).

28. 428 U.S. 52 (1976).

29. 431 U.S. 678 (1977). Of course the ultimate question is autonomy for the mother or the fetus.

30. 431 U.S. 494 (1977).

31. 416 U.S. 1 (1974).

32. 406 U.S. 205 (1972).

33. 431 U.S. 816 (1977).

34. 413 U.S. 528 (1973).

35. Mahan v. Howell, 410 U.S. 315 (1973).

36. 418 U.S. 717 (1974).

37. *See* Columbus Board of Education v. Penick, 443 U.S. 449 (1979); Dayton Board of Education v. Brinkman, 443 U.S. 526 (1979). The sacrifice of local autonomy to the egalitarian crusade clearly comes through in Monell v. Department of Social Services, 436 U.S. 658 (1978).

38. 426 U.S. 833 (1976). Arnett v. Kennedy, 416 U.S. 134 (1974), and its progeny are further steps in cutting back on the constitutionalizing of the welfare state undertaken by the Warren Court, but they are also reassertions of the autonomy of state and local government units in determining just what entitlements they choose to assign their dependents. *See* Paul v. Davis, 424 U.S. 693 (1976); Bishop v. Wood, 426 U.S. 341 (1976).

39. *Cf.* Blasi, *The Checking Value in First Amendment Theory*, 1977 AM. B. FOUNDATION RES. J. 521, who stresses the autonomy but not the private institution aspect of the media.

40. Miami Herald Publishing Co. v. Tornillo, 418 U.S. 241 (1974); *see also* C.B.S. v. Democratic National Committee, 412 U.S. 94 (1973).

41. Houchins v. KQED, 438 U.S. 1 (1978); Pell v. Procunier, 417 U.S. 817 (1974); Saxbe v. Washington Post, 417 U.S. 843 (1974).

42. Gertz v. Robert Welch, Inc. 418 U.S. 323 (1974).

43. Zurcher v. Stanford Daily, 436 U.S. 547 (1978).

44. Branzburg v. Hayes, 408 U.S. 665 (1972).

45. Herbert v. Lando, 441 U.S. 153 (1979).

46. *See, e.g.,* FCC v. Pacifica Foundation, 438 U.S. 726 (1978). *Compare* Miami Herald Publishing Co. v. Tornillo, *supra* note 40, *with* Red Lion Broadcasting Co. v. FCC, 395 U.S. 367 (1969). *See also* C.B.S. v. Democratic National Committee, *supra* note 40. This emphasis on media autonomy is clear in FCC v. Midwest Video Co., 440 U.S. 689 (1979), holding that the Federal Communications Act may not be read as turning the electronic media into common carriers. *Herbert, supra* note 45, may at first glance appear to run very much in the opposite direction because it allows a detailed opening up of the thought processes of editors in the context of libel suits. Like the *Stanford Daily* case, *supra* note 43, the key here is that journalistic

enterprises are treated as autonomous, *private* enterprises whose autonomy must yield to the traditional incursions of the legal process. As several of the opinions point out, the problems that arise in *Herbert* really stem from possibly overgenerous discovery rules that go beyond the traditional incursions of the legal process into private affairs.

47. *E.g.*, C.B.S. v. Democratic National Committee, *supra* note 40.

48. 424 U.S. 1 (1976).

49. 436 U.S. 307 (1978).

50. *See* Couch v. United States, 409 U.S. 322 (1973); United States v. Miller, 425 U.S. 435 (1976).

51. Miller v. California, 413 U.S. 15 (1973).

52. Laird v. Tatum, 408 U.S. 1 (1972).

53. Wyman v. James, 400 U.S. 309 (1971).

54. *See* Wisconsin v. Yoder, 406 U.S. 205 (1972); Bell Terre v. Boraas, 416 U.S. 1 (1974).

55. City of New Orleans v. Dukes, 427 U.S. 297 (1976).

56. Morey v. Doud, 354 U.S. 457 (1957).

57. Ely, *The Constitutionality of Reverse Racial Discrimination*, 41 U. CHI. L. REV. 723 (1974).

58. See *supra* note 22.

59. Fiss, *The Fate of an Idea Whose Time Has Come; Antidiscrimination Law in the Second Decade after* Brown v. Board of Education, 41 U. CHI. L. REV. 742 (1974).

60. Brest, *Foreword: In Defense of the Antidiscrimination Principle*, 90 HARV. L. REV. 1 (1976). *But see* Brest, "Race Discrimination," chapter 6 above.

61. *See* United Steelworkers v. Weber, 443 U.S. 193 (1979).

62. Furman v. Georgia, 408 U.S. 238 (1972); Gregg v. Georgia, 428 U.S. 153 (1976).

63. 433 U.S. 584 (1977).

64. For one slight Burger Court move down the Warren welfare path, see Goss v. Lopez, 419 U.S. 565 (1975).

• Contributors •

Robert W. Bennett is professor of law, Northwestern University School of Law. He is a graduate of Harvard College (1962) and the Harvard Law School (1965). Before entering law teaching, he served as an attorney with the Federal Communications Commission and litigated test cases with the Chicago Legal Aid Bureau. Among the courses he teaches are welfare litigation, contracts, and legislation. He argued one of the abortion funding cases before the Supreme Court. He has been a visiting professor at the University of Virginia Law School and the University of Southern California Law Center. He serves on the Board of Governors of the Society of American Law Teachers.

Vincent Blasi is Corliss Lamont Professor of Civil Liberties at Columbia Law School. He received his B.A. degree in 1964 from Northwestern University and his J.D. from the University of Chicago Law School in 1967. He has taught at the University of Texas, Stanford, the University of Michigan, and the University of California, Berkeley. He is a member of the Board of Governors of the Society of American Law Teachers.

Paul Brest is professor of law, Stanford Law School. He graduated from Swarthmore College in 1962 and the Harvard Law School in 1965. He clerked for Judge Bailey Aldrich and for Supreme Court Justice John M. Harlan. For two years he worked as an attorney with the NAACP Legal Defense Fund in Jackson, Mississippi. He is coauthor of the most innovative teaching materials on constitutional law. He has been a visiting professor at Yale Law School. He serves on the Board of Governors of the society of American Law Teachers.

Robert Burt is Southmayd Professor of Law, Yale Law School. He is a 1960 graduate of Princeton University and a 1964 graduate of the Yale Law School. He also holds a graduate degree from Oxford. He teaches family law, constitutional law, and law and medicine. His book *Taking Care of Strangers* (1979) is a pioneering study of the role of law in doctor-patient relations. Before joining the Yale faculty in 1976, he taught at the University of Chicago Law School and the University of Michigan Law School.

Norman Dorsen is Frederick I. and Grace A. Stokes Professor of Law at

New York University and director of the Arthur Garfield Hays Civil Liberties Program. He is also the president of the American Civil Liberties Union. He received his undergraduate degree from Columbia in 1950 and his law degree from Harvard in 1953. He clerked for federal judge Calvert Magruder and for Supreme Court Justice John M. Harlan. He has argued several cases before the Supreme Court and has been a strong advocate of civil liberties in many other forums. He is the editor of *The Rights of Americans* and coauthor of *Political and Civil Rights in the United States*. He has taught at Harvard, the University of California, Berkeley, and the London School of Economics. He is a past president of the Society of American Law Teachers.

Thomas Emerson is Lines Professor Emeritus at Yale Law School, from which he graduated in 1931. Before commencing his long and distinguished teaching career, he served as counsel for a number of federal government agencies, including the National Recovery Administration, the National Labor Relations Board, the Social Security Board, and the Office of Price Administration. He has been a Guggenheim Fellow and a visiting professor at the London School of Economics. He is coauthor of *Political and Civil Rights in the United States*. His magnum opus *The System of Freedom of Expression* (1970) is already a classic. He serves on the Board of Governors of the Society of American Law Teachers.

Ruth Bader Ginsburg is a judge of the United States Court of Appeals for the District of Columbia Circuit. She is a graduate of Cornell University (1954) and Columbia Law School (1959). Before being appointed to the bench, she was a professor, specializing in constitutional law and women's rights, at Rutgers Law School and Columbia Law School. During her teaching career she coauthored the leading casebook on sex-based discrimination and argued many cases before the United States Supreme Court. She also served as general counsel of the American Civil Liberties Union. She is a former vice-president of the Society of American Law Teachers.

Joel Gora is professor of law, Brooklyn Law School. He received his undergraduate degree in 1963 from Pomona College and his law degree in 1967 from Columbia. Before commencing his teaching career, he served for ten years as associate legal director of the American Civil Liberties Union. He is the author of several books on civil liberties. He is a member of the Board of Governors of the Society of American Law Teachers.

Yale Kamisar is Henry K. Ransom Professor, University of Michigan Law School. He holds a B.A. degree from New York University (1950), an Ll.B. degree from Columbia (1954), and several honorary degrees. His pioneering coauthored casebook on criminal procedure remains after several editions the dominant book in the field. He is also coauthor of one of the leading casebooks on constitutional law. He has taught at the University of Minnesota and at Harvard.

Richard Markovits is professor of law, University of Texas, and director, Center for Socio-Legal Studies, Wolfson College, Oxford. He holds a B.A. degree from Cornell (1963), an Ll.B. from Yale (1968), and a Ph.D. in economics from the London School of Economics (1966). He has taught at Stanford and at the University of Konstanz, Germany. He teaches antitrust law, constitutional law, and microeconomic policy analysis.

Theodore St. Antoine is James E. and Sarah A. Degan Professor of Law, University of Michigan. He is a 1951 graduate of Fordham College and a 1954 graduate of the University of Michigan Law School. Before commencing his teaching career, he practiced labor law in Washington, D.C., for seven years, during which time he argued many cases before the federal courts of appeals and the Supreme Court. From 1971 to 1978 he served as dean of the University of Michigan Law School. He has been a visiting professor at Duke. In addition to labor law, for which he has written a leading casebook, he has taught contracts and property.

Martin Shapiro is professor of jurisprudence and social policy, University of California, Berkeley. He holds a bachelor's degree from U.C.L.A. (1955) and a Ph.D. degree from Harvard (1961). He is the author of a number of books that examine various legal institutions and systems from the perspective of political science. He is one of the founders and directors of the innovative Jurisprudence and Social Policy program at Berkeley. He has taught at Harvard, Yale, Stanford, and several of the campuses of the University of California system.

• Index •